Totalitarian Dictatorship and Autocracy

Totalitarian Dictatorship and Autocracy

by Carl J. Friedrich
and Zbigniew K. Brzezinski

Harvard University Press, Cambridge, 1956

To Lenore and Muška

Preface

The present study of totalitarian dictatorship seeks to give a general, descriptive theory of a novel form of government. It does not seek to explain why this dictatorship came into being, for the authors are convinced that such an explanation is not feasible at the present time, though some of the essential conditions can be described. Some brilliant efforts have been made in this field, but they have remained speculative and controversial. The authors' is a humbler task: to delineate, on the basis of fairly generally known and acknowledged factual data, the general model of totalitarian dictatorship and of the society which it has created. In attempting such a general assessment, they hope to provide a basis not only for more effective teaching but also for a more informed discussion of particular issues and further developments. It might be objected that their study is not addressed to any definite group, that it is too elementary for the scholar, too difficult for the general reader and too learned for the beginner. But is not any study of this kind partly esoteric, partly exoteric? There is no doubt that a book which seeks to delineate in fairly clear and comprehensive form the general nature of totalitarian dictatorship, on the basis of what are reasonably well-established matters of fact, will traverse much ground that is familiar to the specialist. At the same time, its argument will involve recondite matter which may well go beyond the range of interest of the intelligent lay reader and the student. The authors hope, nonetheless, to have succeeded in producing a volume that has something to offer each of these groups, and which may contribute something of an answer to the question—what is a totalitarian dictatorship, and how does it fit into the general framework of our knowledge of government and politics.

This volume is the product of very close collaboration between the authors not only in the course of writing but also in teaching and research. To be sure, the studies of C. J. Friedrich in this field go much further back; the main framework was developed by him in

the late thirties in a nearly completed book-length manuscript, but
the knowledge and understanding of both the Nazi and Soviet dictatorships was then very limited and it was decided not to publish it
when the war broke out. In the years following, Merle Fainsod became associated with him in the course he was then teaching on totalitarian dictatorship—a most fruitful cooperation which grew out
of their joint direction of the Civil Affairs Training School at Harvard. This training effort in turn led to Friedrich's work in military
government and the seminar in this field, taught for several years in
conjunction with the continuing work on totalitarian dictatorship.
For the constitutional dictatorship of Western military government
provided an interesting contrast to the totalitarian pattern. Z. K.
Brzezinski became associated with this seminar in 1951, and out of
their joint work this study eventually emerged.

The main reason for relating this background is to emphasize the
method of joint authorship of which this book is the fruit. Unlike
many books by two or more authors, this one was written by both
authors chapter by chapter, now one, now the other providing the
first draft. The general conception, as outlined in chapter one, is
Friedrich's and was first offered in *Totalitarianism,* a volume of proceedings edited by him for the American Academy of Arts and Sciences in 1953. But even this, dating back to prewar days, was considerably refined in constant discussions between the authors and
with others, notably members of the Russian Research Center and
the many acute students who have participated in the seminar these
past years. Beyond this general beginning, the authors worked out
the book together, and consider it their joint product. As far as concrete material is concerned, the authors' divergent linguistic background and source knowledge combined to provide the necessary
breadth. Brzezinski wishes to acknowledge with sincere gratitude
the generous support given to him in this connection, as in the past,
by the Russian Research Center at Harvard University of which he
is a staff member; similarly, Friedrich wishes to thank the director
and staff of the Institut für Zeitgeschichte at Munich for their critical
reading and helpful criticisms, though neither of these learned bodies
thereby assumes any responsibility for this interpretation. Many
helpful suggestions and criticism were made by colleagues, particularly Professor Merle Fainsod, who read the entire manuscript.
Similarly Dr. Dante Germino read the manuscript, especially the

sections dealing with Fascist Italy, and kindly gave counsel on the basis of his able study of the Fascist Party. Between March 1955 and April 1956, Friedrich directed a research project for the Human Relations Area Files, Yale University, on the Soviet Zone of Germany which has since appeared as one of their studies and contains the names of the numerous collaborators (see item 59.2 in the bibliography). The authors' debt to many others will, it is hoped, be largely apparent from the footnotes, though certain "consultants" of the seminar, notably Hannah Arendt, Sigmund Neumann, Franz Neumann, Adam Ulam, and Alex Inkeles call for special mention. Finally, the authors would like to express their profound appreciation for the help of Miss Roberta G. Hill, the seminar's secretary, who devoted untold hours to editorial and related chores.

The manuscript was completed in December 1955. In view of the events in the Soviet Union surrounding the Twentieth Party Congress, held in February 1956, a few minor revisions and additions to the text were made. But the hard core of the analysis has not been changed; developments up to now do not appear to call for any such revision; as yet no fundamental change seems to have occurred in the Soviet system. The party continues to play its crucially important and predominant role and, indeed, the significance of the party as the mainspring of the system has increased. The leadership is now attempting to shift somewhat from its reliance on terroristic measures to more subtle incentives as the basis for continued drives in "the socialist construction." This search for a new basis of authority, in which the post-Stalinist regime is now engaged, has resulted in some relaxation of police controls over the population, but the use of arbitrary violence against the opponents of the regime has not been abandoned. No effective restraints against the employment of terror have yet been developed. The potential of terror still is present, and the party would not hesitate to use violence to defend its monopoly of power. Nonetheless, it is heartening to see that even Stalin's closest collaborators feel compelled to renounce his activities.

Z. K. B.

April 1956   C. J. F.

CONTENTS

I

Introduction

Chapter One

The General Characteristics of Totalitarian Dictatorship

Everybody talks about totalitarian dictatorships and about totalitarianism. They are said to be tyrannies, despotisms, absolutisms. And yet, the greatest uncertainty surrounds the most elementary aspects of this form of government. One flatters it, actually, when one calls a dictatorship of this kind a tyranny or a despotism. The autocratic regimes of the past were not nearly as ghastly as the totalitarian dictatorships of our time. Yet, one also maligns totalitarian dictatorship by these descriptions, for, whereas tyranny was conducted, according to the definition of Aristotle, for the benefit of the tyrant, it is not very realistic to make that kind of egoism the basis of an interpretation of totalitarian dictatorship.

The truth of the matter seems to be that totalitarian dictatorship is a logical extension of certain traits of our modern industrial society (oftentimes called "capitalism"). It is our purpose in this introductory chapter to trace the main aspects of this novel kind of government and thereby lay out the pattern for the later more detailed treatment. We also propose to indicate by way of contrast how and why totalitarian dictatorships differ from autocracies of the past. Though actually neither a tyranny nor a despotism, totalitarian dictatorship is apparently linked to both in certain important ways, or at least there are significant similarities which justify putting all of these regimes into one common category. This category might properly be suggested to be that of "autocracy."

There have been many types of autocracy in the history of government. The several forms of despotism, often associated with the deification of the ruler characteristic of the Orient, the tyranny of the Greek cities and their replicas in Renaissance Italy, and the absolutist monarchies of modern Europe, are among the more familiar patterns of autocracy. In all these systems, the truly distinguishing feature is that the ruler is not responsible to anyone else for what he does; he is the *autos,* who himself wields power; that is to say, he

makes the decisions and reaps the fruits of them. The logical opposite of autocracy, therefore, would be any rule in which another, an
heteros, shared the power through the fact that the ruler is responsible to him or them. In the modern West, it has become customary
to speak of such systems as responsible or constitutional governments.* Among these, constitutional democracy has become the predominant type, though there have been constitutional monarchies,
aristocracies, and theocracies in the past.

Since any pattern of responsibility must be expressed in rules of
some kind, which together constitute the "constitution," and, as
rules are properly speaking a kind of legal norm, it has been customary since Plato and Aristotle to stress the role of law and to distinguish political systems according to whether or not they are characterized by the subordination of the political rulers to law. From this
viewpoint, an autocracy is any political system in which the rulers
are insufficiently, or not at all, subject to antecedent and enforceable
rules of law—enforceable, that is, by other authorities who share the
government and who have sufficient power to compel the law-
breaking rulers to submit to the law.

This problem of the control of the rulers by the law must be distinguished from the problem of the role of law in a given society.
All human societies, communities, and groups of any sort have some
kind of law, and the totalitarian dictatorships of our time are characterized by a vast amount of "legislation," necessitated by the requirements of a technically industrialized economy and of the masses
of dependent operators involved in such a society. (54a) Similarly
the Roman empire saw an increase, not a decline, in the detailed
complexity of its legal system during the very period when it was
becoming more and more autocratic. This autocracy eventually
reached the point of deifying the emperor, while the detailed development of the legal system continued. Long before this time, all enforceable control of the ruler had vanished and the responsibility of
which the Republic had been so proud had completely disappeared.
The will of the emperor was the ultimate source of all law. This
conception was expressed in a number of celebrated phrases which
eventually became the basis of the doctrine of sovereignty that pro-

* The term *heterocracy* has never been suggested though as it is the genuine logical alternative to *autocracy* there is something to be said for it, in order to escape the
common connotations surrounding the term "constitutional government."

vided the rationalization for the autocracy of absolute monarchs in the seventeenth century.

Autocratic legalism, however, must not be confused with the totalitarian distortion of the notion of law in what is spoken of as the "laws of movement." These are presumably "laws of nature" or "laws of history" (but history understood as a part of nature); they contain an existential, rather than a normative, judgment. The interrelation of existential and normative law has been a central problem in the long history of the law of nature. (56) The totalitarian ideology tends to dissolve the normative in the existential realm, and to consider all ordinary laws merely as expressions of laws of nature and history. "All history is the history of class struggles," for example, would be such a law in terms of which the positive legal order must be structured; it provides the standard by which to measure positive laws, to interpret and if necessary to alter and break them. All laws become fluid when they are treated merely as the emanation of such laws of movement, and their very multiplicity testifies to their normative weakness. (276a) Such fluidity makes them incapable of serving as standards of responsible conduct, since every violation can be argued away by the rulers as merely an adaptation to the higher laws of movement. A similar difficulty attached to the law of nature when it was to serve as a restraint upon absolute rulers, who in the past were allowed to contravene it in case "reason of state" required it.

Thus, as far as this characteristic absence of responsibility is concerned, totalitarian dictatorship resembles earlier forms of autocracy. But it is our contention in this volume that totalitarian dictatorship is historically unique and *sui generis*. It is also our conclusion from all the facts available to us that fascist and communist totalitarian dictatorships are basically alike, or at any rate more nearly like each other than like any other system of government, including earlier forms of autocracy. These two theses are closely linked and must be examined together. They are also linked to a third, that totalitarian dictatorship as it actually developed was not intended by those who created it—Mussolini talked of it, but meant something different—but resulted from the political situations in which the anticonstitutionalist and antidemocratic revolutionary movements and their leaders found themselves. Let us take the third of these points first, treating the second and first afterward.

The fascist and communist systems evolved in response to a series of unprecedented crises, and they have shown a continuous, though intermittent, tendency to become more "totalitarian." There is no present reason to conclude that the existing totalitarian systems will disappear as a result of internal evolution, though this possibility cannot be excluded. The two totalitarian governments which have perished thus far have perished as the result of wars in which they had become involved with outside powers, but this does not mean that the Soviet Union necessarily will. We do not presuppose that totalitarian societies are fixed and static entities, but, on the contrary, that they have undergone and continue to undergo a steady evolution, presumably involving both growth and deterioration.

In terms of historical perspective, three points might be added. First, certain autocracies in the past have shown extraordinary capacity for survival. Not only the Roman but also several Oriental empires lasted for hundreds of years, at least as systems they did, though the dynasties changed. (276b) By contrast, the tyrannies of the Greek city states were usually short-lived, as Aristotle noted. Second, such autocracies have as a rule perished in consequence of foreign invasions. Third, their autocratic features have usually been intensified over long periods, the reason being that violence is readily available for dealing with the tensions and breakdowns that occur. In short, some of these autocracies were not stable, but lasting.

To the uncertainties about the end correspond the controversies about the beginning of totalitarian dictatorship. The debate about the causes or origins of totalitarianism has run all the way from a primitive bad-man theory (22a) to the "moral crisis of our time" kind of argument. A detailed inspection of the available evidence suggests that virtually every one of the factors which has been offered by itself as an explanation of the origin of totalitarian dictatorship has played its role. For example, in the case of Germany—Hitler's moral and personal defects, weaknesses in the German constitutional tradition, certain traits involved in the German "national character," the Versailles Treaty and its aftermath, the economic crisis and the "contradictions" of an aging capitalism, the "threat" of communism, the decline of Christianity and of such other spiritual moorings as the belief in the reason and the reasonableness of man—all have played a role in the total configuration of factors contributing to the over-all result. As in the case of other broad developments in history, only a multiple-factor analysis will do. But at the present time, we cannot fully explain the rise of totalitarian dictatorship. All we can do is to explain it partially by identifying some of the antecedent and concomitant conditions. Broadly speaking, totalitarian dictatorship is a new development; there has never been anything quite like it before.

Now concerning the second point, it is very important to explain somewhat at the outset why the totalitarian dictatorships, communist and fascist, are *basically alike*. What does this mean? In the first place, it means that they are *not wholly alike*. Popular and journalistic interpretation has oscillated between two extremes; some have said that the communist and fascist dictatorships are wholly alike, others that they are not at all alike. The latter view was the prevailing one during the popular-front days in Europe as well as in "liberal" circles in the United States. It was even more popular during the Second World War, especially among Allied propagandists. Besides, it was and is the official Soviet and Hitler party line. It is only natural that these regimes, conceiving of themselves as bitter enemies, dedicated to the task of liquidating each other, should take the view that they have nothing in common. This has happened before in history. When the Protestants and Catholics were fighting each other during the religious wars of the sixteenth and seventeenth centuries, they very commonly denied to each other the name of "Christians," and argued about each other that they were not "true churches." Actually, and from the viewpoint of the sectarians whom they both persecuted, they were indeed that.

The other view, that communist and fascist dictatorships are wholly alike, is presently favored in the United States and in Western Europe to an increasing extent. Yet they are obviously not wholly alike. For example, they differ in their proclaimed purposes and intentions. Everyone knows that the communists say they seek the world revolution of the proletariat, while the fascists proclaimed their determination to establish the world dominance of a particular nation or people, or at least their imperial predominance in a region, as in the case of the Italian Fascists. The communist and fascist dictatorships differ also in their historical antecedents: the fascist movements have arisen in reaction to the communist challenge and have offered themselves to a frightened middle class as the saviors from the communist danger. As we shall have occasion to show in the chapters which follow, there are many other differences which do not allow us to speak of the communist and fascist totalitarian dictatorships as wholly alike, but which suggest that they are sufficiently alike to class them together and contrast them not only with constitutional systems, but also with former types of autocracy.

Before we turn to these common features, however, there is another difference which used to be emphasized by many who wanted "to do business with Hitler" or who admired Mussolini and therefore argued that, far from being wholly like the communist dictatorship, the fascist regimes must really be seen as merely authoritarian forms of constitutional systems. It is indeed true that more of the institutions of the preceding liberal and constitutional society survived in the Italian Fascist than in the Russian Communist society. But this is due in part to the fact that no liberal, constitutional society preceded Soviet Communism. The promising period of the Duma came to naught as a result of the war and the disintegration of tsarism, while the Kerensky interlude was far too brief and too superficial to become meaningful for the future. In Czechoslovakia and in the Soviet Zone of Germany (German Democratic Republic) we find precisely such institutions as universities, churches, and schools surviving. It is likely that, were a communist dictatorship to be established in Great Britain or France, the situation would be similar, and that here even more such institutions of the liberal era would continue to operate for a considerable initial period at least. Precisely this argument has been advanced by such British radicals as Sidney and Beatrice Webb. The tendency of isolated fragments of the preceding state of society to survive has been a significant source of misinterpretation of the fascist totalitarian society, especially in the case of Italy. In the twenties, Italian totalitarianism was very commonly misinterpreted as being "merely" an authoritarian form of middle class rule, with the trains running on time, and the beggars off the street. (13) In the case of Germany, this sort of misinterpretation took a slightly different form. In the thirties, various authors tried to interpret German totalitarianism as either "the end phase of capitalism" or as "militarist imperialism." (148a) These interpretations stress the continuance of a "capitalist" economy whose leaders are represented as dominating the regime. The facts as we know them do not correspond to this view (see Part V). For one who sympathized with socialism or communism it was very tempting to try and depict the totalitarian dictatorship of Hitler as nothing but a capitalist society and therefore totally at variance with the "new civilization" that was arising in the Soviet Union. These few remarks have suggested, it is hoped, why it may be wrong to consider the totalitarian dictatorships under discussion as either wholly alike or basically different. Why they are basically alike remains to be shown, and to this key argument we now turn.

The basic features or traits which we suggest as generally recognized to be common to totalitarian dictatorships are six in number. The "syndrome," or pattern of interrelated traits, of the totalitarian dictatorship consists of an ideology, a single party typically led by one man, a terroristic police, a communications monopoly, a weapons monopoly, and a centrally directed economy. Of these, the last two are also found in constitutional systems: Socialist Britain had a centrally directed economy, and all modern states possess a weapons monopoly. Whether these latter suggest a "trend" toward totalitarianism is a question which will be discussed in our last chapter.

These six basic features, which we think constitute the character of totalitarian dictatorship, form a cluster of interrelated traits, intertwined and mutually supporting each other, as usual in "organic" systems. (8) They should therefore not be considered in isolation or be made the focal point of comparisons, such as "Caesar developed a terroristic secret police, therefore he was the first totalitarian dictator," or "the Catholic Church has practised ideological thought control, therefore . . ."

The totalitarian dictatorships all possess the following:

1. an official ideology, consisting of an official body of doctrine covering all vital aspects of man's existence to which everyone living in that society is supposed to adhere, at least passively; this ideology is characteristically focused and projected toward a perfect final state of mankind, that is to say, it contains a chiliastic claim, based upon a radical rejection of the existing society and conquest of the world for the new one;

2. a single mass party led typically by one man, the "dictator," and consisting of a relatively small percentage of the total population (up to 10 per cent) of men and women, a hard core of them passionately and unquestioningly dedicated to the ideology and prepared to assist in every way in promoting its general acceptance, such a party being hierarchically, oligarchically organized, and typically either superior to, or completely intertwined with the bureaucratic government organization;

3. a system of terroristic police control, supporting but also supervising the party for its leaders, and characteristically directed not only against demonstrable "enemies" of the regime, but against arbitrarily selected classes of the population; the terror of the secret police systematically exploiting modern science, and more especially scientific psychology;

4. a technologically conditioned near-complete monopoly of control, in the hands of the party and its subservient cadres, of all means of effective mass communication, such as the press, radio, motion pictures;

5. a similarly technologically conditioned near-complete monopoly of control (in the same hands) of all means of effective armed combat;

6. a central control and direction of the entire economy through the bureaucratic co-ordination of its formerly independent corporate entities, typically including most other associations and group activities.

The enumeration of these six traits or trait clusters is not meant to suggest that there might not be others, now insufficiently recognized, but that these are universally acknowledged to be the features of totalitarian dictatorship to which the writings of students of the most varied backgrounds, including totalitarian writers, bear witness.

Within this broad pattern of similarities, there are many significant variations to which the analysis of this book will give detailed attention. To offer a few random illustrations, at present the party zealots play less of a role in the Soviet Union than the party bureaucrats, as contrasted with an earlier stage; the ideology of the Soviet Union is more specifically committed to certain assumptions, because of its Marx-Engels bible, than that of Italian or German fascism, where ideology was formulated by the leader of the party himself; the corporate entities of the fascist economy remained in private hands, as far as property claims are concerned, whereas they become public property in the Soviet Union.

Let us now turn to our first point, namely, that these systems are historically "unique"; that is to say, that no government like totalitarian dictatorship has ever before existed, even though it bears a resemblance to autocracies of the past. It may be interesting to consider briefly some data which show that the six traits we have just identified are to a large extent lacking in historically known autocratic regimes.* Neither the Oriental despotisms of the more re-

---

* Autocratic regimes, as defined above, should be clearly distinguished from the broader category of "authoritarian" regimes of which some of them form a sub-

mote past, nor the absolute monarchies of modern Europe, neither the tyrannies of the ancient Greek cities, nor the Roman Empire, nor yet the tyrannies of the city states of the Italian Renaissance and the Bonapartist military dictatorships of the last century exhibit this design, this combination of features, though they may possess one or another of its constituent traits. For example, efforts have often been made to organize some kind of secret police, but they have not been even horse-and-buggy affairs compared with the terror of the Gestapo or of the OGPU (MVD today). Similarly, there have been both military and propagandistic concentrations of power and control, but the limits of technology prevented any thoroughgoing development along totalitarian lines. It is very evident, we trust, that the six distinctive features here sketched, and to be developed in what follows, sharply differentiate contemporary totalitarian dictatorships from past autocratic regimes. Certainly neither the Roman emperor nor the absolute monarch sought or needed a party to support him nor an ideology in the modern party sense, and the same is obviously true of oriental despots. The tyrants of Greece and Italy may have had a party—that of the Medicis in Florence was called *lo stato* but they had no ideology to speak of. And, of course, all of these autocratic regimes were far removed from the very distinctive features which are rooted in modern technology, from the terror to the centrally directed economy.

Something more should perhaps be added on the subject of technology. This technological aspect of totalitarianism is, of course, particularly striking in the matter of weapons and communications, but it is involved also in the secret police terror, depending as it does upon technically enhanced possibilities of supervision and control of the movement of persons. In addition, the centrally directed economy presupposes the reporting, cataloging, and calculating devices provided by modern technology. In short, four of the six traits are technologically conditioned. To envisage what this technological advance means in terms of political control, one has to think only of the weapons field. The Constitution of the United States guarantees to every citizen the "right to bear arms" (Fourth Amendment). In the days of the minutemen, this was a very important right, and the freedom of the citizen was indeed symbolized by the gun over

division. Thus both monarchy and tyranny may be said to have been authoritarian, but the difference has long been decisive.

the hearth, as it is in Switzerland to this day. But who can "bear" such arms as a tank, a bomber, or a flame-thrower, let alone an atom bomb? The citizen as an individual, and indeed in larger groups, is simply defenseless against the overwhelming technological superiority of those who can centralize in their hands the means with which to wield these modern arms and thereby physically to coerce the mass of the citizenry. Similar observations are easy to make regarding the press, the radio, and so forth. "Freedom" does not have the same potential, resting as it did upon individual effort, which it had a hundred and fifty years ago. With few exceptions, the trend of technological advance implies the trend toward greater and greater size of organization. In the perspective of these four traits, therefore, totalitarian societies appear to be merely exaggerations, but nonetheless logical exaggerations, of the technological state of modern society.

The same cannot be said with respect to the first two distinctive features of totalitarian dictatorships, for neither ideology nor party have any significant relation to the state of technology. (This may not be strictly true, since the mass conversion continually attempted by totalitarian propaganda through its effective use of the communications monopoly could not be carried through without it.) However, the party, its leader(s), and the ideology link the totalitarian dictatorship to modern democracy. It is the perversion of democracy. Not only did Hitler, Mussolini, and Lenin build typical parties within a constitutional, if not a democratic, context but the connection is plain between the stress on ideology and the role which platforms and other types of ideological goal-formation play in democratic parties. To be sure, totalitarian parties developed a pronounced authoritarian pattern while organizing themselves into effective revolutionary instruments of action; but, at the same time, its leaders, beginning with Marx and Engels, saw themselves as constituting the vanguard of the democratic movement of their day, and Stalin always talked of the Soviet totalitarian society as the "perfect democracy"; Hitler and Mussolini (205) made similar statements. Both the world brotherhood of the proletariat and the folk community were conceived of as supplanting the class divisions of past societies by a complete harmony—the classless society of the socialist tradition.

Not only the party but also its ideology harkens back to the democratic context within which the totalitarian movements arose. Ideology generally, but more especially totalitarian ideology, involves a high degree of convictional certainty. As has been indicated, totalitarian ideology consists of an official doctrine which radically rejects the pre-existing society in terms of a chiliastic proposal for a new one. As such it contains strongly utopian elements, some kind of notion of a paradise on earth. This utopian and chiliastic outlook of totalitarian ideologies gives them a pseudoreligious quality. In fact, they often elicit in the less critical followers a depth of conviction and a fervor of devotion usually found only among persons inspired by a transcendent faith. Whether these aspects of totalitarian ideologies bear some sort of relationship to the religions which they seek to replace is arguable. Marx denounced religion as "the opium of the people." It would seem that this is rather an appropriate way of describing totalitarian ideologies. In place of the more or less sane platforms of regular political parties, critical of the existing state of affairs in a limited way, totalitarian ideologies are perversions of such programs. They substitute faith for reason, magic exhortation for scientific knowledge. And yet, it must be recognized that there is enough of these same elements in the operations of democratic parties to attest to the relation between them and their perverted descendants, the totalitarian movements. That is why these movements must be seen and analyzed in their relationship to the democracy which they seek to supplant.

In summary, these regimes could have arisen only within the context of mass democracy and modern technology. In the chapters that follow, we shall deal first with the party and its leadership (Part II), then take up the problems of ideology (Part III), and follow them with the terror and propaganda (Part IV). Part V will be devoted to the issues presented by the centrally directed economy, while the monopoly of communications and of weapons will be taken up in special chapters of Parts III, IV, and VI. Finally, Part VI will deal with certain areas which to a greater or lesser extent have managed to resist the totalitarian claim to all-inclusiveness; we have called them "islands of separateness" to stress their isolated nature. In a conclusion we propose to consider the problem of stages of totalitarian development and to consider the possibility of projecting such developmental models into the future.

I I

Dictator and Party

Chapter Two

The Totalitarian Dictator

The idea of totalitarian dictatorship suggests that a dictator who possesses "absolute power" is placed at the head. Although this notion is pretty generally assumed to be correct and is the basis of much political discussion and policy, there have been all along sharp challenges to it; it has been variously argued that the party rather than the dictator in the Soviet Union wields the ultimate power, or that a smaller party organ, like the Politburo, has "the final say." (224a) Similarly, it has been claimed, that the power of Hitler or Mussolini was merely derivative, that "big business" or "the generals" were actually in charge, and that Hitler and his entourage were merely the tools of some such group. While the dictatorships of Mussolini and Hitler as well as that of Stalin were intact, there existed no scientifically reliable way of resolving this question, since the testimony of one observer stood flatly opposed to that of another. We are now in a more fortunate position. The documentary evidence clearly shows that Mussolini and Hitler were the actual rulers of their respective countries. Their views were decisive and the power they wielded was "absolute" in a degree perhaps more complete than ever before. And yet, this documentary material likewise shows both men to stand in a curious relationship of interdependence with their respective parties—a problem which we shall return to further on. As for Stalin, comparable evidence has now become available. Earlier, the large body of material which skillful research in a number of centers had developed suggested that Stalin's position, particularly after the great purges of the Thirties, was similarly decisive. A number of participants in foreign policy conferences with Soviet leaders have remarked on the fact that only Stalin was able to undertake immediately, and without consultation, far-reaching commitments. Furthermore the personal relationships between Soviet leaders, to the extent that they could have become apparent at such meetings, also indicated clearly that Stalin's will could not be questioned. In terms of Soviet internal politics, the available information on Soviet purges again seems to confirm Stalin's unquestioned personal dominance.*

It might be objected, however, that, had Stalin's position been indeed so predominant, the transition of power following his death would not have been quite so smooth. This objection is not valid for, in fact, the transition was not altogether smooth. And the transitional period may still not be over, according to some indications. Stalin's death led to the attempted Beria coup, which manifested itself first of all in seizures of power by the Beria elements on the republican levels. It was only through decisive action at the very top, and almost at the last moment, that the Party Presidium succeeded in decapitating the conspiracy. (18a) Likewise, Malenkov's "resignation" early in 1955 suggests that the succession still remains to be securely settled. The fact, however, that the Soviet system continued to maintain itself after Stalin's death is significant, but it points not to the lesser significance of Stalin but to the high degree of institutionalization of the totalitarian system through an elaborate bureaucratic network, operated at the top by the political lieutenants of the leader. It is they who pull the levers while the dictator calls the signals. With the dictator gone, they have undertaken also, so far successfully, the task of calling the signals.

The reader may wonder why we do not discuss the "structure of government," or perhaps the "constitution" of these totalitarian systems. The reason is that these structures are of very little importance; they are continually changing, and they do so accordingly to the old French adage: "tout ça change, tout c'est la même chose." The "structure of government" has no real significance because the power of decision is completely concentrated, either in a single leader or in a collective body, at least for a limited period. More specifically, a constitution has, under these conditions, largely propagandistic value. It is not a constitution in the functional Western sense of providing a system of effective, regularized restraints, (55j) but a disguise by which a "democratic" framework is being suggested, a kind of window-dressing for the totalitarian reality. Such bodies of the Soviet Union and the several satellites as appear

---

* The most recent and dramatic illustration of this was the secret speech delivered at the Twentieth Party Congress by Nikita Khrushchev, which, however, might somewhat exaggerate Stalin's role in order to minimize the responsibility of the successors.

in the garb of "legislative bodies," or the Reichstag of Hitler's Germany, are essentially there to acclaim the decisions made. Similarly, the judicial machinery, devoid of all independence, is actually part and parcel of the administrative and bureaucratic hierarchy. The very shapelessness of the vast bureaucratic machinery is part of the technique of manipulating the absolute power which the dictator and his lieutenants have at their disposal. It is therefore necessary to say something more about these sub-leaders.

It is this significant role played in the totalitarian system by the political lieutenants of the dictator that suggests an additionally unique feature of the system. These political lieutenants wield the levers of control that hold the totalitarian dictatorship together, and are instrumental in maintaining the dictator in power. Yet in spite of this crucial function most studies of modern totalitarianisms tend to ignore the political phenomenon of the dictator's lieutenants. A notable exception to this is Sigmund Neumann's path-breaking *Permanent Revolution*. In it Neumann attempted the first analysis of the totalitarian lieutenant and pointed to the four decisive elements which "make up the composite structure of the leader's henchmen." (149a; 115) These, he suggested, were the bureaucratic, feudal, democratic, and militant.

The bureaucratic element, in the light of this analysis, is the outstanding feature of the totalitarian leadership elite. Modern totalitarianism, unlike the more traditional dictatorships, is a highly bureaucratized system of power (see Chapters 3 and 17). Without this complex bureaucracy the total character of the system could not be maintained. The party organization in particular is a hierarchically structured political machine, and the efficient bureaucrat is an indispensable political lieutenant of the dictator. In this respect the similarity between such men as Bormann and Malenkov is more than striking—they were both capable and efficient bureaucrats who held their positions by virtue not only of administrative ability but, and this in totalitarianism is more important, "because they were found worthy of the supreme leader's confidence." (149b)

The feudal element, in terms of Neumann's analysis, is involved in the system of delegation of power to local satraps, be they *Gauleiters* or *Obkom* secretaries, who then act on behalf of the dictator. Such "feudal" vassals are not only territorially distributed; they also operate on the top levels, manipulating important levers of power such as the secret police. Himmler, Bocchini, and Beria were thus responsible for making sure that no internal challenge to the dictator's power arose, and the dictator at all times had to make certain that such posts were filled by men of unquestionable loyalty. In return, all of these lieutenants shared in the system of spoils, and every effort was made to develop in them a vested interest in the continued maintenance of the dictator's power.

The third feature of this leadership elite is its internal democratic element. That is not to say that it is subject to the customary democratic processes of selection and election. "Dictatorship is democracy for the insiders alone. Brutal and merciless as the lieutenants usually are toward their enemies, strutting like the gods of vengeance, they had better not play the boss within the circle of their associates." (149c) This is actually an oligarchic rather than a democratic equality. The lieutenants must accordingly be careful not to appear to crave excessive popularity. Such a craving can have disastrous effects also in so far as it may challenge the dictator's own domain. And the totalitarian dictator tolerates no trespassers on his power. The political lieutenants must thus limit themselves to the function of providing the dictator with the necessary contact with the masses and acting as his gauges of public opinion.

The final element, growing out of the revolutionary character of totalitarianism, is the militancy of the leadership. The political lieutenants must act as subleaders in the struggle for the achievement of the totalitarian society. Each in his particular sphere, the totalitarian lieutenant must attempt to break down all resistance to the implementation of the ideological-political goals of the regime. He must lead the "battle of the grain," or he must strive for higher accomplishments in "socialist competition." He may even have to encourage women to increase the number of their pregnancies. And it is through such battles, be they local or national, that the political lieutenants are weaned, steeled, and promoted.

The general aptness of this analysis is illustrated, with some obvious reservations, both in the case of Soviet internal politics and the present Communist leadership of the captive nations of East-Central Europe. The men who surrounded Stalin prior to his death, and who since have risen to the top, were precisely of this type. They provided the dictator with an efficient bureaucratic machine and substituted its filing indexes for many a machine gun. Men like Malenkov, who worked at the apex of the political *apparat,* or Khrushchev, who acted for many years as a feudal vassal in the Ukraine, produced for the dictator an efficient core of loyal supporters, who were not likely to challenge his political supremacy. They came to the fore only when the inexorable laws of human life removed from the picture the familiar, and dreaded, face of the dictator.

The present Soviet leadership, which, in many ways, is a leadership of the second lieutenants operating without the leader, has also its own body of able and hardworking political assistants. The careers of men like Ponomarenko and Brezhnev are illustrative of the efforts of the new leadership to surround itself with efficient and trustworthy political bureaucrats. Ponomarenko during the late forties served as Party Secretary in Byelorussia until his adoption into the top circle of the *apparatchiki* (members of the *apparat*) in Moscow. At the Nineteenth Party Congress in October 1952 he was promoted to the new Party Secretariat and the Party Presidium, which replaced the Politburo. Following Stalin's death he was dropped from these bodies—presumably by the party old guard (18b)—but became Minister of Culture under Premier Malenkov. In March of 1954 he was appointed to the important post of First Secretary of Kazakhstan Party Committee in the place of an older Stalinist, Shayakhmetov. In 1955 he was appointed ambassador to Poland, the most important European satellite of the USSR. Brezhnev is another such typical new *apparatichik* whose career took him in the last four years from the post of a regional party secretary (in Dnepropetrovsk), to Moldavia as First Secretary, and then to Moscow following the Nineteenth Congress as member of the Secretariat and candidate member of the Party Presidium. After Stalin's death he was dropped from both posts and appointed head of the Political Administration of the Navy. In March of 1954 he assumed the post of Second Secretary in Kazkhstan under Ponomarenko. A year later, when Ponomarenko was shifted, he became First Secretary and at the Twentieth Party Congress in 1956 was again appointed to the top party organs. Both typify the younger generation of the political lieutenants of the present leadership.

Their counterparts are to be found in the satellite Communist leadership of East-Central Europe. During Stalin's life, efforts were made to focus the spotlight of totalitarian propaganda on certain local leaders, and to build them up in the image of the central dictator

—Stalin. Admittedly this was only a half-hearted attempt. They were never allowed to claim the mantel of the dictator in such crucial matters as ideological definition and they were continually expected to affirm their allegiance to the "Teacher and Leader of World Communism." Nonetheless, men like Bierut or Gottwald or Rakosi were pictured as outstanding leaders and they far outshone their colleagues in the allotted quotas of propaganda limelight. Following Stalin's death and the emergence of a nonpersonal type of leadership in the USSR, it was felt in Moscow that the prominence of the Bieruts and the Gottwalds could constitute a threat to the unity of the Soviet bloc. Indicative of the subservience of these Communist parties to Moscow is the noteworthy fact that within half a year of the proclamation of the principle of collective leadership in the Soviet Union, a de-emphasis of personal leadership was apparent in the satellites. To take the case of Bierut, instead of combining in one person the posts of premier and party secretary, Bierut, in the Soviet pattern, was restricted only to the latter. There has been a corresponding de-emphasis of his personality in the press. Similarly in Czechoslovakia, where the convenient death of Gottwald helped to remove him from the picture, the new President Zapotocky does not personally control the party machine.

These satellite political lieutenants of the central leadership (and formerly of the dictator himself) differ from their Soviet counterparts in one important respect. There is considerable evidence to indicate that decision-making in the USSR is highly centralized and is the prerogative of the men at the top of the party *apparat*—the Party Presidium. The Soviet political lieutenants have little discretionary power and generally operate either on the basis of direct orders or relatively specific instructions. Their colleagues in the captive nations naturally also operate within the framework of specific instructions but these generally tend to be somewhat more flexible in their local application. Furthermore, the satellite satraps tend to base their decision-making to a certain extent on the anticipated reaction of the central Moscow leadership, which is not able at all times to provide direct supervision. This gives the national Communist leaders a greater degree of responsibility, although also increasing their occupational risks.

Both the Soviet and the satellite political lieutenants, however, seem to fit the categories suggested by Neumann's analysis. They operate on behalf of the central leadership to which they pay ideological and material obeisance, and in most cases are its direct appointees. A somewhat more difficult and complex situation is presented by Mao Tse-Tung. His rise to power, his leadership of the revolution, and his control over the vast masses of China puts him in a somewhat more independent position. Until Stalin's death, Mao Tse-Tung acknowledged Stalin's ideological supremacy and in this respect appeared in the guise of an apostle. He was accordingly somewhere on an intermediary level between a political lieutenant and a totalitarian dictator in his own right. Stalin's death left Mao Tse-Tung in unquestioned political and ideological control of the Chinese Communist Party, which, however, continues to acknowledge the common ideological as well as power-political bonds with Moscow. His position thus no longer fits the more restricted standards set for the category of political lieutenant of the central dictator.

With this problem of the lieutenants clarified, let us now return to the position of the leader. Hitler, in the opinion of Alan Bullock, author of the most carefully documented recent biography, exercised absolute power, if ever a man did. (22b) He thus confirmed a report given by the former British ambassador, Nevile Henderson, who wrote that Goering told him that "when a decision has to be taken, none of us count more than the stones on which we are standing. It is the Führer alone who decides." (77a) In support he quotes the notorious Hans Frank as writing: "Our Constitution is the will of the Führer." The Nuremberg trials produced massive evidence in support of this conclusion. The position of Mussolini, according to Ciano's diary, was very similar. (179a) This concentration of power was an element of decided weakness as well as strength. A number of Hitler's gravest errors of judgment, such as the attack upon Poland and later upon the Soviet Union, were arrived at without any kind of consultation, let alone by group decision. All available evidence suggests that, had there been such group action required, the errors would not have been made. This truly absolute power of Hitler manifested itself during the war in his assumption of military tasks for which he was wholly unprepared. He came to picture himself as one of history's great strategists, and placed himself in the position of making ultimate decisions in this field, which proved the undoing of the German army. (78; 65)

The position of overwhelming leadership that the totalitarian dictator occupies makes it necessary to inquire into the kind of leadership he wields. It is also necessary to explore more fully the relation of the dictator to his party following. The two questions are to a considerable extent interrelated, but for purposes of clarification they must nonetheless be treated as distinct. There have been a number of approaches to the problem of leadership. One of the more comprehensive schemes of classification is that offered by Max Weber. Since his theories have had much influence, it seems desirable to state that the totalitarian leader fits none of Weber's categories. However, Hitler has, by a number of writers, been described as a "charismatic" leader. (148b) Since in Weber's view, Moses, Christ, and Mohammed were typical charismatic leaders, it is quite evident that Hitler does not fit the type. Arguments that the common factor is the inspirational and emotional appeal he had for his following is misleading in a double respect. In the first place, Weber's conception of charisma implies a transcendent faith in God which was characteristically lacking both in Hitler himself and in the typical follower of his creed; the same was true of Mussolini and other Fascist leaders, like Peron in Argentina. In the second place, the believed-in charisma is not a primarily emotional "appeal," but a faith of genuine religious content, metarational in its source, rational in its theology. But the fact that Hitler was not a charismatic leader does not mean that he was therefore *either* a "traditional" leader or a "rational-legal" leader—Max Weber's other two types. For the traditional leader is typified by monarchs like Louis XIV or Henry VIII, while the rational-legal leader is exemplified by the president or prime minister of a constitutional democracy. (247b) The emergence of the totalitarian dictator proves the Weberian typology inadequate. This is part of the unprecedented, unique quality of totalitarian dictatorship which has been stressed before. The problem of the kind of leadership therefore persists.

It is evident from the experience to date that totalitarian leadership is built upon metarational emotional appeals that are cast in strongly rational terms. The analysis of ideology will show that this leadership is believed to be an executioner of history, of forces that arise inevitably from the predestined course of social events. It is the consequent sense of mission that has led to the interpretation of this leadership as charismatic. Such a view entirely overlooks that this "appeal" is reinforced by factors that are totally absent in the case of genuine charisma, more especially the control of mass communications and propaganda, and the terror apparatus (see Chapters 11 and 14). Both these features fully mature only in the course of the effective seizure of total power, but they are present from the start. The early history of the Fascist and Nazi movements is replete with the technique of mass propaganda and the manipulation of coercive violence. The notorious whippings, burnings, and castor-oil orgies of the Italian Fascists are paralleled by the *Saalschlacht* (lecture hall battles) of the Nazi storm troopers which led to large-scale intimidation of both followers and outsiders long before the actual seizure of power. The tactics of Lenin (see also Chapter 9) also were violently coercive and made of the Bolshevik "party" a conspiratorial military brotherhood rather than a group competing in the market place with discussion and argument. We are not implying here that the conditions of tsarist Russia were favorable to such "bourgeois" or liberal conduct; the facts are, however, that propaganda and terror cradled the Bolshevik party, as well as the Fascist parties. Still another type of totalitarian leadership, more obviously noncharismatic, is that of Stalin, who certainly cannot be discarded, since he represents the most effective man in the group. From the period of Lenin's death to the great purges of 1936 to 1938 there was certainly no question of a "charismatic" appeal exercised by Stalin on the masses. His climb to power was made possible purely by internal bureaucratic measures, augmented by firm doses of terror and coerced propaganda, while the appeal which rationalized his claim to power was phrased in terms of collectivization, industrialization, and preservation of the Soviet Union. But this appeal was made possible only through intra-Party maneuvers, and it was organization and not popularity—for Trotsky was certainly more popular— which provided the basis for Stalin's seizure and consolidation of power.

As a result of this organizational interaction between leader and following, the peculiar nature of this leadership is inseparable from the mythical (or, perhaps more precisely, magical) identification of leader and led. In the early days of the Nazi movement, a book appeared which was characteristically entitled *Hitler—A German Movement.* (31) The concept which helped the Nazis to accomplish this feat of collective identification was the "race." The race, as we have seen, is not to be confused with the Germans; the Aryans are to be found among a variety of peoples, and their discovery is possible only on the basis of their identification of such persons with the leader. The corresponding concept in the communist armory is that of the proletariat, which does not consist solely of those who actually work, except in a marginal sense. By introducing the idea of class-consciousness, the actually existing mass of the workers is transcended, just as the Germans are in the Aryan race concept, and only those workers who are ready to identify themselves with the leader, Marx, Lenin, Stalin, are truly class-conscious and hence intrinsically involved in the process of totalitarian leadership.

There is no particular reason for inventing a weird term to designate this type of leadership, other than to say that it is "totalitarian." It represents a distinct and separate type, along with the "traditional," the "rational-legal," and the "charismatic." It may be helpful, considering the pseudo-religious emotionalism of these regimes, to designate this kind of totalitarian leadership as "pseudo-charismatic." It bears certain resemblances to still another distinct type, also not adequately developed by Weber and his followers, the "revolutionary" leader. Indeed, it may be argued that the "totalitarian" leader is a kind of "revolutionary" leader. Certainly, the characteristic features of Hitler or Stalin are more nearly comparable to those of Robespierre or Cromwell; but a detailed analysis would lead us too far afield.

In any case it might be said in conclusion and by way of a summary that the totalitarian leader possesses more nearly absolute power than any previous type of political leader, that he is completely identified with his actual following, both by himself and by them, in a kind of mystical union, that he is able to operate on both these levels as he does because he is backed by mass propaganda and terror— coercive cohesion and that therefore his leadership is not to be confused either with tyranny, or despotism, or absolutism in their historical forms (see Chapter 1).

Chapter Three

The Nature and Role of the Party

To call a totalitarian leader's following a party is quite common. And yet it is a rather bewildering use of words, for the totalitarian following is decidedly different from the kind of party usually found in constitutional democratic regimes. The totalitarian movements outwardly adopted the forms of such parties, but their inner dynamic is quite different. They do not freely recruit their membership, as democratic parties do, but institute the sort of tests which are characteristic of clubs, orders, and similar exclusive "brotherhoods." They correspondingly practice the technique of expulsion, usually on the basis of an autocratic *fiat* by the party leader, whereas in democratic party life the expulsion, if employed at all, is the result of a formalized judicial process. Within the party, there is no "democracy" either. The party following does not decide even if they vote or elect the leadership; it is subject to autocratic direction in matters of policy, and to hierarchical control in matters of leadership.

The first to formulate and to set in motion the operational principles of a totalitarian party was Lenin. In his fanatic insistence on strict party discipline, total obedience to the will of the leadership, and unquestioning acceptance of the ideological program (as formulated by the leader), Lenin charted the path so successfully later followed by Stalin. In his *What is to be Done* (1902) Lenin outlined the centralist organizational pattern which his movement was to adopt, and rejected firmly the idea of a broad popular party with open membership. "Everyone will probably agree that 'broad democratic principles' presuppose the two following conditions: first, full publicity, and second, election to all functions. It would be absurd to speak of a democracy without publicity, that is, a publicity which extends beyond the circle of the membership of the organization . . . No one would ever call an organization that is hidden from everyone but its members by a veil of secrecy, a democratic organization." (113e) Such an open organization, under tsarist conditions, he considered absurd, and his conviction about a disciplined paramilitary party did not waver despite the split it produced in the Marxist ranks. The basis for the first totalitarian movement was thus laid. It is seen, in so far as Lenin was right in justifying his course by reference to conditions in tsarist Russia, that the autocracy of the tsars is thus mirrored in totalitarianism. This must be borne in mind in considering the general problem of the totalitarian party.

Following Max Weber, but eliminating his normative aspect of "free recruitment" from the general definition of a political party, it may be characterized as follows: A political party is a group of human beings, stably organized with the objective of securing or maintaining for its leaders the control of the government, and with the further objective of giving its members, through such control, ideal and material benefits and advantages. (55b; 106c; 225a) It must be stably organized in order to distinguish it from temporary factions and the like; the control of the government should be understood to cover other than political government, for example, church government; and it is very important to include both ideal and material advantages, since no party can exist without some advantages of both kinds accruing to its members. The familiar distinction between parties oriented toward ideology and patronage is sound only if the two criteria are understood as "predominating" rather than exclusive. But another distinction must be drawn in the light of the facts of totalitarian dictatorship, and that is the distinction which may be expressed as that between cooperative and coercive parties. The latter are exclusive (elitist), hierarchically organized and autocratic. This too is not an absolute contrast, but a question of the prevailing tendency. (136)

These traits of the totalitarian party have at times been rationalized in terms of the fighting position of such groups. Since, generally speaking, any group organization tends to be more tightly autocratic as the group encounters more difficulty in its fight for survival, there is some ground for thus explaining the autocracy of totalitarian movements. But what concerns us primarily here is the *fact* of such autocratic leadership, not its explanation. It would, in any case, not hold after the seizure of power, for, even after the party has achieved complete control, it does not become less autocratic. On the contrary, it becomes the vehicle for transforming the entire society in its image. This well-known dynamism shows that there are other drives involved besides the needs of a fighting group.

In the matured totalitarian society the role of the party is a distinctive one which bears little resemblance to the role of parties in democratic societies. As has been pointed out in the preceding chapter, it is the role of the party to provide a following for the dictator with which he can identify himself. According to a well-known phrase of Mussolini, the party has the function of the "capillaries" in the body; it is neither the heart, nor the head, but those endings where the blood of party doctrine, party policy, and party sentiment mingles with the rest of the body politic. In a sense, the party may be pictured as the "elite" of the totalitarian society, if the word elite is taken in a very neutral sense.* In view of the total dependence of the party as a following upon the leader at its head, it can be argued that the party does not possess any corporate existence of its own. It is in this respect comparable to the Hobbesian state, in which all the separate members of the society are severally and totally dependent upon the sovereign. But somehow such a view seems not to do justice to the collective sense of the whole, and the almost complete loss of personal identity which the party members suffer, or rather enjoy, as they feel themselves merged in the larger whole. This feeling seems to contradict another aspect of these movements, namely, the unquestioning obedience. Fascists and Nazis never wearied of repeating Mussolini's formula: "Believe, Obey, Fight"— these were the focal points of Fascist and Nazi education. In this kind of military subordination, the individual seems to confront the commander as an alien and wholly detached being. The answer to this seeming paradox, fascist writers found in what they conceived to be the "style" of the new life. This "style of living" was in Nazi Germany proclaimed, as it had been in Italy, to be that of the "marching column," it being indifferent for what purpose the column was being formed. (287a)

The Soviets, on the other hand, never weary of proclaiming that their communist party is a democratically organized movement composed of class-conscious workers and peasants. Unlike the Fascists or the Nazi Party, the organization of the Communist Party is thus designed to give the outward appearance of inner party democracy,

* Such a usage would, however, conflict with that suggested by Lasswell and Kaplan (106), p. 201, where an elite is defined as those "with most power in a group"; it is contrasted with the "mid-elite" who are those "with less power" and the class which has "least" power. Following such a definition, the party would be the "mid-elite."

with the final authority resting in the hands of the party membership through the party congress. The congress, which is to meet every three years, and is composed of delegates from all the party organizations, is the highest legislative body of the party. It elects a Central Committee as its permanent organ to legislate on behalf of the congress during the lengthy intersession periods. The executive organ is the Party Presidium, known until October 1952 as the Politburo, and the Party Secretariat is the chief bureaucratic organ of the party. Under these central party organs, there are the 15 republican party organizations (for example, that in Georgia), each with its own Central Committee, Presidium, and Secretariat; 8 *Krai* organizations; 167 regional and 36 *okrug* organizations; 544 city organizations; 4,886 district and 350,304 primary party organizations.* (271b) All of these, according to official interpretation, operate in the spirit of "democratic centralism," that is to say, that there is full freedom of discussion prior to the determination of policy, but once policy is determined subsidiary organizations are expected to execute stated policy in full.

In fact, however, authority and decision-making is highly centralized, and during the Stalinist era, the power of the dictator was certainly no less than in Germany or Italy. But the rise of Stalin was made possible by his skillful exploitation of the position of general secretary of the party. In the internal struggle for power he knew how to manipulate the personnel of the party organization, to put his henchmen into key positions, to demote or denounce the henchmen of his rivals, and generally to utilize all the resources of a large organization, including its files, as so many weapons.† During his rule, an inner party bureaucracy, the *apparat,* composed of full-time party members in a position to wield most power, steadily developed and expanded to its present tremendous size and importance, but even by 1925 some 25,000 party members were full-time employees of the party *apparat.* (47a) Consequently, on Stalin's death a small

---

* See also Chapter 17 on bureaucracy for some estimates of the number of party bureaucrats. In 1956, in addition to the fifteen republican party central committees, a special bureau was set up in the Moscow Central Committee for RSFSR party affairs, headed by Khrushchev.

† Khrushchev's secret speech of February 1956 revealed that even the Politburo was broken up by Stalin into smaller committees (e.g., the "Sextet" for Foreign Affairs) which Stalin himself co-ordinated, and that Stalin sometimes arbitrarily forbade Politburo members to attend its sessions.

group of individuals in the Party Presidium, who took over control of the party, shared the dictatorial power. Control over the party today is concentrated in the hands of this small group of men in the Presidium, and particularly in the hands of the First Secretary of the party (and presumably chairman of the Presidium), N. S. Khrushchev, who, through his Secretariat, controls the work of the various sections of the Central Committee of the party. These sections deal with a variety of functions: there is the section on party appointments (so important to Stalin's rise to power); a section on political controls over the military, on foreign affairs, the special section dealing with police matters; there are the sections on industrial development, propaganda and agitation, and so forth. (47b) These sections, as can be seen from the preceding, not only control the life of the party but also supervise the functions of the respective ministries of the government. In fact, the top party leaders often assume personal direction for various phases of state activity: Mikoyan over foreign trade, Beria formerly over police and also over the Caucasus region, Kaganovich over railroads, planning, and the Ukraine, and so on.

This bureaucratization of power is also duplicated on lower levels. The regional party committee, for instance, also reflects through its organizational pattern both the concentration of power in the hands of the party bureaucrats and the control of the state bureaucracy by the party. The regional party committee accordingly, in addition to its own Secretariat, has various sections dealing with such matters as propaganda and agitation, industry, roads, agriculture, trade unions, trade organizations, enlightenment. It is no exaggeration to say that the regional committee is constantly in charge of the entire life of the region, either through actual direction or supervision. As a result the party leaders are frequently swamped with work, and sheer paper work reaches fantastic proportions. This, of course, impairs the zeal and the revolutionary quality of the party. There is thus constant ambivalence in party declarations on this subject; in one sense, the party warns its officials against becoming overinvolved in operations of the governmental bureaucracy; yet, not to become involved is to let power slip from its hands. Thus, for instance, the official journal of the Central Committee, in an article entitled (in translation) "Raise the organizational role of the party apparat," emphasized the necessity for supervision and stressed that party officials should not work for others—that is, the state bureaucrats—and should guard against red tape. (265a) Yet, the Central Committee explicitly urged the party members "to put a decisive end to a liberal attitude toward violators of state discipline . . . to replace them by active organizers . . . to intensify the guidance of industry, to strive for concrete results in improving the work of enterprises." (252a) While there may appear to be little contradiction between these two positions, attempts to implement both might result in some headaches for the party bureaucrat.

The party bureaucracy is thus both the brains and the blood stream of the Soviet system. Without it, it is not only likely that the political regime would crumble, but probably the entire economic life of the country would come to a standstill. In that sense, the party bureaucracy is far more important, and indeed crucial, to the system than its counterparts in both the Nazi and Fascist states. Since the death of Stalin, the *apparat* has become even more important as a mechanism of modern dictatorship. To quote an eloquent assessment of one of the foremost students of the Soviet scene:

It provides the organizational cement which holds the Party together. Out of the evanescent magic of personal despotism, a new design of government has been forged. The personal dictatorship of the leader has embodied itself in the Party dictatorship of the apparatus. Like Frankenstein's monster, the apparatus has acquired a momentum of its own, a vested interest in its own survival which promises to outlive its creator and to perpetuate his system of rule long after the forces which shaped it have been forgotten. (47c)

This, however, does not mean that the individual party member is unimportant. On the contrary, the Communist Party puts the greatest emphasis on individual eligibility, personal loyalty, and political consciousness of a candidate for membership. "It must not be forgotten that to enter the sacred door of the Party one must be spotless not only in his public life but in his personal life as well." (271c) That this sacred door opens the way to greater career opportunities is an additional factor enhancing the prestige of party membership, which, however, is not devoid of hardships and obligations. Indeed, one of the outstanding features of Communist Party membership is the pressure put on the members to make them active participants in the organization's collective as well as individual undertakings. This point was strongly re-emphasized at the Nineteenth and Twentieth Party Congresses, and Khrushchev spared no words in his castigation of those party members who fail to perform their tasks. Party members are accordingly expected to participate constantly in various study circles, reading sessions, special seminars, and discussions. They are utilized in stimulating "socialist competition" in their places of work. They are expected to proselytize among their relatives, friends, and colleagues. They must be active in setting up small study-groups among nonmembers to familiarize them with the teachings of Marxism-Leninism.

At the regular party organization meetings, the prime concern of those attending is to report on the failure or success in meeting their *partnagruzka* (party duty or obligation). In such meetings the individual members must fully account for their activities, admit any shortcomings and criticize themselves for them. In this they are assisted, either spontaneously or by prearrangement, by their colleagues, who report also their own delinquencies, while criticizing one another. These critical mutual self-examinations are not restricted to the performance of *partnagruzka* only. The party is also a paternal institution concerned, albeit for motives of efficiency, with the moral and personal life of its members. Accordingly, such meetings quite often develop into dissecting operations in which a member's personal life is scrutinized and castigated. Excessive drinking, sexual promiscuity, rudeness, and vulgarity to subordinates and/or family are subjects which crop up constantly at such party meetings. And all of this is recorded faithfully in extensive protocols and individual *kharakteristikas* (individual personal files) which are kept in the party archives, and copies of which are forwarded to upper party organs. During periods of accentuated militancy and crisis such sessions often produce expulsions from the party and subsequent arrests, although such are not as frequent as the imposition of reprimands.

Party members are furthermore obliged to participate in the special campaigns, such as the Soviet elections or the 1954 agricultural campaign. In the course of these mass operations the party members agitate, propagandize, and work for the fulfillment of the tasks set. This they do after work, during lunch breaks, and in their leisure time. They thus set the example for the masses with their energy, spirit of self-sacrifice, and complete devotion to duty. All this, of course, is very time-consuming and physically exhausting. One of the frequent complaints of party members, expressed after they have defected to the West and evident also in Soviet materials, is that they are overwhelmed, overburdened, overused. Yet, at the same time, all this generates considerable enthusiasm. The membership is made to feel part of a constructive machine, led by dynamic leadership, achieving unprecedented goals. Their personal identity is submerged in the totality of the party, and the might of the party becomes a source of personal gratification. That this gratification frequently takes the form of more rapid promotion seems further to enhance its value, while a sense of unity and integration frequently obscures the more seamy aspects of the system.

While such total identification of the party with the leader and its related capillary function is quite common to all totalitarian regimes, significant differences appear when we ask about the relation of this organization to the government. This relationship is frequently pictured as simply one of control, but the actual situation is more complex. The divergence between the Bolshevik, the Fascist, and the Nazi regimes is symbolized by the position of the respective leaders in them. Stalin for many years and until World War II was the General Secretary of the Communist Party of the Soviet Union. Mussolini proudly called himself for many years the Capo del Governo (head of the government), while Hitler was the Führer (leader) of the movement and president and chancellor of the Reich at the same time. The relation of the party to the government corresponded to this set of titles. In the Soviet Union the party was superior to the government, and the heads of government departments were correspondingly "people's commissars." In Italy the government was for many years superior to the party; this corresponded to the Hegelian emphasis on the state in fascist ideology (see Chapter 7). But, as Germino (64b) has observed, "although at the outset Italian Fascist theorizing on the party differed markedly from Nazi and Soviet ideology, these contrasts became less sharp as the non-totalitarian wing of Fascism became silenced and the party, in accordance with what appear to be the imperatives of totalitarian rule, expanded to wield extensive power independently of the governmental services."

In Hitler's Germany, party and government stood in a position of rough equivalence to each other and the same was true of Italy in the late thirties. The German situation was strikingly characterized by

Ernst Fraenkel when he undertook to interpret the Nazi system as that of a "dual state," or, more properly speaking, a "dual government." One of these he designated as the prerogative state in which everything was arbitrarily decided by party functionaries from the Führer on down; the other continued to function along the lines of the established legal order. Fraenkel leaves no doubt, however, that the prerogative state was the superior in his opinion, that it had "the last word" in that it could at any time break into the other, set aside its rules, or superimpose others. (54b) This situation was perhaps best illustrated at the time when Hitler is said to have exclaimed, after a court had found Pastor Niemöller not guilty, that "this is the last time a German court is going to declare someone innocent whom I have declared guilty." He had Niemöller rearrested by the Gestapo. But, precisely because it was Hitler himself who had the last word and who was both leader of the party and chief of the state, something of a coequal status prevailed in the lower echelons.

It looked at the end of war, and immediately thereafter, as if a similar situation was developing in the Soviet Union. As Premier of the Soviet Union and Marshal of its Armed Forces, Stalin appeared in the dual role similar to that which Hitler occupied until his death. However, since that time, the party secretariat and the premiership have fallen into different hands, making it more feasible to assess their respective roles. It appears that on all levels of Soviet life, from the agricultural collectives through the secret police to the Foreign Ministry, exertions are being made to strengthen the role of the party through the introduction of party functionaries into leading posts, thereby maintaining the dynamic role of the party in the system. Indeed, there are no indications that the influence of the party is on the wane. Recent efforts to revitalize its militancy, such as a new ideological campaign and a membership drive for workers and peasants, suggest clearly that the party remains the political and ideological standard-bearer and continues to supervise the activities of the state apparatus. Among the first to bear the brunt of this attack resulting from a re-emphasis of party predominance were the intellectuals, who were curtly reminded that it is the party which sets their tasks and determines their doctrinal compliance. Similarly, the state officialdom was attacked for its bureaucratic attitudes and ordered to mend its ways. Symptomatic of the party's crucial role is also the fact that it is the first secretary of the party who is leading the current agricultural "battle" for increased grain production.

The administrative-political role which the party plays in the USSR, acting as a sort of super-bureaucracy controlling and penetrating the purely administrative institutions, would seem to indicate that its predominance, in so far as the foreseeable future is concerned, is not likely to be challenged. Periodic purges as well as new campaigns restore to the party the necessary degree of *élan* and consequent cohesion, while maintaining at the same time its revolutionary fervor. How to maintain this *élan* and revolutionary fervor was, furthermore, not nearly as acute a problem in the USSR as it was in Nazi Germany, or Fascist Italy, where large numbers of people were admitted into the NSDAP by *fiat*. In the USSR, membership in the Communist Party still is a privilege. And while the state apparatus maintains the system in function, it is the party or rather its leaders which sets new goals and keeps the totalitarian grip on the population. Without it the Soviet system would become brittle and sterile, and would be likely to lose its vitality. The recurrent emphasis on *partiinost* (literally, partyness) serves as a reminder to those who would like to forget it.

In order to work effectively, the party must be restricted in size. It must be an honor worth striving for to belong to it. Neither the Bolshevik party nor the Italian Fascist party were very large at the time power was seized by their leaders. They were both subsequently enlarged. The Nazi Party, on the other hand, strove to increase its size as long as it was engaged in competition with other parties, and the same holds true today of the Communist Party in Italy and France, among others. In such cases, the membership ought after the seizure of power to be reduced; the fact that this did not happen in Germany explains in part the position the party occupied. Yet, in a sense the blood purge of June 30, 1934, was such a reduction of party membership; the storm troopers of Captain Roehm became an inferior group in the party hierarchy.

The Communist Party in the Soviet Union increased its membership very gradually during the twenties, then grew rapidly between 1928 and 1933, reaching a high of 3.5 million in 1933. It declined sharply during the purges of the thirties, although by 1941 it again reached its 1933 level. During the war there occurred a rapid step up to about 6 million, as the leadership hoped to secure greater support for the war effort by conferring the coveted party membership to a large number of people. During some of the war months the party actually was growing at the rate of a 100,000 people per month. Since the end of the war there has been increased concern shown by the leaders about the low political literacy of the membership and a number of local purges have occurred, particularly in the national republics. The over-all party membership remained rather static, growing slowly by the end of 1952 to 6.9 million and by the end of 1955, to about 7.2 million. All in all, the Soviet Union's party has constituted only 2 to 4 per cent of the population.

The Italian Fascists similarly represented only a small percentage of the total population. There were about a million members by 1927, somewhat over 2 per cent of the population. Up to that year, the party had remained formally "open." Recruitment was "free," in Weber's sense, which was logical enough, considering that not until sometime after 1926 did the Fascists achieve absolute, totalitarian power. Soon afterwards, the ranks were closed. But they were opened again for some months in 1932–33, and some groups, such as government officials, were actually forced to join. Salvatorelli remarks that after 1932 membership became "more than ever a necessary condition not only for government employ . . . but . . . for all positions of any importance in industry, commerce, and culture." (179b)

The growth of the Fascist Party was due to yet another circumstance. Due to Mussolini's stress on youth (*giovinezza*), an annual contingent of several hundred thousand members were admitted from the youth organizations. By October 1934, it had reached 1,850,777, and by October 1939, 2,633,514, according to official figures issued by the party. This figure would still be only 5 per cent of the population, but it constituted about 17.5 per cent of the total electorate. Actually, during the war, membership rose rapidly, and by June 10, 1943, had reached 4,770,770. This was due to the removal of all restrictions for soldiers after the outbreak of war. But the Fascists, like the Soviets, soon realized their mistake, and in 1943 attempted to reverse this trend, and once again tried to make the party a selective one which would be composed of "fighters and believers," "the custodian of the revolutionary idea." (275a) In any case, the Fascist militia, with its half-million members, was the real heart of the Fascist Party, reinforced by the "old guard" and some of the more zealous youth. This militia, characteristically, always contested the secret polices' monopoly of terroristic procedures.

The German NSDAP went further, both in enlarging its size, and in developing a hard core of fanatics. For one thing, it was a mass party at the time of Hitler's accession to power; it had reached approximately one million by 1933. Financial as well as general political considerations led Hitler to build it into the largest political party ever built in Germany, measured not only by votes, but by membership as well. There was a rush into the party immediately after the seizure of power in 1933; a further expansion took place in 1937, when all government officials were forced into the party by "law." Since the Nazi Party was thus watered down into a fairly nondescript agglomeration, hardly animated by genuine enthusiasm, the inherent need for such an elite corps reasserted itself in the SS (Schutzstaffeln) of Heinrich Himmler. The SS were at first merely a part of the brownshirted storm troopers, but after the eclipse of the latter in 1934, the SS became separate and predominant. Indeed, this order rather than the National Socialist Party must be considered the dynamic core of the Nazi system. The SS remained always quite restricted, even though during the war the organization of the Waffen-SS (see Chapter 14) diluted it somewhat. (287b)

Generally speaking, these facts show that the party and/or special cadres within it will be highly selective and elitist in a totalitarian dictatorship. This tendency toward elitism reinforces the strictly hierarchical structuring of the totalitarian parties we have noted above. The rigid hierarchy and centralized power are the result of an evolutionary process; everywhere there is at first considerable impact from below; later the party following becomes more and more subdued, until finally its influence is negligible. This is part of the maturing process of totalitarian regimes. Rotation of party leadership becomes a very real problem in connection with this solidifying of the hierarchy. Both in Italy and Germany, the fact that the same leader remained in control throughout the existence of the dictatorship undoubtedly inhibited such rotation. Yet, a purge occurred in both regimes by which some of the older sub-leaders were eliminated. Others would no doubt have followed after the war, if several confidential statements to that effect by Hitler, Himmler, and others are allowed to stand. (See Chapter 15 for how the purge in the Soviet Union has developed into a regular instrument.) But such crises notwithstanding, the party constitutes the mainstay of totalitarian dictatorship. Without his party's support the dictator would be inconceivable; his unquestioned leadership gives the party its peculiar dynamic, indeed fanatical, devotion to the dictatorship, and the spineless attitude of subjection of its members toward the man at the top is merely the psychological counterpart to the party's ruthless assertion of the will and determination to rule and to shape the society in its image.

Chapter Four

Youth and the Future of the Dictatorship

The totalitarian dictatorship, because of its sense of mission, is vitally concerned with the transmission of its power and ideological program to the younger generation. Indeed, it is upon the young that the hopes of the dictatorship are focused, and the totalitarian regime never tires of asserting that the future belongs to the youth. Feeling little or no commitment to the past, the totalitarian regimes are unrestrained in emphasizing the failures of yesterday and the utopian quality of tomorrow. Stalin put it in a way that would fit Hitler and Mussolini just as well. "The youth is our future, our hope, comrades. The youth must take our place, the place of the old people. It must carry our banner to final victory. Among the peasants there are not a few old people, borne down by the burden of the past, burdened with the habits and the recollections of the old life. Naturally, they are not always able to keep pace with the party, to keep pace with the Soviet government. But that cannot be said of our youth. They are free from the burden of the past, and it is easiest for them to assimilate Lenin's behests." (199d) The imaginations and the energy of the youth, the leadership hopes, will thus be harnessed to aid, and later carry on, the program of totalitarian reconstruction launched by the party. The intensity of the efforts to convert and discipline the youth have no parallel in the recent traditional dictatorships, which were much more concerned

with the problem of immediate political and social stability. Only
some philosophic constructs like the Platonic Republic come close
to matching the totalitarian myths for, and indoctrination of, the
young.

All the totalitarian movements have been concerned with the indoctrination of the young. *Giovinezza* was one of the key slogans in
Mussolini's rhetoric. Both the Italian Fascists and their German imitators organized youth before their advent to power. When Hitler
said that the National Socialist state would have to take care that it
obtained, through an appropriate indoctrination of youth, a generation ready to make the final and greatest decisions on this globe, he
was merely echoing views which Mussolini had expounded from the
beginning. The Italian Balilla organization, although formally
embodied into the governmental apparatus by the law of April 3,
1926, formed the training ground for the Fascist party. (64c) The
law establishing it declared that Fascism considers the education of
youth one of the fundamental tasks of the revolution, in an "atmosphere of discipline and service to the nation." Hitler, when he came
to put forward the National Youth Law on December 1, 1936, could
do little better than paraphrase these sentiments, stating that on the
youth depends the future of the German people (*Volkstum*). The
age groups in the Hitler youth were somewhat higher than in the
Balilla, but otherwise the story was largely the same.

All Fascists stress the training of youth outside family and school
for the tough life of warriors and conquerors who are continually
on the march and must be ready to endure all the hardships of such
an existence. Hitler proclaimed dramatically at the party meeting
of 1935: "The German youth of the future must be as hard as the
steel from the plants of Krupp. The development of mental capacity is only of secondary importance." Both the Balilla organization
and the Hitler youth (216) were considered essential branches of the
party, even though the Balilla remained within the framework of
the government until 1937, when the secretary of the Fascist Party
personally assumed the leadership of the organization. But from
1926 onward Fascist youth was actually led by Renat Ricci, a key
member of the party directorate who also directly reported to the
Capo del Governo. In Germany, Baldur von Schirach became
Reich Youth Leader in 1933 and likewise reported directly to the
Führer. However, the German Youth organization always re-

mained much more definitely a distinctive party organization. Both
organizations aspired to and eventually largely achieved the total
control of youth. The German law of 1936 explicity stated that
"the totality of German youth must be prepared for its future du-
ties," but only in April 1939 made membership obligatory for all
German youth. The O.N.B. (Balilla) did the same in 1937. We
do therefore find a close parallel in objectives: they are stated
for O.N.B. as military, physical, technical, spiritual and cultural—a
significant ranking of priorities. In keeping with this stress on the
warrior task and the warrior virtues, both organizations engaged in
a great deal of paramilitary activity. It is a melancholy thought that
much of the idealism and love of adventure which is perhaps the
best part of boyhood was thus channeled by these organizations into
activities which stimulated the lower instincts. The free organizations of the democratic countries, whether boy scouts or religious or
artistic groups, and even those connected with political parties,
though at times outwardly resembling these youth organizations,
are yet very different; even when the slogans they use are similar,
when they stress character and sports and the benefits of outdoor
life, the purpose is individual improvement and a finer personality
rather than the brute objectives of war and conquest.

The growth of these youth organizations under the inducements
and pressures of the fascist regimes was striking: in January 1924,
the membership of Italian Fascist youth organizations was 60,941,
while in July 1937 it was 6,052,581. In Germany, the total at the
end of 1932 was 107,856, while early in 1939 it was 7,728,259. Considering the relative population of Italy and Germany, it can be
seen that the Italian organization was even more successful in its effort to absorb the entire youth of the country. However, in the
course of the war, the Germans caught up and their total by 1942
approached 10,000,000.

Within the context of these vast organizations, a rigid selective
process was organized. Boys and girls were put through various
tests before they could graduate to the next higher group, and these
graduations, in Italy called *Leva Fascista,* were accompanied with
solemn ceremonies and highly emotionalized totalitarian ritual. Of
course, the final test was whether a member of one of the youth organizations qualified for membership in the party, or better, the SS
or the Armed SS (Waffen-SS), Himmler's military formations (see

42 DICTATOR AND PARTY

Chapter 13). Indeed, within the German Hitler Youth, by the year 1939, an inner core of superior fellows was organized, known as the Stamm-HJ, or trunk of the Hitler Youth. Members of this nucleus were presumably carefully selected and had to fulfill "the same racial conditions which the Nazi Party insists upon for its members." Thus was the total enlistment of youth in the Fascist regimes made a key factor in the long-range maintenance of the regime. But since these regimes did not last, we cannot be sure whether those programs would have succeeded. There are some indications that they might not. But for a more conclusive story we must turn to the USSR.

According to an official Soviet interpretation the powerful appeal of the Communist Party is derived from the fact that "it is linked with the broad masses by vital ties and is a genuine party of the people, that its policy conforms to the people's vital interests. The role of such mass organizations as the Soviet Trade Unions and the Young Communist League has greatly increased in rallying the working people around the party and educating them in the spirit of communism." (271d) The party, with its subsidiary organs, penetrates every branch of Soviet society, sucking into itself what are believed by the leaders to be the best and most able elements. This process of selection begins with the young to whom the elite character of the organization has a special attraction. The youth are made to understand that membership in the organization involves a special state of communion with the Soviet body politic, and the official acceptance of a young boy or girl into the Soviet Pioneers (9 to 14 age group) is accordingly a ceremony celebrated with pomp and solemnity, and marks the first step in their career.

The occasion has been described in a Soviet publication, cited by Fainsod, in the following manner:

The celebration is attended by all the Pioneers of the school, their leaders, teachers, the school director, and honored guests. The assembly hall is decorated with portraits of Lenin and Stalin. The Pioneers march into the hall in quasi-military formation. One of the honored guests, an old Party member, presents each initiate, arrayed in his new uniform, with his red kerchief, his Pioneer badge, and his membership card. As the presentation is made, the symbolism of kerchief and badge is explained. The three corners of the triangularly folded kerchief stand for Party, Komsomol, and Pioneer, pillars of the Soviet state. The badge is decorated with a red flag on which are the hammer and sickle and a camp fire of five logs burning with three flames symbolize the Third International with its promise of the future world revolution. The new recruits are greeted with the slogan, "To battle for Lenin and Stalin—be ready." Rendering the Pioneer salute they reply with the slogan emblazoned on the Pioneer badge, "Always ready." The ceremony is concluded with speeches, recitations, and songs designed to impress the initiates with their new estate. (100; 47d)

The significance and the impact on the young of all this need not be stressed. In the Pioneer organization, which now embraces almost the entire age group eligible, the young are taught to merge their individuality in the collective effort, and their leaders are exhorted to remember that "it is very important to teach the Pioneers to subordinate their personal interests to those of the group." (256a)

The emphasis placed on indoctrinating the young follows quite logically from the position of the Communist Party that the people, in order to be "liberated," must be made "conscious" of their role and position. The process of making them "conscious" ought to start at the earliest possible time, and for this reason the party, through its affiliates, must pay special attention to the young. However, unlike the Fascists and the Nazis, the Bolsheviks could not operate as a mass youth movement prior to the seizure of power. The tsarist oppression made necessary a conspiratorial formation, and in that situation any form of organized activity for the Russian youth was out of the question. Furthermore, most of the conspirators were young men anyway. The first steps in organizing a youth movement were taken after the seizure of power, in November 1918. At that time, the first congress of what later came to be called the Komsomol was held. It was, however, not until the second congress in October 1919, that the youth movement was made, both in terms of program and organization, into an affiliate of the Communist Party, a relationship continuing to this time.

The history of Komsomol, in many respects, is a reflection of the problems and difficulties which the party faced. (47e) There was a period of disillusionment during NEP when many young stalwarts thought the revolution was being betrayed; there was the time of considerable Trotskyite support in the ranks; then came the enthusiasm and the challenge of the First Five Year Plan and the collectivization. The party employed the energies of the young in combating inertia, old traditions, and the peasants in pushing through its program. The industrial center, Komsomolsk, far in east Asiatic Russia, was built under most difficult climatic conditions by the young Komsomolites. Then came the purges and the decimation of the thirties, particularly those of the Yezhov period. The Komsomol suffered its casualties like the party (see Chapter 15), but at the same time the purge opened up new career opportunities. When the war came, Stalin once again relied heavily on the youth for the partisan war, and for ideological leadership in the armed forces. (114) The young Komsomolites became guerrilla leaders and political officers; many were promoted into party membership. And after the war, they were called upon to help in the task of reconstruction.

Today, in 1956, the party is harnessing the Komsomol for yet another task: to combat the growing juvenile delinquency in Soviet cities. This problem, common to urbanized societies, is becoming a source of major concern to Soviet leadership, and the Komsomol is called upon to show the way to "Soviet morality." Nonetheless, there are signs that some of the revolutionary qualities of the Soviet youth are on the wane, and that even among the Komsomol there are those whose interests tend more toward jazz, dances, good living, than to efforts "to build communism." The following harangue, which was published recently in the Soviet Union, illustrates the difficulties. "A playboy is recognized by his special style of slang speech and by his manners; by his flashy clothes and impudent look . . . the female of the playboy species wears tight-fitting clothes which reveal her figure to the point of indecency. She wears slit skirts; her lips are bright with lipstick; in the summer she is shod in Roman sandals; her hair is done in the manner of fashionable foreign actresses . . ." (279) The Soviet press has been forced to acknowledge that even Komsomolites have been guilty of criminal activities. However, the current agricultural campaign in the virgin lands (see Chapter 21) has given the Komsomol an opportunity to appeal again to the imagination of the Soviet youth, and to channel the energies of the younger generation into tasks that benefit the Soviet state. The Soviet press since 1955 has been full of accounts of young Komsomolites leaving the cities and going east, to build new state farms in Kazakhstan and central Asia. This movement, although officially inspired, doubtlessly has occasioned some enthusiasm among some of the young; many young people see in this kind of work a new opportunity for heroic struggle on behalf of communism.

That the party continues to expect the Soviet youth to lend its energies to the many and continuing tasks of building "communism" was demonstrated by the following words of Nikita Khrushchev, addressing in April 1956 the All-Union Conference of Young Builders:

Comrades! Hundreds of thousands of new workers will be required for the major construction projects of the Sixth Five-Year Plan. To provide the personnel for these construction projects the Party Central Committee and the Soviet government will appeal to Soviet youth to send their finest comrades to build the most important enterprises.

The Y.C.L. [Young Communist League] has 18,500,000 members. Will the Y.C.L., then, not be able to assign 300,000 to 500,000 members from its ranks? I believe they will be quite able to do so. (*Stormy applause.*) We believe in the energy of the Y.C.L. and the young people; we believe in their militant spirit. We know that our young people aren't afraid of cold weather or the Siberian taiga. (*Applause.*) (271q)

The Komsomol today is a mass movement embracing the great majority of the Soviet youth. It is so organized as to provide organized direction to the Soviet youth from the time that they begin their education. A child first joins "the Little Octobrist," then at the age of nine he becomes eligible for membership in "the Pioneers." In this organization, athletics, hiking, and camping, are combined with the first stages of more serious political education. At the age of fourteen, if considered qualified, the Pioneer is allowed to join the Komsomol proper, where the actual training for ultimate party membership begins. In fact, both in organization and in operation, the Komsomol is a younger replica of the party. The party relies heavily on it in its various propaganda and agitation campaigns, in its political controls over the military, and in educational drives. Those who are most able become party members; in the words of the Komsomol statutes, "a Komsomol member considers it the greatest of honors to become a member of the Communist Party of the Soviet Union and in all his work and studies prepares himself for Party membership." (256b) Like the Fascist organizations the Komsomol has increased steadily through the years: in 1936 it numbered 3,800,000; in 1949, 9,300,000; in 1951, 13,380,000, and in 1954, 18,825,000. (45; 256c) Thus the party has ample reserves to draw upon, and only those considered most able, or, as it happens sometimes, those with the best connections, can hope to become members.

Those who have had contact with the Soviet youth of today testify that the regime appears to have been successful in making many young people identify their future with that of the system. In view of the magnitude of the effort just described, this is hardly surprising. It points to the conclusion that the totalitarian regime, given time, might succeed in transforming the thinking and the attitudes of an entire society—a scheme never attempted by the more traditional autocracies—and thus perpetuate itself for a long time. There is one further aspect of the Communist approach to youth which sharply differs from the Fascist. The regime does not limit its efforts to the young living within its own confines. Appeal is also made to the youth of the world, and an international youth movement, paralleling the internal totalitarian youth organization, was set up as early as November 1919. This organization, known as KIM (Communist Youth International), after the failures of revolutionary upheavals in Germany, Poland, and Hungary did not assume world-wide importance until 1945, when the old KIM *apparat* was reorganized into the World Federation of Democratic Youth (WFDY) under the control of its Soviet affiliate, the Anti-Fascist Committee of Soviet Youth, which is the foreign branch of the Komsomol.* The close link existing between this organization and the CPSU is illustrated by the fact that in East Germany the WFDY organization was first set up in 1945 by Ulbricht and Hiptner, old Komintern agents. At present, the WFDY claims 83,000,000 members, which includes, however, the 19,000,000 Komsomolites and many more millions in the satellite and Chinese youth organizations. Its activities, be it "anti-germ" propaganda or the Stockholm peace appeal, follow closely the foreign policy propaganda line of the USSR.

Even this cursory review shows how keen is the interest of all totalitarian dictatorships in the development of youth. If such a regime should succeed in capturing the minds and the energies of the young, it may be able to continue the mission that the totalitarians dedicate themselves to execute. In all the totalitarian regimes, the

* Kochemasov, its head, became member of the Komsomol secretariat in 1949.

party has assumed full responsibility for the ideological training of the younger generation, and has used the youth movement both as a training ground and as a recruiting device for ultimate party membership. Only the USSR, however, has had the opportunity to maintain its system for a longer time-span than one generation. Over this period, the Soviet leadership has devoted ceaseless efforts to assure itself of the loyalty and support of the youth. Indications are that, given the complete monopoly of communications, constant unremitting pressure, and simultaneous appeals to the future through grandiose projects, it is difficult for the young to resist the totalitarian temptations.

Chapter Five

The Problem of Succession

The history of government as a formal scheme of organization tends to obscure the problem of what happens when those who hold effective power disappear. The problem can be stated also as that of establishing a convincing identification between the departed ruler(s) and the newly instituted one(s). In the modern West, two schemes have predominated: that of the traditional monarchy, and that of the constitutional republic; constitutional monarchy, which from the late seventeenth until the middle of the nineteenth century was seen as a happy synthesis of the schemes of Locke and Benjamin Constant, proved to be an unstable transitional form. In a monarchy of the traditional Western type, the problem of succession is solved by a law which provides that legitimate blood descent should, as in private property, be the basis of succession. In a constitutional republic, the problem of succession is, in a sense, eliminated, because the rulers are periodically changed as the result of constitutionally organized elections, while the constitutional order is considered as self-perpetuating under an amending procedure which the constitution itself provides for. In totalitarian dictatorships, on the other hand, the problem of succession presents itself anew with real insistence. (142a; 18c)

In so far as totalitarian dictatorship retains the outward, formal features of a constitutional republic it may be able to fall back upon certain procedures in the crisis necessarily precipitated by the death of the leader. In a way, this may be the most important aspect of the retention of "constitutions" in totalitarian dictatorships, apart from the propaganda value which the making of such constitutions has for pressing the claim that the totalitarian dictatorship is a "democracy." But it would be folly, indeed, to assume that the succession to Lenin or Stalin was actually settled in a democratic process "from below," since all the dynamics required for the functioning of this process, like freedom of expression and competing parties, are nonexistent in the totalitarian state.

The action of the larger, more popular bodies, like the Supreme Soviet, is therefore purely acclamatory. This still leaves open the question of how succession is to occur. The build-up of adulation for the totalitarian leader and the development of the vacuum around him create a most dangerous hiatus the moment this mortal god goes "the way of all flesh." In the nature of things, the leader has not been able to designate a successor of his choice; even if he had, it would leave such a person without real support after the leader is dead. Indeed, such designation might well be the kiss of death. As we have seen, persons very close to Stalin, such as his private secretary, have been "eliminated" by the group which found itself in control of the actual source of physical power after the death of the leader.

The documentary evidence we have on the subject of succession is rather scanty. Besides the story of Stalin's rise to power after Lenin's death, when the Soviet Union was not yet fully developed as a totalitarian state, we have only such documentary evidence as has come to light regarding potential successors to Hitler and Mussolini. As far as the available evidence allows a conclusion, it is this: the problem of succession was unsolved, the question of who might take over was an open one, and there is little doubt that in Germany there would have taken place a sharp struggle between the military men and Himmler and his SS. Who would have won is hard to say. If the Soviet Union gives any clue, the army might have made common cause with certain key party leaders, such as Goering, and eliminated Himmler. The fact that a military man took over from Hitler cannot be cited as conclusive evidence in support of such a contention. In the case of Mussolini, the army's attempt to supersede him was foiled, but it was foiled by Nazi intervention, and so that case is even more inconclusive. It is rather interesting that earlier in his career Mussolini had sought to dictate his successor. After 1929, it was to be the Grand Council's task to pick a successor; various leaders, like Ciano, Italo Balbo, Bocchini, and Buffarini as well as the party secretary, Starace, were mentioned from time to time. In any case, all signs point toward the conclusion that in Italy, too, a bitter struggle would have ensued among various contenders. Furthermore, both Hitler's and Mussolini's cases are vitiated by the fact that they were defeated in war, and therefore their true successors were the victors.

It now seems pretty clear that, after the death of Lenin, the hiatus was at first filled by no one. Into the breach stepped a party clique of top leaders who immediately proceeded to compete with each other for ultimate control. In light of the evidence which Fainsod and others have sifted (47f; 142b; 24b), it seems that Trotsky, as heir apparent who considered himself entitled to the succession, immediately aroused the mute antagonism of Stalin. The fight was focused on a disagreement of policy; whether this disagreement precipitated the antagonism or whether the antagonism begat the disagreement in policy is an idle question; the two were obviously part of the same total situation. Stalin, after having isolated Trotsky and destroyed his power and support, as well as that of his associates, then turned on those who had assisted him in this task, and in turn isolated and destroyed them. At the end of three years, he emerged as the totalitarian leader in effective control of the system.

His emergence in control of total power was facilitated by the absence of an established and well-functioning state bureaucracy and by his ability, as party secretary, to manipulate the party organs. The local party organs had by the twenties already assumed important local administrative functions. These functions were not infringed upon either by the secret police (still in its diaper stage) or the army, then weakly organized on a territorial militia basis. (231a) And in so far as the party was highly involved in local administrative-operational problems, a central headquarters—the Secretariat and the Secretary—tended to assume paramount importance in questions not only of patronage but also of occupational loyalty. Stalin's vital capacity for such work, as well as his actual position, was hence crucially important to this subsequent seizure of power.

This experience, while of course not conclusive, suggests that it would be rather risky to draw any inferences from the present state of affairs in the Soviet Union. It is too soon, presumably, to know what is going to be the outcome of the struggle over succession. But we are, in the light of the foregoing analysis of totalitarian dictatorship, justified in doubting that anything like group control or collective leadership has been permanently substituted for monocratic leadership. It is, as we have seen, at variance with the inner dynamics of the system. Basing our views only on available evidence, it would appear that the same thing has happened as did after Lenin's death: a group of insiders has taken over control, and these insiders seem to be those who possess powerful positions in either the party or the army. A struggle within this group is going on.

The fluid character of the situation produced by the death of a totalitarian dictator is demonstrated by the change which occurred in the top Soviet leadership circles after March 1953. Five distinct phases of development in the succession struggle seem, on the basis of available evidence, already apparent. The first stage, lasting only a few days, resulted in Malenkov's inheriting most, if not all, of Stalin's mantle. During this brief interlude, Malenkov basked in the sunshine of Soviet press acclamation and, more concretely, held the crucial posts of Premier and Party Secretary. In a notorious photomontage *Pravda* portrayed him in an intimate huddle with Stalin and Mao Tse-Tung; all other participants were eliminated from the original photograph. This stage, however, was short-lived. The other second lieutenants apparently quickly gathered together to prevent the emergence of a new dictator who subsequently might wish to promote his own second lieutenants. Malenkov was forced to concede one of his power posts, and Khrushchev replaced him as the Party Secretary. The principle of collective leadership was proclaimed, and *Pravda* declared that "collectivity is the highest principle of party leadership" and that "individual decisions are always or almost always one-sided decisions." (271e)

This second stage, however, was short-lived too. For obscure reasons, Beria, the head of the secret police, felt it necessary to assure his own safety through further acquisition of power. (18d) The third phase was thus one of a power struggle between Beria and the other leaders, apparently headed by Malenkov. Despite initial successes, mirrored particularly in increased control over some of the national republics (notably Georgia and Ukraine), Beria and his colleagues were finally arrested and liquidated. His removal from the "collective leadership" necessarily involved an internal reshuffling, which inevitably produced subsequent shifts. The pattern as seen in the fourth phase in 1954 appeared to point in the direction of a polarization of power between Malenkov and Khrushchev, in the respective capacities of Premier and First Secretary of the party, especially in view of the former's commitment to a consumer-goods policy and the latter's emphasis on agricultural and heavy industrial expansion. The fifth phase was initiated early in 1955. Khrushchev's control of the party *apparat* proved decisive and the January 1955 session of the Central Committee fully endorsed its boss's position. Malenkov resigned early in February and Bulganin, backed by the military, but a willing collaborator of Khrushchev's, became Premier. The highly developed and bureaucratized state administration and the party accordingly are like two Greek columns supporting the edifice of the Soviet state. The arch that keeps them together, and also prevents them from crashing, is provided by the other lieutenants in the "collective leadership." Such a situation appears rather unstable and further conflicts over the succession appear more than likely, although their final outcome cannot be predicted on the basis of our present knowledge.

There is ample evidence, however, to suggest that the present "collective leadership" is agreed on one particular thing: there is to be no Stalin in their lifetime. The significance of this is lessened by the consideration that the present leadership is clearly a transitional one: it is composed of men in their sixties and therefore any arrangement they make must be viewed in that perspective. Nonetheless, their efforts to dethrone Stalin could have significant consequences. The present anti-Stalin campaign certainly is likely to make the claim to power of any future would-be totalitarian dictator that much more difficult. This campaign, in full swing as this book goes to print, began in fact a few days after his death. References to Stalin soon became quite scarce, greater emphasis began to be placed on Lenin,* collective leadership was contrasted with the harmful effect of one-man rule. The open attack came in February 1956. At the Twentieth Party Congress Mikoyan frankly criticized a number of Stalin's

---

* References to Lenin soon became idolatrous. At the Twentieth Congress he was constantly referred to as "the immortal Lenin," "immortal teacher," and "the source of all the successes of the Party."

basic tenets while also referring to some purged victims of Stalinism as "comrades." Then a few days later, at a secret night session of the congress, Khrushchev came out with a detailed and allegedly emotional attack on Stalin, charging him with a variety of offences. These ranged from inept leadership in the war against Hitler to charges of terrorism and murder. The stage was thus set for the disintegration of the idol.

Reports of his speech spread rapidly throughout the Soviet orbit, and special meetings were held with party members to whom a Central Committee letter on this subject was read. In some places, particularly Georgia, convinced Stalinists reacted very unfavorably. There were reports of demonstrations and shootings in Tbilisi. An even greater stir occurred in the satellites, where the attacks on Stalin were even more energetic. One of the secretaries of the communist party of Poland (United Workers Party), Jerzy Morawski, openly wrote in the party paper of the terror and damage wrought by Stalin and of his paranoiac tendencies. In some cases past grievances were denounced and previously purged (and hanged) communists rehabilitated.

In so far as succession is concerned, this development makes the emergence of an absolute ruler an unlikely prospect in the immediate future. It certainly excludes the possibility of anyone claiming the mantle of Stalin, although one cannot exclude entirely an alternative of this type. The more likely prospect, however, is that the present leadership will continue to claim that it has returned to true Leninism and has abandoned the "cult of the personality." But Leninism does not, as the record shows, exclude the possibility of one-man rule, and it would be possible for a new ruler to claim that he is enforcing a Leninist policy while in fact maximizing his own power. For the moment, all appearances suggest that Khrushchev succeeded in effectively strengthening his own power in the party *apparat* and the Twentieth Party Congress has resulted in an extensive purge of the Central Committee (about 40 per cent of its members were dropped) and was preceded by similarly thorough purges of the republican central committees. At the congress Khrushchev delivered the political report in which he severely criticized some of his colleagues and, in recent international appearances—in Belgrade, Geneva, New Delhi, London—he played the leading role. Voroshilov once explicitly referred to him as the head of the Soviet delegation, which included Bulganin, to Jugoslavia. All accounts agree that he took the initiative everywhere and the other Soviet leaders followed. His hand has been felt in the recent party shake-ups, his Ukraine favorites have been rising, his past opponents have been slipping down the power ladder. And such processes, given their totalitarian setting, tend to be cumulative. Others notice, and react either by joining to oppose or by demonstrating their fealty. We do not know whether there is any opposition to Khrushchev on the Party Presidium. It is quite conceivable that some day he could be removed as First Secretary and accused of attempting to subvert collective leadership. But for the time being, the Twentieth Party Congress gave some indications that a number of the *apparatchiki* are beginning to pay special attention to whatever the First Secretary says. Within the context of great emphasis on collective leadership, Khrushchev's report on behalf of the Central Committee drew, according to *Pravda* reports, such plaudits as: "Comrade Khrushchev's report described with great force and very convincingly . . ." (Shepilov); ". . . in his speech comrade Khrushchev reported clearly, profoundly, and exhaustively . . ." (Suslov); "In the report of comrade Khrushchev with definitive clarity and profundity he . . ." (Brezhnev); ". . . comrade Khrushchev with definitive clarity and conclusive profundity . . ." (Furtseva). It appears that expressions for Khrushchev's "profundity" were more widespread among the lower echelons of the *apparat* than among Khrushchev's own colleagues on the Presidium. Potentially even more important was his role as the reviser of party doctrine, a role which he again played on behalf of the Central Committee but nonetheless of which he was the articulator. As his speech is being reprinted in millions of pamphlets and widely distributed, the party membership will not be able to avoid thinking of "comrade Khrushchev's teachings." He thus appears to be at least a *primus inter pares,* but there is no doubt that a future leader, if there will be one, given Khrushchev's age (b. 1895), can come only from among the younger generation on the Party Presidium. Among these, Brezhnev, Pervukhin, or Malenkov are considered by observers to be among the ablest.

In view of the inconclusive nature of the empirical evidence on succession, it may be worthwhile to consider the question from the standpoint of the inherent rationale of the totalitarian system. For it would seem that succession necessarily rests upon the legitimation of a government's power. It exposes a regime's authority to its greatest strain, since the passing away of the ruler calls not only his, but the system's, authority into question. The broad problems of authority go beyond our present purpose; but it should be noted that authority may result from brute force; it may also be the consequence of rational persuasion or effective participation in the choice of it. Authority of the kind resting on force is most readily transferred, because all that is needed is to pass over the means of coercion.

It would seem that, since the dynamic focal point of the totalitarian dictatorship is the leader-party interdependence, the party would provide the key to the succession problem, not as a democratic and cooperative group of free individuals, but as a bureaucratic apparatus with an hierarchical structure of legitimacy. Hitler himself spoke of a body of his lieutenants acting like the Vatican Council. (84c) Far be it from us to suggest any kind of identity between the Catholic Church and totalitarian dictatorship, but, with all due allowance for the fundamental differences, the doctrinal cohesion of the faithful upon which the legitimacy of the hierarchical leadership rests allows for some analogical questions. Is not the election of a pope as spiritual head of the organization by the college of cardinals an indication of how succession in totalitarian dictatorship may become formalized, if totalitarian dictatorship lasts as a governmental organization? Is not the very absolutism of the pope legitimized by this choice made by his peers in the hierarchy of the believers? Is not such a procedure "convincing" in terms that fit both the ideology and the power structure of the totalitarian dictatorship? Against such a hypothesis, weighty arguments have been advanced in support of the contention that the police having gained the upper hand in the totalitarian dictatorship will manipulate the succession. (59a; 3c) But what is the basis of the claims on the part of the police? Must not the police seek to demonstrate its orthodoxy, and how is it to accomplish this task, except by appealing to the party? There may be much cynical mocking among actual power holders in such a system, but do we find even a Himmler ever abandoning the key ideological framework of the party-in-being? * It would seem that there is a rather simple explanation for this phenomenon.

* When he finally did, in his secret negotiations with Count Bernadotte, it was only to save his skin in the face of imminent defeat.

The "commissars" ruling within such a totalitarian system are eminently practical men; they are as far removed from contemplative, theoretical studies as they can be; they are never yogis (Koestler). This would predispose them to avoid ideological controversy or even reflection upon party slogans. Changes in these slogans will become necessary from time to time, but it is never a total rejection or even a rejection of the major part of the established set of formulas which have been learned by all those who adhere. It would make little sense to try and appeal to others, to the inert and intimidated masses who are not adherents and organized in the dominant party. In short, the party would seem to fill the breach, bridging the hiatus created by the death of the leader, and only he who fully understands its role has any chance of succession. And who will win in the ensuing struggle is a question of personality, of effective control over the *apparat,* of skillful manipulation of the various competitors. Just as the purge is needed to rejuvenate the *apparat,* so the succession which involves rejuvenation at the very top of the hierarchy cannot be managed except in interaction with and support by the *apparat.*

It is thus from this inner sanctum of the system, this *apparat* which is its mainspring, that a new leader will finally emerge. This process of emergence may be brief or long, depending on the interaction of the many variables involved. And during the interregnum of undetermined succession effective leadership is provided, symbolically, by the party—as the personification of ideological continuity—and, effectively, by the top levels of the *apparat.* Within this *apparat* maneuverings for power, as already seen in the Soviet experience after Lenin's and Stalin's deaths, are likely to be vicious and deadly. Such internal intrigues and struggles, furthermore, are not merely limited to the period following the dictator's death. The history of both the fascist movements and the communist regime shows that even during the dictator's life a considerable amount of internal shuffling and backstabbing occurs in the top party levels. The struggles between Goering and Bormann, of Zhdanov and Malenkov are cases in point. Indeed, the dictator may even encourage and secretly promote some of those conflicts, thereby maintaining internal mobility among his second lieutenants and preserving a fluid situation, not likely to endanger his own undisputed power.

The struggle for succession, however, is not likely to disintegrate the totalitarian system, as so many are inclined to hope. Failure in such a struggle is apt to be fatal and consequently it is to be waged with caution. Beria's lack of prudence, possibly because of circumstances beyond his control, thus probably united the other leaders against him and led to his fall. All of those concerned, however, have a vested interest in the continued maintenance of the system and are not likely to tear it apart recklessly. The closing of the ranks that occurred after Stalin's death is an illustration in point. In the initial period after the dictator's death compromise and mutual adjustment are accordingly likely to be the policies followed. A political principle of mutual "no trespassing" is to prevail with due warnings and penalties for those who trespass against their colleagues.

This, in a sense, tends to produce a frightening Orwellian image of an entire system, embracing millions of politically controlled masses, being ruled by an impersonal collective, without individual faces and individual voices. The masses have no real indication of internal relationships and developments within this closed circle. They know only what they read and see in the official newspapers, which dutifully publish on every state holiday a somber photograph of the "collective leadership"—a group of stony-faced men. Changes within that group become apparent only after they have physically manifested themselves—through fall from the *apparat* and subsequent liquidation. A careful reader is then able to plot, *ex post facto,* the internal web of intrigue. But even within a few years all references to the fallen colleague are expunged from the record and he ceases to have existed.

This element of secrecy and total separation from the masses is precisely what makes the disintegration of a totalitarian system through a struggle for succession unlikely. Political struggles will occur within the *apparat*—this secret grouping divorced from the people by a curtain of darkness—as they must between humans wielding power and wanting more. But no leader will be able to break out and make a mass appeal. No ideological conflict of the pretotalitarian scale of Stalin versus Trotsky will be possible. Totalitarian monopoly of all communications and all arms will make it unfeasible. The intricate system of cross-controls will make it difficult for any one leader to gain uncontested support of a power structure, like the army, for his cause. The internal struggles will thus be resolved within the *apparat,* and only its aftermath is likely to reach the masses, as was the case with Beria. By then the question of disintegration will be meaningless. (59b)

Political power, however, is never static. A collective leadership of a totalitarian system is likely to be subject to gradual elimination of its fringe elements, and a tendency toward the emergence of central contestants in time is likely to manifest itself. The logic of power points toward its monopolization and the history of the two Soviet successions seems to confirm this. The process of decision-making, and consequent accountability, in time unavoidably leads to internal inequalities in the "collective leadership," and true leadership again begins to assume a personal veneer, even if still contested by two or more competitors within the closed circle of the *apparat*. But it is within the *apparat,* and not on barricades of ideological conflict, that new totalitarian leaders are begotten, destroyed, or eventually made triumphant.

Chapter Six

The Totalitarian Dictatorship and the World

"Workers of all the world, unite!" is the summary slogan of the *Communist Manifesto*. It is the call to world revolution to which the Soviet Union has at least ideologically steadfastly adhered. "Today Germany, tomorrow the world!" was the battlecry of the Nazi Party, as Hitler set out for aggression and war. These virulent world-revolutionary appeals are an innate part of totalitarian dictatorship. They correspond to the "passion for unanimity" which these regimes display in their dealings with the people already under their control, and also indicate their inherent propensity for disturbing the peace. There can be little doubt that without an outward projection against a real or imaginary enemy, these regimes could not marshal the fanatical devotion which their system requires for survival. They are in a permanent state of emergency and cause other countries to be similarly afflicted. How to cope with the constant emergency created by the totalitarians has therefore become one of the most serious problems of all constitutional and democratic regimes.

This problem has been aggravated by the inability of democratic states to adjust themselves to the fact that the totalitarians completely reject the traditional patterns of diplomatic behavior in the international arena. Such behavior patterns, institutionalized by custom and usage of many years, require a certain ritual and the adoption of certain consequent niceties. In a sense, therefore, diplomatic protocol—guiding the general conduct of international affairs and conferences—serves to limit the area of diplomatic warfare to certain accepted fields of battle, and the actual conduct of the warfare to certain mutually accepted weapons. The totalitarians accept all these to the extent that such rules and conventions do not limit their freedom of action; the moment they do they reject them unhesitatingly.

The totalitarian dictator thus proclaims total freedom of action for the achievement of his total goals. The startled world, accustomed, during the last one hundred years at least, to traditional diplomatic manners, thought it extremely bad taste for Ribbentrop, when presenting his credentials as Nazi Ambassador to the Court of St. James, to greet the astonished English monarch with a resounding "Heil Hitler!" The world probably forgot, however, that a similar act of scornful rejection of established international manners had already occurred more than fifteen years earlier, when the first Soviet delegation arrived at Brest Litovsk to negotiate with the stiff and formal German delegates. For as soon as the Soviet delegation had detrained and exchanged official greetings with the Imperial German representatives, Radek, who accompanied the Soviet delegation, broke loose and began to distribute revolutionary tracts among the curious German military onlookers gathered at the station.

The democratic states are thus confronted with a pattern of behavior completely at variance with their own. The totalitarian operations are designed always in terms of their goals, and restrictions are only reluctantly accepted. The diplomatic notes of totalitarian regimes, for instances, are usually couched in a language which a few decades ago would have constituted a *casus belli* for any self-respecting nation.* Abuse, tendentious lies, and vituperation are all

---

* One need only to cite the famous Ems Dispatch and the Franco-Prussian war of 1870 as an example.

part of the normal contents of a note from a totalitarian dictator, be it from Nazi Germany a few years ago or from Communist China today. Yet to a student of modern totalitarianism this should come as no surprise. For such notes, mirroring in part the actual totalitarian vision of the world, are not really meant to further understanding between nations as the citizens of a democratic state would desire. They are tools which are aimed either at forging domestic opinion or shattering the morale of the opponent. This attitude has become so embedded in totalitarian practice that now even notes designed to influence wavering foreign opinion, as for instance the 1954 Soviet notes to France on the EDC, cannot fail to scatter a few vituperative remarks about capitalist aspirations.

Similarly in international conferences the totalitarians have succeeded frequently in substituting competitions in vituperation, in which they have a definite edge, for a more formal type of negotiation. At the same time, much to the amazement of more conventional statesmen, negotiators of the totalitarian dictator, particularly communist ones, utilize such meetings for open appeals to the populations of their opponents urging them to rise and revolt. It was truly two baffled men, who, in the persons of Ambassador Kuehlmann and General Hoffman, reported to Berlin in January 1918 on the first negotiations with the Soviet delegates. What perplexed them, presumably, was that the Brest Litovsk conference had become the first international gathering where a green table was used as a soap box for agitatorial addresses. It was there that Trotsky declared on his and his colleagues' behalf that "we do not belong to the diplomatic school. We should rather be considered as soldiers of the revolution." (240) And to this day Soviet leaders use foreign conferences, as well as domestic occasions, to couple denunciations of the leaders of the West with ringing appeals to the "brotherly" English and American peoples.

A recent demonstration of the agitational character of totalitarian diplomacy has been provided by the Khrushchev-Bulganin visit to India and Burma in November and December 1955. Western diplomats were literally appalled by the brutal tone and mendacious character of the speeches delivered by the Soviet leaders to throngs of cheering Indians and Burmese. Completely disregarding the possibility that their remarks might embarrass their hosts, Khrushchev and Bulganin used every opportunity to vilify the West, accusing it

of a variety of imagined crimes ranging from helping Hitler attack
Russia to planning to subvert the newly-won freedom of the Asiatic
peoples, most of which had been granted by the West. What the
Western observers had failed to learn is that totalitarian leaders refuse to consider state visits in the light of traditional western diplomacy, which harks back to ancient customs of royal courtesies and
polite exchange of hospitality. To them, such an occasion is another
opportunity to undermine the enemy. Seen in that light, Bulganin
and Khrushchev were acting according to expected form.

Naturally, then, normal exchange of diplomatic representatives is
considered by the totalitarian dictator to be part of the total struggle. His diplomats, while insisting on the customary diplomatic
privileges, do not hesitate to serve as organizers of Nazi Fifth Columns or Communist underground cells and espionage networks. At
the same time, efforts are made to deny even the customary privileges to democratic diplomats in the totalitarian zones of influence;
instead they cause continuous trouble ranging from severe travel restrictions to such wanton acts as the imprisonment of the American
Consul Lester Ward in Mukden or the murder of the Polish Consul General Matusinski in Kiev in 1939. This, to a totalitarian dictator, is merely a question of tactics, and what follows may help to
illustrate the fundamental operational differences between democratic and totalitarian relations with the world.

A review of the intricacies of totalitarian foreign policy in its detailed development is beyond the scope of our analysis. (57; 7; 52)
But it is of great importance to study the general problems which
this world-revolutionary premise of the totalitarian dictator presents. Before we consider the similarities between the different systems, one basic difference between fascist and communist dictatorships must be pointed out. It is found in the field of ideology.
(See Chapter 7) The fascists of all shades glorify war. The glorification of war by Mussolini, as he preached the resurrection of "the
grandeur that was Rome" is well-known. The theme was elaborated upon by Hitler. War was the necessary school for men, Hitler insisted, and only through the trials of the warrior could the
manly virtues be developed and maintained. His views were echoed in speeches and writings of Nazi sub-leaders again and again.
"Every German who by his blood belongs to the great community of
the German people is first a soldier, a fighter for his nation," Victor

Lutze, Chief of Staff of the SA, told a group of foreign diplomats and press representatives on January 24, 1936. In an official publication on the training of German youth for military service by Hellmut Stellrecht, published in 1935, we read that "it is absurd to make a man a soldier for two years only, and after he is grown up. The preparation for military service ought to begin in the earliest possible years of youth, and should be continued and extended until the culminating point of training is reached by service in the army." Similarly, the Italian Balilla had stated: "Therefore, everyone of you must consider himself a soldier, a soldier even when he is not wearing the green-gray uniform, a soldier also when he is at work . . . a soldier bound to the rest of the army . . ." (50a) In lieu of many other such passages, Mussolini may be cited for the key proposition, later reiterated again and again by him as well as other Fascists and Nazis: "Fascism . . . believes neither in the possibility nor the utility of perpetual peace . . . War alone brings up to its highest tension all human energy and puts the stamp of nobility upon the peoples who have the courage to meet it. All other trials are substitutes, which never really put men into the position where they have to make the great decision— the alternative of life and death." (50b) This glorification of war and the warrior, which rests upon the ideological stress laid upon a collective commanding the total dedication of the individual (see Chapter 7), stands at the center of the fascist view of man. It contrasts sharply with the communist emphasis on the worker. For the communist, war is primarily the war of classes rather than of nations. But this class-war which culminates in revolution is not considered in itself a good. Indeed, the eventual world order of communism is a peaceful order, although communism rejects the possibility of peace between communism and capitalism. This rejection is the result of what the Soviets consider a realistic view of capitalist warmongers and their plots against the "socialist fatherland." Bolshevik readiness to prepare for war is due to its bellicose view of man as a class-bound being, motivated by economic interest; but somehow all this bellicosity will, they claim, end when the world revolution has been consummated. War is a necessary means to the end the Bolshevik strives for; it is not an end in itself.

That is why the communist leaders are able to profess simultaneously, and probably with some degree of sincerity, their contradictory beliefs in the possibility of coexistence of the communist and capitalist worlds and in the inevitability of conflict between the two, ending in the total extinction of the capitalist world. Soviet leaders have frequently gone on record as believing in peaceful coexistence, and endless quotations to this effect could be cited. Thus in replying to Elliot Roosevelt's no doubt well-meaning question whether coexistence was possible, Stalin was widely quoted as stating firmly:

Yes, of course. This [coexistence] is not only possible, it is reasonable and fully realizable. At the most tense times during the war differences in form of government did not prevent our two countries from uniting and conquering our enemy. To an even greater degree it is possible to retain these relations in peace time. (260)

Stalin's position follows quite logically from what we have previously said concerning communist conviction in the ultimate victory of their cause. It is precisely because they assume, on allegedly *scientific* grounds, that capitalism is doomed that they are willing to coexist with it. For coexistence to them is by no means a static situation. In the communist conception of reality, coexistence does not stop the unfolding of history which the communists feel they must further, and the fall of capitalism still remains the object of feverish activity despite the absence of armed conflicts. Indeed, war is a means but only one of many; other means frequently as effective are social and economic decay, anticolonial eruptions, and racial strife. Only when they fail may war be necessary. Thus Molotov was not contradicting Stalin when he declared that "the feverish efforts of imperialists, under whom the ground is giving way, will not save capitalism from its approaching doom. We are living in an age in which all roads lead to Communism." (271f)

Does any practical importance attach to this difference in outlook? To the democratic statesman, confronted with the Soviet Union today, the difference is primarily this that it makes the Soviet Union a more dangerous enemy in the long run. While it was foolish to doubt the warlike propensities of Hitler, and to assume that they could be appeased, it is probably unwise to assume that the USSR will seize the first chance that is offered by atomic superiority to attack the United States. The Soviets, as they gain strength, may become more bold in challenging the United States position in contested areas; they are likely to remain circumspect about a general war. One does not have to accept at face value the protestations of those who claim that the leaders of the Soviet Union are so confident about the eventual victory of Marxism, anyhow, that they will not see any reason for starting wars. Stalin, at one point, is said to have told an English visitor who queried him on this point that every so often a kick well administered might help a lot. But such kicks, such limited wars, are means toward achieving the overall end of world revolution; they are not something to be gloried in for their own sake.*

The struggle for world conquest which is the totalitarians' natural bent has certain affinities with the imperialism of a preceding age, but must not be misunderstood as identical with it. Mussolini, to be sure, wrote that "imperialism is the eternal immutable law of life." To him, the would-be warrior, imperialism was "at bottom, nothing other than the need, the desire, and the will to expansion which every individual, and every live and vital people possess." He added that "imperialism is not, as is usually thought, necessarily aristocratic and military. It may be democratic, pacific, economic, spiritual." (50c) But such a broad conception of imperialism blurs the significant features. Hannah Arendt rightly observed that "imperialism is not empire building and expansion is not conquest." (3d) They are all related, but should be clearly distinguished. And the conquest of the world for a totalitarian movement is something else again. While the older imperialism was an outgrowth of the industrial economy, the will to conquer the world which animates the totalitarian systems is intimately linked with their ideological preoccupations. It is the outward thrust of that "passion for unanimity" which brooks no disagreement with what the movement has proclaimed as "the truth."

As a consequence, the totalitarian attack is a continuing one. It takes the form of organizing subversive activities within the communities abroad, based upon the ideology of the movement. The Italian Fascists and the German Nazis tried to mobilize these elements in countries like the United States, which by background and

---

* The only Marxist writer of note who leaned in this direction is Georges Sorel who, in his *Reflexions sur la violence,* stressed the value of bloody combat for the development of the morale of the proletariat. Mussolini acknowledged his indebtedness to Sorel. Cf. the illuminating preface to the English edition by E. A. Shils, Glencoe, 1950.

tradition "belonged." At one time, immediately preceding the United States entry into World War II, all the programs in the Italian language which were broadcast in Boston were in the hands of Fascist agents. (246) The Nazi Bund sought to provide effective support for Hitler's party line, especially among German-Americans. (10) Similar activities were carried on, wherever there were German minorities that could be organized for this purpose. A particularly dramatic instance was the large-scale subversion carried on by the Sudeten German organizations of Nazi bent which eventually comprised a large percentage of the German-speaking population of Czechoslovakia. (17) Hitler acknowledged this development in the spring of 1938 and made it the basis of an annexationist appeal. In his speech before the Reichstag on February 20, 1938, he spoke of ten million "Germans" who lived in Austria and Czechoslovakia and announced that the protection of their personal, political, and convictional freedom was a national interest of the German Reich. (85; 104)

These efforts, while dangerous enough, were child's play compared to the world-wide movement of Communist parties, because of the limited appeal which the supremacy of a particular "folk" has for the rest of the world. In some countries, the party has been outlawed, but there is no country in the world in which there does not exist a Communist party and in some of them it is large enough to affect vitally the nation's political decisions, whenever a major disagreement develops. The substantial majority for the European Defense Community which existed in France outside the Communist ranks was routed by the Communists when they made common cause with its opponents from other quarters. This is only perhaps the most striking instance of the "enemy within" effectively determining a country's foreign policy by parliamentary means. Similar results are continually achieved in France and Italy, though rarely in many other countries where the Communist party is not strong enough. In these places, the Communist party is devoting its efforts to infiltrating the government services, the educational institutions, and more particularly the trade unions. This latter effort can be very serious, if the unions concerned happen to operate vital key industries which might cripple an effective defense effort. Even in the United States, where Communism is notoriously weak, some unions have been under Communist domination. (30; 188)

Communist infiltration in the United States reached also the upper government levels, it is alleged, and included, during the thirties and the forties, some key officials of the Treasury and of the State Department. It is precisely this ability of the Communists to recruit local supporters that makes them much more effective and dangerous than the Nazis. Communist control over the captive nations in Eastern Europe, so much more stable than the Nazi occupation, owes a great deal not only to the actual Soviet military occupation, which was instrumental in seizing power, but also to the ability to raise local cadres, which then could penetrate easily any attempts at developing an anticommunist underground. Under these circumstances repressive measures are much more effective.

This "strategy of terror," which has been made even more unsettling by the development of the atomic bombs which presumably could be placed in strategic centers by a relatively small group of saboteurs without too much difficulty or even danger of detection, has not so far been met by any significant countermoves by those opposed to the totalitarian dictatorships. The timid efforts to broadcast cheering bits of information into the totalitarian lands, while probably of some limited value, can in no way be compared in their effect with totalitarian subversion. Consequently, extension of Soviet control over one bit of territory after another has been proceeding since 1945 with almost the annual regularity of the seasons. After the big grab of that first year netting Poland, Rumania, Hungary, and Jugoslavia, there have been the additions of Czechoslovakia, Eastern Germany, China, Korea, and now Indochina. Comparable efforts in Greece, Iran, and Indonesia have been stopped for the time being, but it seems to be only a matter of time until the next victim is "bagged."

The only significant breach in the Soviet forward march has been made in Jugoslavia, which however, despite a temporary alienation from the Soviet bloc, still remains a Communist dictatorship. The reason for this is twofold: first, Jugoslavia never left the Soviet bloc, but was expelled much against its hopes; and second, Jugoslavia was probably the most communized satellite in Eastern Europe by the time of the break in 1948. The loss of Jugoslavia stemmed from a surprising miscalculation of Stalin and, allegedly, Zhdanov. The Soviet leaders assumed that because of the high revolutionary fervor and strength of the Jugoslav Communist Party and its ambitious political and economic goals, the very thought of separation from the Soviet bloc would make the party reject Tito's leadership and replace him with more amenable successors. The expulsion of Tito from the Kominform, however, did not produce his fall from power. The reason for this may be found in precisely what was assumed to be the ground for so confidently expecting his fall: the Jugoslav Communist Party was sufficiently strong and sufficiently rooted not to need outside assistance by 1948. Despite the expulsion of its leader, it could maintain its cohesion and still hold its power. (215) The breach is in the process of being healed, since the dramatic visit of Khrushchev and Bulganin to Belgrade in the spring of 1955. This should be sufficient to suggest also that talk of Titoism in China is based on two fundamental errors: it construes Titoism as a defection and not as a miscalculated expulsion; it assumes that the Soviet leadership is foolish enough to make the same egregious error twice.

The relations between the totalitarian dictator and the world are accordingly those of constant struggle, varying only in place and intensity. The world-revolutionary aspirations of the communist movement have become intertwined with the ancient Russian imperial propensities, based upon historical reminiscenses and geographical inducements, the so-called necessities of geopolitics. (120) This novel combination results in providing the Russian imperial expansion with an ideological underpinning far more potent than the older Panslavist and Third Reich ideologies. This must be kept clearly in mind, especially as a number of well-known writers have claimed the opposite. Hannah Arendt, for example, argued that "Nazism and Bolshevism owe more to Pan-Germanism and Panslavism (respectively) than to any other ideology or political movement," and she has further alleged that "this is the most evident in foreign policies, where the strategies of Nazi Germany and Soviet Russia have followed so closely the well-known programs of conquest outlined by the pan-movements." (3e; 96) Miss Arendt's views are always entitled to respect, but it seems difficult to agree with her that the USSR *owes more* to Panslavism than to Communism, even if one agreed that their policy followed the Panslavist "program of conquest." Neither China nor Germany played the role in these programs which they do in Soviet policy and ideology. Yet there has developed a significant shift toward nationalism since 1934 and there are some curious points of kinship between the thoughts of the panslavist Danilevsky and those of Stalin. They both saw the struggle between the Slavic world and the West as inevitable, wanted Russia to turn to the Asians for support, and were profoundly convinced that the prolonged war with the West would end in Russian victory. But these thoughts were framed, in Stalin's mind, in the rigid dialectical formulas of orthodox Marxism-Leninism, and completely lacked the romantic note which is such a curious feature of Panslavism. (130)

In this connection, a word might be added on the "explanation" which the Russian philosopher Nikolai Berdyayev has given in his *The Origins of Russian Communism* (Chicago, 1948). He, too, tried to link communism to the ancient Russian dreams of world domination:

> Communism was the inevitable fate of Russia, the inward moment in the destiny of the Russian people . . . The old consecrated Russian Empire fell and a new one was formed, also a consecrated empire, an inverted theocracy. Marxism, itself so un-Russian in origin and character, assumed a Russian style approaching slavophilism. Even the old Slavophil dream of transferring the capital from St. Petersburg to Moscow, to the Kremlin, was realized, and Russian Communism proclaimed anew the old idea of Slavophils and Dostojewsky—*ex Oriente Lux*. Light shines from Moscow, from the Kremlin, to lighten the bourgeois darkness of the West.

Such poetic parallels ought not to be allowed to hide the fact that the present totalitarian rulers are very far from any such romantic notions that may possibly play a role, but surely a minor one, in the minds of the Russian masses. Panslavism has always been more of a topic of conversation for the intellectuals than a mass sentiment in Russia and other Slav nations. Actually such world-missionary notions are a recurrent theme in the history of nations, and not only in the West; for China too has had such a tradition of world empire. It may be argued that at some point in the course of a conceivable transformation of the USSR, such panslavist ideas may be made to furnish convenient substitutes for the fading appeal of communist formulas. But such a day seems to be relatively remote, and whether it would mean a substantial change in the totalitarian dictatorship is more than doubtful.

There is more of a direct relation between the Nazi position and Pan-Germanism, since Hitler explicitly acknowledges in *Mein*

Kampf his indebtedness to von Schönerer, the Austrian leader of the Pan-German movement. (82a)   To claim it as the primary ingredient of Nazi ideology, however, is surely not feasible.   While Hitler's writings and speeches often use Pan-German slogans, the key to Nazi ideology is the race myth, as we shall see (Chapter 7), and this race doctrine is, in spite of some antisemitism in the ranks of the Pan-German League, a far cry from the old-fashioned imperialism of this league, which never had any substantial popular support.   Pan-Germanism lacked the emotional depth of Panslavism, as it lacked historical roots.   It possessed a shrill quality and a demagogic superficiality which contrasts unfavorably with the romantic dreams of a Danilevsky or a Dostoievsky. (228)

In conclusion we might say that the dictator's aspiration to world rule is inseparable from the ideology of the movement and from the party which provides the framework for the dictator's operation in this as in other fields.   It is, conversely, quite evident that the possibility for peaceful coexistence of the nations peopling this world presupposes the disappearance of the totalitarian dictatorships. Since, according to their own loudly proclaimed professions, their systems must be made world-wide, those who reject the system have no alternative but to strive for its destruction.   Any relaxation of the vigilance required to face such ideological imperialists as the totalitarians is likely to result in disasters such as the Second World War, or worse.

III

The Nature and Role of Ideology

Chapter Seven

Types of Totalitarian Ideology

"Ideas are weapons," in the view of many. But are they only weapons? The cynic answers "yes," because the truth has no meaning for him. Totalitarians tend to be such cynics. Yet they are fanatics when it comes to maintaining their own ideas. They seem to believe passionately in *their* truth. But are passionate belief and fanaticism signs of the strength of one's conviction? One does not argue violently with a man, let alone assault him, because he refuses to agree that two and two make four. Nor is the Christian who is firm in his belief intolerant of the man who cannot see the truth of his beliefs. The history of religion, as indeed the history of ideas generally, shows that periods of witch-hunting are periods of declining faith, of doubt, uncertainty, and anxiety. Ideas become weapons when they are no longer firmly seen as true.

Marx and Engels described the whole range of ideas as "superstructure." Religion, law, and other value systems were seen by them as nothing but camouflage, surrounding the bare and brute facts of economic controls, the "control of the means of production." They served as weapons in the class struggle, by which the ruling class buttressed its position of power. Thus Marx wrote: "The ruling ideas of each age have ever been the ideas of its ruling class," (126) and again: ". . . every historical period has laws of its own, . . . as soon as society has outlived a given period of development, and is passing over from one given stage to another, it begins to be subject to other laws." (125) Clearly, according to them, the prevailing ideology of any particular epoch was both the outward rationalization of that epoch's economic organization and also the tool used by the dominant class to stop history from continuing on its inevitable path. For, as Marx and Engels saw it, history was a perpetual progress through time, propelled irresistibly by the class struggle, though at varying rates of advance. The struggle produced the historical momentum and established the economically dominant classes in a position of power and then toppled them from it. "All history is the history of class struggles," the *Communist Manifesto* declared. Throughout this unfolding pattern of dialectical change, combining revolution and evolution, ideology served both to mask and then to unmask "objective reality."

Though we can readily see that this communist approach to history and the ideas at work in it was the product of a specific historical period, Marx and his followers believed its unique quality to be that it was more than an ideology. To them, their thought embodied the science of history, and as such constituted an unprecedented insight into the true course of development. As such, it provided those who fully grasped it with a key for understanding not only the past and the present, but also the future. And because its view of the future was said to be scientifically accurate, and because it asserted that the future would be better than the present, it readily became a compelling call to action. The future, thus clearly perceived and rightly valued, must be hastened; its advent must be assisted with all available means. Dialectical materialism (or *Diamat,* in current Soviet parlance) offers, according to the communists, not only an infallible perception of the meaning of the interrelationship of social forces, but also a clear guide to the character of inevitable social change. It combines moral indignation against the Today with a fiercely fanatic conviction that the Tomorrow, which is bound to come, will be a higher, indeed a near perfect, state of society. (157)

Marx and Engels, by making ideas depend upon the economic system, raised the issue of what has come to be known as the "sociology of knowledge"—or, the study of the social conditioning which causes and thereby explains the rise and growth of ideas, of notions regarding values, of scientific discoveries, and of practical programs of social reform. By claiming that all such knowledge is essentially superstructure, of which the substructure is the system of economic controls, the Marxist makes knowledge a dependent variable which changes with the economic system. This is a sweeping sociological generalization and it was natural that not only scholars should question it and ask in turn: how true is this proposition? To what extent is the economic system primary, the first cause of all other changes in the intellectual field? Indeed, the obvious query suggested itself: is this true of the Marxist system itself?

We are not now going to go into this vast problem of intellectual

creativity and its relation to environmental conditioning, but wish
to make quite clear at the outset that these issues are involved in
the problem of ideology and its role in the totalitarian dictatorships
of our time. The Soviet dictatorship, more particularly, rests upon
this belief in the instrumental nature of ideas and ideology. Far
from reducing the role of ideology, this conviction has led to its explicit cultivation and to the large-scale indoctrination of the masses.
An intense concern with ideological conformity is the paradoxical
consequence of the doctrine that ideas are nothing but weapons.

But before we further elaborate a typology of totalitarian ideologies it is necessary to define the term. The problem of totalitarian
ideology must be seen within the more general context of the role of
ideology in the political community. Some would define it as "a
general system of beliefs held in common by the members of a collectivity, i.e., a society, or a subcollectivity of one—including a movement deviant from the main culture of the society—a system of
ideas which is oriented to the evaluative integration of the collectivity and of the situation in which it is placed, the processes by which
it has developed to its given state, the goals toward which its members are collectively oriented, and their relation to the future course
of events." (153a) Such a definition makes an ideology a characteristic feature of any politically organized community, equivalent in
function to a rationalization in an individual, and serving the purpose of integration. The wisdom of so broad a definition of the
term ideology may well be doubted. Ideologies are of much less
general and more recent significance. They arise in connection with
parties and movements maintaining explicit systems of thought;
they are a product of the age of mass communication.

Even more dubious is another definition which would sharply
contrast ideology and utopia. Deriving their thought from Karl
Mannheim's well-known work (123a), these writers would maintain that ideology serves as the "political myth," which is further defined as the "pattern of basic political symbols." It is the function of
this political myth "to preserve the social structure." It should be
clearly distinguished from an "utopia" whose function it is "to destroy the social structure." (106a) As a consequence, it is then argued that, "with the seizure of power, utopian symbols become ideologies." This contrasting and juxtaposing of ideology and utopia
is confusing, to say the least. It obstructs an understanding of the

actualities of totalitarian politics.* And it has the further incon-
venience that the same set of ideas are at some fixed point in time
changed from an utopia into an ideology, when as a matter of fact
they serve as both, before and after the seizure of power. This may
be manageable in a case like the Soviet Union, but it is perplexing in
the case of Hitler's *Mein Kampf,* which would be an utopia before,
and an ideology after, January 30, 1933. Actually, *Mein Kampf*
contains the utopian ideology of the German Fascist movement both
before and after that date.

It would seem best, in the light of all the facts, to restrict the term
ideology to that of a set of *literate ideas.* An ideology thus defined
is a reasonably coherent body of ideas concerning practical means of
how to change and reform a society, based upon a more or less
elaborate criticism of what is wrong with the existing, or antecedent, society. And a totalitarian ideology would then be one
which is concerned with total destruction and total reconstruction,
involving typically an ideological acceptance of violence as the only
practicable means for such total destruction. It might accordingly
be defined as "a reasonably coherent body of ideas concerning practical means of how totally to change and reconstruct a society by
force, or violence, based upon an all-inclusive or total criticism of
what is wrong with an existing or antecedent society." This total
change and reconstruction in its very nature constitutes an "utopia"
and hence totalitarian ideologies are typically utopian in nature.
(276c) Totalitarian ideologies, in this perspective, are a radical form
of a development which, although there are precedents, is typically
modern; they must not be confused with traditional notions, beliefs, and customs prevalent in older traditional societies.

Consequently, we also reject the suggestion of Mannheim that we
speak of an ideology as "total" when "we are concerned with the
characteristics and composition of the total structure of the mind of
this epoch, or of this group." (123b) He informs us that the idea
of a total ideology is "intended to designate the outlook inevitably
associated with a given historical and social situation, and the

---

* In a special discussion on conservatism Karl Mannheim argued (*Essays on Sociology and Social Psychology,* London, 1953) the point involved in Lasswell's generalization, by particular reference to the Italian Fascists. Actually, the "conservative"
note in Italian fascism turned up soon after 1919, long before the March on Rome.
Mr. Germino suggests that one might even argue that fascism was conservative before
and utopian after the attainment of power.

Weltanschauung and style of thought bound up with it." (123c) Mannheim would contrast with this total ideology "particular" ideologies, which would include "all those utterances, the falsity of which is due to an intentional or unintentional, conscious, semiconscious, or unconscious deluding of oneself or of others, taking place on a psychological level and structurally resembling lies." (123d) This dichotomy of two kinds of ideologies, total and particular, which is based upon psychological and moral aspects shared as a matter of fact by all systems of ideas, is quite unfortunate.* It is therefore not surprising that Mannheim in the later sections of his work drops the "total ideology" as a valid conception, observing that "we shall, as far as possible, avoid the use of the term 'ideology,' *because of its moral connotation,* and shall instead speak of the 'perspective' of a thinker." This "perspective" Mannheim considers the proper subject of the "sociology of knowledge." (123e) What remains as Mannheim's notion of ideologies is that they are "utterances" and that they "structurally resemble lies." But the "structure" of a lie is typically that of a statement which does not correspond to what can be known as a true statement, such as "all men arc crcated cqual." While such an uttcrancc is undoubtedly part of democratic ideology, it receives its "ideological" significance from the fact that it carries the implication that hereditary privileges are bad and should be abolished and that a society without such privileges is good and should be so constructed.

In short, ideologies are essentially action-related systems of ideas. They typically contain a program and a strategy for its realization and their essential purpose is to unite organizations which are built around them. (109a)

The rise and development of such ideologies appears to be a feature of the democratic age, as we have said, and seems to be associated with the development of parties. Parties of reform especially tend to develop such ideologies, which they propose to put into practice upon their assumption of power. In this process, adaptations take place and some of the more utopian aspects of the ideology are eliminated as a concession to reality. (4a) Totalitarian parties are an extreme instance of this general trend. By their elimination of

---

* When seen as creations of finite minds, all ideas are limiting in scope, selecting aspects of an infinitely complex reality, and hence may be described as "deluding one's self and others."

all rivals (see Chapter 3), they monopolize the field and convert their group ideology into a governmental one. But the process of adaptation to "reality" still takes place even though a persistent effort is made to maintain the myth that the ideology is intact, and that the concessions are temporary. Thus Hitler found himself obliged to compromise with big business and indeed to strengthen its position of monopolistic control in the German economy, although his ideology called for "socialism" in the sense of the state protecting the interests of the lower middle classes and the workers. By mobilizing the idea of "leadership" and by making the factory owner or manager the "leader" of the enterprise, he tried to straddle the ideological conflict.

Similarly in the Soviet Union the regime had to face the problem of adjusting the hallowed concept of "withering away of the state" to the new "socialist realities." This concept, highly utopian in its appeal, had been repeatedly stressed in Lenin's writings, in which he quoted Marx and Engels as his authority and emphasized himself that "the proletariat needs only a state which is withering away, i.e., a state so constituted that it begins to wither away immediately, and cannot but wither away." (113a)

The abyss between this statement and current Soviet reality is obvious, and the Soviet leaders have not been blind to it. The concept has consequently been redefined to suit the imperatives of power without prima facie invalidating it. Stalin merely stated that

[the concept] is correct but only on one of two conditions: 1) *if* we study the socialist state only from the angle of internal development of the country, abstracting ourselves in advance from the international factor, isolating, for the convenience of investigation, the country and state from the international situation; or 2) *if* we assume that *socialism* is already victorious in all countries, or in the majority of countries, that a Socialist encirclement exists instead of a *capitalist encirclement,* that there is no more danger of foreign attack, and that there is no more need to strengthen the army and the state. (199a)

These illustrations serve to show that an ideology can be more or less "rational" in its elaboration. The Soviet ideology, based as it is upon the allegedly "scientific" findings of Karl Marx and Friedrich Engels, as elaborated by N. Lenin and others, appears to be decidedly more rational than either that of Fascist Italy or Hitler Germany. In the last two instances, the ideology was distinctly "personal," resting, in the case of Mussolini, upon his journalistic writings and more especially his article on fascism in the *Encyclopedia Italiana* (1932) (150a); in the case of Hitler, upon *Mein Kampf* (82) written in 1923–24 during his sojourn in jail, and maintained ever after as the gospel of National Socialism. An analysis in terms of antecedent intellectual influences and the like would incline one to differentiate further and call Mussolini's creed more rational than that of Hitler. The degree of "rationality" here involved is that of a rationality of means, rather than ends. For the values in all three ideologies are of a highly emotional sort. This may not make much difference to the skeptic who considers all value judgments beyond rational discourse, but in any case there are differences of degree, and it is certainly permissible to assert that the value judgments at the base of Thomism, Confucianism, and modern constitutionalism are more rational than those of the totalitarian creeds, even if they are not wholly rational.

These totalitarian ideologies can also be classified according to their ultimate values, and this is the more usual and conventional procedure. We then arrive at the very well-known differentiation between the Soviet ideology which is universal in its appeal— "Workers of all the world, unite!"—and the fascist ideologies— which address themselves to a particular people in terms of their grandeur, power, and historical role. In the Soviet ideology, the place of the national group is taken by the proletariat, which is invested with the historical role of liberating mankind from the shackles of industrial capitalism, but Marx and Engels make it very clear that this proletariat, by overthrowing the existing class structure, ultimately eliminates itself and ceases to exist as a proletariat. From this standpoint, social justice appears to be the ultimate value, unless it be the classless society which is its essential condition; for the fascist, this ultimate or highest value is dominion, eventually world dominion, and the strong and pure nation-race is *its* essential condition, as seen by its ideology. Since there are many nations and races, there can theoretically be as many fascisms, and this has actually proven to be the case. Wherever fascism has raised its head, whether in France, England, or the United States, the strength and the purification of the particular nation involved has been in the center of ideological attention. This aspect is an element of weakness in fascist ideologies, as contrasted with the communist ones.

The latter have the advantage of an inherent universalism and the consequent ability to cope more readily with the extension of power to other nations (the Soviet Union vis-à-vis Poland, Czechoslovakia, Germany, and so forth, China vis-à-vis Korea, Indochina, and so forth).

It is precisely this doctrinal catholicism which makes communism an effective weapon of combat, not only between nations, but also, and generally unlike fascism, within nations. Fascism, when a spontaneous product of local combustion, by necessity tended to accentuate national distinctiveness and national sovereignty. It emphasized frequently the biological superiority of the given community. Fascism, when imposed on several nations, produced, as it did during World War II, the most vigorous reactions from those nations which it enveloped. Universality based on a restricted nationalist appeal is a contradiction in terms. Actually, Italian Fascism had a good deal of appeal beyond Italy. Similar movements cropped up in Austria, Hungary, Rumania, Spain, France, and Great Britain, and one must not forget that Italian Fascism was, after all, the inspiration for many of Hitler's followers as well as for Hitler himself. Peron also followed the basic line of Italian Fascism. There is a very interesting item in the Italian Fascist catechism used in the youth organizations: "Question: Is Fascism exclusively an Italian phenomenon? Answer: Fascism, as far as its ideas, doctrines and realizations are concerned, is *universal,* because it is in the position of saying to all civilized people *the word of truth without which there cannot be lasting peace in the world; therefore it is the sustainer and creator of a new civilization."* It should be noted, however, that with this kind of "universalism," while it may be able to arouse imitators, each of the resulting fascist movements will itself seek world, or regional, dominion, and hence be creating obstacles to the extension of effective control by the "creator." Presumably, a fascist France or England would have been at least as vigorous a rival of Italian aspirations to dominion in the Mediterranean as the democratic regimes of these countries were. (64a)

Communism, on the other hand, has been markedly successful in operating on the national base for the sake of supranational goals. For communism, unlike fascism, operates simultaneously on two levels: one is the universal, "orthodox," and philosophical plane, which at this time is still the private domain of Soviet leadership, notwithstanding some modest contributions of Mao Tse-Tung to the concept of the revolution. The other level is the practical, the tactical. On this level communism may vary, temporarily at least, from country to country. Thus the nature of the communist appeal is markedly different in, let us say, France from that in India. Similarly, even in the captive nations of Eastern Europe and in China, great stress was laid on the distinct nature of their communist development. In Poland, for instance, in the immediate postwar years, the official party declarations stressed the fact that communism in Poland was to be implemented in "the Polish way." (263a) Indeed, it became the standard weapon of the parlor communist in Eastern Europe to emphasize the distinctive, allegedly more democratic, character of the development of a communist society in Eastern Europe as contrasted with past Soviet history.

Such an attitude, at that time, was not heresy. It was merely an acknowledgment of the "fact" that history moves by stages, which according to Marxism are contradictory to one another, and that the Soviet Union at the given moment was operating on a higher plane of social development. The Tito affair, however, soon forced the Soviet leadership into the rigorous affirmation that past Soviet experience is binding on all communist parties, notwithstanding their local circumstances. The theoretical journal of the Soviet Communist Party, *Bolshevik,* stated in this connection that:

The assertion that every country advances towards Socialism along its own specific path cannot be recognized as correct, as well as the contention that there are as many roads in this direction as there are countries. To utter this means to deny the international portent of the Bolshevik experience. The general laws of transition from capitalism to Socialism, discovered by Marx and Engels, and tested, put to concrete use and developed by Lenin and Stalin on the basis of the experience of the Bolshevik Party and the Soviet State, are binding upon all countries. (243a)

Nevertheless, significant local variations of a practical nature are to this day evident, as for instance in the treatment of the Catholic Church or the farmers in Poland, or the redefinition of the concept of the elite in China. The crucial determinant of ideological loyalty is the ultimate implication of the local variation: if it serves to further the over-all goals of the universal ideology, without fragmenting the power bloc on which the ideology rests, the practical deviation is tolerated. If not, it is excised.

Throughout the discussion of types of totalitarian ideology, we have alluded to certain historical antecedents which helped to shape the ideas that are contained in these ideologies. We must now turn to this problem. What are the historical roots of these ideological movements? And what is therefore the importance of "ideas" as such in the ideologies? Should certain groups or thinkers be "blamed" for the rise of totalitarian ideologies in the sense that, if they had not written, the ideologies could not have been fashioned?

Chapter Eight

The Historical Roots of Totalitarian Ideology

In seeking to trace the roots of totalitarian ideology, every kind of link has been argued. (97) Marx and Hegel, Nietzsche and Hobbes, Kant and Rousseau, Plato and Aristotle, St. Augustine, Luther, and Calvin—all have been charged with having forged the ideas that became weapons in the arsenal of the totalitarians. Since the thinkers thus involved are in turn related to many other intellectual trends and views, it is not too much to suggest that the sum of all the arguments is plainly this: totalitarian ideology is rooted in the totality of Western thought and more especially its political thought. To be sure, the key points of emphasis, such as equality, justice, freedom are of so general a nature that they do not lend themselves to very precise analysis in this context. But even more specific points, like the stress on democracy or the state, are similarly elusive. This situation should not surprise anyone, for the programs of action which the totalitarians proclaim are programs cast in terms of the antecedent states of European and American society (with interesting variations introduced in cases such as China) and they must therefore be related to the patterns of ideas associated with these antecedent states. Moreover, since ideology has an instrumental function, as we have seen, totalitarian leaders will fashion their ideological tools to fit the states of mind of the masses they are addressing. For example the idea of progress, so peculiar a product of the Western mind, is embedded in the totalitarian thought so deeply that it would collapse if this idea were eliminated.

It should be clear that this entire discussion of the roots of totalitarian ideology rests upon what answer is given to the question: what is the role of ideas in history? Do ideas have demonstrable effects or are they merely incidental to reality, like the froth on top of the waves of an agitated sea? Many of the writers who have placed major emphasis upon the ideological background of totalitarian movements have failed to realize the full implications of this view. For if ideas are assumed to have significant causal effects upon the course of events, a spiritualistic interpretation of history easily becomes part of the story. A stress upon religious ideas is most especially prone to carry that implication. The common argument that men act in terms of the ideas in their minds does not settle the question of where such ideas come from. If some such notion as inspiration is introduced—Trotsky wrote that revolution is the mad inspiration of history—then one must ask: whose inspiration and by whom inspired? It is evident that many contemporary formulas are merely thinly disguised, feebly secularized ways of saying the same thing that the old Jews had in mind when they claimed that God had given the Tables to Moses. The several totalitarian ideologies are basically trite restatements of certain traditional ideas, arranged in an incoherent way that makes them highly exciting to weak minds.

Their roots are as varied as the backgrounds of the people who expound them and who listen to them. One might illustrate this by the recurrent references in Hitler's *Mein Kampf* to the notion that the end of national glory justifies any means appropriate for its achievement. This "Machiavellism" has been charged to Machiavelli and some of his followers. But what was in Machiavelli, at least for his time, a novel and fairly sophisticated doctrine becomes in Hitler's treatment a crude and banal thought.

In other words, any effort to relate totalitarian ideology more specifically to antecedent thought reveals that the antecedent thought is either distorted to fit the proposition, or completely misrepresented. Thus Hegel is made an exponent of the doctrine that "might makes right," when as a matter of fact, he explicitly and sharply rejected it. Or Hobbes is claimed to believe in the "state regulating everything," when it is quite evident to a casual but unprejudiced reader, that Hobbes was inclined to restrict the sovereign to the police function, that is, to the function of maintaining peace in a given society. If one were to argue all the various statements which have been set forth on this score, one could fill volumes. Such arguments may have a certain value in the market place, where the fighting about these ideas takes place; but on the whole, it is a hopeless enterprise, because the history of ideas is a particularly difficult field of scholarship which is fully mastered by few. In any case, the problem of what an author actually said, and, in the saying of it, what he meant calls for a never-ending search, and the more comprehensive the author, the more divergent the answers. Nonetheless, the discussion of whether the activities of the Soviet Union fit the ideas which Marx and Engels expounded is a source of continuing controversy and debate. A volume such as *The God that Failed* is almost entirely concerned with a discussion of the true meanings of Marxian teachings.

There is no doubt that Marxism owes a great intellectual debt to the traditions, and particularly to the modes of thought, of the French Revolution. The intellectual climate of Europe, of which both Marx and Engels were very much a part, had been fired not only by the slogans, but also by the philosophic content of that great enterprise. As a result, though surely not for the first time in the history of Europe, the intellectual, in his role of interpreter of the past and of the present, reached out to shape the realities of tomorrow. To acknowledge that Marxism is part of that stream is not, however, to establish a causal relationship, for to do so, as some have, is to engage in ex post facto attempts to interpret the ideas and even motivations of eighteenth-century thinkers in terms of categories imposed by the nineteenth- and twentieth-century realities. Nonetheless, it can be shown that the Rousseauistic concept of total democracy can easily degenerate into total dictatorship when the Legislator ceases to be a transient educator and becomes a permanent vanguard acting in behalf of the people. Such concepts as "knowledge" are not far removed from "consciousness," of a class variety, and both need to be instilled in those "who are born free and yet everywhere are in chains." The emphasis on unity, unanimity, and ceaseless participation are suggestive—but no more than that—of the twentieth-century "passion for unanimity" (see Chapter 13) characteristic of the totalitarian systems. And, what is more, it was the French Revolution which gave an outlet to the feeling of rationalistic revolutionaries that society must, and can be, remade in its totality to assure man the liberty which is inherently his. Indeed a dialectical relationship to the religious zealots of the past suggests itself. Like Saint-Just, in the French Revolution, such individuals become the self-appointed guardians of virtue and truth; genuine conflicts of opinion are excluded, and disagreement is condemned as absolutely wrong.

Similarly, the Marxist dialectic contains not only Hegel, but Babeuf and his primitive notions of class struggle. At the same time, Marxian doctrine divorced the utilitarian emphasis on self-interest from the individual, welded it to an economic class, and made it the focal point of the historical movement. Thus various antecedent notions borrowed from different writers and movements were fitted to the requirements of the industrial age and the peasant reaction to the machine. One need not linger, however, on the relationship of Marxism to preceding thought in the western political heritage to prove how complex is the task of establishing meaningful intellectual causation. Within Marxism itself, which developed, as we shall see later on, through schismatic clashes, the problem of elaboration or distortion is continually disputed. For instance, the formation of the new communist regimes in central Europe and Asia, bringing with it the problem of transition from a bourgeois or feudal society to a communist one, has perplexed Soviet ideologues in recent years. For various practical reasons, the theory of the dictatorship of the proletariat, mentioned only once by Marx in his *Critique of the Gotha Program* and developed by Lenin into something of utmost importance, has become unsuitable for these regions. A completely new terminology and a new interpretation, evolving around the term "People's Democracy" has been developed. The relationship between this terminology and Marx's own view of the postrevolutionary situation is open to dispute.

Disappointed believers in some of the ideas contained in a particular ideology recurrently constitute very strong opponents of the regime based upon such ideology. This is a phenomenon familiar from the history of religion. After all, the story of Christianity is to a considerable extent the story of successive disagreements over what Christ meant, and over the true import of his message. From these disagreements have resulted the successive dissents leading to new sects and churches. Considering the relatively short time that totalitarians have been actively at work, it is surprising how many divergent interpretations have already been expounded and made the basis of schismatic movements.

And yet it is these schisms which provide a real clue to the meaning of the term we have been using—totalitarian ideology. The splits and disagreements on the basic tenets of Marxism, for instance, have served to accentuate the democratic and nondemocratic aspects of that theory. Through a process of political adaptation, differences in degree have become differences in kind, despite the original uniformity of view. Are not then social democracy and communism possibly the products of the same intellectual roots? Do they not claim ancestorship of a common family tree? Are not their basic assumptions to be found essentially in the same body of writings? Despite the necessarily affirmative answers, the distinction between the two schools of thought, when translated into actual practice, becomes fundamental and far-reaching—one is totalitarian, the other not.

The translation of an ideology into practice usually serves to reveal certain inadequacies inherent in human foresight. Attempts to picture the future and to prescribe the methods of achieving it clearly cannot conceive of all eventualities, of all possible situations, and communism is further handicapped by the general looseness of its philosophical structure. Consequently the schismatic movements which developed immediately as attempts were made to transform Marxism into political practice were, apart from pure power factors, the inevitable product of such an attempted implementation. When theory is applied to a real-life situation, there are usually only two alternatives: one is to modify theory so as to make it more compatible with the prerequisites of practice, and the other is to attempt to force reality to fit the theory. The totalitarians, by their almost complete rejection of the *status quo,* are inclined to attempt to force history to fit their conception of it.* And when such a conception involves a far-reaching idea of the desirable, that is,

---

* See Chapter 7 for our definition of totalitarian ideology. The totalitarians are particularly vehement and violent in their criticism of "existing" [antecedent] societies. Their effort to change history does not, however, prevent them from making specific concessions in their ideology when such are necessitated by expediency. See Chapter 9.

historically inevitable, scheme of social organization, the efforts to mold society to fit it, and the consequent measures to break down the resistance to it, result in totalitarianism.

Not all the original supporters of such an ideology, however, are willing to go quite so far. This is particularly well demonstrated by the Marxist schism on the issue of evolution *versus* revolution. Marxism embodies both concepts, which are said to be historically inseparable. "Revolution is the midwife of every society," said Marx, but before the midwife sets to work, a lengthy evolutionary process precedes the climactic spasms of the revolution. The inner contradictions of capitalism have to ripen lest the revolution fail by coming too soon. And it is precisely on this time element that conflicting interpretations have clashed. When is the precise moment for revolutionary action?

Bernstein and the so-called Revisionists felt that precipitate revolutionary action would merely intensify the blood flow in the corroded veins of capitalism and thus prolong its life. Key to success, according to Bernstein and the Social Democratic school, was ability to wait, while exacting concessions through participation in the democratic process. Socialism would in time supplant the capitalist order and the revolutionary stage would, in effect, become merely the technical act of taking over. Capitalism would die of old age, and therefore need not be slaughtered. The revolutionary act would consist in burying it, and not in killing it.

The Social Democrats have therefore been unwilling to engage in drastic measures to destroy the capitalist society. Their optimism in the certainty of their success makes them patient and willing to work within the framework of constitutional-capitalist society. Having accepted the perspective of an inevitable historical victory, they are content with the thought that the *status quo* is not going to last.

The totalitarians, however, having announced that the *status quo* is doomed, proceed to prove the correctness of their analysis through measures to effect it. To them, willingness to wait is sheer treason. "Reformism . . . which in effect denies the Socialist revolution and tries to establish socialism peacefully, . . . which preaches not the struggle of classes but their collaboration—this reformism is degenerating from day to day, and is losing all marks of socialism." (198) Lenin and the Bolshevik revolutionaries, accordingly, emphasized that revolutionary action was the key to historical salvation, and that only direct measures aimed at overthrowing the capitalist order would produce its fall. "Great historical questions can be solved only by *violence*," exclaimed Lenin (113b), calling upon the revolutionaries to act as the gravediggers of history and to help repose the remnants of capitalism in the dustbin of antiquity. For, unless a revolutionary party acting as the vanguard of the proletariat acts firmly, the working classes will develop a pacifist trade-union mentality and become the unwitting tools of capitalist measures of self-preservation.

In the Nazi movement, the socially more radical elements were strongly represented in the Storm Troopers, called the Brown Shirts. The SA men were under the command of Captain Roehm, who at the time liked to suggest that all they needed to do was to turn their swastika armbands around to make them red. To be sure, all this argument remained on a very low level, as did the ideological discussion in the Hitler movement generally, but it nonetheless represented a characteristic ideological conflict pointing to the divergent strands in the official creed. There developed also a "leftist" deviation in Italian Fascism which was headed by Giuseppe Bottai, Edmondo Rossoni, and Ugo Spirito. Giovanni Gentile was eventually prevailed upon to make common cause with this group, and his last work, *Genesi e struttura della societa,* expounds the group's general theory. (19b) Two reviews, edited by Bottai and Rossoni respectively, expressed these views in a veiled fashion, but it should be noted that these ideas had no support in the inner circles of the party.

In both the Fascist and Nazi movements, actually, the physical presence of the men who formulated the programs prevented the emergence of major splits.* The essential postulates of both movements—stressing the leadership principle, the traditional and historical values of the people as contrasted with the "bourgeois" degeneration, the *Etatismo* of Italy and the *Volk* veneration of Nazism, state corporatism but private ownership, the mystic quality of the soil, and last, but not least, the race principle—generally remained unchallenged during their relatively brief existences.

---

* The same was essentially the case with the Peronista movement in Argentina. The dictator was the official promulgator of the *Justicialismo* ideology, which appears to be a further vulgarization of Fascist corporatism. (155)

It is noteworthy, however, that both communism and fascism are characteristized by their insistence on the revolutionary fulfillment of the "truths" of their doctrines, and it is this insistence that leads to the further conclusions on the necessity of a disciplined party— the elite of the proletariat or of the nation. This party was to eliminate the remnants of the vanquished. Its infallible leadership, through "intuition" or "science," was to effect the conditions which, according to the ideology, are considered necessary for the achievement of its utopian apocalypse. It is precisely this attempt to impose on society a rationally, or rather pseudorationally, conceived pattern of distinctly novel forms of social organization that leads to the totalitarian oppression. And since this oppression is justified in terms of the ideology, this ideology is totalitarian.

The fact that the totalitarian ideology is rooted in the totality of Western ideas raises the question of its relation to democracy and Christianity. On the face of it, these two bodies of thought are the patent antithesis to fascist and communist ideology. The conflict with Christianity was highlighted in the Soviet Union by the Movement of the Godless; in Nazi Germany it led to protracted struggles to establish control over both Protestant and Catholic churches (see Chapter 23). With regard to democracy, the situation is somewhat more confused since both communists and fascists like to consider themselves true democrats; but, if democracy is defined in constitutional terms as characterized by a genuine competition between two or more parties, a separation of governmental powers, and a judicially enforced protection of individual rights, the conflict is fairly obvious on both the ideological and the practical levels. Yet in spite of these sharp conflicts between totalitarian ideologies on one hand and the Christian and Democratic heritage on the other, it is only within the context of this heritage that the ideologies can be fully understood. Communism is not Christian, but it could not have taken root without the foundations laid by Christian belief in the brotherhood of man and social justice. Perhaps even more important than these substantive links are the habits of mind established by Christianity, and the other religions with a formal theology, such as Buddhism and Mohammedanism, for they establish the cultural habit or trait of relating action programs and norms to elaborate "rational" frameworks. These rational frameworks of theology are then secularized and become ideologies. There is, to put it another way, a style of living involved that calls for transcendent explanations of what is right. When the theological explanations become untenable as a result of the decline of religious faith, these "secular religions" then fill the vacuum. (3a) When seen in this perspective, it becomes evident why the totalitarian ideology has become potent even in China, which is not at all a Christian country. The argument is reinforced by the consideration that China inherited, but did not invent, the communist ideology. It seems more than doubtful that Chinese thought would have produced this kind of ideology, and all of Mao's presumed originality in interpreting the Marxist-Leninist heritage provides little more than an attempt at applying it to specific Chinese conditions. (76; 185a) It may be well to add that communist ideology has, in a sense, a similar relation to Chinese traditional culture as Christian creeds have had: it is a missionary body of alien thought.

It must be pointed out finally that the relation of the totalitarian ideology to Christian and democratic ideology is a "dialectic" one, that is to say, the relation is antithetical. But, just as antithesis in logic cannot be conceived except in juxtaposition to its thesis, so also in the movement of ideas the root is often the thesis of which the idea or ideology in hand is the antithesis. The importance of this kind of relationship lies not only in the consequent "consanguinity," enabling human beings to shift back and forth between these ideologies, but it also may provide a clue for the next step in the dialectic.

All in all, our discussion has shown that the roots of the totalitarian ideologies, both communist and fascist, are actually intertwined with the entire intellectual heritage of modern man, and that all specific links should be seen, not in terms of causation—of this or that thinker or group of thinkers being "responsible for" the totalitarian ideologies—but as strands of a complex and variegated tapestry. The specific totalitarian ingredient, namely, the employment, even glorification, of violence for the realization of the goals which the ideology posits, is largely absent from the thought of those whose ideas these ideologies have utilized, and, in utilizing them, distorted.

Chapter Nine

The Change and the Corruption of Ideologies

In the discussion of the role of ideology in totalitarian societies, some deny, as we noted, that ideology plays any significant part in the thinking of the leaders. Those who argue thus usually dwell upon the changes in ideology that they feel are in fact corruptions, proving the insincerity of the leaders. The key leadership groups are said not to take the ideology seriously, but to manipulate it, to change it arbitrarily to suit their shifting policy lines. (3) But change need not be corruption; it can be genuine adaptation and meaningful change. It must, however, be admitted that in the case of Hitler, a strong case can be made for such a claim, because of Hitler's own cynical statements about the matter. Certainly, several well-known passages in Hitler's *Mein Kampf* as well as remarks reported by Rauschning in *The Revolution of Nihilism,* (164) lend color to the proposition that Hitler's attitude toward ideology was "manipulative." On the other hand, Hitler's secret talks (86a) give a different impression, even though ideology does not play a decisive role; in these monologues Hitler clearly stays within the framework of his racist ideology.

Whatever may be the conclusions concerning Hitler's opinions, it appears quite clear that Soviet leadership, and Communist leadership generally, has continued to attach considerable importance to ideology. In spite of the vigorous denunciations of Trotskyite and other opposition elements, one is obliged to conclude that ideology plays a significant part in Soviet life, and that the leaders are sincerely exercised over ideological issues. All the ingenuity of the opposition has actually only been able to prove that there are important *changes* in the ideological pattern employed by the leaders.

Some of the key controversies in these ideological clashes revolved around the question of the spread of the revolution, the issue of democracy *versus* dictatorship, and the nature of the party's organization and operations. The first controversy, that of world revolution *versus* socialism in one country, was resolved for the Bolsheviks more by necessity than by doctrinal decision. Notwithstanding this, the issue gave rise to most vehement clashes and bitter disagreements.

Originally, most of the revolutionary leaders were hopeful that the revolution would spread from Russia to the West. Trotsky spoke glowingly of how "the working class of Russia, by leading in the political emancipation, will rise to a height unknown in history, gather into its hands colossal forces and means and become the initiator of the liquidation of capitalism on a global scale . . ." (210; 36) Brest Litovsk, dictated by German bayonets, clearly implied, however, that the revolution was territorially limited to Russia proper. This gave rise to a serious intraparty crisis. Bukharin declared it to be a blow aimed at the international proletariat which caused him and his supporters to "turn aside with contempt." Lenin's reply was characteristic: "Yes, we will see the international world revolution, but for the time being it is a very good fairy tale, a very beautiful fairy tale—I quite understand children liking beautiful fairy tales." (113c)

Bolshevik hopes soared high for a brief period after the Armistice and the consequent collapse of Austro-Hungarian and German imperial power. Central Europe became a political vacuum, torn by social and political strife. The situation seemed ready-made for communism. By January 1919, the commander of the Red Army, Leon Trotsky, was boasting: "It is no longer the spectre of communism that is haunting Europe . . . communism in flesh and blood is now stalking the continent." (213) He was re-echoed, albeit in a less ringing fashion, by Lenin, who observed hopefully that the "revolution has begun and is gaining strength in all countries." (111c)

Yet this was not to be. The revolution failed to spread, but still succeeded in Russia. Its failure as an international move led to the birth of the theory of socialist victory in one country at a time. This view was at first propounded cautiously and halfheartedly, and Soviet leaders continued to emphasize that it was merely a transitional point in historical development. In one of his earlier statements Stalin expressed it as follows:

While it is true that the *final* victory of Socialism in the first country to emancipate itself is impossible without the combined efforts of the proletarians of several countries, it is equally true that the development of the world revolution will be the more rapid and thorough, the more effective the assistance rendered by the first Socialist country to the workers and laboring masses of all other countries. (199b)

The Soviet Union accordingly became the base of world communism. This issue was somewhat overstressed by the struggle between Trotsky and Stalin which, because it operated within an ideologically oriented setting, necessarily took the form of a theoretical clash.

Similarly the controversy on the issue of democracy *versus* dictatorship gave rise to charges (later repeated by Tito) that the Bolsheviks here again had abandoned true communism. In a sense, it was out of this conflict that the Bolshevik Party was conceived. It is not idle, however, to emphasize again that Marxism is subject to varying interpretations, and the divergent lines developed by the Bolsheviks and the Mensheviks offer a striking illustration. Lenin stressed that during the revolutionary period it is pointless to talk of democracy because "broad democracy in party organization amidst the gloom of autocracy . . . is nothing more than a useless and harmful toy." (111d) And once the revolution has been achieved, terror is needed to eliminate the remnants of the bourgeoisie. The dictatorship of the proletariat, therefore, will not tolerate any restrictions on its freedom of action against the fallen, but still not liquidated, foes. Lenin put this quite flatly, thus:

Dictatorship is power based directly upon force and unrestricted by any laws. The revolutionary dictatorship of the proletariat is power won and maintained by the violence of the proletariat against the bourgeoisie, power that is unrestricted by any laws. (113d)

The question of dictatorship is inherently related to the conflict over the nature of the party which was to lead the proletariat. The issue is again as old as the Bolshevik movement itself. The split between the Mensheviks and the Bolsheviks was precisely on this crucial issue, and some of the severest attacks ever launched by fellow Marxists against Lenin were uttered during the development of this schism. Trotsky's famous charge, often erroneously cited as aimed at Stalin, was to reverberate over and over again, whenever this question came to be discussed by Marxists: "Lenin's methods lead to this: the Party organization . . . at first substituted itself for the Party as a whole; then the Central Committee substituted itself for the organization; and finally a single 'dictator' substituted himself for the Central Committee." (212)

But since all this vituperation failed to prove that Lenin's insistence on a disciplined, paramilitary party organization is un-Marxist, it is not surprising that it was the Leninist view that prevailed, and it was the Leninist Party which seized power in 1917. Political events proved Lenin to be right and among the first to acknowledge it was Trotsky himself. Lenin, too, despite his earlier doctrinal misgivings, had accepted by 1917 Trotsky's concept of the permanent revolution, as political events again suggested its doctrinal correctness.

If one considers this range of ideological conflict—these changes which are essentially corruptions—one is struck by the fact that the issues are political rather than economic. This is due at least in part to the fact that Marx and Engels were inclined to minimize the political problem which arises once the proletariat has "seized power" (see Chapter 7). The *Communist Manifesto* seems to envisage a purely cooperative living-together, without any government. "The state withers away," Engels wrote, and he meant, of course, the disappearance of the bureaucracy. Marx and Engels concentrated their ideological effort on the criticism of the existing state of society, that is to say, upon the second aspect of ideology defined here, and as proud students of economics they dealt in detail only with the analysis of economic reality, treating political problems only incidentally. This is in a way curious, considering that the two men had been harshly critical of earlier socialists as "utopian" because they did not give due attention to political realities and, more especially, "the state." Likewise, Marx's controversies with the anarchists focused upon the latter's failure to appreciate the power of existing states and the effort required to overthrow them.

One might further add that the gigantic task of industrialization which confronted the Soviet leaders in Russia called for state planning on a comprehensive scale, regardless of any doctrinal positions. The Marxist doctrine, economically speaking, is elaborate only in regard to "capitalism"; to say that Marxist dogma is "closed" or finished on the economic side is certainly incorrect. Such generalities as "to each according to his need, from each according to his capacity" are general social slogans, not economic theory.

Generally speaking, the ideological changes in the Soviet Union need not be seen as "corruptions" of ideology, as they have been by the USSR's socialist and, more especially, its Marxist opponents. They may be interpreted as "adaptations" or "modifications" and thus may be seen as a sign of vitality, as suggested by cultural comparison in other spheres. Adaptability and flexibility are thus virtues, provided they do not lead to empty opportunism. There are a number of passages in Marx and Engels suggesting such adaptations.

Soviet policies over the last several decades likewise serve to illustrate the adaptability (or corruptibility) of communism. On such fundamental issues as equality, authority, nationality policy, or foreign relations, striking adaptations to the imperatives of political reality have been made. To take one example only, the Soviet Union is today, as Barrington Moore correctly calls it, "a system of organized social inequality" despite its almost fanatic fulminations against capitalist inequality. (141a) This Soviet inequality involves not only a highly differentiated scale of rewards, which creates distinct classes of "haves" and "have-nots," but, even more than that, distinct levels of opportunities for advancement on the social scale. (141b)

The problem of adapting the communist theory of equality to fit this Soviet reality could not, because of the importance of this doctrinal facet, have been evaded. But neither could this principle be repudiated. The current Soviet rationalization accordingly runs along the lines of the *Pravda* article on socialism and equality, which states in part:

The idea of equality is not an unshakeable eternal truth. It was born of certain definite social relationships. Its content changes with changes in the latter. The sense of the demand for equality lies only in the abolition of inequality. With the disappearance of inequality, the content of the demand for equality is lost. (271a)

In other words, with the elimination of class oppression and class struggle, equality is said to be accomplished. The countless manifestations of inequality in the USSR are accordingly, in the light of this Soviet analysis, not indications of inequality at all, but the necessary concomitants of a complex industrialized society.*

A recent elaboration of Marxist, or rather Soviet, doctrine occurred at the Twentieth Party Congress, in February 1956. It again illustrates the plasticity of Bolshevik ideology, a virtue about which the Soviet leaders frequently boast. At this congress, Khrushchev jettisoned the Leninist concept of the civil war as a *necessary* stage in any society's transition to socialism; he declared that the necessity for civil conflict depends upon how determined and strong the oppressing classes are. If these classes are weak and are faced by powerful, united labor masses, then "the winning of a stable parliamentary majority backed by a mass-revolutionary movement of the proletariat and of all the working people could create for the working class of a number of capitalist and former colonial countries the conditions needed to secure fundamental social changes." Needless to add, the Soviet leaders were probably not unaware of the favorable response the above statement would draw in some postcolonial and neutralist circles.

Why do we not find any comparable pattern of ideological change in the fascist states? Apart from their shorter life, it might first of all be suggested that both Mussolini and Hitler were available to "interpret" their own thought. The situation resembles that of the Socialist International at the time Marx and Engels were still alive and could be consulted. Certain alterations in their own views certainly were acknowledged by these fascist dictators. And although logically at variance, they could be claimed as a natural sequel to what the leader himself asserted had been his purpose and intention all the time. It is, nonetheless, striking that in certain areas sharp differences of opinion could develop over ideological questions. Thus Mussolini's concordat with the Catholic Church was felt by a number of fascist subleaders to be a betrayal of fascist ideology; no less an ideologist than Gentile took this view. The varying attitudes adopted by Hitler toward the Protestant churches led, on the one hand, to sharp conflicts with Protestants, who had accepted his leadership on the strength of his alleged purpose of revitalizing Christian religion, while, on the other, alienating some of his more

---

* It is of interest to note in this connection the considerably greater pay variation between the officers and men in the Soviet Army and comparable scales in the "capitalist" United States Army.

decidedly pagan followers (see Chapter 23). We have already alluded to the potential conflict with brownshirted "socialists" whose rebellious spirit was quelled in the "blood purge" of 1934. The difficulties in this sector of relations between "capital" and "labor" never ceased to plague the Nazis; a series of uneasy compromises were struck.

Even more perplexing is the antisemitic aspect of Nazi ideology. It was, of course, central to Hitler's early ideological position, as developed in *Mein Kampf*. According to Hitler, it was his "studies" on the Jewish question that transformed him "from being a feeble world-citizen" into a "fanatical anti-Semite." (83a)   To Hitler, antisemitism was inherently linked with anticommunism, and he firmly believed that "if the Jew, with the help of his Marxist creed, conquers the nations of this world, his crown will be the funeral wreath of the human race, and the planet will drive through the ether . . . empty of mankind." (83b)   Hitler himself has attributed his own conversion to certain Austrian leaders and acknowledged their inspiration—more especially the then mayor of Vienna, Dr. Lueger.   While Hitler found ready responses to this antisemitism among the peasantry of Germany, it was a double-edged sword.   At least one investigator, Abel, has offered striking evidence in support of the proposition that Hitler gained his adherents not because of, but in spite of, his antisemitism.   Considering this fact, as well as the extent to which antisemitism proved a handicap in his foreign policy, it is striking with what radical determination Hitler pursued this "ideological" goal to the bitter end. The wholesale extermination of Jews during the war was, no doubt, in part motivated by Hitler's belief that the Jews were responsible for British and American opposition to him and his policies, and hence it was an act of revenge.   However, the ideological aspect remained of central importance; in the secret talks recorded at the height of his power and triumph he expounded it with fanatical zeal.   It appears, in some ways, the inner "rationale" of his entire conduct.

It is possible, especially in the light of the catastrophic end of Hitler's enterprise, to argue that his failure to adapt his ideology to the realities of both German and international politics was a source of weakness, perhaps even the greatest source of weakness.   Timely "corruption," such as was argued at times by Goering and others of his sub-leaders, might have saved him. He was not a complete purist; for he enunciated the curiously paradoxical doctrine that no one whom he proclaimed an Aryan could be a Jew. Several men of his immediate entourage were, according to the available evidence, non-Aryan in the Nazi sense of having some Jewish ancestry. This fact provided not only occasions for mockery to the opponents of the regime, but it troubled the race purists. But since it was not worked out ideologically, but put in terms of a fiat of the Führer's godlike will, the believers in the Third Reich could argue that such Aryan non-Aryans were purified by the "divine touch."

It might finally be suggested that a certain flexibility lends an appearance of infallibility: positions which are brought forward as developments of an underlying theme, no matter how illogical, can be made to reinforce this theme. As long as the ultimate goal remains pure, the adaptations appear to strengthen it.

Since both communism and fascism are "success philosophies," built upon the confident assumption that history is on their side, ideological factors are weapons in the struggle for men's minds. (See Chapter 11.) In the past, the role of ideology in strengthening the body politic had always been played by religion and tradition, and by the symbols and myths in which religion and tradition were embodied. In modern totalitarian societies, the leaders must carefully create and control the ideological weapons useful to their political existence; ideological adaptations and corruptions are ultimately tested by the role they play in the propaganda and education of totalitarian societies.

Chapter Ten

Symbols and Myths

Hammer and sickle, swastika and fasces are the familiar symbols of the totalitarian movements. They are well-known to many who have no clear conception of the movements for which they stand. Each of these symbols embodies an element of its ideology which has central importance, and its importance to the totalitarian deserves consideration. The symbol gives concrete form and focus to an abstraction, while the abstraction serves to illumine for the faithful the "meaning" of the symbol. The hammer and sickle stand rationally enough for the workers and peasants who together constitute the new society which the USSR aims at. Swastika and fasces (the bundle of sticks which the Roman lictor or police officer used to carry) symbolize the ancient tribal world to which Nazism and Fascism wished to seem linked, the barbaric heathens in the woods of pre-Christian Northern Europe, and the Romans of the early times. While the swastika is a ritual symbol of uncertain origin, quite common in primitive societies, the fasces are an image of the harsh discipline of sober and archaic Rome which presumably provided the basis for the city's eventual greatness. It is probably not an accident that the symbol of the Soviet Union and its satellites is a constructed symbol, invented by the leaders of the movement and pointing to the future, while the Fascist and Nazi symbols are ancient and inherited forms relating the movement to a mythical past.

In the recent attempt to establish a totalitarian regime in Argentina, the symbolic appeal tended to focus on the personal magnetism of the regime's leaders—Peron and his wife, Evita. Their pictures appeared with the same frequency that the swastikas adorned Nazi buildings or that the Red Star blazes on Soviet structures, homes, and vehicles. The Peron regime, in its use of symbols, tended to utilize the religious inclination of its predominantly Latin population. Thus, for instance, after Evita's death, the Peronista Party and particularly the Peronist trade union movement sponsored an Evita Peron cult—the living symbol of Peronist *Justicialismo*. All references to Evita were always in the present tense—"Evita says, Evita orders, Evita cares . . ."—her pictures were sold throughout the country like religious relics, little shrines to her were set up. "Peron cumple, Evita dignifica"—these words, appearing on huge posters, accompanied the Argentinian everywhere, reminding him of his debts to the Peronist regime.

This inclination to identify the living person of the dictator with the symbolism of the regime became very marked in the USSR toward the end of Stalin's life. His seventieth birthday became the signal for a veritable orgy of celebrations, gifts, panegyrics, and declarations of faith which continued until his death. The following quotation from a Soviet magazine is by no means an extreme one:

I approached Stalin's portrait, took it off the wall, placed it on the table and, resting my head on my hands, I gazed and meditated. What should I do? The Leader's face, as always so serene, his eyes so clear-sighted, penetrated into the distance. It seems that his penetrating look pierces my little room and goes out to embrace the entire globe. I do not know how I would appear to anyone looking at me at this moment. But with my every fibre, every nerve, every drop of blood I feel that, at this moment, nothing exists in this entire world but this dear and be-loved face. What should I do? "The Soviet government handles the enemies of the people with a firm hand . . ." These are thy words, comrade Stalin. I believe them sacredly. Now I know how to act. (267; 139)

After the death of Stalin in 1953 his successors proceeded to de-emphasize him as a symbol of Soviet rule and in 1956, after the Twentieth Party Congress, they openly attacked him as a paranoiac tyrant who brutally suppressed "party democracy" in the later stages of his rule. Feeling apparently that Stalin and Stalinism were a handicap to them and to their foreign relations, Stalin's successors openly cut loose from their former master and proceeded to blame him for many real and imagined crimes. At the same time, how-ever, in a vivid demonstration of the symbolic significance of a personal leader, the new Soviet leaders spared no effort in empha-sizing that they were the "faithful," "loyal" pupils of Lenin, whom they portrayed as a "genius," "great leader," and "the creator of the Communist Party." Of course, it is one thing to glorify a living leader, another to glorify a dead one. The present campaign of emphasizing Lenin leaves the Soviet leadership ample room for de-fining what Leninism is, while a living leader constantly defines his own premises and policies. In that sense, Soviet collective leader-ship strengthens its own broad appeal while not limiting its ma-nipulative capacity in policy formulation.

An additional important symbol for all the totalitarian regimes is the negative one of the stereotyped image of the enemy. For the Nazis it was the fat, rich Jew or the Jewish Bolshevik; for the Fas-cists, it was at first the radical agitator, later the corrupt and weak, degenerate bourgeois; for the Soviets it is the war-mongering, atom-bomb wielding American Wallstreeter; for the Chinese Commu-nists it is the Yankee imperialist and the western colonial exploiters. These negative images tend to accentuate by contrast the positive values of the totalitarian regime that protects its people from these dangerous and ever-conspiring monsters.

All these symbols are closely related to myth. A myth is typically a tale concerned with past events, giving them a specific meaning and significance for the present and thereby reinforcing the authority of those who are wielding power in a particular community. They may carry a lesson, explicit or implied, for the future course of events. Such myths may be invented or they may "just grow," but they play a vital role in totalitarian dictatorship. Though certainly not found only in totalitarian dictatorship (4b), the question therefore arises as to whether these totalitarian myths have a specific quality. This is indeed the case. They are pseudoscientific. The communist myth rests upon the notion that its view of history is beyond criticism (see Chapter 7), while the Nazi myth claims biological superiority for a particular race. Naturally, considerable difficulties arise when these signs are confronted with reality. This process has been ridiculed by George Orwell in *1984;* here a Ministry of Truth is staffed with officials who are always at work shaping and reshaping the record of the past to bring it into consonance with the particular situation and the exigencies in which the dictatorship finds itself. There has been enough of this actually happening to make the caricature significant. When, after Stalin's death, it became important to highlight certain new men, like Malenkov, their pictures appeared associating them closely with the deceased. In fact, some of these were forgeries manufactured for the purpose of establishing a firm link between the new rulers and the old. Stalin himself had, at an earlier date, engaged in similar tricks to establish the myth of Lenin's appreciation for him; fortunately, Trotsky among others saw to it that the uncomplimentary views which Lenin had from time to time expressed about Stalin were not lost to posterity. (24a; 234) But such forgeries should not blind us to the important and very real place which the myth has in all political societies, including totalitarianism. It is the result of a spontaneous response of men who possess power and seek authority and who wish others subject to that power to accept it as legitimate.

The myths that have played an important role in the dictatorships are numerous. For the Soviets they are in part at least embedded in Marxist writings. Myths being tales, the stories that they tell are usually stories about the past or stories about the future. *Diamat,* or dialectical materialism, provides the key myth of the communists. In the laborious words of Stalin, ". . . if the passing of slow quantitative changes into rapid and abrupt qualitative changes is a law of development, then it is clear that revolutions made by the oppressed classes are quite a natural and inevitable phenomenon. Hence the transition from capitalism to socialism and the liberation of the working class from the yoke of the capitalism cannot be effected by slow changes but only by a qualitative change of the capitalist system, by a revolution." (199c)   That all past history is a history of class warfare is part of this general myth of the communist world; that Lenin detested Trotsky and was anxious to rid the movement of his counterrevolutionary plots is a specific myth; both are related to the past; they are historical myths.   That there will eventually be established an anarchic paradise of freely cooperating individuals is a similar general myth referring to the future; another, but more specific, futuristic myth is that the Soviet Union will liberate peoples falling under its sway, that it will abolish class distinctions, and so forth.

In the case of the Nazis, the role of the myth was specifically proclaimed as constitutive of the movement and the regime.   Harking back to certain notions popular since the days of the Romantics, Alfred Rosenberg expounded in his often mentioned, but seldom read, *Der Mythos des Zwanzigsten Jahrhunderts* (The Myth of the Twentieth Century) a rather confused racial doctrine.   This doctrine is the "myth" of the century:

> Soul means race looked at from within.   Conversely, the race is the outside of a soul.   To awaken a race-soul and bring it to life means to recognize it as the highest value, and to assign to the other values their organic position under this dominant value: in the state, in art and in religion.   This is the task of our century, to create out of a new myth of life a new type of man. (171)

To this myth is related the other myth that the Germans as a cultural nation stand guard against the Slavic barbarians who, for some unexplained reason, are denied the status of a race which has a historic function.   The abysmal hatred of all things Slavic, which was also such a strong impulse of the Sudeten Austrian Hitler, produced in the Baltic German Rosenberg the mystifications of his

Mythos, which read like the fulminations of a madman now, but which were acknowledged by all adherents of the Nazi movement as gospel truth. Hitler himself, however, admitted that he had never read this book. (84b) "The German mission" was rooted in this race myth, which according to Rosenberg always is centered in a metaphysical idea. His wordy generalities about India, Persia, and the rest of the Nordics and Aryans, in the manner of Stewart Houston Chamberlain, culminate in the proposition that honor and spiritual freedom are the metaphysical ideas which are shaping the Germanic myth. As is typical of myth, the glaringly illogical inconsistencies and downright absurdities remain wrapped in a consciously mystifying language. Like the *Diamat* myth of the communists, they represent painfully corrupted versions of popularized Hegelian notions.

In Italian Fascism we find a similar mysticism and conscious stress on the myth. One early interpreter went so far as to misunderstand this to the extent of writing that "fascism represents a religious revival." Having a pragmatic view of religion, this writer immediately added, however, that he did not mean this in the sense of fascism developing a new theology, but only in "that it has given to thousands of Italian youths an ideal for which they are ready to sacrifice all." (183) If this were a valid criterion for determining whether a movement were a religious one, it would only be consistent to conclude that all totalitarian movements are religious movements, for they certainly make their youthful members ready to sacrifice all. In point of fact, it is crucial to distinguish clearly between religion and a political myth. In another chapter (Chapter 23) we shall deal with religion and the churches, but the political myth of fascism is the idea of "the grandeur that was Rome," sometimes seen as a synthesis of the Roman Empire at its glory, reinforced by the Roman Catholic Church as its spiritual guardian, but more typically divorced from the latter. The love all Italians feel so passionately for their country was projected in terms of conquest and imperial violence, which were sanctified by the memories of a historical past. History itself was, as in the case of the Germans, "spiritually conceived," that is, similarly distorted and seen as revolving around Italy—the Latin nation par excellence, the center of all civilization, the "light of the world."

That Mussolini's stress on the creative force of the myth goes back to the inspiration he derived from Georges Sorel and Vilfredo Pareto is apparent in all his utterances. Sorel, in his *Reflexions sur la Violence* (195; 42), had argued that the general strike is or should be "the myth in which socialism is wholly comprised." He had defined such a myth as "a body of images capable of evoking instinctively all the sentiments which correspond to the different manifestations of the war undertaken by Socialism against modern society." Heroes and martyrs are woven into the general myth to give concreteness and consequent appeal to the masses.

This viewpoint had been put into the broader perspective of a general view of society by Vilfredo Pareto (152), who stressed "nonlogical conduct" as characteristic of such political, and other social, life and assigned to myths, of which he examined many historical variants, an essential role in organized mass activity. Although practical applications were rather far removed from Pareto's scientific interests, he was obviously implying that a man who wants to build a political movement would do well to create myths calculated to satisfy the human craving for metarational beliefs in terms of which man's emotions can be organized for action.

Writers, such as Charles Merriam, Harold Lasswell, and Talcott Parsons, have tended to stress symbols rather than myths in their general analyses. The work of anthropologists has led to the discovery of "systems of 'symbols'" corresponding to systems of culture and systems of value. (See Chapter 7.) Myths may in fact be interpreted as symbols. We saw that in a sense they are "images" which picture the past or the future in panoramic ways. Thus seen, myths are mental "symbols," if symbols are taken in the broad sense of "signs." Parsons observes that "even the most elementary orientation of action on animal levels involves signs which are at least the beginning of symbolization. This is inherent in the concept of expectation which involves some sort of 'generalization' from the particularities of an immediately current stimulus-situation." (153b) That is to say, without signs there could be no orientation, no selection among alternatives. Parsons believes that symbolization is the necessary condition for the emergence of culture. This is no doubt historically valid. But we see in the consciously manipulated symbol manufacture and the myth-making activities of ministries of truth, so-called, of contemporary totalitarianism (which some of the more unscrupulous activities of hucksters and political propagandists everywhere rather painfully resemble) that symbolization, that is, the process of symbol formation, can also become the condition for the destruction of culture and the emergence of a Kafka-like "hall of echoes" in which all words and other signs tend to lose their meaning. If it is true that "the high elaboration of human action systems is not possible without relatively stable symbolic systems where meaning is not predominantly contingent on highly particularized situations" (153c), then it would seem that totalitarian societies cannot last, because the frantic striving for unanimity betrays great instability of the symbols (and myths), precisely because meaning *is* predominantly contingent on the highly particularized situations with which the totalitarian dictatorship is continually confronted (see Chapter 13). Only experience will tell.

Too broad a conception of symbols and myths implies another danger. If constitutions, charters, laws, treaties, and other products of rational-legal political authority are included under symbols, a serious confusion is apt to result. (106b) To be sure, a constitution may well in the course of time become *also* a symbol; when an American refers to *the* constitution without actually knowing what the United States Constitution says on the subject he is discussing, "the constitution" has become a symbol of some vague mystical entity, such as "Americanism," which is surrounded by myths and symbols. (55a) But apart from this symbolic aspect, such things as constitutions retain a significant and indeed politically predominant core, in their rational-legal function and content, to which anyone can refer. This fact may be of great political importance in situations where the constitution is symbolically abused, because it enables those who disagree with the distorters to call them to account.

It seems more appropriate and useful, therefore, to restrict the meaning of symbols to the metarational signs, such as memorial days and monuments, songs, flags, decorations and uniforms, ceremonials and rituals, mass demonstrations and parades. (133) In all these matters, the totalitarians have gone further than more traditional societies, although none of these features are lacking in any body politic, nor could they be. But the exhibits of dead leaders, like Lenin, the special memorial days, like the anniversary of the revolution, the special flags and elaborate uniforms all contribute their share to a massive and effectively manipulated symbolization, which culminates in the great parades of the party gatherings in

Red Square or Nuremberg. We might conclude with a vivid description of one of these.

The most important Soviet holiday is the May Day celebration. What follows is a description of it by a former American foreign service officer, whose embassy window faced the Red Square, the focal point of this symbolic ritual:

At exactly 10 a.m. the parade marshal appears . . . to see that the troops are ready. "Hoorays" thunder as he inspects them. Then there is a brief ten-minute "hate" speech and after that many "Long Live's" to May Day, to the Communist Party, to the Soviet state, and to Stalin. Then the military parade lasts for about forty minutes . . . At the same time the air show takes place . . . Throughout the day the loudspeakers are on everywhere in the city. The programs vary from the "Soviet Hymn" and march music to wild accordion dances, from mass choral music to high sopranos, and as background to all this loud-speaker noise is the constant roar of the paraders; chanting and cheering and singing for eight hours in a row. In the parade itself, there are not many bands. The costumes and banners and flags are in all colors. However, dominant among these is red . . . The tomb (Lenin's and Stalin's) itself is tightly fenced off by close-packed M.V.D. troops, almost all of whom are officers, and it is noticeable that when the civilian parade and demonstrations start, these troops are reinforced immediately. These M.V.D. troops are placed in elaborate formation, one facing in, the next out—all of which is a double-precaution . . . All day long from the early hours before sunrise until late hours after sunset, the "spontaneous" paraders pour into the square, coming from all directions along the main boulevards and side streets which converge onto the few thousand cobblestones which are the center of Russia. (175)

I V

The Psychic Fluidum:
Propaganda and the Terror

Chapter Eleven

Propaganda and the Monopoly of Mass Communications

The psychic fluidum—that is, the peculiar atmosphere of totalitarian dictatorship—is created by two closely related phenomena, namely propaganda and the terror. Because the terror reinforces the monopoly of mass communication, and indeed a good part of all communication, totalitarian propaganda can be understood only within this context. And conversely the terror assumes its all-pervading quality because it is spread about through continuous repetition of the official propaganda lines. This linkage of propaganda and terror distinguishes them from all comparable phenomena in nontotalitarian systems of government.

The nearly complete monopoly of mass communication is generally agreed to be one of the most striking characteristics of totalitarian dictatorship. It is also one of the features which clearly differentiates it from earlier forms of despotic rule, as we have noted. Modern mass communication media, the press, the radio, and the film, have been developing gradually and have, under competitive conditions, been looked upon as an essential condition of large-scale democracy. For, without the possibility of communicating a great deal of information which is beyond the reach of the immediate community, even the casual participation in policy determination which the citizen of the modern state is called upon to perform would be impossible.

In totalitarian dictatorships, all these means of communication are centrally controlled by the government, regardless of whether they are also actually owned by the government, as in the Soviet Union, or continue in "private" ownership, as in fascist countries. Even typewriters fell into this category, as indicated by the following decree issued in 1950 by the communist regime in Rumania: "All institutions, enterprises, state and private stores, public or private associations, offices for copying documents, and all private persons

who possess typewriters and duplicating machines such as gestett-
ners, mimeographing machines, photo-engraving machines, hand
presses, as well as material necessary for duplicating various texts,
such as stencils, fluids, and other similar materials, are required to
register them at the Ministry of Interior, General Administration
of Police, within 30 days of the publication of this decision." (244)
Effective control over the content of communications is vested in
the "state," which in fact means the top party functionaries, who
usually possess, as a result of previous revolutionary agitation, considerable know-how in the field of propaganda.

Propaganda as such is not a peculiarity of totalitarian dictatorship. It has become increasingly recognized as an integral part of
all organizational activity in a highly literate society. Propaganda
has been defined in different ways, depending in part upon what it
was to be distinguished from. It should be pointed out here that
the Soviets make a clear distinction between propaganda and agitation. Some of what we mean here by propaganda would, in Soviet terminology, be more accurately called agitation. To the
Soviets, propaganda is restricted to a more refined, rational, documented appeal, designed to convince rather than to induce. Agitation tends to be more vehement, striking, and is generally aimed at
the masses. Hence the frequent references in Soviet publications
to mass agitation. It has been said that "propaganda is the other
fellow's opinion." In line with such a superficial notion, many
people think of propaganda as essentially untruth. But no propagandist worth his mettle will prefer an untruth to a truth, if the
truth will do the job. This is the vital test of all propaganda activity: does it do the job? and what is the job? The needs, interests, and requirements of the organization for which the propagandist works determine the answer to this question. If it is the
Red Cross, the "job" may be to secure contributions, if the *Ladies'
Home Journal,* it may be subscriptions. The latter example shows
that propaganda, under competitive conditions, resembles advertis-
ing; the two today are often referred to eulogistically as "public relations." In short, propaganda is essentially action-related; it aims to
get people to do or not to do certain things. That action focus may
be either very visible or it may be hidden away. But it always is
there and needs to be inquired into, if propaganda is to be understood. And since propaganda is carried on in behalf of an organiza-

tion, it is equally important to inquire into who finances it. Many propagandists are reluctant, therefore, to reveal the source of their funds. (58a)

In totalitarian dictatorships, virtually all propaganda is directed ultimately to the maintenance in power of the party controlling it. This does not mean, however, that there are not many sharp conflicts between rival propagandists. As will be shown later, the final integration of totalitarian dictatorship does not preclude the occurrence of many internecine struggles; on the contrary, it lends to these struggles a fierceness and violence which is rarely seen in freer societies. This issue of the rival component elements in the particular totalitarian society poses very difficult problems for the over-all direction of propaganda. The chief propagandist often has to opt between such rival groups. (In Goebbels' Ministry of Propaganda and Public Enlightenment, these rival claims to some extent found expression in the organization of the "desk," that is to say, of different bureaus which would report on different sections of the society and would thus mirror the conflicts.) (38a)

The documentary evidence which has become available since the war tends to support earlier views regarding the inner workings of Goebbels' propaganda organization. (193a) There is no need here to go into the details of the organization, but some outstanding features deserve brief comment. Perhaps the most important aspect of this "monopoly" control was the dualism of government and party. Each had its elaborate propaganda setup, headed by Dr. Goebbels, who succeeded in maintaining a measure of effective coordination. But on the whole, it would seem that the Ministry of Public Enlightenment and Propaganda and the party office of propaganda were in a co-ordinate position. Key officials of the Ministry, who stood in sharpest antagonism to Goebbels, however, like Otto Dietrich, the press chief of the Hitler government, also occupied pre-eminent posts in the party's propaganda machine, and this "personal union" extended fairly far down the line. The relationship has been described as follows:

The task of the Propaganda Ministry in the whole machine for controlling and creating public opinion might be compared with a Ministry of War. It coordinates, plans, and is responsible for the smooth carrying out of the whole propaganda effort of the German government. The Party Propaganda Department, on the other hand, is comparable to the General Staff of an army which actually directs operations and musters and organizes the forces and their supplies and ammunition. (193b)

It is seen from this and other evidence that the two organizations had different functions within the regime, comparable to the difference between party and government. The aggressive boldness of a leader of the National Socialist movement was as much a quality required of Goebbels as the forceful caution of a leading government official. It is generally agreed that the most important arm of Goebbels in planning and co-ordinating all the far-flung activities of his two organizations was the Coordination Division of the Ministry. Here was centered the conflict between the rival requirements of the two organizations; here, if possible, such difficulties were solved by the key officials of the Division, or if necessary, by Goebbels himself. But it was never an easy task to draw together the various divergent strands of the propaganda apparatus and the difficulties experienced by the Ministry of Propaganda reflected the tensions of the moment. It is an ever present problem when total monopoly control exists.

The same problem, often in aggravated form, confronts the totalitarian propagandist in the field of foreign relations. While he gains the advantage of controlling all channels of information to other countries, he suffers under the distinct disadvantage of having little chance of securing the confidence of people abroad, including the foreign governments themselves, for any information reaching them about the country. Hitler showed considerable awareness of these difficulties. At one time, talking among intimates, he noted that a sharp distinction must be made between handling the domestic and the foreign press. Radio messages for foreign countries must similarly be differentiated. Such messages, if intended for Britain, should contain musical offerings, since they appeal to English taste and would accustom the British public to tune in to German broadcasts.

As regards news-bulletins to Britain, we should confine ourselves to plain statements of facts, without comment on their value or importance . . . As the old saying has it, little drops of water will gradually wear the stone away. (84d)

Goebbels added that the opinion of people who have confidence in their leadership can be effectively swayed by pointed and unequivocal value judgments. He therefore recommended that in messages to the German people reference should be made again and again to "the drunkard Churchill" and to the "criminal Roosevelt."

This attempt to create stereotype images of the enemy has been developed to a fine point in Soviet propaganda. All discussions and pictorial representations of the enemy stress some specific feature and characteristic suggesting the enemy's alleged criminal nature and evil intent. Operating on a huge scale and addressing its appeal to the great masses of the Soviet people, Soviet propaganda strives to present a simple, unrefined, and strikingly negative portrayal, so as to create the politically desirable conditioned reflex in those to whom it is directed.

During the war, for instance, in anti-Nazi propaganda the prefix "Hitlerite" was usually associated with such terms as "vermin" or "beast," frequently with corresponding illustrations. The anti-American campaign has similarly tended to restrict itself to certain oft repeated terms, such as "war-mongering," thus playing on the Soviet people's fear of war. *Krokodil,* the "humor" magazine, has become a real rogues' gallery of various criminal types, with beastly faces, dressed either in United States Army uniforms or top hats and morning coats, their fingers dripping with blood and threateningly grasping an atomic bomb. These excesses against foreign nations also cause considerable difficulty. For in external propaganda, the Soviet Union never fails to draw a distinction between the people as such and the leaders, who are the one who fit the stereotype.

The nearly complete control of all means of mass communication gives the totalitarian dictatorship the very great advantage of being able to shift its general point of view rather radically over short periods of time. This is especially helpful in the field of foreign affairs. After the Hitler-Stalin Pact of 1939, Communist and Nazi propagandists were stressing all of a sudden the common features of these "popular" regimes and their contrast with the "Pluto-democracies" of the West. Various points were brought forward in this connection—such as that the Russians and Germans were both "young" and "vigorous" as contrasted with the decadence of the West. Even more striking is the recent turn in regard to Stalin. Such complete reversals in official propaganda lines are inconceivable under competitive conditions. It should be noted, in this connection, that while these shifts may work in the Soviet Union, they certainly tend to bring on a crisis in the communist movement in other countries. Many of the communist followers including important men, have changed sides in the past and may do so again. After the Hitler-Stalin pact twenty-one French Communist deputies out of a total of seventy-two abandoned the party. (14) Similarly, Nazi sympathizers in a number of countries, especially the United States, were deeply disturbed, and anti-Nazi activities were assisted by this change.

The reverse took place when Hitler suddenly decided to invade the Soviet Union in the summer of 1941 on the flimsiest of pretexts. We find that Hitler was much pleased with his success in accomplishing this *salto mortale*. "I am proud that it was possible with these few men [himself, Goebbels, and a few aides] to shift course by 180°. No other country could do the same." (86b; 84e) In this instance, we know from postwar documentation that the effect on German public opinion was quite mixed. For, while some men who had previously stood aloof decided that in a life and death struggle with communism they must support Hitler, others concluded that the game was up and joined what became a dangerous and large-scale opposition movement. Detached analysis suggests that it was not so much the propaganda as the very facts themselves which had the greatest effect. (174a; 39a)

This instance serves to illustrate what is probably a very important aspect of all totalitarian propaganda. The fact of monopolistic control gradually causes in the general public a profound distrust of all news and other kinds of information. Since people do not have any other source of information, there develops a vast amount of rumor-mongering as well as general disillusionment. And since man cannot think without having valid information upon which to focus his thought, the general public tends to become detached from all general questions. This in turn leads to a phenomenon more fully discussed below, which we may call the "vacuum" which increasingly surrounds the leadership. In the manner of Harun al-Rashid, who is said to have stalked Bagdad at night disguised as a commoner to find out what was going on, totalitarian dictatorships have tried to break through this vacuum by a variety of devices. The recently discovered records of the German Gestapo contain many "reports" rendered by local Gestapo men about the developing public attitude. Some of them are very realistic appraisals, showing how the propaganda was breaking down as an effective instrument of public control. They reported at times that there were not two in two hundred citizens who could be trusted.

There is little data of this type available with respect to the USSR. Some Soviet documents, however, including secret police reports, have fallen into Western hands and consequently permit a limited insight. The most curious thing about these secret police reports is their almost complete candidness. Reports of decline in morale among party personnel, or hostile attitudes toward specific Soviet policies, or accounts of particular reactions among workers or peasants to a given measure were made, according to the information available, in a very matter-of-fact fashion, with little or no attempt to embellish the facts with more palatable dressing. Provided these reports are not unique in their accuracy (and there is no reason to believe that they are), and provided they receive the attention they merit, the Soviet regime can, when it wants to, judge the responsiveness of its population to its propaganda with a surprising degree of accuracy. One is bound to wonder whether the recent changes in the Soviet Union were not, at least in part, motivated by reports about the dissatisfaction with the regime. There is one major problem, however: as the totalitarian regime maintains its internal coercion and indoctrination, the degree of spontaneous expression will in time diminish, and the secret police will find it much more difficult to assess the true attitude of the population. There is no doubt that the Soviet population is today much less spontaneous in its expressions and reactions than a generation ago. This naturally makes information-gathering less reliable.

Goebbels was by no means unaware of the difficulties he was confronting. In *The Goebbels Diaries,* published by Louis Lochner after the war (67), the problem is a recurrent theme. They also show how well he knew how to exploit the clumsy views which were being aired by the Allies regarding the German people as a whole, particularly the demand for unconditional surrender. As the plain facts of the Allies' successful air war against Germany mounted, the "unconditional surrender" formula remained as one of the few propaganda weapons to fall back upon. Another one was provided by the "Morgenthau Plan" put forward at Quebec in

September 1943. But not only the Western Allies provided desperately needed propaganda weapons; the Soviet Union, by repeatedly demanding that ten million Germans be furnished for reconstruction purposes in the Soviet Union, allowed Goebbels to note: "Demands like that are wonderful for our propaganda. They stir German public opinion deeply. The idea that our soldiers might not return home at all but might have to remain in the Soviet Union as forced labor is a terrible thought for every woman and every mother. The German people would prefer to fight to their last breath." (67a) Incidentally, this is an illustration of the fact noted above that a propagandist prefers a good fact to the best lie.*
But in spite of such aids, the task of propaganda became ever more desperate as the war continued. What evidently kept Goebbels going was that he himself believed in the Führer's ability to avert disaster, at least until the end of 1943.

Otto Dietrich has described the difficulties which resulted from Hitler's hostility to the press. This contrasted curiously with Hitler's avid interest for reading press reports from abroad. (38b) But although they were brought to him almost hourly, they failed to influence his modes of expression and his basic propaganda lines. It is interesting that Dietrich believes that these propaganda lines were detrimental to the regime. His comments indicate a typical clash of views between the professional propagandist and the ideologue, whether educator or party fanatic, who is preoccupied not with the survival but with the advance of the totalitarian movement. Dietrich's comments are so revealing that they deserve quoting *in extenso:*

I was of the firm conviction at that time that a national socialist Germany could live in peace with the world, if Hitler had been restrained in his actions, had bribed the radicalism internally, and had externally an objective propaganda which took account of the interests of other nations. The provocative demonstrations, unnecessary in their extent . . . the anti-semitic excesses, the inciting and tolerating of, and the world propaganda of Goebbels as embodied in the tone and content of his Sportpalast demonstrations were psychologically unsuited to gain support abroad for national socialist Germany and to cause other na-

---

* A more recent indication of this is the Soviet exploitation in Poland and Czechoslovakia of the American unwillingness to dissociate itself from some West German territorial claims. This has given the Soviets a propaganda advantage which the U. S. has consistently underestimated.

tions to recognize the good side of national socialism. These tactless and offensive outbursts decisively influenced world public opinion against Germany immediately after 1933. (38c)

Dietrich probably is right, but he overlooks the fact that Hitler was not primarily interested in the German people—a fact which he elsewhere recognizes—but was basically motivated by his totalitarian mission, as he conceived it, and for this the German people were merely the tool.

Another important feature of totalitarian propaganda is its all-pervasiveness. It is, of course, the direct result of the propaganda monopoly. Not only the members of the party and the more or less indifferent masses, but even the more or less determined enemies of the regime, fall prey to its insistent clamor, to the endless repetition of the same phrases and the same allegations. A general pattern of thought, almost a style of thinking, proves increasingly irresistible as the regime continues in power. A German doctor, for nearly ten years a Russian prisoner and employed in various concentration camps where political enemies of the regime were detained, has recently given a very telling account of his observations. He notes the extent to which avowed enemies of the regime think in terms of the established phraseology of Marxism-Leninism. (201a)

It has been, as a matter of fact, the frequent experience of interviewers of former Soviet citizens to find that even those who profess the most violent hostility to the Soviet system tend to think in patterns instilled into them by that regime. Their attitudes on such matters as freedom of the press or the party system are often inclined to mirror, even by contradiction or negation, official Soviet propaganda. Similarly, in such matters as word usage, words laden with propaganda-derived value judgments are used as part of their daily vocabulary. They thus serve unconsciously as unwitting propagandists for the regime they abhor.

This singular success of totalitarian propaganda is the result of constant repetition. Soviet press, radio, oral agitation, and propaganda operate ceaselessly, supplementing the party and Komsomol activities and the ideologically oriented training system. (89a) Soviet newspapers, controlled centrally, repeat day after day the political themes set by *Pravda,* the organ of the Central Committee of the CPSU, and *Izvestia,* the organ of the Soviet Council of Ministers. *Pravda* itself, with a circulation of well over three million, is read and studied throughout the Soviet Union, particularly in the party cells, where it is compulsory reading. Local newspapers, many with circulations of several hundred thousand, such as *Radyans'ka Ukraina* and *Leningradskaia pravda,* re-echo the essential points of the Moscow daily, often reprinting its editorials and commentaries. The local press is also sometimes given special instructions about the handling of the news and the sequence in which the various statements of the leaders are to be presented. For instance, after Malenkov's "resignation" in February 1955, radio Moscow issued such special instructions to all the provincial papers. In addition to the two central newspapers, *Izvestia* and *Pravda,* there are a large number of specialized papers for youth, the trade unions, the military, and others, published centrally and distributed throughout the USSR. All these newspapers, with a combined circulation of over forty-seven million, play an important role in the Soviet process of indoctrination. (255a)

This process is backed by the other two basic media of propaganda and indoctrination: the radio and personal agitation. The radio, with an estimated listening audience of about forty million, quite naturally devotes a great deal of its time to political matters. (89b) A reliable estimate places the amount of time devoted to political and scientific broadcasts at 28 per cent of the central radio program time. One of the most important Moscow radio broadcasts is the morning reading (7:00 a.m.) of the *Pravda* editorial which is relayed simultaneously by all other Soviet stations. (245a) Soviet radio publications openly admit the political importance of radio broadcasting, as seen in the following statement:

Radio helps considerably in the Communist education of the workers. It is one of the most important means of disseminating political information, of spreading the all-triumphant ideas of Marxism-Leninism, popularizing the most advanced industrial and agricultural techniques and the achievements of socialist culture, science, and art. (274)

News and editorial programs particularly are designed to complement the press propaganda coverage, and highlight the important points in the current propaganda themes. Foreign news is rarely given prompt treatment, and it is usually presented as a commentary. Furthermore the use of radio-diffusion speakers, which work on the basis of wire transmission and are therefore useless for listening to non-Soviet stations, is promoted. This, of course, insures complete monopoly for Soviet broadcasting, and about 70 per cent of all sets in the USSR are of this type. (89c) Similiar sets are now being introduced in the satellite regimes of central Europe.

The third, and, in some ways, the most important device is that of direct, personal agitation. This involves literally millions of agitators, some full-time, some part-time during special campaigns, who organize mass meetings, give lectures, visit families in their homes, distribute literature, set up study and discussion groups, and, in general, attempt to draw everyone into active participation in the indoctrination process. The estimated number of regular agitators is around two million, thus providing one agitator for every hundred Soviet citizens (including children). (89d) In a sense, this mass indoctrination constitutes an effort to conduct a nationwide process of "brain-washing," which only a very few succeed in completely avoiding. It is on these propaganda processes, as well as on the educational training system, that the regime depends for the achievement of total ideological integration of its people. It is these instruments of mental molding that are used by the administration to produce a generation of true totalitarians, thinking and acting in disciplined unison.

The corresponding aspect of Nazi and Fascist propaganda techniques was the emphasis placed upon the spoken word. Hitler himself had supported this method emphatically in *Mein Kampf* and it became a key policy of the Goebbels operation. One whole section of the party's propaganda apparatus was dedicated to the training of speakers, and there was a deliberate effort made to cultivate oratory rather than written communications. Thousands of men were thus trained to emulate Hitler in developing the technique of rousing the mass assembly, with its emotional outbursts and its vague longings, to violent action against the Jew, the Marxist, and the November criminal.

All in all, the system of propaganda and mass communication developed in the totalitarian systems is of crucial importance for the maintenance of the regime. It may be doubted whether it could function at all well without the terror, but it cannot be doubted that as it actually functions it is highly effective. In a very real sense, it dehumanizes the subjects of the regime by depriving them of a chance for independent thought and judgment.

Chapter Twelve

Education as Indoctrination

We have shown, when discussing the party, how the totalitarian organization extends to the young and even the very young. Komsomol, Hitlerjugend, and Ballila all seek to organize and indoctrinate the child at the earliest possible age. But besides engaging in this party activity, the totalitarians also transform a large part of the educational process itself into a school for their particular brand of ideology. The entire educational process becomes an adjunct to the propaganda efforts of the regime and is perverted to this purpose in ever larger measure as the totalitarian nature of the dictatorship unfolds. This is true even though the educational system, especially on its higher levels, provides an important haven for dissidents and serves as an "island of separateness" from which a certain amount of opposition emanates. We shall discuss this aspect of education in another place. (See Chapter 24.) Here we wish to consider its operation as a technique for "making fascists" or communists.

In considering totalitarian activity in this field it is important, however, to recall that a certain amount of this kind of thing is found in all political societies. In a well-known study, Charles Merriam explored this problem in its various ramifications and undertook to formulate certain generalizations. (132) It is quite evident that all political societies must instill a love of the country and its institutions in its citizens in order to generate that degree of loyalty without which there cannot be effective cooperation. And since no political regime can last without a certain degree of effective cooperation from most of its members, the development of this loyalty has been the concern of all governments. This was emphasized by Aristotle, who devoted some significant pages of his *Politics* to this "making of citizens." But there is a vital difference between employing the educational system to develop in youth the ability and inclination "to think for themselves," as the conventional phrase goes, and using education for the purpose of making all those who come within its grip think alike. There can be no question that time and again civic educational programs in free countries have tended to overstep the boundary suggested by this contrast. Patriotic organizations often seek to pervert education, even in the democracies, into some kind of propagandistic indoctrination, "to develop a burning faith," or in some other way to restrict free inquiry and to confine it within the bounds of a particular political (or religious) orthodoxy. But such activities are fairly generally recognized for what they are and, even though they may temporarily prevail under the impact of a war crisis, they are at length repudiated by the citizens at large.

In the nature of the case, no such criticism is possible under totalitarian dictatorship. Teachers and pupils alike are continually exposed to the pressures emanating from the totalitarian apparatus. And when, in the course of the totalitarian dictatorship's development, more and more teachers become absorbed into the movement, often by formal recruitment into the party itself, the distinction between education and propaganda becomes increasingly blurred, at least as far as broadly moral and social fields of study are concerned. (28) Education, like ideology, becomes an instrument in the hands of the regime that takes upon itself the definition of the truth. This process reached its extreme point in Stalin's celebrated concern with language. In his *Marksizm i voprosy iazykoznaniia,* Stalin completely rejected the hitherto official Soviet doctrine of linguistics, branding it as "un-Marxist." Until Stalin's 1950 statement, the official line, enunciated by academician N. Ia. Marr, was that language was part of the superstructure derived from the economic basis. As such, it was subject to the same process of dialectical development. Stalin declared that, on the contrary, language was an independent phenomenon, not to be confused with the superstructure. Party propagandists, quickly taking the cue, declared that the Russian language was the international language of the age of socialism, just as Latin, French, and English had been the common languages of past epochs. Similarly, in the case of the now discredited Lysenko theories, it was through the official intervention of the regime, particularly in the person of Zhdanov, that an obsolete environmental approach to biology was proclaimed to be in keeping with Marxism. The attempt to force various fields of culture into line with the party orthodoxy, had of course very serious deleterious effects upon the educational system. The same was true with the Nazi claim that the theory of relativity was a "Jewish" deviation from truth, and that certain trends of modern mathematics and physics, not to speak of biology, must be rejected because they were in conflict with the race myth of the official ideology.

In order to be able to direct an educational system to respond to such metarational directives, it is necessary to organize it in strict subordination to the official hierarchy. Beyond the general bureaucratization characteristic of all modern society (see Chapter 17), it becomes necessary to force all teachers into membership in the party or into related organizations, such as the National Socialist Union of Teachers, the Fascist Association of Teachers, or the Soviet professional unions for academic workers. But what is even more important is that the entire educational system be permeated by the "spirit" of the movement. From the elementary school to the university, the system must be responsive to the propaganda appeals at the top, as they elaborate and adapt the official ideology. At the same time, it must be geared to creating the "Soviet man," the "new man" who would be an idealizing projection of certain key features of the ideology, such as the class-conscious worker in the Soviet regime or the "warrior" in the Fascist regimes. (69; 6; 109b) This notion of the infinite pliability of human beings is, of course, an important premise of totalitarian emphasis on education as the long-range arm of propaganda. (58b)

The organization of the educational system of the Soviet Union underwent considerable change after the first postrevolutionary phase. The original ideologues, more especially Lunacharsky, were fired with a genuine enthusiasm for educational reforms, which bore a resemblance to what has become known throughout the West as "progressive education." They believed in freeing the child of the fetters of traditional authority, and hoped that a system of complete freedom in the schools would be suitable to the molding of the future Soviet citizen. Sidney and Beatrice Webb, themselves committed to this Western progressivism, have written movingly of this early phase of Soviet educational effort. It was combined with a vigorous attack upon analphabetism, which had been so doleful an aspect of tsarist autocracy. (224b) It is evident, in retrospect, that this phase of Soviet education predates the consummation of totalitarian dictatorship in the USSR.

It was marked by a spirit of revolt against the disciplinarian traditions of the tsarist schools and resulted in the shattering of school authority. Pupil self-government was considered the best method of instilling a sense of responsibility in the young; the authority of the teacher was minimized, homework and examinations were abolished, and in many schools a state of semi-anarchy prevailed. This somewhat destructive phase ended, however, as early as 1923, and was followed by a similarly unsuccessful era of organized experimentation designed to develop a uniquely Soviet educational process. The new Soviet education was to be a manifestation of the class relationships prevailing in the USSR, and hence was to favor the laboring masses. Discriminatory practices became widespread against the children of white-collar workers, ex-aristocrats, and others. At the same time, efforts were made to give the children the benefits of political education at the earliest possible age. Even kindergarten children were expected to participate in discussions involving, for instance, the relationship of the military to the bourgeoisie, and so on. Traditional subjects, on the other hand, were neglected. (71; 209; 232)

The big change occurred in the early thirties. It was a part of the general process of totalitarianizing the system, marked by the party purges, collectivization, and the suppression of the opposition. It occurred also in the midst of a tremendous expansion of educational facilities, as the following figures for primary- and secondary-school attendance indicate: 1914: 7,800,000; 1928: 11,952,000; 1939: 32,000,000; 1950: 33,000,000; 1954: 29,000,000. (37)

The number of teachers also grew rapidly: 1914–15: 23,007; 1938–39: 1,270,164. (286a) By 1932 the regime had acknowledged the failure of its experimental educational policies, and an about-face was made. Professorial ranks were re-established in an effort to give the academic profession more prestige, salaries were rapidly increased, traditional subjects (such as history or literature) reappeared, the Komsomol was called upon to help assert the authority of the teacher, and the process of political education was rationalized. On the youngest levels it was abandoned altogether, while it received growing emphasis in the upper academic classes. In 1938 the official, short course History of CPSU, a remarkable falsification of the past, was made obligatory study matter for the older students. The purges removed from the scene many nonparty teachers, and the others were made fully subject to party control through the professional teachers' unions. The internal atmosphere of the schools became characterized by the strictest discipline and great respect for the teacher as a representative of the state. Indeed, an American high-school student would be surprised by the regulations which bind his Soviet counterpart as per the decree of the RSFSR (Russian Soviet Federated Socialist Republic) of August 2, 1943, which we quote in full:

Every student is bound to:

1. Stubbornly and persistently master knowledge in order to become an educated and cultured citizen and as useful as possible to the Soviet Fatherland;
2. Duly learn; attend classes regularly; not be late at the beginning of school occupations;
3. Obey unquestioningly the directives of the director of the school and of the teachers;
4. Come to school with all required textbooks and writing materials; be completely ready for the class before the entry of the teacher;
5. Come to school clean, with hair well-groomed, and tidily dressed;
6. Keep his place clean and orderly;
7. Enter the classroom immediately after the ringing of the bell and take his place (one may leave or enter the classroom during class only with the teacher's permission);
8. In the classroom sit erect, not lean on his elbow, not sprawl, listen with attention to the teacher's explanations and to the answers of other students, not talk and not indulge in any extraneous matters;
9. When the teacher or the director of the school enters the classroom or leaves it, greet him by rising;
10. While answering the teacher, rise, keep erect [this and #9 is also true of university students], and sit down only with the teacher's permission; raise one's hand when wishing to give an answer or ask a question;
11. Enter in a notebook the exact notation of the assignments made by the teacher for the next day and show this notation to his parents; do the entire homework by himself;
12. Show respect to the director and the teachers; when meeting the director of the school or a teacher in the street, greet him by a respectful salutation, the boys by taking off their headwear;
13. Be courteous with elders, behave modestly and decently at the school, in the street and in public;

14. Not use swear or rude words, not smoke; not play any games for money or any objects of value;
15. Take care of the school property; take care also of his own and his colleagues' property;
16. Be attentive and obliging with old people and children, with weak or sick persons, let them pass and give them one's seat, assist them in every way;
17. Obey parents and help them in taking care of small brothers and sisters;
18. Keep one's room clean, and one's clothes, shoes, and bed linen in good order;
19. Always carefully keep the student's card, not give it to other persons, and produce it at the request of the director or a teacher of the school;
20. Cherish the reputation of the school and of one's class as much as one's own.

Students are liable to be punished, including expulsion from the school, for violation of these rules. (33; 103a)

The internal atmosphere of the school was thus made to correspond to the general emphasis on discipline so characteristic of authoritarian societies.

More recently, according to the instructions voiced at the Nineteenth Party Congress, increased emphasis has been paid to technical and vocational training, at the expense of literature and the humanities. (284) At the same time the regime has made it clear that not all the high-school students can expect that their studies will lead them to higher institutes of learning. On the contrary, in keeping with the swing initiated in 1940, admission to higher institutes is becoming increasingly difficult, not only through the introduction of fees, but also through raising admission standards.*
The USSR has no shortage of candidates for higher training, and it would be dangerous for all pupils to orient themselves purely in terms of higher academic training. The schools are to instill in the pupils "a desire to join the ranks of the toilers," (262a) and high-school graduates are now being sent directly into industry or agri-

---

* It appears, however, in the light of the 1956 Twentieth Party Congress that fees will be abolished; standards of admission will remain very high. Special boarding schools will be set up for the especially gifted students; these schools will stand out by their comforts and high standards. Whether they become places for the children of the privileged elite remains to be seen.

culture. This is particularly true in the agricultural regions, where many pupils complete their education at the age of 11 and are allowed to work. In the urban areas the minimum work age is 14. (280) The educational process in the USSR has thus evolved into a manipulative organ of the regime, which uses education not merely to enlighten the minds of men, but also as a method of channeling both brains and manpower to meet the current requirements. The administration of the educational system, needless to add, is highly centralized, despite the sham autonomy of the republics in the field of education. Textbooks, educational programs, and the ideological line emanate from the center, and the intellectual activity of the scholars is closely supervised. Recent years, for instance, saw repeated attacks on many historians in the various Soviet republics for their alleged "nationalist deviationism." On the whole, however, it would be erroneous to conclude that, because of the emphasis placed on political indoctrination, the Soviet school fails in the function of training and preparing specialists, technicians, and generally alert Soviet citizens. Indeed, the remarkable and dangerous conclusion is that Soviet totalitarianism seems well on the way to doing both. (282)

The National Socialists, although they almost immediately attacked the educational task in totalitarian terms, did not really have sufficient time to mature such a system. Even though they were vigorously aided by the Hitler Youth (see Chapter 4) from the very beginning, schools and more especially universities maintained a degree of passive resistance (see Chapter 24). Nevertheless, the liberal and humanistic educational system, which had been the pride and glory of Germany in the past, was revamped. Physical education was placed in the center, and the kind of personality in which the Nazis believed, where loyalty and honor were invoked to cultivate an unquestioning obedience to the Führer, was not only encouraged, but coercively imposed. This unquestioning obedience was given a meaningful underpinning by inducing the pupils to identify themselves completely with the Führer and his regime. The process of building such an identification meant, where it succeeded, that education was completely "politicized." Not only the content of various subjects, such as history, literature, and biology, but also their range of priorities of preference, was determined by such political considerations as could be derived from the party

ideology. The key concept in this connection became action (*Tat*)
—a thoroughly pragmatic attitude which may be indicated by para-
phrasing an old American saying: "We don't know where we're
going, but Hitler does and anyhow we're on the way." This education for action and active obedience appealed, in a sense, to an
older strand of passive submission to traditional authorities which
the few years of the Weimar Republic had not succeeded in up-
rooting despite the efforts of the men then in charge, like Doctor
Becker, Minister of Education in Prussia for several years. But it
must not be confused with it, as was done by wartime propaganda.
For the new activist outlook committed the person who accepted
it to the values and beliefs involved. The identification which it
asked for could have become the stepping-stone for a more independent viewpoint, once the identification had disintegrated; but,
while it lasted, "the mystique" of "service" and of "loyalty" made
the submission to the "will of the people and of the state," as per-
sonified by Hitler, and to the orders of functionaries and officials
appear not only as naturally right, but also as "morally obligatory."
(105a) This "mystique" or ideology possessed, of course, strongly
militaristic and imperialistic overtones which helped to convert the
entire educational system into a school for aggressive war and
conquest.

The Nazis made short shrift with the former local autonomy in
the field of education. They soon organized their Ministry of Education, in which all educational authority was centralized. (This
centralization of educational policy decisions is one of the more
striking kinships between Nazism and Jacobinism.) This Reich
Ministry did not succeed in completing a revolution of the methods and organization of education, which merely became again
somewhat more authoritarian and rigid. But it imposed upon the
schools a welter of politically oriented subject matter which even in
its headings is revealing: family sociology, race theory and practice,
genetics, population policy, ethnography, prehistory, current events,
colonial politics, planning, civil defense, aeronautics, social aid. (293)
It will be recognized that some of these subjects may well be useful additions to a curriculum of a modern school, if taught in the
spirit of experimentation and free inquiry. By the Nazis they were
made vehicles for the transmission of their ideology of "blood and
soil."

The situation in Fascist Italy, while resembling that of Nazi Germany, was characterized by the struggle between the government and the church over the control of the schools. The Fascists actually sought to counterbalance the continuing influence of the Catholic Church in the schools by a compulsory service in the Fascist youth organizations (see Chapter 4). In the course of this struggle, they developed approaches which the Nazis never improved upon; indeed in this whole field of education, the Italians were the originators, led as they were by a man of unusual learning and ability, Giovanni Gentile. It must be said at once, however, that his "reforms" were perverted by the needs of the totalitarian dictatorship. One commentator has written that Gentile's reforms were "designed to reduce the domination of the textbook, and of learning by rote, and to bring the tang of actual life, and the problems of conduct, into the schools." And he comments rightly that "this is the crucial issue in education all over the world." (50d) But what the totalitarians have done is exactly the opposite. They have substituted for the scholarly text of the humanist tradition the domination of the party program-textbook, the learning by rote of rituals and of propagandistic formulas, all seemingly unbookish—to bring the tang of life and conduct, as seen by totalitarians, into the schoolrooms. In short, they revealed the great danger to all education implicit in these well-sounding phrases. Time and again the theme song was repeated: "The School is life and Italian life is the enthusiasm of faith and Fascist discipline."

The wearisome details of teacher regimentation and pupil indoctrination need not be described further. The story is essentially the same as in the other totalitarian regimes. The schools became in effect branches of the Fascist party, dedicated to the task of "making Fascists." (184) There were pictures of the Duce everywhere, commemorative altars, and tablets, celebrations, songs, parades, and the ever repeated slogans of Fascist propaganda. The Teachers' Association issued guides to help the teachers keep up the continuous barrage, and the textbooks were full of the same slogans. Herman Finer has summed up his impression of these texts in a rather effective manner:

Why are you a Balilla? Why are you a "Little Italian girl?" It is not enough to have a membership-card and the uniform! You must be sincere in heart and educated to Fascism! For example, you must learn to obey. What is the first duty of a child? Obedience! The second? Obedience! The third? Obedience! The Fascist celebrations are explained. The Flag and the rods are illustrated . . . The life of the Duce is retold under the caption: "The Child Prodigy" . . . An entire legend of Mussolini as a war hero is created. The impression is given that the war was fought at his wish and under his direction . . . (50e; 40a; 122a; 218)

The same theme song was repeated over and over again throughout the years from elementary and high school into the universities. And although much rigorous intellectual training of the formal continental sort continued in Italy's schools, the essential framework was provided by this typically totalitarian adulation of leader, party, and system. (The universities are dealt with in Chapter 24.) It seems astonishing, in view of this record, that further reforms in this direction were envisaged by the proposed school reform (*Carta della Scuola*) of 1938 (122b) put forward by Giuseppe Bottai. Bottai at the time called for an "organic union of party and school through the youth organization" which would "finish forever the age of the agnostic school . . . we decisively want a Fascist school, a Fascist pedagogy—Fascist teaching to create the Fascist man, by the thousands upon thousands." (275b)

How nearly alike in method and effect the communist and fascist approaches to school education are is dramatically shown by developments in the Soviet Zone of Occupation in Germany. Only the controlling elite cadres and the ideology differ—and these not as much as is pretended. The development of educational reform started with a genuine impulse toward democratization. A number of former teachers and school officials, mostly members of the Social Democratic Party and committed to the progressive educational idealism of the Weimar Republic, were put to work and produced the "law for the Democratization of Education," in 1946. Rejecting the traditional concepts as those of a *Standesschule* (class school), and professing a sharply antifascist outlook, the law provided: "The German school must be organized so as to guarantee the same right to education, according to their abilities, to all youth . . . regardless of the estate of their parents." And, consequently, it demanded that "the form of public education is a system of schools which is equal for boys and girls, is organically structured and democratic." (105b) So far, so good. But as the evolution of

the Soviet zone of Germany veered toward totalitarianism, the interpretation of the term "democracy" became increasingly that of
the Soviet Union. Democratic school reformers left or were ousted,
and the entire school system was permeated with the spirit of the
class struggle, that is to say, it became politicized and was made into
an arm of the propaganda machinery of the dictatorship. All teachers were enrolled in the official organizations, the students were exposed to a variety of strictly pragmatic subjects related to the tasks
of the dictatorship, and loyalty was made part of the test of admission to the higher ranges of the educational system. At the same
time, the students were subjected to rigid and doctrinaire discipline.

The experience of Eastern Germany is part of a general process,
undertaken in all the European satellites of the USSR, of politicizing education and making it part of the indoctrinating function of
the party. In all these regimes, the schools have been subjected
to intensive purges designed to weed out both the recalcitrant
teacher and the hostile student. The most notorious, but certainly
neither unique nor most extreme, example is that of the Communist
Action Committee screening and expelling professors and students
of the ancient Charles University in Prague, after student demonstrations on behalf of the Beneš government. In all of the satellite
systems, political loyalty has been made the prerequisite consideration for admission to higher institutes of learning. Candidates are
screened in an oral examination designed to test their political consciousness and to ascertain the level of their ideological maturity.
A curiously frank insight into these practices is given by a short
story published in *Nowa Kultura,* the official literary organ of the
communist regime in Poland. The author describes the emotions
and experience of a peasant boy facing the examining board. Prior
to departure from home, his mother pins on him a holy picture,
which his father silently removes just before they arrive in town for
the examination, and his uncle warns him—"our times are political;
remember to say everything as you should, just like we read in the
papers . . ." (264)

But admission is dependent not only on the ability of the candidate to convince the examiners that he is suitable for higher education in the "people's democracy." According to *Trybuna Ludu,*
the official organ of the party in Poland, "applicants [of peasant
origin] for the first year of studies in higher institutions of learning

should attach to their application an official certificate showing the degree to which their parents or guardians have fulfilled their assigned delivery quotas." (281) And a special system of priorities has been set up designed to keep out of the higher institutions those whose class origin makes them potentially enemies of the new system. In that discriminatory spirit, Anna Jungwirthova, a member of the Czech Parliament, suggests that ". . . if the children of bourgeois origin are healthy enough, they should choose manual work, the kind of work in mines and factories which their class gladly left to the proletariat . . . There, deep underground, applying the drill to the coal, or in the harsh glare of the foundries near the molten iron, they will see a new world, a world of versatile work. There they will find their new higher schools and colleges: there we will be able to mould and re-educate them into builders of socialism." (258; 21)

In conclusion, it could perhaps be said that the profession of teacher is profoundly changed under a totalitarian dictatorship. From a democratic standpoint, in terms of the ideals of the teaching profession in a free society, this profession may be said to be totally incompatible with the totalitarian conception of teaching. As in so many other fields, totalitarianism totally alters the meaning of the terms used. The teacher becomes the long-range indoctrinator, the instiller of an ideology that is intended to subjugate the students intellectually and commit them for the rest of their lives to a doctrinal orthodoxy. But, unlike quite a few other features of totalitarian dictatorship, this is not a new notion. Plato expounded it in his *Laws,* and argued that a stable community depended upon such firm indoctrination (161; 68), and various churches, including the Roman Catholic, the Greek Orthodox, and the Mohammedan churches have taken this view with varying intensity over the centuries. But so have the Confucians and Buddhists, and the Mandarin bureaucracy of the Chinese Empire was built upon the doctrinally fixed teaching of virtue in a manner strictly analogous to Plato's views. It is evident from all this that the totalitarians in their approach to teaching and education have returned to what has been the predominant tendency of the past. Where they differ is in asserting that these ideological doctrines are "scientific" rather than transcendentally inspired by religious experience. They allege them to be rational and hence in keeping with the modern world. Unfortunately for them, true science is forever on the move, and even those genuinely scientific insights that were involved in the totalitarian movements' original positions have since been superseded by new ones. It is difficult to forecast what this will do to the stability of the totalitarian structure in the long run, but it cannot be doubted that it contributes to their long-range difficulties.

Chapter Thirteen

The Terror and the Passion for Unanimity

Totalitarianism is a system of revolution. It is a revolution which seeks to destroy the existing political order so that it can subsequently be revolutionized economically, socially, and culturally. Totalitarian movements, motivated by the general goals which their ideologies outline, have thus not stopped at the seizure of power, as frequently was the case with earlier dictatorships which were concerned with the mere maintenance of the *status quo*. Such dictatorships, after seizing power, usually devoted the rest of their energies to the preservation of the existing order, without setting in motion any further fundamental changes. And when such changes occurred, as the result of the logic of counteraction, they were more often than not produced in spite of the efforts of the dictator.

The totalitarian movement, having seized power, seeks to extend this power to every nook and cranny of society. Thus change becomes the order of the day. This change, which is not meant to stop with the fulfillment of the first Five Year Plan, is intended to be the task of generations. The process of building communism is not finished with the mere physical liquidation of the capitalists. The revolution continues, as Soviet leaders still emphasize, with each accomplished task giving birth to another. Similarly, victory in World War II was not to be the signal for Hitler's Nazis to sit down and contemplate the "Thousand Year Reich." It was to be followed by gigantic schemes of reconstruction for the whole of Europe, of vast resettlements, of constant colonization, of a relentless struggle for an increased Teutonic birthrate. The present is never good enough—the totalitarian movement is always concerned with the future.

This futuristic orientation of the totalitarian movement, to repeat, is based firmly on the totalitarian ideology, with all its pseudoscientific doctrines and all its actual twists. Whether it be the "inevitable" laws of Marxism-Leninism, or the equally inaccurate "intuition of the Führer," the totalitarian movement goes ahead confident in the blissful thought that it is marching in step with history. The constant rejection of the present for the sake of grandiose schemes of social reconstruction and human remolding thus provides the basis for the total extension of totalitarian power to all segments of society.

It is this determination to achieve total change that begets the terror. Change always entails opposition; in a free society total change cannot occur, because it would bring forward massive resistance from a variety of groups and interests. In a totalitarian society opposition is prevented from developing by the organization of total terror which eventually engulfs everyone.

The totalitarian schemes for the destruction of the existing society are indeed total, as any reader of communist or fascist literature can tell. In every respect, human life and the nature of social existence are to be subjected to extensive revisions, provided for in the ideology and supplemented by the subsequent operationally expedient requirements of the regime. These revisions need not be embarked upon all at once—indeed, the history of totalitarian systems tells us that usually a step-by-step program, gradually increasing in violence, is adopted. And this violence which leads to terror is almost inevitable within this context. For life in society is composed of closely interlocking and overlapping groups. It is almost impossible to subject one social group to punitive, or as totalitarians would call it, "re-educative," measures without producing a hostile reaction not only from the group concerned, but also from overlapping and interlocking units, whose vested interests dictate this response. The totalitarians really have no choice but to intensify their efforts.

Thus the repressive measures of the totalitarian regimes, which aim first at eliminating their open enemies, are gradually extended, in snow-ball fashion, to other sections of society. Totalitarian terror grows by leaps and bounds. It not only becomes a political prophylaxis of the regime, aimed at anticipating political resistance —it becomes the fundamental method of achieving the total goals of the regime and of maintaining the permanent revolution without which the regime would lose its total character, and probably also its power. (59c) Totalitarian terror is, therefore, the vital nerve of the totalitarian system.

This system, because of the alleged ideological infallibility of its dogma, is propelled toward an increase of terror by a violent passion for unanimity. Since history tells the totalitarian he is right, he expects all others to agree with him, thereby vindicating the correctness of his historical insight. This passion for unanimity makes the totalitarians insist on the complete agreement of the entire population under their control to the measures the regime is launching. This agreement, which finds expression in coerced plebiscites and elections, must not be passive; on the contrary, the totalitarian regimes insist that enthusiastic unanimity characterize the political behavior of the captive populations. Thus periodic elections in the USSR consist not only of the mechanical act of depositing a single-name ballot in the electoral box. For weeks before the election, intensive agitation is conducted by literally millions of party members and Komsomol youths. The population is expected to attend mass meetings, pass appropriate resolutions, and approve the past and future policies of the regime. The election day itself becomes a joyful event—a holiday—in which the masses are expected to celebrate the 99.9 per cent support they give to the regime.

Plebiscites are not an invention of the totalitarians. It was an important feature of the dictatorial rule of the first Napoleon. The practice grew out of the revolutionary consultations of the people, which were supposed to embody Rousseau's ideas on direct democracy. But Napoleon went further. At certain crucial moments in his career, such as his election for life as First Consul and his assumption of the emperorship, he called for popular plebiscites. These were held openly, with much coercion. Even so, the French proved too independent, and therefore Napoleon personally "corrected" the result to improve on what local intimidation and fraud had failed to accomplish. (55c) The practice was revived by the third Napoleon with comparable results, though there was even greater lenience allowed those who were determined to register their opposition.

These plebiscites of the Napoleons and of their imitators must not be confused with the terroristic practices of the contemporary totalitarian regimes, though they perhaps inspired them. Even the official sources show the difference in approach. According to a Nazi authority, "the meaning of such a 'consultation' of the people by the Führer was to be seen in the fact that the relation of confidence between the leader and the people as followers receives tangible political expression on the occasion of important political decisions." The decision is made by the leader, in other words, and the people merely "register" their agreement. The magical unity of leader and led receives its symbolic consecration. Here is one of the roots of the passion for unanimity. Any dissent is like an act of desecration which must be "stamped out," if it cannot be prevented by terrorization beforehand. Mussolini stated this quite frankly, before the 1929 plebiscite, saying that even if the majority voted, "no," the Fascists would not step out, that a plebiscite could "consecrate" but not overthrow a revolution.

The National Socialists used the plebiscite repeatedly to demonstrate a thoroughly metarational state of affairs: a people completely in the grip of passion, the passion of self-assertion and self-realization. They talked of the "boiling soul of the people" (*Kochende Volksseele*) as one might talk of an erupting volcano—a force of nature at once formidable and irresistible. When Hitler, in the fall of 1933, decided to quit the League of Nations and the Disarmament Conference, he appealed to the people to express their feelings. The move was designed to prove to the whole world that this demand for "equality of treatment" was backed by the boiling folk soul. But it was also, and even more importantly, intended to commit as many Germans as possible to the folk community of the Nazis by making them feel united in their national passion. The referendum, which was held on November 12, 1933, produced the desired results: of 45,176,713 qualified voters, 43,491,575 or 96.39 per cent participated in this ballot, and of these 40,622,628 or 95.1 per cent were reported as voting in the affirmative; 2,101,191 or 4.9 per cent as voting in the negative; the remainder as invalid. We spoke of the "desired result"; actually this result was still far from the 99.9 per cent which was eventually achieved after the technique had been applied again and again. When Hitler, after Hindenburg's death in July 1934, took over all the powers of the presidency, when

Hitler occupied the Rhineland (1936), when Hitler forced the *Anschluss* of Austria (1938), the decision was "submitted" to the people for "ratification" in a "free plebiscite." (55d) Elections served the same purpose in Fascist Italy. There, too, the desperate search for a magic unity through patent uniformity exemplified the totalitarian passion for unanimity. Basically, the Italian electorate at large remained as indifferent as elsewhere, while the cadres of the party organization were gripped by a veritable frenzy for seeking support. Their "capillary action," to use Mussolini's phrase, became intensified at such times to the point where terroristic acts of violence, large and small, were the order of the day. (50f)

But why should the leaders of such all-powerful regimes invariably demand the support of more than 99 per cent of the population? What causes this passion for unanimity? Could it be that this is itself a propaganda weapon? Does a Goebbels consider that a feeling of apartness and loneliness in those who are not satisfied with the regime should be fostered as an effective means of discouraging and eventually completely disorienting them? Such an effect would presuppose that opposition elements believed the results of such plebiscites and accepted the figures as *bona fide*. Why should they, when they distrust all official news?

Such concern for unanimity could, however, be explained in other ways. There is the totalitarians' concern with the judgment of history, as in Orwell's *1984,* where the totalitarian propagandist of the Ministry of Truth finds himself rewriting history by manipulating the reports. There is the further probability that this urge for unanimity results from the desire to delude themselves about the actual extent of their support. Furthermore, with overwhelming support the totalitarian leadership may feel justified in committing the most outrageous crimes. They hide, so to speak, in the womb of a solid collectivity.

Another, at least partial, explanation of the passion for unanimity is the totalitarian belief in the big lie as a propaganda technique. Hitler, Goebbels, and others are on record as believing that if you have to tell a lie, tell a big one, and the mass of the people will be more ready to believe it because it appeals to their superstitiousness. Thus the 99.7 per cent ayes in a plebiscite compel belief in a highly favorable result, even though the actual figure is assumed to be exaggerated. Evidence from the Soviet experience seems to indicate that the compulsive emphasis upon the total support of the regime may actually have succeeded in convincing many, even among those who are highly suspicious.   But in the last analysis, the passion for unanimity seems to spring from the pseudoreligious fervor of the totalitarian ideology.   The great universal religions conceive of their mission as that of converting all mankind to their faith as the only means to salvation in the world to come.   The totalitarians similarly believe in the universal validity of their secular mission. The drive toward unanimity manifested itself in the Middle Ages in the persecution and extermination of sectarians and heretics, such as the Waldensians and the Albigensians, and more recently in the recurrent pogroms instituted against the Jews.   Such dissent was felt to be an intolerable offense to the majesty of the divine order that all the faithful accepted.   The dissenter in a totalitarian dictatorship is in a similar position; he too is an intolerable offense to the grandeur of the totalitarian enterprise and must be liquidated, because, according to the ideology, he has no place in the world the totalitarian movement is bent upon building.

We can see clearly why totalitarian terror and total unanimity are thus interdependent.   The passion for unanimity, characteristic of a mass movement, demands tools to enforce it.   And according to totalitarian ideology all "normal" members of the society will naturally be part of that unanimity.   Only scattered social misfits—be they bourgeoisie (historically doomed) or Jews (racially deformed) —remain outside that unanimity, joined possibly by a few traitors. The terror makes certain that the masses are not infected, while the "social misfits" are liquidated.   In this way, all the brutal, premeditated violence of the terror becomes rationally justified to the totalitarian.

Totalitarian terror has not only this negative function to perform. Operating within the context of enforced unanimity, it becomes a stimulant to more enthusiastic expressions of support for the regime. It classifies men's behavior according to degrees of loyalty, and mere absence of opposition to the regime becomes insufficient as proof of devotion to it.   Positive action is demanded, and men compete in loyalty.   It is no accident that secret police files in the USSR stress, first of all, whether a given individual is passive or active. Needless to add, one can be active in a totalitarian society only on behalf of the regime.   A remark on someone's *kharakteristika* that he is passive represents a major question mark as to his loyalty. The Communist Party of the Soviet Union particularly stresses the fact that *partiinost* (literally "party-ness") demands active, very active support of the regime, measured by concrete achievements.

The same was true in the Fascist and Nazi dictatorships. In the election campaign after the murder of Matteotti there was a great deal of pressure, of violence, of the parade of uniformed force. Whether one agrees with Finer that these "secured the triumph of the party," there is no question that he is right in stressing the extent to which party activity was made the test for remaining after the victory had been won. (50g) "No compromise, no quietism, no cowardice in the face of the responsibilities imposed by the party"— thus Finer sums up the party member's role. Outward conformity to certain changes in style of speaking and eating were made the test of party enthusiasm and members who did not conform were not only rebuffed, but at times expelled, beaten up, or imprisoned.

In National Socialist Germany, the party was so large that its membership failed to display some of the characteristics of complete dedication just described. As a consequence, the elite guard (SS) increasingly stepped into this role of being the unquestioning, enthusiastic supporter of the regime. It was the SS in its three distinct formations that embodied, for the masses of the subject people, the terroristic apparatus of the regime, symbolized by the dagger that every member received upon his initiation into this "elite." From a recent careful analysis (287c) it becomes clear that the SS embodied a more satanic outlook on life and politics than was represented by the ordinary Nazi and SA men. Indeed, there was at work a distinctly anti-intellectual trend in the SS which was fully shared by Himmler, their boss. These anti-intellectuals infiltrated the government, the military and economic cadres, and the party which they sought to control. (110) After the abortive *putsch* of the underground opposition, the SS succeeded in taking over the key controls of the armed forces. Its style of "the marching column" triumphed. The SS was essentially an "order." Its attitude was pointedly summed up in the demand, "Believe, obey, fight!" All ideas were reduced to the sloganized framework of an ossified ideology to be enunciated, and perhaps restated, by the Führer at his pleasure. Any dissent must be ferreted out and crushed with ruthless terror.

It is a curious and frightening fact that totalitarian terror increases in scope and violence as the totalitarian system becomes more stable and firm. In the initial period after the seizure of power, the major energy of the machinery of terror is directed at the obvious enemies—such as the Social Democrats in Germany, the Mensheviks or "bourgeoisie" in Russia, the democratic parties in Eastern Europe (see Chapter 14). Only when these are destroyed is the sword of the regime turned against the broad masses; only then does mass terror gradually develop. Hannah Arendt observed that

the end of the first stage comes with the liquidation of open and secret resistance in any organized form; it can be set at about 1935 in Germany and approximately 1930 in Soviet Russia. Only after the extermination of real enemies has been completed and the hunt for "potential enemies" begun does terror become the actual content of totalitarian regimes. Under the pretext of building socialism in one country, or using a given territory as a laboratory for a revolutionary experiment, or realizing the *Volksgemeinschaft,* the second claim of totalitarianism, the claim to total domination, is carried out. (3f)

It is at this latter stage that totalitarian terror comes into its own. It aims to fill everyone with fear and vents in full its passion for unanimity. Terror embraces the entire society, searching everywhere for actual or potential deviants from the totalitarian unity. Indeed to many it seems as if they are hunted, even though the secret police may not touch them for years, if at all. Total fear reigns.

The total scope and the pervasive and sustained character of totalitarian terror are accordingly its unique qualities. By operating with the latest technological devices, by allowing no refuge from its reach, and by pentetrating even the innermost sanctums of the regimes (see Chapters 14 and 16), it achieves a scope unprecedented in history. The atmosphere of fear it creates easily exaggerates the strength of the regime and helps it achieve and maintain its façade of unanimity. Scattered opponents of the regime, if still undetected, become isolated and feel themselves cast out of society. This sense of loneliness, which is the fate of all, but more especially of an opponent of the totalitarian regime, tends to paralyze resistance and makes it much less appealing. It generates a universal longing to "escape" into the anonymity of the collective whole. Unanimity, even if coerced, is a source of strength for the regime.

Of course, it would be a gross over-simplification to claim therefore that in all places and at all times the citizens of a totalitarian regime are subject to immediate arrest and live in a spine-chilling fear for their lives. First of all, terror can become internalized; the people become familiar with a pattern of conformance, they know how to externalize a behavior of loyalty, they learn what not to say and do. Second, reliance on force can decrease as a new generation, brought up in loyalty and fully indoctrinated, takes its place in the totalitarian society. But terror as a last resort is always present in the background, and the potentiality of its uninhibited use does not disappear. That seems to be, for instance, the situation in the USSR in 1956.

It should be apparent from the preceding analysis that totalitarian terror cannot be compared to the occasional outbursts of violence and terrorism which occur sometimes in constitutional societies. Such outbursts, unfortunate as they are, usually represent sporadic responses to specific crises. Even when institutionalized by legislative process, they operate with a definite goal in view and apply to a small and sharply delimited segment of society. Such situations are open to abuse and, indeed, history tells of many cases of injustice. Yet to compare these outbursts, as some are inclined to do, to totalitarian terror is to underestimate the latter and grossly exaggerate the former. The total scope of totalitarian terror and its pervasive and sustained character, operating in an atmosphere of ideological compulsion, makes it a unique feature of modern totalitarianism.

Chapter Fourteen

The Secret Police and the People's Enemies

"When the old society dies, the corpse of bourgeois society cannot be nailed down in a coffin and put in the grave. It decomposes in our midst, this corpse rots and contaminates us," warned Lenin. (238)

To the totalitarian, this "rotting corpse" of the *ancien régime* is still a mortal enemy from whom the people must be protected. It makes no difference whether the people desire such protection or not. The totalitarian is convinced either that the masses are with him, or that they ought to be. And in either case, they have to be defended from the enemy who makes every effort to impede the process of indoctrination—to teach people to perceive the totalitarian "truth"—and even to overthrow the totalitarian system. This struggle against the enemies is a constant one and, as suggested in the preceding section, often grows in intensity as the totalitarian regimes become stabler and firmer. The regime can then afford greater violence, and initial patience and expediency give way to unbridled terror.

Who are the enemies? It would be a lengthy list that might include all the various categories of enemies, spies, saboteurs, and traitors that the totalitarian regimes scourge day after day. Each totalitarianism, or pseudototalitarianism, has its own special key enemy, and a whole cast of additional foes who appear and disappear from the scene, depending on the given political and international climate. Thus the Nazi system had one arch-foe: "the international, capitalist, Jewish conspiracy." This conspiracy was said to include Jewish Bolshevism, except for a brief interlude during the Stalin-Hitler Pact. In addition, the enemies of the Nazis were the various non-Teutonic races: the Slavs who were to be destroyed; the Latins, with the exception of the Italians, who were said to be generally lazy and effeminate; the Americans, who were said to be largely negroid, and so on. Domestically, there were the communists, the Social-Democrats, the racially impure (partly Jewish), and the churches, which acknowledged a higher deity than the Führer. This by no means exhausts the list, but it does suggest that the "enemies" are numerous, and constant means to remove them are therefore necessary.

Similarly the budding totalitarianism of Peron's Argentina emphasized the need to protect the people—the shirtless ones, as Peron affectionately called them—from the invidious plots of the *Oligarquía.* The *Oligarquía,* in the words of Peron, stand for the *ancien régime:* the wealthy landowner in the provinces, the old families of Buenos Aires, the rich and the privileged who conspired against the "social justice" of Peronismo, and last, but not least, the priests. The people had to be protected from the *Oligarquía* which, on the international plane, was aided and abetted by "Yankee imperialism." The enemy was powerful—the struggle, ceaseless.

But probably the most imposing roster of "enemies of the people" is provided by the history of the struggle of the Stalinist regime against its many and varied foes. The entire capitalist order, with its countless satellites, is said to be the enemy of the Soviet Union. On the international plane, it supposedly organizes successive systems of capitalist encirclements and plots, ringing the Soviet Union with air bases and military establishments, planning war and destruction. It is sufficient to read the daily Soviet press to perceive a most terrifying picture of "war mongering" and conspiracies against the USSR. This, the Soviet leaders assure their people, has internal repercusions also. The last remains of the bourgeoisie, they say, take heart and proceed to sabotage "the great socialist construction," endangering the people.

"The enemy of the people" is a familiar phrase in Soviet terminology. It appears in the press, in speeches, in secret archives. At various stages of Soviet development it has embraced former Mensheviks and liberals, disaffected elements in the Communist Party, supporters of the opposition against Stalin, local nationalist leaders, unsuccessful Soviet industrial managers, defeated generals, purged party, police, and military leaders. And as Soviet influence has expanded westward, the former leaders, political, intellectual, and professional, of the captive countries have also become enemies of the people. Anyone in contact with the "bourgeois international conspiracy" is an enemy of the people, and it is symptomatic that among the orders issued to the NKVD at the time of the occupation of Lithuania in 1940, one was to arrest all Esperanto students and foreign stamp collectors.*

The totalitarian regimes, however, do not proclaim the total destruction of all the enemies of the regime. In the case of some of them, the totalitarians' official purpose is to "re-educate" them, though the Nazis seem to have been less hopeful than others about their capacity to do this. The "enemies of the people" have sinned, it is true, but now that the totalitarian regimes are firmly in power and the environmental situation is different, some of them may actually be deemed and re-educated. Such a process, of course, demands sacrifice from those concerned, and it was because of this cynical spirit that the inmates of the Auschwitz and Dachau death

---

* The NKVD officer-in-charge was the present Col. General Serov, head of the State Security Committee.

camps were met by signs proclaiming "Arbeit macht frei"—"Labor makes free."

In practice, however, the "enemies of the people" are usually found to be "incorrigible." Then their liquidation becomes the standard practice, and may be decreed for large groups of people as well as for individuals (see Chapter 15). Such violence is, of course, not peculiar to totalitarianism. Particularly dangerous individuals have been singled out for arrest and subsequent liquidation under all forms of autocracy. Such liquidation of individuals is particularly characteristic of the initial totalitarian period, after either the seizure of power or the occupation by a foreign power, when such individuals still stand out. Much more typical and indeed unique in its scope is the liquidation of vast masses of people, categorized in an arbitrary fashion as "enemies of the people" and therefore unsuitable for further existence in the totalitarian system. Such was the fate of the Jews killed by the Nazis in the death camps, or of the Polish officers murdered by the Russians in Katyn, or of the Chechen-Ingush deported *in toto* to Siberia for allegedly having fought against the Soviet Union.

All of this, of course, demands an elaborate machinery of terror, and the history of the totalitarian regimes is to some extent mirrored in the gradual evolution and perfection of the instruments of terror. In the Soviet Union one of the early acts of the regime was to organize a special body with the task of stamping out its enemies. This "Extraordinary Commission to Fight Counter-Revolution," or Cheka, from its first two Russian letters—Ch. K.—was set up in December 1917, and was charged with combatting "counter-revolution and sabotage." (271g) The bourgeoisie, it was said, was aided and abetted by the Entente, plotting a come-back, and constant vigilance was therefore required. The abortive attempt in August 1918 by the Social Revolutionaries to assassinate Lenin gave the Bolsheviks an excellent practical justification for the intensification of terror. Mass arrests followed, and the shooting of hostages became widespread. Terror did not cease with the conclusion of the Civil War but, as suggested previously, grew with the growing stabilization of the regime. The official label of the secret police was changed occasionally, as political circumstances made it expedient: first Cheka, then GPU—State Political Administration, then NKVD—People's Commissariat of Internal Affairs, then MVD and MGB—

Ministry of Internal Affairs and Ministry of State Security, and in 1954 MVD and the Committee of State Security. (47g)

The greatest impetus to the expansion of the Soviet secret police was provided by the collectivization of the early thirties and the great purges of the Communist Party and the state apparatus which operated almost incessantly for a decade, until the Eighteenth Party Congress in 1939. The opposition of the peasants to the collectivization program resulted in the adoption of stringent repressive measures. The GPU, in cooperation with local party organizations, arrested and deported literally millions of so-called kulaks, some of whom were merely resettled in the distant regions of the USSR, and some of whom provided the backbone for the developing network of NKVD labor camps (see Chapter 15). Police organization naturally expanded in proportion to the demands of this task. The importance of the secret police was similarly maximized by the mass purges, launched by Stalin, to clean up the CPSU and the state bureaucracy by removing former deviationists and potential opponents. These great purges accounted between the years 1933 and 1938 for some two million of the three and a half million party members in 1933. (18e) As the purge became more hysterical and violent, it ceased being merely a party operation, and the secret police became the prime agent. Indeed, the period 1936–1938 is known in common Soviet parlance as the period of the *Yezhovshchina,* named so after Yezhov, the head of the NKVD. By 1938 the situation had become so strained that, if it had not been for the timely liquidation of Yezhov and his close associates, the secret police might have swallowed up the party.

Between 1939 and 1953 the Soviet secret police was headed by Lavrenti Beria. During his rule its forced labor operation expanded tremendously, with the mass deportations from Poland and the Baltic States. At the same time, the NKVD carried out the "pacification" of territories acquired through the Ribbentrop-Molotov pact, particularly by eliminating the local intelligentsia in the newly acquired territories. The Katyn massacre is only a specially dramatic and better-known instance of this policy. After the war, similar policies were carried out in the Central European areas controlled by the USSR. The satellite police forces have been closely linked, through personnel and direct supervision, with the Soviet MVD.

After Beria's arrest in 1953, there were some indications that the role of the secret police diminished somewhat. Precise information is still unavailable (201b), but we know that the secret police has no longer a personal spokesman in the highest party organ—the Presidium (formerly Politburo)—as it did for so many years. The administrative organ for meting out sentences, the so-called Special Board, was quietly abolished. Another change was the division of functions between the MVD and the newly established Committee of State Security. This measure, however, was probably made necessary by considerations of administrative efficiency. The vast functions of the secret police were thus split into two separate entities, very much like the former division between the MVD and the MGB. Under the existing arrangement the MVD is charged with the broad functions of policing the interior and maintaining its elite troops. The Committee of State Security performs the more specialized tasks of investigation, espionage, counterintelligence, and the like. Needless to add, this change not only might result in greater administrative efficiency, but certainly makes the emergence of a state within a state—as some have called the secret police— more unlikely.

As a further safeguard and also to prevent excessive abuse of power, a special division in the Chief Prosecutor's Office was set up in April 1956 to supervise and investigate the activities of the secret police. In the past, the prosecutor's office was expected to perform such a function; the need for a special division suggests that it did not. Only time will tell whether this new agency will be more successful. The secret police, nonetheless, continues to play a great role in Soviet life. Khrushchev explicitly underscored this in April 1956 —two months after criticizing "Stalinist terror"—by declaring in a speech to the Komsomolites that: "Our enemies are hoping that we will relax our vigilance, that we will weaken our state security agencies. No—this will never happen! The proletarian sword must always be sharp . . ." (271r)

In both fascist movements, the original instrument of the terror, designed to intimidate opponents, as well as eventually the governments, were uniformed armed bands, called Blackshirts of Squadristi in Italian Fascism, Brownshirts or SA (storm troopers) in Nazism. They committed various acts of violence: broke up meetings of opponents, administered castor oil to their leaders, beat up persons whom they considered undesirable, and so forth. Both movements eventually became concerned with these "revolutionary" elements, and sought to subdue them. The Nazis were more success-ful in this than the Fascists, the reason being that Heinrich Himmler succeeded in replacing the Storm Troopers (SA) with his Elite Guards (SS, or Schutzstaffeln) and in turn assumed the control of the police and eventually superseded it, using the SS to do so. At the beginning the Secret State Police (Gestapo, or Geheime Staatspolizei) was the key arm of the government and was under the control of Hermann Göring as head of the Prussian government, but Himmler succeeded on June 17, 1936, in taking it over. Just before the war (May 26, 1939) the merger of the Gestapo and the SS was in fact complete; for by a decree of that date the leadership of the two was made identical, although distinct tasks were presumably assigned to them. The police at that time contained two organizations: the Ordnungspolizei (ordinary police) and the Sicherheitspolizei (security police); both were headed by immediate subordinates of Himmler and key SS men. The Gestapo, which formed an integral part of this complex organizational whole, had by 1936 become part of the prosecutor's office, was removed from judicial control, and had assumed theoretical control and operation of the concentration camps. It actually had, however, little to do with the operation of the concentration camps which in 1939 were placed under the Economic Office of the SS. The Gestapo perverted the notion of "protective custody" and used it for the arbitrary arrest and confinement in a camp of anyone whom they wished and for as long as they wished; it thus became the most dramatic symbol of the terror and of totalitarian dictatorship at its worst. Cooperating closely with it and soon exceeding it in arbitrary violence was the Security Service (S.D., or Sicherheitsdienst) of the SS. Many of the worst excesses, such as the management of the slaughter houses at Auschwitz (Oswiecim), were placed in their hands.

The Italian development was quite different from the Nazi. As we said, the party activists or *squadristi* remained a factor in the Fascist dictatorship, committed to and committing violence. The secret police, on the other hand, was run as a *state* service, and on the whole tended to oppose the more extreme party elements. The party, in fact, continued to maintain its own investigatory services, while the Secret Police, organized after 1926 as *Opera Volontaria per la Repressione Antifascista* or OVRA, operated as an arm of the government not even exclusively staffed by Fascists. It was headed until his death in 1940 by Arturo Bocchini, who never achieved anything like the position of Himmler in the Councils of Fascism (117), thereafter by Carmine Senise. Throughout, the relations between party and police were fraught with tension. Actually, the party continued to operate its own secret police units, and to try and control the political aspects of the OVRA. Its special service of Political Investigation was lodged with the Militia which contained the party stalwarts. It had direct control of the Special Tribunal which took charge of cases of anti-Fascists. It also administered, together with the state police, the *confino* or confinement, the Italian version of protective custody, by which persons who had incurred the displeasure of the party or the regime would be confined either to a locality or (in more serious cases) to the penal islands, which took the place of the Nazis' concentration camps. Though conditions were not as serious, they were surrounded by the same air of terrifying mystery, and when combined with the common practice of beating up individuals at random sufficed to create the characteristic atmosphere of totalitarian terror. Ciano tells in his *Diaries* of the beating up of an individual merely because he had used *Lei* (he) instead of the Fascist-decreed *Voi* (you). The police, remaining independent of the party, as well as of the Ministry of the Interior, illustrated well the relation between government and party in Fascist Italy (cf. Chapter 3).

Germino, in his discussion of the police (64e), draws attention to a passage in Ignazio Silone's *Bread and Wine* which describes the all-pervading tentacles of the terror:

It is well-known [says Minorca] that the police have their informers in every section of every big factory, in every bank, in every big office. In every block of flats the porter is, by law, a stool pigeon for the police. In every profession, in every club, in every syndicate, the police have their ramifications. Their informers are legion, whether they work for a miserable pittance or whether their only incentive is the hope of advancement in their careers. This state of affairs spreads suspicion and distrust throughout all classes of the population. On this degradation of man into a frightened animal, who quivers with fear and hates his neighbor in his fear, and watches him, betrays him, sells him, and then lives in fear of discovery, the dictatorship is based. The real organization on which the system in this country is based is the secret manipulation of fear.

In Italy as elsewhere, party and police shared in this manipulation of fear, though on the whole the system was less total, less frightful, and hence less "mature" than in Germany and the Soviet Union, and in China and the satellites today.

The machinery of terror, defending the "people" from its "enemies," and glorified in totalitarian publications for its heroism and efficiency, relies on a rather elastic criminal code which makes the category of political crime a broad one. Thus even industrial failure frequently becomes a political offense for which the guilty ones must be found.

Recent Soviet press articles have again tended to emphasize the dangers of subversion and have been stressing the merits of constant vigilance. In a recent article, "Vigilance—Our Weapon," printed in the organ of the Central Committee of the CPSU, *Partiinaia Zhizn,* the party membership was exhorted to remain ever vigilant against foreign efforts to undermine the Soviet Union. The article describes in detail United States attempts to parachute saboteurs into the USSR and emphasizes that Soviet security organs demand the cooperation of the population in their efforts to defend it against such enemies. (265b) Careful scrutiny of the Soviet press also reveals that in all regions there are now operating, parallel to local MVD offices, Plenipotentiaries of the Committee on State Security.

Failure to meet the norms or financial manipulations have usually been treated as sabotage. Indeed, in all the totalitarian states there occurs a tremendous expansion in the area of penal or criminal law in which the attorney of state brings suit, and a resultant reduction of civil law. Matters that in constitutional societies are subject to suit between individuals become the concern of the state and, thus having been absorbed into the general framework of totalitarian justice, are considered on the basis of political standards. There inevitably develops a close liaison between the secret police and the prosecuting and defense attorneys. The judicial system is thus politicized and the political objectives of the regime replace substantive law. The communist Czech Minister of Justice stated this quite bluntly: "The real task of those employed in the administration of justice is to be the realization of every word of party and government resolutions, but particularly the consolidations of the socialist legal structure and the modeling of our courts on the shining example of the courts of the Soviet Union." (277)

The abject degradation of judicial procedures is hence a very characteristic feature of modern totalitarianism. (102)*

In serious political cases, the principle of collective responsibility has been frequently adopted by the totalitarians. In 1934 it was officially made a part of Soviet law with respect to cases involving deserters to foreign powers. The totalitarian secret police is furthermore given a free hand in political cases, and the Soviet MVD and the German Gestapo dispensed "justice" through administrative processes from which there was no appeal. Confinement in concentration camps, or even execution, is in most political cases handled that way. The Soviet secret police often exercises its prerogative of forcibly resettling suspected "enemies of the people" in outlying districts of the Soviet Union, from which they are not allowed to depart. This method has been used particularly frequently with those "enemies of the people" who are condemned *en masse* as a hostile category, such as the Volga Germans in 1941.

In terms of the development of totalitarian terror techniques, the Soviet secret police has generally been more sophisticated in its operations and more successful in eliminating opposition than the Gestapo, especially in relation to foreign peoples. The MVD has been able to penetrate the subject population much more thoroughly with networks of police informers, and consequently the experience of underground movements in communist-controlled nations has been altogether unhappy. Relying more on local cadres than the Gestapo was able to, the MVD has been generally successful in nipping in the bud any organizational moves by incipient opposition elements. And unlike the practices of the Gestapo, there have been no mass street arrests, shootings of hostages, public square executions, which serve only to intensify resistance. Soviet arrests are

* That this is still true in 1956, despite the campaign for "socialist legality," is suggested by the following attack on two defense attorneys for having apparently taken their tasks too seriously. *Trud,* April 10, 1956, after reporting the conviction of two criminals, adds: "Mention should be made of the behavior of comrades Rumiantsev and Rybakov, the defendants' lawyers. Instead of helping the court to establish the truth and to throw an objective light on the facts, they tried to cast doubt on the witnesses' facts and behaved tactlessly during the trial. Even when it was clear to all that the hoodlums had been identified as criminals, the lawyers stubbornly denied the obvious facts and made every effort to whitewash their clients, forgetting the Soviet lawyer's basic duty of being always truthful and conscientious. An opinion has been drawn up concerning the behavior of lawyers Rumiantsev and Rybakov . . . "

quiet, usually by night; liquidations are performed in the privacy of MVD death chambers or of a secluded forest. Direct opposition is avoided and precautions are usually taken to avoid open resistance. Thus, for instance, when in 1940 the NKVD arrested the head of the Polish Military Underground, it did so by a clever subterfuge designed to mask its intention: when the door of the hide-out was opened in reply to a knock, a militiaman (not NKVD) came in bringing with him two white-aproned millers, with their hands raised. These two promptly pointed to the underground leader and identified him as a black-marketeer. He was politely requested to come down to the station for further check, which he readily agreed to, as his papers were perfect. As soon as he entered the police wagon, he was arrested by the two "millers," who identified themselves as NKVD colonels. There are, of course, literally hundreds of similar occurrences, many of them buried in the archives of the secret police.

Besides the enemies of the people inside a totalitarian society, there are, of course, the even more formidable enemies who lurk beyond the frontiers of the totalitarian systems. Apart from the foreign policy of the regime, there are many activities which the terroristic apparatus of the totalitarian regime engages in to cope with these enemies. These activities fall into two major categories. There are the activities, usually criminal in nature, by which a totalitarian regime seeks to remove, through murder or abduction, outstanding individual enemies of the regime. The Soviet secret police eliminated, so it is generally believed, Leon Trotsky by the hand of a murderer in Mexico. Other similarly notorious cases involve two deserters from the Soviet secret service: Ignace Reiss and W. G. Krivitsky. Reiss deserted the NKVD network in Western Europe because of the purges in Russia, reacting particularly to the execution of Marshal Tukhachevsky in June 1937. He succeeded in evading NKVD murderers until September, when his body was found riddled with bullets on a lonely Swiss road. Swiss police established the fact that he was killed by an NKVD liquidation squad. Krivitsky, an NKVD general and head of its Western European spy network, deserted soon afterwards, and succeeded for four years in evading repeated attempts at assassination or kidnapping but finally died a mysterious death in an American hotel.

A second, and in many ways more dangerous method, is that of organizing subversive groups which, since the Spanish Civil War, have been known as "Fifth Columns." These became particularly notorious in connection with the Hitler conquest of Europe. In all the countries which Hitler eventually attacked, movements sprang up and were supported by the Nazi secret police, whose avowed aim it was to organize their country on a Fascist model and to cooperate with Hitler to the point of surrendering national independence, if necessary, to accomplish the goal of fascistization of the country. By this growth of Fifth Columns, the "people" are really extended to include a world-wide population of sympathizers. This process of "universalizing" the people is evidently more easily consummated when the ideology itself is universalist and rests upon the slogan, "Workers of all the world, unite!" But it was actually at work in the case of the Nazis, and on a considerable scale. Its psychological effects upon the "enemy" of the totalitarian regime were very much greater, however, than was warranted by the actual strength of the movement, and the same terrorizing effect can at present be observed in connection with the communist "cells" in the United States. A careful student of this entire Fifth-Column activity has been able to show from the documents now available that only in the instances of Czechoslovakia and Austria were the Nazi movements a genuinely effective factor in the conquest of the country. But their effectiveness in terrorizing the enemies of the people" as seen by the totalitarians was phenomenal. In Holland, in Belgium, in France, in Norway, in Denmark—everywhere, the "enemy within" was believed to be the real explanation of the sudden collapse of a country which had been believed defensible. (35) This enemy, who when seen from the Nazi side was "the people on the march," consisted of German soldiers and officers, police agents and saboteurs, disguised as every imaginable kind of native, aided and abetted by the native quislings, as they came to be called. The atmosphere soon acquired under such conditions the eerie quality of a novel by Kafka.

Chapter Fifteen

Purges, Confessions, and Camps

The purge is a refinement of the totalitarian terror and a distinctive feature of totalitarian dictatorship. But, unlike the terror which pervades the entire totalitarian society, the reach of the purge is limited to those within the totalitarian movement, grasping in its often fatal grip only those who appear, on the surface at least, to be quite loyal to the regime. The purge itself is a product of both the imperatives of power of the totalitarian leadership and the dictates of the official ideology, as interpreted by that leadership. It is the interaction between these two manifest tendencies that makes the purge a unique instrument of totalitarian government, not paralleled in more traditional dictatorial systems.

As we have seen, totalitarian terror maintains, in institutionalized form, the civil war that originally produced the totalitarian movement and by means of which the regime is able to proceed with its program, first of social disintegration, and then of social reconstruction. The pulverization of the opposition, both actual and potential, makes room for a coerced public enthusiasm for the official goals and introduces into the system a vigorous competition in loyalty to the regime. The purge, however, is more restricted in scope. Jews or capitalists cannot be purged because by definition they are not part of the system. The purge can be applied only against those who are already anointed, who have accepted the totalitarian ideology, and who are, directly or indirectly, associated with the movement.

The purge, furthermore, is an expression of the resilience and energy of the totalitarian movement and not, as many erroneously claim, an indication of its corruption and of its forthcoming disintegration. Soviet leaders frequently proclaim that the party strengthens itself by purging itself, and empirically speaking, the monolithic unity of the party has indeed been forged through a recurrent recourse to the technique of the purge. Elements which could possibly have challenged the will of the leadership were removed, often brutally, and an inner cohesion established. From an outside point of view, such procedures may be morally unacceptable, but totalitarianism produces its own ethic, sanctifying success and power.

It is noteworthy in this connection that purges have generally not occurred when the totalitarian parties were either weak or engaged in crucial power conflicts. They have occurred only during periods of relative political stability, when the leadership could afford the luxury of such an operation. Also, when the purge was part of an inner struggle for power, its violent, explosive, and more widespread manifestations appeared only as an aftermath of that struggle, and signified the victory of one of the competitors. Being then essentially a clean-up operation, the purge is certainly not a manifestation of weakness.

Soviet totalitarianism is much more fully developed in this connection than its Nazi or Fascist counterparts. Because of its longer life-span, Soviet totalitarianism has had time to undergo a considerable internal evolution, and has passed through phases of totalitarian development that were forestalled by the outbreak of the war in both Germany and Italy. The Fascist institution of the "Changes of Guard," however, was in fact a mild form of purge and served the same purpose. The Soviet regime has been able to launch its own ambitious schemes of social reconstruction, and has already been faced with two crises of succession, which produced their own peculiar repercussions. Clearly, all this did not happen in the Fascist (64f; 11; 18f) and Nazi dictatorships which remained, until their military and political disintegration, still in the preliminary stages of development and continued to be guided, unto doom, by their original initiators. We speak, of course, of the Roehm purge by which Hitler smashed the smoldering opposition of his leftist following in the storm troops, incidentally eliminating a number of prominent enemies of the movement, such as General Schleicher. (Dr. Heinrich Brüning, the former chancellor and inveterate foe of the Nazis, was also slated for extermination, but escaped beforehand, having been warned by the British intelligence.) But this purge did not possess the functional characteristics which we have just indicated as those of the developed totalitarian purge. A similar observation might be made concerning the large-scale executions following upon the attempt, on July 20, 1944, to kill Hitler. The extensive resistance movement which had been developing among

Germans in all walks of life—trade unionists, businessmen, government officials, university professors, as well as army officers—was a natural consequence of the defeats Hitler had suffered in the war he had provoked, and of the certain loss of the war and the large-scale destruction of German cities by the bombing. (174b; 39b; 169a; 53) But that those implicated in an armed revolt, especially in wartime, should be executed, is an event in no way peculiar to a totalitarian dictatorship, although the cruelty, ruthlessness, and savagery with which the punishments were administered are truly totalitarian. All things considered, the sequel to July 20, 1944, would seem not to be a purge, in the sense here defined as an "institution" of totalitarian dictatorship, but a punitive action resulting from the rapid disintegration of the regime. Consequently, we have to conclude that no real purge technique developed under the Hitler regime, and the same holds true for Italian Fascism. For this reason, any analysis of the purge must rely more on Soviet experience, though China has also recently staged a genuine purge. However, because of certain generic qualities of totalitarian rule, the Soviet lesson may serve as a basis for broader conclusions.

The experience of Soviet purges suggests not only that the more accentuated manifestations of the purge are essentially an indication of the resilience of the totalitarian movement, but that there is also a purging continuum in the totalitarian system. In a sense, therefore, the purge is like the undulating motion of the seas, ever active, but only sometimes stormy. The history of the Communist Party of the USSR suggests that the leadership of the party, operating in a context devoid of the democratic devices for assuring efficiency through open electoral competition, is faced with the dilemma of resolving the problem of efficiency, while maintaining the elite status of the party. Since the latter excludes any open political competition, the problem has to be resolved internally by the device of the purge. This purge then operates continually, on the basis of constant interaction of personal motives, group manipulation, and power pressures. The purge is in a sense permanent. (18)

In specific crises, the purge may be utilized for the achievement of particular power objectives and may, if need be, become quite violent and far-reaching. Thus the period of transition of the Soviet dictatorship into a modern industrial totalitarian regime, with far-reaching social objectives, made the thirties a period of violent purges in which countless individuals perished. It is not within the scope of this chapter to set forth a detailed account of this period, but suffice it to say that, from the time of the assassination of Kirov in 1934 to the liquidation of Yezhov in 1938, some one million party members were purged, and many of them, particularly the higher officials, were executed. The consolidation of the Stalinist dictatorship was thus achieved and Stalin was not boasting idly when he declared that

when it had smashed the enemies of the people and purged the Party and Soviet organizations of degenerates, the Party became still more united in its political and organizational work and rallied even more solidly around its Central Committee. (190a)

What he neglected to add, however, was that the Central Committee itself lost about 75 per cent of its membership.

Subsequent years did not witness such drastic applications of the purge. Nonetheless, after the conclusion of the hostilities in 1945, a series of quiet purges swept the Communist Party *apparat,* as well as the intellectual circles, and reached, after Zhdanov's death in 1948, people of such stature as Voznesensky and other close collaborators of the deceased heir-apparent. Such purges continued on the republican levels until Stalin's death in 1953, which immediately gave them a more specific political connotation. The most striking purge after 1953 followed the aftermath of the struggle for succession between Beria on the one hand and the other members of the collective leadership, set up in March 1953.

While the full story of this period is still to be told, it now appears clear that Beria felt himself to be in an insecure position, probably because of the original implications of the "Jewish doctors' plot" of January 1953. At that time, it was clearly hinted in the Soviet press that the "Jewish doctors' conspiracy" against the leading personalities of the Soviet regime was tolerated by the secret police. Beria probably felt that he must therefore buttress his position in the power hierarchy by placing his own men in key positions throughout the USSR. In this manner he would be able to neutralize the elements which sponsored the January intrigue aimed apparently at him. But efforts to do this provoked, after a while, a reaction from the other leaders, who, in turn, felt endangered by Beria's maneuvers. The situation was brought to a climax in June

1953, and Beria was arrested. During the summer and early autumn efforts were made to remove his supporters from office, and a number of them were imprisoned. Beria and six of his closest associates were executed in December 1953. This episode again illustrates both the continuing nature of the purge as well as its recurrent outbursts in the aftermath of a crisis situation.

The satellite experience also supports this thesis. The major satellite purges occurred after the regimes were solidly installed in power, and their intensity was most marked in those countries whose communist parties were the strongest. Thus in Poland, for instance, the violence of the purge of Gomulka and his supporters was much less than that of Slansky in Czechoslovakia, Rajik in Hungary, or Kostov in Bulgaria.

The purge accordingly appears to be inherent in modern totalitarianism. It is produced both by the existential conditions of the system and by the subjective motivations of its leadership. The purge serves to invigorate the movement, which often is clogged with careerists and flatterers. It restores it to a healthy revolutionary fervor. It insures fresh blood—what Pareto called a circulation of the elite. It releases the inherent tensions of a closed system, and, indeed, it has been noted that the purge evokes from the masses a grim feeling of satisfaction at the sight of the downfall of frequently oppressive bureaucrats and party officials. This "equalization" of suffering makes the burdens of political oppression somewhat more palatable to the average man before whose eyes the masters, formerly invincible, are made to bite the dust.

At the same time, the purge is utilized to prevent the stabilization of political forces around the totalitarian leadership and to prevent the development of local satraps in the provinces which could weaken the central control of the leadership. An artificial instability is accordingly created among the upper levels of the party, and existing deficiencies are transferred from the shoulders of the leaders to convenient scapegoats. This, in turn, allows the totalitarian leadership considerable freedom of action, not hampered by stable group interests. The elimination of the Red Army High Command in 1937 was, in part at least, motivated by that objective. No potential alternatives to the leader are allowed to mature, while the institutionalized competition in loyalty insures the perpetuation of unchallenged supremacy of the leadership.

The purge is thus an important and unique instrument of totalitarian government. But it has to be handled carefully; Soviet experience in 1937 shows that it can easily get out of hand. The purge, being a political instrument, operates with the human element, and the forces of hysteria, the drive for power, and sheer brutality can easily get hold of it. The purge can develop a momentum of its own and reach such proportions as to endanger the system itself. Its supporters may be swept away by panic and their loyalty may wane. This is precisely what happened in the Soviet Union during the years 1937 and 1938, and ever since then the Soviet leadership has been careful to avoid using the purge on a total scale.

As the purge operates within a political context, the changing nature of that context influences the character of the purge. Thus originally, during the first decade of communist rule, the purge was restricted to the party alone and was handled by party procedures. (239) With the growing totalitarianism of the system and the fundamental social and economic changes of the thirties, the purge increased in scope and violence and became, at the same time, primarily a secret police function. After World War II, during the period of consolidation, the purge operated quietly in cleansing the party of undesirable elements admitted during the conflict, and did not erupt violently until the struggle for succession. But even then it tended to be restricted to the upper levels of the regime. This development suggests the possibility that, with the institutionalized concentration of power at the top and the general totalitarianism of the system, future purges may remain restricted to the upper levels of the *apparat* where all conflicts will be resolved, violently if necessary. The public will learn of such conflicts only in their aftermath, as official announcements are made about who was purged. This already appears to have been the experience with the Soviet purges of 1953.

But whatever the future character of the purge may be, modern totalitarianism requires the purge for the sake of operational efficiency, and one of the indictments of the system may be the fact that it cannot operate efficiently without it. For better or for worse, the two are linked in indissoluble union.

A curious sequel to the purge has been the confessions. "I do not want clemency. The proletarian court must not and cannot spare my life . . . I have only one desire, to stand with the same calmness . . . on the place of execution and with my blood to wash away the stain of a traitor to my country," so pleaded a former Bolshevik revolutionary before a Stalinist court in 1937. (167)   And the State Prosecutor mused: "Time will pass.   The graves of the hateful traitors will grow over with weeds and thistle, they will be covered with eternal contempt . . .   But over our happy country, our sun will shine with its luminous rays as bright and as joyous as before." (166)

The confessions, the vulgar abuse by the prosecutor, the verdicts of death, and the announcements of execution—all made for a fearful pattern which dominated Soviet life during the notorious years of the Great Purge.   The confessions were particularly mystifying and troublesome.   Here were men who had spent their lifetimes in danger, who had faced death on innumerable occasions, but who were now cringing, admitting their guilt, beating their breasts.   And yet none of them *appeared* to have been tortured, drugged, beaten. Why did they confess, and why did the Soviet regime want them to confess?

Before an attempt is made to answer this, it must be pointed out that the Soviet techniques of obtaining confessions and staging public trials evolved gradually toward the stage of refinement reached by the mid-thirties.   It is also noteworthy that the emphasis on the role of confession in public trial parallels closely Stalin's rise to a dominant position in the party.   Thus the first large trials which received considerable publicity and in which the defendants pleaded guilty and cooperated with the prosecution occurred only at the end of the twenties and in the beginning of the thirties.   In 1928 a political conspiracy against the Soviet regime was "unmasked," and the accused confessed to having hatched crude plots to seize power.   A much improved version of such a confession trial came two years later with the so-called "Industrial Party Trial."   In it leading Russian technicians confessed to elaborate schemes of sabotage and wrecking, designed to upset Soviet economy.   But even here, the secret police slipped up on occasion, as in the instance involving two alleged contactmen for the conspiracy, who, in fact, had died five years earlier.   Another set-back occurred in 1933 at the Metro-Vickers trial when some of the accused foreign technicians repudiated their confessions, taking courage in the intervention on their behalf by the British government.   Their Russian colleagues, completely at the mercy of the regime, remained faithful to their confessions.

A number of other trials occurred before the "big shows" of 1936–1938. The growing competence of the prosecution, the more elaborate nature of confessions, the instances of dramatic confrontation and confirmation displayed in the trials testified that the secret police was successfully mastering its art. This process generally paralleled the further totalitarianization of the political system and the consequent need to eliminate the last possible alternatives to Stalinist rule. It is this developmental factor which probably explains why similar large public trials were not staged in Nazi Germany. The Germans entered the war within six years of the Nazi seizure of power. It was only after the unsuccessful July coup of 1944 that the People's Courts were let loose with full vengeance on actual or potential opponents of the regime, and show trials, with all their terroristic qualities, were staged.

In dealing with the general problem of confession in the totalitarian public trial it ought to be noted, first of all, that not all of the political prisoners are actually brought to trial. Many of them perish and only their alleged admissions of guilt are actually brought to trial. This indeed has been the case with some of the leading Soviet officials purged both under Stalin and under Malenkov-Khrushchev. The military leaders, notably Marshal Tukhachevsky, were executed after a trial *in camera* in June of 1937, and such was also the fate of Beria and his henchmen in December of 1953. The possibility that they may have refused to confess clearly suggests itself. Admittedly, however, a great number of the accused do confess. And they include men who, by normal standards, could not have been considered as weaklings, cowards, or fools. Therefore the question of why they confessed still demands an answer.

Any attempted explanation of this phenomenon must be, quite naturally, both speculative and inconclusive. There is sufficient data, however, from former prisoners as well as secret policemen to suggest the basis for at least a partial analysis. (204; 151; 143) It appears that confessions are brought about by two parallel and overlapping processes: the wearing down of the prisoner both physically and mentally. The former technique tends to be more important with non-Communists, the latter with Communists. But both are used simultaneously, differing only in degree of application.

The wearing-down process, on the basis of available evidence, consists of four main methods. First, there is sleeplessness, induced by such devices as night-long lighting of the cell, prohibition of keeping one's hands under a blanket, and the obligation to lie, when trying to sleep, flat on one's back, with the face upwards, toward the electric light. Sleep, under such conditions, is not easy. A second physical discomfort is coldness, caused by poor heating. The cell is never really cold, but always chilly and sometimes somewhat damp. This again makes relaxation unlikely. Third, systematic undernourishment keeps the person above the starvation level, but never gives him enough. Food consequently becomes an obsession, obscuring all other thoughts. Finally, there are endless examinations, lasting often for ten hours without interruption and conducted by relays of investigators, all expressing their belief in the prisoner's guilt. These interrogations may often include beating and torture of the prisoner.* Added to this are such devices as the tomblike silence prevailing in the prison, solitary confinement, occasional screams of those led to the execution chamber. All of these, clearly, tend to break down the prisoner's physical resistance.

The other aspect, much more important in terms of the actual trial, involves the technique of intellectually pulverizing the prisoner. Through a process of intellectual attrition the prisoner is gradually induced to question his own judgment, his own memory, even his own motives. He is confronted with witnesses who repeat in detail alleged conversations with the prisoner, attesting to his evil intentions or acts. In time, with the physical factors also playing their role, the prisoner either begins to realize the futility of further resistance or may even actually begin to accept the interpretations pressed upon him by the secret police. Once this happens, he is ready for the public exhibition at the trial.†

* The use of physical torture, according to Khrushchev's secret speech of February 24–25, 1956, was specifically ordered in the mid-thirties by Stalin himself as a method of interrogating "obvious enemies of the people."

† Recent psychological studies conducted in conjunction with the National Institute of Mental Health give a more scientific validation for the above hypothesis. These studies involved experiments in which the subject was placed in a water tank face down (with an oxygen mask) and left there to float. At first this created a sensation of great delight and relaxation. After a while, however, his mind began to go blank and his thinking became disorganized. At that point, the subject was ready for a process of "feed-in" of information from those in charge of the experiment and the subject would absorb this information as his own thinking, without being able to

This latter intellectual distortion of reality is something much more likely to be effective with believing Communists than with nonmembers. The communist way of thinking, operating on the basis of the dialectical process, generally tends to make no difference between such aspects as prediction and preference. Thus, for instance, to predict Soviet collapse is to favor it, as the following exchange between Vishinsky and Radek, at the latter's trial, clearly shows:

Vishinsky: Were you in favor of defeat in 1934?
Radek: In 1934, I considered defeat inevitable.
Vishinsky: Were you in favor of defeat in 1934?
Radek: If I could avert defeat, I would be against defeat.
Vishinsky: You consider that you could not have averted it?
Radek: I considered it an inevitable fact.
Vishinsky: You are answering my question incorrectly. Did you accept the whole of Trotsky's line given to you in 1934?
Radek: I accepted the whole of Trotsky's line in 1934.
Vishinsky: Was defeat part of it?
Radek: Yes, it was a line of defeat.
Vishinsky: Trotsky's line included defeat?
Radek: Yes.
Vishinsky: Did you accept it?
Radek: I did.
Vishinsky: Hence, since you accepted it you were in favor of defeat?
Radek: From the standpoint . . .
Vishinsky: You headed for defeat?
Radek: Yes, of course.
Vishinsky: That is, you were in favor of defeat?
Radek: Of course, if I say yes, that means we headed for it.
Vishinsky: Which of us, then, is putting the question rightly?
Radek: All the same, I think that you are not putting the question rightly.
Vishinsky: In 1934 you were not against defeat, but in favor of defeat?
Radek: Yes, I have said so. (168)

The prisoner is thus forced to admit that the situation he expected to come about was the one he desired. And having desired it, he was, therefore, working for it. Therefore, it would not do to explain

---

distinguish truth from falsehood. The parallel between this and the material described above in our text suggests a most striking and frighteningly real explanation for the pattern of confessions.

that one wanted precisely to avoid such a situation, for as Lenin said, ". . . it is not at all a matter of your wishes, thoughts, good intentions . . . What matters is the results" (111e)

All of these factors together, plus the likely elements of threats and promises of deals, made the prisoners confess or, as often was the case, cooperate with the prosecution while attempting to evade some part of the responsibility. (108) But why was the regime so anxious to have them confess? The answer probably lies in the mass character of modern totalitarianism, which operates on the basis of mass slogans and simple explanations. The trials and confessions are accordingly very useful devices in the "educational" programs of the regime, and give the masses simple explanations for all the existing evils, while justifying the might and wisdom of the leadership. To permit the prisoners to defend themselves, to deny the accusations, to cross-examine one another would only complicate matters, would create heroes, would confuse the public. The confession, buttressed by subsidiary testimony, eliminates such an eventuality and makes the public trial into an important educational function of terror.

Similar confessions are notably lacking in the case of the fascist dictatorships. It is a subject of speculation why this should be so. Do they belong to a later phase of totalitarianism? * Are they part of the peculiar dogmatic fanaticism of the Bolshevik creed? All these and other explanations have been given, but all we know for sure is that they did not take place, under fascism, but have occurred in the western satellites, though less frequently. An interesting case has recently been advanced for the proposition that something analogous happened in Tudor times. (253)

The concentration camp is another significant and familiar feature of totalitarian terror. The concentration camp is one of the unique aspects of these systems, not paralleled in the traditional co-

* The possibility that confessions are a feature of a specific period of totalitarian development which needs terroristic persuasion may be suggested by the fact that in April 1956 the Soviet legal journal *Sovetskoe gosudarstvo i pravo* criticized Vishinsky for having developed this practice. The fact that he alone was certainly not to be blamed for it (and is conveniently dead) suggests that such criticism has to be taken with a grain of salt. Only the future will tell how real it is; but possibly at some trial some associates of Vishinsky will *confess* to having initiated this invidious practice of confession.

ercive institutions of the constitutional or absolutist regimes. In a sense, one of the tests of the "totalitarian" character of a regime is the presence or absence of concentration camps. These concentration camps are designed to accommodate those social elements that, for one reason or another, are allegedly incapable or unwilling to adjust themselves to the totalitarian society (see Chapters 13, 14). In the concentration camp they are to be given an opportunity to redeem themselves and to make themselves useful again to society. That most of the victims perish in this process is, according to the totalitarian point of view, merely incidental.

According to Eugen Kogon, who has written much the most penetrating study of the concentration camp (limiting his analysis to Nazi Germany, however), these camps (called Kazett—Kz, from *Konzentrationslager*) were the sharpest expression of the system of terror, and at the same time its most effective method. (95; 176) He believes that their purpose was to eliminate all actual, potential, and imagined enemies of the regime, by first separating them, then humiliating, breaking, and destroying them, killing ten innocents rather than allowing one "guilty" one to escape. He allows that there were a number of collateral purposes; among these he notes that the Kz's were intended to provide a training ground for the Himmler "elite"—men who would learn how to be hard and ruthless, specialists in brutality, whose instincts of hatred, domineering, and exploitation would thus be developed. There also was the purpose of providing the SS leaders themselves with readily available slaves who would serve their masters in cringing terror as long as it pleased them to keep them alive.

The camps started from relatively modest beginnings, about a dozen of them, with no more than about one thousand inmates each. The acts of revolting torture which are sufficiently attested to even at the very outset did not constitute a system at first. They were the result of brutality of individual guards, but Heinrich Himmler and his SS soon caught on and began to systematize these practices into an elaborate ritual. They were administered from one center, under the direct control of Himmler. Eventually, there were three layers of camps, the labor camps which were relatively the mildest, a much more severe second group, and finally those which bore the name of "bone-mills," which very few people survived. But these distinctions are really not of very great importance. For example Dachau which always remained in Group I, as a labor camp, actually was among the worst.

It is still not possible to be at all definite about the number of persons placed in camps over the years. Kogon is convinced that millions went through the camps in the course of the Nazi regime. Since at least 3.5 to 4.5 million were killed in Auschwitz (Oswiecim) alone, 8 to 10 million does not appear to be a fantastic figure. But probably there were never more than about one million in the camps at any one time, considering that even the large original camps, such as Dachau, Buchenwald, and Sachsenhausen rarely had more than 100 thousand inmates. It seems that toward the end, Himmler at one point mentioned a figure of about 600 thousand in a decree, at a time when approximately half a million inmates had already been liberated by the Allied armies.

Which were the main categories of human beings placed into these camps? According to the SS conception, there were four main groups: (1) political enemies of the regime, (2) members of inferior races and persons who seemed "biologically inferior," (3) criminals, and (4) "a-social persons." It is evident that these were quite flexible categories, which were by no means interpreted by courts or judicial bodies, but simply by discretion of the SS leadership. Under (2) we find, until 1939, largely Jews and people related to Jews. Criminals were not necessarily men who had committed crimes, but also those who might commit or had in the past committed crimes. Among the "a-socials" there were, besides tramps, drunkards, pimps and the like, many who had done nothing worse than being late for work and offending some Nazi. Among the political enemies of the regime, a great variety of people, including dissident Nazis, clergymen (especially Catholics), and Jehovah's Witnesses were found.

Kogon, Rousset, and others have shown that the SS camp directors and their minions depended to a very considerable extent upon the inmates themselves for the running of the camps. They developed a fine art of setting one group against another; communists were encouraged to maltreat socialists, and the criminals more especially were given frequent opportunities to practice their various "arts" upon fellow prisoners. In response to this system, a variety of secret organizations developed among the prisoners and extensive defensive mechanisms were worked out to cope with the gruesome realities of camp life. Compensating, in a higher sense, for the depravity of the SS and its helpmates in the camps, there developed opportunity for selfless comradeship and heroic sacrifice. The world of the camps, so incredible from the viewpoint of a liberal and civilized society, reduced human beings to their ultimate essence; unspeakable viciousness, corruption, and debauchery were counterbalanced by acts of saintliness, and a display of the finest and most noble in man.

Soviet labor camps began developing on a large scale during the thirties in order to accommodate the hundreds of thousands of deported kulaks. These dispossessed peasants were herded together into large-scale makeshift camps and were used as cheap labor in the construction of such projects as the Stalin canal in the semi-Arctic north. Needless to say, the mortality rate was high. Parallel to this came the gradual increase in the number of political prisoners, starting first with the oppositionist elements in the party and then embracing the many thousands arrested during the great purges of the thirties. Soviet concentration camps gradually took on more of a political character, and became the main repositories for imprisoned, alleged enemies of the Soviet system. During the war, these prisoners were joined by hundreds of thousands of arrested Poles, Balts, Finns, and—later on—other Central Europeans, and even a sprinkling of Americans and Britons. The only exceptions to this practice were those executed outright, such as four thousand Polish officers massacred in the Katyn Forest, and those considered important enough to be put into solitary confinement in the main secret police prison, Lublyanka, in the center of Moscow. (140)

In theory, Soviet concentration camps are styled "corrective labor camps," designed to "purify" the prisoner and to train him for acceptance as a Soviet citizen. All accounts of former prisoners, however, emphasize that the mortality rate is very high, and that few political prisoner are ever released. (79; 66) As a consequence, consignment to camp means for most victims a dragged-out death sentence. The camps themselves are run by the Main Administration of Camps (GULAG) of the Ministry of Internal Affairs (MVD). It is the MVD which sets the work quotas, standards of living, internal regulations, and disposition of prisoners. GULAG also makes an important contribution to the Soviet state economy. According to the Soviet "State Plan of Development of the National

Economy of the USSR for 1941," captured by the Germans, the secret police share of the projected capital investment amounted to about 18 per cent of the total planned. (47h) This did not include such well-known MVD undertakings as the lumber industry in the North, or goldmining in Kolyma. Clearly, such vast enterprises demand many prisoners, and the various estimates of forced labor in the USSR range in the millions. (237)

Another striking feature of the Soviet forced labor system is the fact that not infrequently the secret police hires out its prisoners to local agencies for the purpose of carrying out some local project. When this happens, elaborate contracts are drawn up between the two parties, specifying all the details and setting the rates at which the secret police is to be paid. At the conclusion of their task, the prisoners, or more correctly the slaves, are returned to the custody of the secret police.

After Stalin's death in 1953, and particularly after Beria's arrest in June of the same year, a wave of unrest swept the camps, culminating in a serious outbreak in the Vorkuta coal-mining camps in the north. The regime successfully quelled the revolts, or strikes, but viewed them with sufficient seriousness to warrant some reforms. The administration of the camps, according to some reports, was taken over by the Ministry of Justice, and efforts were made to improve their internal conditions somewhat. The criminal prisoners were no longer allowed to terrorize and suppress the political prisoners, and those prisoners who overfulfilled their work norms had their sentences shortened accordingly. That in turn, of course, helped to raise the productivity of the prisoners, a matter not alien to the interests of the regime.

In the fall of 1955 the post-Stalin regime engaged in the first large-scale releases of political prisoners. The scope of this amnesty is not yet certain; it has not, as far as is known, resulted in the liquidation of the labor camps, and that odious institution still plays its role in the Soviet arsenal of terror. Nonetheless, as a result of this new policy a number of political prisoners arrested during the purges regained their freedom. Some of them included old Bolsheviks who have spent the last twenty years behind barbed wire. Also many of the foreign prisoners were released, although there is evidence in this case that the amnesty, at best, was only a partial one. Among the leading groups were two very dissimilar ones: Polish underground fighters seized by the Soviet secret police in 1945 and 1946, and who, after fighting the Nazis for five years, spent their postwar years doing forced labor; and about 10,000 German prisoners, classified by the USSR as "war criminals." The number of people released is, however, small compared to the hundreds of thousands of prisoners who, not released, have probably perished.

In so far as the over-all impact of the concentration camps is concerned, recent psychological studies seem to imply that fear of the camp is far greater on the outside than on the inside of the camp. This, to some extent, is produced by the totalitarian practice of maintaining a curtain of mystery around the concentration camp. The very few prisoners who are released are pledged, on pain of severe penalties, to keep silent about their experiences. As a consequence, the concentration camps represent to the great masses of the population the great and fearful unknown. The occasional public trial, with the mystifying spectacle of the confession, further enhances this feeling, so much a part of the pervading atmosphere of totalitarian terror.

Purges, confessions, and camps are thus part of the equipment of a developed totalitarian system. They are present in various degrees of intensity, depending on the given stage of development, in all totalitarian systems. They have been developed to the highest point in the communist dictatorships where social changes, mass elimination, and succession struggles within the Party went the furthest. But available evidence suggests that, had the Nazi regime endured beyond Hitler, the succession struggle and ideological conflict between Bormann and Goering and Himmler would likewise have produced large-scale purges in their aftermath. For the totalitarian system the purge provides the mechanism of elimination and stimulation within the movement of the "chosen," the confessions are useful to vilify the opposition and underline the infallibility of the leadership, while the camps provide cheap labor and a tool for the liquidation of the "enemies of the people." All three make their contribution to the all-pervading atmosphere of terror by which the totalitarian regime attempts to construct its allegedly happier future.

Chapter Sixteen

The Limits of the Terror:
The Vacuum

The terror in all its forms is so formidable that there appears to be no escape. When reinforced by totalitarian propaganda, it conjures up the spectre of a population of millions thinking and talking and acting in uniform ways. Yet there are limits, and, although they are fluid, they are quite significant. Besides the "islands of separateness" which will be discussed in the last part, there is a reaction pattern which falsifies the communication between rulers and ruled all the way down from the dictator to the lowest party functionary, and indeed beyond him, affecting all relationships of subordination and corroding and eventually destroying all genuine authority. (247c; 59d)

This failure to communicate effectively, both within the hierarchy and with the rest of the people and the world, we have called the phenomenon of the vacuum. There develops within the regimes a kind of empty space around the rulers, which becomes more and more difficult to penetrate. A slow disintegration affecting all human relations sets people against each other and causes mutual distrust so that ordinary people are alienated from one another, all the bonds of confidence in social relationships are corroded by the terror and propaganda, the spying, and the denouncing and betraying, until the social fabric threatens to fall apart. The confidence which ordinarily binds the manager of a plant to his subordinates, members of a university faculty to each other and to their students, lawyer to client, doctor to patient, and even parents to children as well as brothers to sisters is disrupted. The core of this process of disintegration is, it seems, the break-down of the possibility of communication—the spread, that is, of the vacuum. Isolation and anxiety are the universal result. And the only answer the totalitarian dictatorship has for coping with this disintegration of human relationships is more organized coercion, more propaganda, more terror.

Among the folklore of despotism, there is a legend that was

meant to glorify the wisdom of the ruler, but which at the same time illustrates this problem of the disruption of effective communication as power becomes absolute. Harun al-Rashid, so the tale goes, was wise enough to realize that his subordinates would be prone to abuse their great power, and instead of employing it for the good of the community and the commonwealth, would oppress and exploit the people. But since he had no reliable way of ascertaining the common man's views through regular channels as all of these were controlled by the very subordinates whom he wished to check up on, the great Kalif disguised himself from time to time and mingled, in the dark of night, with the folks in taverns and streets to listen to their tales of woe. And on the basis of what he had heard, he would bring those to trial who had been talked about as vicious and corrupt. This problem of check-up occurs, of course, in all human organization, but under orderly constitutional government (and the corresponding patterns of responsibility in private organizations), such check-up occurs readily and continuously as a result of the open criticism which is being voiced by members not only in formal meetings, but informally through press, radio, and all the other channels. Under the conditions of totalitarian dictatorship, the check-up becomes exceedingly difficult, if not impossible.

It might be suggested that the totalitarian dictatorship could adopt some such institutional device as the censorate in Imperial China. These censors were men surrounded by tradition and imperial protection, men with the greatest degree of independence, who would travel about the provinces of the Empire and hear complaints from anyone who felt himself oppressed or exploited. They would bring even the governor of a province to trial without ado. The notion was, evidently, that these censors were actually acting in place of the Emperor himself, and the reverence shown to them was accordingly great. But the functioning of the censorate clearly rested upon the Confucian belief system, with its stress upon a static public good, upon *li* and its emphasis on tradition, custom, and good manners. In a way, it is difficult to picture anything more diametrically opposed to the totalitarian dynamism than the Confucian Empire. A censorate in a totalitarian dictatorship would at once become either an empty ritual or a rival center of power.

Something of the function of the censorate, the check-up function, has been from time to time assigned to the secret police in totalitarian systems. We know today that the SS of Himmler made extensive check-ups on the attitude of the German population during the war. Many of these reports show a remarkable candor about the faltering and eventually the vanishing support for the regime. But there is every reason to believe that these reports never reached Hitler, even in abbreviated form. It is not even clear how many of them became available to Himmler. The terror which permeates the party and secret police cadres, no less than the general population, operates as an inhibition to truthful reporting. Blockwardens falsify their reports, and do so in the hope of currying favor with their superiors. We shall note, later, how this tendency to pretend that results are better and more favorable to the regime and to make adjustments, not only in reports about attitudes, but also in those about production and maintenance of industrial plant, interferes with industrial planning (see Chapters 18, 19).

A similar situation arose in Italy. We learn from Leto's *Memoirs* that only Rocchini among Mussolini's lieutenants had the courage to tell him that the Italian people were bitterly opposed to entering World War II; Starace even claimed that almost all Italians would unite behind the Duce. (116a) The Duce was similarly misinformed about the state of Italy's military preparedness; his subordinates preferred to flatter their chief by presenting rosy estimates, suggesting the prowess of his regime. (116b)

This tampering with reports also affects the USSR's intelligence work and hence their foreign relations. It appears that Soviet intelligence is somewhat handicapped by the fact that, in some respects at least, it must work with and through local communist parties. If it tried to do without them, it would soon find itself in difficulties, particularly with reference to the problem of recruiting agents and contacts, as well as penetrating the government institutions of the foreign powers. (177) But when the intelligence service employs the local communist party organization, it is exposed to the effect of this process of falsification, rooted both in fear of the Moscow center and in ideological blindness. Local communist leaders, fearful of Moscow disfavor and subsequent purges, might easily develop a tendency toward overestimating their strength and the degree of inner disintegration of the capitalist order. Soviet miscalculations in France and Italy in 1947 and 1948 are the more recent of many examples, dating back to the days of the Komintern and the unsuc-

cessful Soviet venture in China. Also at the time of the blockade of
Berlin, undertaken by the USSR in June 1948 in order to counteract
the currency reform which the western Allies had instituted after
lengthy Soviet obstruction (27; 241a), it became clear that the Soviet
Union, on the basis of SED information, had confidently counted
upon the Germans in Berlin to abandon the Allied cause and submit to the Soviet position, when as a matter of fact, even elementary
intelligence work could have informed them to the contrary. In
fact, there is reason to believe that the entire Soviet policy in Germany was, to some extent, the result of such failure of intelligence,
because of excessive reliance upon German communist information.

It would be a mistake, however, to conclude, therefore, that Soviet
intelligence, both at home and abroad, operates like a man wearing
red-colored blinders. Soviet leadership, as conclusive evidence
clearly shows, makes special efforts to develop alternate channels of
information and control in order to eliminate precisely this element
of coloring and distortion. Soviet espionage abroad, apart from col-
laborating with the local communist outfits, also operates independent networks, which report directly to Moscow. The espionage revelations of Guzenko and Petrov show that there are normally at least
five such networks in a country subjected to intensive Soviet espionage: one working through the local communist parties, another
run by the MVD, a military intelligence network, a commercial espionage network, and finally the foreign service intelligence network. Excessive discrepancies can thus be more easily detected
when all such reports are processed in Moscow and submitted to the
policy makers. Similarly, in their domestic espionage, the Soviet
rulers are careful not to make themselves dependent only on one
source of information. Apart from the secret police and the ordinary channels of the party, there exist the Party Control Commissions, which investigate party activities in all walks of life, the Ministry of State Control, which is specially concerned with keeping in
touch with administrative functions and making independent reports on their operations, and the Prosecutor General and his subordinates, who have recently been given additional investigating
powers. (285) There is also the technique known as *samokritika,* or
self-critique, according to which Soviet officials and functionaries as
well as the people in general are encouraged to criticize the opera-

tions, but *not the policy,* of the party, of the state administration, and of economic enterprises.* This not only serves as a vent to pent-up aggression, but is also useful to the rulers in detecting current weaknesses, abuses and public opinion attitudes.

All this notwithstanding, the Soviet regime is not entirely free, although it appears to be freer than its Nazi counterpart, from the curse of the vacuum. It seems, however, that this is due more to an over-all ideological dogmatism than to sheer lack of adequate and accurate information. The way objective facts are put together and interpreted is predetermined by the ideological requirements of the system. The most classical example is the famous Varga debate, in which an accurate assessment of the American economic situation was castigated as false, and Varga was forced to retract the assertions he had made after World War II that the United States was not facing an imminent economic crisis. As a result, the Soviet Union continued to act on the assumption that the United States would be forced to make political concessions to the USSR for the sake of continued economic relations, and even grant the USSR a loan to avoid a crash of the United States economy. Whether the present Soviet leadership can raise itself above this kind of handicap remains to be seen.†

A similar point might be made with reference to Hitler's policy toward Britain and the United States. Though he was a constant reader of foreign press clippings, Hitler received no sound information either about the probable course of British and American policy, nor about the trend of opinion in both countries. When he arrived at his decision to go to war with Poland, he did not seem to have expected the British to do much more than make a gesture of action, and he hoped until the last to be able to keep the United States out of the war. The efforts of certain qualified persons, especially in the Foreign Office, to furnish Hitler with more adequate data, were thwarted by the predominant party cadres. (186; 234) This circum-

---

* Self-critique is preferable to the more frequent translation of self-criticism. There is a Russian word *krititsizm* which means criticism. *Kritika* means critique, and the Soviet regime is interested in promoting the technique of critique, but not in encouraging a critical attitude through criticism.

† After the Khrushchev-Bulganin visit to England it was reported that the Soviet leaders indicated their surprise at the high level of the standard of living (*New York Times,* April 30, 1956), which would suggest serious misconceptions about conditions abroad.

stance does not, of course, lessen his moral responsibility, but it shows the catastrophic effect of the factor we are here analyzing, as an unintended consequence of totalitarian terror. There exists an unconfirmed anecdote about Hitler at the time of Munich, which fits very well into this pattern. According to this tale, Hitler was taking a cruise with some top-ranking Nazis and businessmen in the summer of 1938. He was at the time entertaining Admiral Horthy, on board a Nazi battleship. Among all those present, there was a general belief that a war would be disastrous for Germany, and that it was necessary to warn Hitler of the probable course it would take, in view of the foreseeable attitude of Britain and the United States. The anecdote then records with considerable relish how each of the men in turn insisted that the other was best qualified and most advantageously placed to inform Hitler: Goering, because he was the next in the hierarchy; Himmler, because he had access to all kinds of secret information; the top businessman, because he was free of official concerns; and so forth. In the end, no one did inform Hitler because no one wanted to incur the Führer's wrath by telling him something that he would not like to hear. Similarly, at the time Hitler decided to go to war, in the fateful August days of 1939, Hitler isolated himself, and no advisers, not even Goering, let alone foreign diplomats—according to Sir Nevile Henderson's pitiful account—could secure access to Hitler. (77b)

Not the vacuum specifically, but the effect of it on the totalitarian rulers has caused one leading student of these problems to make the following comment:

Where the instruments of public enlightenment are wholly under the domination of the active elite of power, the controllers of the media develop a fantasy world in which the images communicated to the people have little relationship to reality. The stream of public communication becomes dogmatic and ceremonial to such a degree that it is inappropriate to think of communication management as a propaganda problem. It is more accurate to think of ritualization than propaganda . . . (59e)

Undoubtedly this kind of ritualization exists to some extent. On the other hand, repeated shifts in the actual lines of communication that are issued, involving serious self-contradictions of the leadership, suggest that large amounts of propaganda as such continue to be issued. The "fantasy world" in which the dictator lives, and which is a product of the vacuum that the terror has created around him plays its role in competition with the real world which he seeks to master.

As in nature, so in society, the vacuum is relative. And since the totalitarian dictators, no less than Harun al-Rashid, realize to some extent at least their isolation, various efforts are made to reduce the "thin air" around them. This is a problem both of intake and outgo. As far as the latter is concerned, there has been developed the technique of whispering campaigns. A high party official will get in some of his friends a little further on down the line in the party and, in strict confidence, tell them something highly startling or secret. He knows perfectly well that they will go and tell somebody else, in similarly strict confidence, and so on. This technique was and is employed also for the purpose of reaching and misleading foreign correspondents. The technique is, of course, not unknown in other societies; but in them it serves a purpose radically different from that in a totalitarian dictatorship. It is the means of penetrating a fog, rather than permeating a vacuum.

The vacuum has another curious effect, as far as outgo is concerned. People in totalitarian dictatorships become so suspicious of all communication, suspecting every news item of being propaganda, that even paramount facts are disbelieved. Thus it appears that, as late as September 12, 1939, Germans professed not to know, or rather not to believe that Britain and France had declared war upon Germany. To the blatant headlines of Dr. Goebbels' press their reaction evidently had been: "Another of Goebbels' propaganda stories." At the time of the Franco rebellion, when the papers reported, quite truthfully, that the British Navy was demonstrating in the western Mediterranean, a widespread public reaction in Germany created a genuine war scare, because people were convinced that the British Navy was demonstrating, not in the western Mediterranean, but on the North Sea coast of Germany. (67b) Goebbels in his diaries reports a number of other instances of this kind and the entire diaries provide a striking illustration for the vacuum theory; as the war went on, the problem of reaching the German populace became more and more perplexing.*

---

* Actually, this problem also plagued the people in charge of wartime propaganda in the Western democracies, for during the war "constitutional dictatorships" were

In the Soviet Union the war gave rise also to many rumors which swept the population by means of the OWS news agency—a translation of the popular and symptomatic abbreviation for the Russian phrase "one woman said . . ." During the period of initial Soviet reverses, much exaggerated accounts of Soviet defeats, flights of leaders, and so forth were passed from mouth to mouth, contradicting the official radio broadcasts and newspaper communiqués. Later on, by 1943 and 1944, as a corollary to the many promises of a happy future made during the war by the Soviet leaders, rumors circulated that the Soviet government had decided to end collectivization of agriculture and release all political prisoners. Possibly such rumors were even originated purposely by the regime itself in order to gain public support for the war effort. In any case, some interviews with former Soviet citizens suggest that these rumors were widely believed, and the population was quite disappointed by the postwar harshness of the Stalinist policies.

It would seem from all the evidence at our disposal that the vacuum works like a cancer in the totalitarianism systems. That means that its growth endangers the continued existence of the totalitarian scheme of things. It may even catapult such a dictatorship into a calamitous foreign adventure, such as Hitler's wars. Stalin's ignorance of the agricultural situation similarly made the food problem in the USSR very much more acute, according to Khrushchev's recent revelations. Reality is hard to perceive in a vacuum created by fear and lies, buttressed by force.

---

instituted, and the controls over news resulting from this temporary concentration of power caused the public to become increasingly suspicious.

V

The Directed Economy

Chapter Seventeen

Totalitarian Bureaucratization

Whether the battle-cry is "expropriation of the exploiters" or "the common good before selfishness," * the totalitarian dictatorships develop a centrally directed economy as the sixth feature in their syndrome of traits. This centrally directed economy, to which we shall turn now, calls for an increasing number of public officials to attend to all the various functions which such an economy needs. But in addition to the appointment of all the actual public officials, there takes place a bureaucratization of large segments of organizational activity beyond the formal governmental system. The Germans proclaimed *Gleichschaltung,* that is to say, co-ordination of all organizations, one of the goals of the regime. By this they meant that, in accordance with the leadership principle, the "leaders" of all organizations should be appointed by the government and these chosen leaders should then wield the same kind of absolute authority within their organization that the leadership principle called for all up and down the line of the official hierarchy. The idea of the corporative state served a similar purpose in Italy, as far as the economy is concerned; all organizations, whether business corporations or labor unions, were made part of one hierarchical structure with the Duce at the head. We shall describe these systems in greater detail (Chapters 19, 20, 21). It is evident that by such a setup the functionaries of almost all organizations are in fact becoming bureaucrats; the difference between them and actual governmental officials is not one of formal prerequisites, such as pension rights and status, but rather of actual political function. When looked at in this perspective, the function of a business manager in a fascist-controlled corporation and a factory manager in a Soviet trust is very similar. They are both dependent functionaries of a vast governmentally controlled apparatus. In short, we have before us what may be called total bureaucratization.

* *Gemeinnutz geht vor Eigennutz* is not, in its alliterations, readily translated; "common benefit goes before (precedes) individual benefit," though literal, is weak.

And yet, there are conflicting trends. If one studies the bureaucracy of the totalitarian regimes from the standpoint of a developmental concept of bureaucracy, such as is implicit in Max Weber's well-known analysis (225b; 154; 226; 134a), one is forced to the conclusion that totalitarianism, while extending bureaucracy, also corrupts it. The six aspects or elements which recur in a developing bureaucracy of the modern Western type are centralization of control and supervision (hierarchical aspect), differentiation of functions, qualification for office, objectivity, precision and continuity, and secrecy (discretion). The first three are organizational aspects or criteria, the last three behavioral ones. We can speak of them as criteria when we employ them as measuring rods for determining the extent of bureaucratization; for all of them may exist to a greater or lesser degree, and it is this degree which determines the degree of bureaucratization. They are never fully attained, of course; in the nature of the case, there could not be in actual administration complete centralization, complete differentiation, and so forth.

What we find, under totalitarian dictatorships, is, however, a marked deviation and a retrogression where previously a higher degree of bureaucratization existed. Centralization of control and supervision yields to a conflict between party and governmental bureaucracy, centralization is superseded by local satraps, like the *Gauleiters,* and party loyalty replaces professional qualification for office.

In terms of such a concept of a developed bureaucracy, then, totalitarian systems do appear to be retrogressive. The subjection of the bureaucracy to party interference and controls, the insistence that not only the key policy posts, but officials up and down the line, and in the fascist case those in the "co-ordinated organizations," be active members of the totalitarian party, and similar trends (see Part II and also Chapter 24) all argue that the totalitarian dictatorships are less rational and legal, and hence less fully developed from a bureaucratic standpoint than, for example, the governmental services of some absolute monarchies in the eighteenth century.

In the Soviet Union, the supremacy of the party, described earlier, had created parallel governmental and party bureaucracies. Fainsod has succinctly stated that "the development of the Communist Party apparatus as an extension of the long arm of the dictator constitutes one of the most impressive and formidable organizational achievements of modern totalitarianism." (47i) Its members become the *apparatchiki*. Ever since Stalin's appointment as secretary of the party, its inner apparatus has been expanding at a steady pace, so much so that today the Secretariat of the Central Committee constitutes an imposing super-bureaucracy, with its tentacles reaching into every aspect of Soviet life. It was by skillfully manipulating the appointing organs of the Central Committee that Stalin succeeded in outmaneuvering his opponents, and solidifying his hold on power. Under Stalin's management the *apparat* became the key instrument of political power in the USSR. It is indeed a manifestation of this fact that the current Soviet leaders, Khrushchev, Bulganin, Malenkov, all came up through the *apparat*. And again, it was by virtue of his control of this *apparat* as Party Secretary that Khrushchev emerged in 1955 as the top man in the Soviet hierarchy.

The *apparatchiki* are then the important bureaucrats of the Communist Party. Their counterparts, more numerous as time goes on, exist also on the lower levels of the party bureaucracy. At the top there are the heads and workers of the various sections of the Central Committee which supervise the ministries and control the party operations; then there are the republican party secretaries with their staffs and workers; there are the secretaries of the two hundred-odd provincial and regional party committees and their staffs; there are the secretaries and staffs of 544 city party committees; there are the secretaries and staffs of the 4,886 district party committees (271h; 47j); there are finally the thousands of party workers who head the primary party organizations on the collective farms, in government institutions, and in military units. A recent calculation put the number of party secretaries on all the party levels (and it is to be remembered that each party committee above the primary level has more than one secretary) at about 327,000. (245c) This figure would have to be increased appreciably if the sizable number of committee members were to be added to it. They are all part of the web spun around the Soviet Union by the Secretariat of the CPSU in Moscow.

This party bureaucracy operates parallel to, and also penetrates, the state bureaucracy, the rapid extension of which has created the characteristic problems of bureaucratization, including status rigidity and privileges. Already, by 1926, the *Large Soviet Encyclopedia* gave the total governmental service as 2,500,000. By 1939, it had grown to some 10,000,000. (141c) This process of expansion, however, was not without its growing pains, and the history of the Soviet bureaucracy is one of constant attempts to adjust to the theoretical and political requirements of the regime.

Prior to their seizure of power the Bolsheviks proclaimed their violent determination to smash the existing state machinery. The state as an instrument of class oppression had to go, and the bureaucracy, being its most direct manifestation, bore the main brunt of this attack. Lenin soon found himself attempting to rationalize the need not only for a state (see Chapter 7), but also for a bureaucracy. He did so both by denying that the Bolsheviks had a bureaucracy and by admitting that they had bureaucrats but, of course, bureaucrats devoted to, and recruited from the people:

Soviet power is a new type of state, in which there is no bureaucracy, no police, no standing army, and in which bourgeois democracy is replaced by a new democracy—a democracy which brings to the forefront the vanguard of the toiling masses, turning them into legislators, executives and a military guard, and which creates an apparatus capable of reeducating the masses. (113f)

The setting up of this Soviet bureaucracy created immediate problems. Personnel recruitment was the obvious one. A large number of tsarist civil servants had to be kept, lest the machinery crumble, until new Soviet cadres were trained. The commanding positions were, of course, taken over by party zealots, but the regime still remained uneasy, and it was not until two decades later that the bureaucracy became fully sovietized. The second problem, at that time seemingly more urgent, was how to maintain the egalitarian façade, an intrinsic part of the doctrine, in the face of the requirements of bureaucratic organization and, more especially, the hierarchical principle. Moore tells how the workers of the newly set-up People's Commissariat of Foreign Affairs at first thought that now they would legislate collectively on the conduct of foreign affairs. Such idle dreams, however, were soon dispelled. Lenin, using Engels as his authority, blandly stated that "any demand for equality which goes beyond the demand for abolition of classes is a stupid and absurd prejudice." (111a) Centralization of command and hierarchy, therefore, were not incompatible with equality.

This problem, however, was not solved so easily. Sizable segments of the party opposed the rapidly developing tendencies toward centralization of power, and the early party congresses became forums for frequently violent discussions on the merit and theoretical orthodoxy of unity of command (*edinonachalstvo*) versus collegiate management, the latter being a concession to the demands for collective decision-making. This collegiate management, although dropped quite rapidly on the lower levels, persisted until the thirties when the Stalinist drives made necessary the complete centralization of command. Since then the Soviet bureaucracy has been operating in an atmosphere of strict discipline and highly stratified hierarchy.

During the early years of Soviet power, the party bureaucracy remained suspicious of the state bureaucracy, and particularly of its former tsarist civil servants. As a safeguard, the Party Control Commission, set up by the Tenth Party Congress in 1921 to check the operations of the party bureaucracy, began to look into the operations of the state bureaucracy too. Efforts were also made to promote into it, as rapidly as possible, loyal party members to replace the tsarist holdovers kept purely for expediency. Thus, for instance, in 1930, out of some 450,000 civil servants screened for security, about 30 per cent were dismissed. (252b; 18h) As late as 1932, however, some Soviet administrations still had staffs, about 50 per cent of which were made up of former tsarist bureaucrats. (141d) It was not until the great purges of the *Yezhovshchina* that this cleansing process could be considered complete. At that time, a large number (running into hundreds of thousands) of young technicians and students were promoted to responsible state posts. (190b)

Since that time the Soviet bureaucracy has been staffed essentially with loyal party members or individuals screened by the party and considered to be sympathizers. Yet even this "reliable" type of bureaucrat remains subject to intensive control. Fainsod describes it thus:

The plan under which he operates must be approved by the State Planning Committee. His staff arrangements are controlled by standards established by the State Civil Service Commission. His financial transactions are subject to the scrutiny of the Ministry of Finance. The Minister of State Control maintains a check on his efficiency, enforces strict control over the expenditure of funds, and makes certain that he is fulfilling all government orders and decrees. The Procurator General watches the legality of his actions. The secret police of the Ministry of Internal Affairs (MVD) keeps him under constant observation to ensure his political reliability. The whole range of his activity, as well as that of the control organs, is always under careful surveillance by representatives of the party. It is not too far-fetched to describe this complex network of controls as a system of power founded on cross-espionage and the institutionalization of mutual suspicion. (47k)

Political loyalty is the primary criterion for assessing a governmental bureaucrat's competence. This is not to say that other more objective standards are entirely ignored, but the political assessment is the primary and fundamental prerequisite to a favorable report on the competence of such a bureaucrat. The fact that such assessments are made primarily by outside party organs necessitates constant re-adjustment between the party and the state bureaucracy. There is a growing tendency, which the party officially combats, for the government bureaucrats to "pass the buck" to party officials and thus avoid responsibility for decision-making. The party organs, as studies of Soviet archives show, become as a result swamped with minutiae. Some of the protocols of party committees, which became available to foreign scholars as a result of World War II, indicate that even most obviously bureaucratic concerns are being usurped by party organs. Local party leaders, instead of attending to party affairs, become involved in such matters as gasoline for tractors, leaves of absence for the bureaucrats, and housing conditions. Party officials also decide on local bureaucratic appointments which must be cleared with the party committee. The party leadership, troubled by this, makes constant efforts to minimize such tendencies. The party organizations are exhorted not to intervene directly in governmental operations, but merely to set the example by maintaining and insisting upon high standards of performance. Party functionaries are thus to lead and to check but not to usurp the functions of duly constituted government bodies. The paper of the Central Committee of the party in a recent editorial entitled, significantly, "Raise the organizational role of the Party Apparatus" specifically attacked the tendency of some members "to work for others" and to turn party workers into office clerks, instead of keeping them on the level of organizers. (265c) The problem, however, seems to be inherent in the political situation, and it is doubtful that it can ever be resolved by a totalitarian system which puts a premium on a politicized bureaucracy.

A further problem that besets the Soviet bureaucracy is the tremendous expansion of its functions and scope. Given the totalitarian nature of the system, the Soviet bureaucracy reaches every organization, every institution, every collective farm, and indeed anyone connected with any activity involving a group of people. As a result, there is an apparent tendency in the state apparatus to respond to every urgency by creating a new body to deal with it. This is as true of the lower levels as of the ministerial hierarchy, where the number of ministries currently is over fifty. From time to time, a drastic curtailment is made, as after the death of Stalin, but then a new expansion occurs. As a result paper-work and division of responsibility continue to plague the Soviet bureaucracy. One regional agricultural administration, for instance, reported that during 1953 it received from the Ministry of Agriculture no less than 7,569 letters; in 1954, 8,459, and on the average about 30 instructions per day. (265d) The Ministry of Agriculture, itself, was, as of December 1954, organized into 422 administrations. (278)

Such a situation affects the bureaucrats adversely. They are still expected "to deliver," but they can only do so by operating in a manner not prescribed by regulations and hierarchy. A complex system of evasion accordingly develops. They minimize in their reports the capacity of their organizations to produce so that the plans will be set lower; they maximize their achievements by taking short-cuts on standards or by actually falsifying records; they organize informal arrangements among themselves, based partially on bribery, to avoid control and to exchange necessary items. (273a)

There is, accordingly, a continuing game of hide-and-seek played between Soviet bureaucrats and the Ministry of State Control, the task of which is to detect such happenings. To combat such procedures as described above, "the Ministry of State Control has been given the right to impose disciplinary penalties on officials guilty of not fulfilling the government's instructions and orders, of neglecting accounts, of wasteful management, wasteful spending of supplies and funds, and also of giving incorrect information to state control agencies." (278b) Power of removal and of turning over the guilty to prosecution is included in this grant.

Such a situation, naturally, affects not only efficiency but also

morale. There seems to have been a steady decline in the ideological *élan* of the Soviet bureaucrats. The party journals have become
increasingly concerned with the low level of political consciousness
among the Soviet civil servants, and examples of bureaucrats igno-
rant of the basic works of Marxism-Leninism have been duly cited.
The party does not want the Soviet bureaucrats to develop an *esprit
de corps* purely their own, with their own standards of efficiency and
performance. The Soviet bureaucrats are exhorted to remember
that

the Soviet executive is a representative of the socialist state, a leader in
whom is invested the people's trust. He must approach problems politically and work creatively and with a purpose in view. A communist
ideological outlook and the ability to organize in practice the carrying
out of Party and government decisions and to create conditions for increasing the initiative and creative activity of the masses are inseparable
features of a Soviet executive. (255b)

The Communist Party of the Soviet Union thus continues to
strive to create an efficient, but ideologically conscious and politically
loyal state bureaucracy. All three criteria have, to some extent, been
achieved. It is difficult, however, to reach and maintain all three
at their optimum.

All in all, it is evident that the trend in the Soviet Union is a
mixed one. We observe a rapid bureaucratization, if this term is
taken to mean an increase in the role of the bureaucracy. But this
bureaucratization has occurred in two distinct spheres: the government and the party. In a sense this may be compared to the dual
development of bureaucracy in democratic capitalist countries, where
we can observe a steady expansion of bureaucracy both in the government and in the nongovernmental sphere of group life, especially business and trade unions. But, whereas in these democratic
countries the bureaucratization in both spheres continues to be subject to a variety of controls, such as elections, representative bodies,
and stock-holders' meetings, the rival bureaucracies of the totalitarian dictatorship may to some extent check each other, but they are
free from control from below. The bureaucracy of the democracies
is responsible, the bureaucracy of the Soviet Union is not. And the
same is true, of course, with minor variations in the satellites and in
China.

A similar trend can be observed in the Soviet Zone of Germany.

It is particularly interesting from our viewpoint, because its bureaucratic developments are superimposed upon the bureaucratization process under the Nazi dictatorship. Because of this setting, it may be well to turn first to the problems which the bureaucracy encountered after Hitler took over the government.

Hitler's advent to power was soon followed by a law, rather oratorically described as intended to "cleanse the civil service of political favorites"; its official title was the Civil Service Restoration Act. Passed April 7, 1933, it was followed by another act in June which addressed itself to making sure that a civil servant "gives a guarantee that he will at all times fully identify himself with the state of national resurgence." These initial assaults upon the professional bureaucracy, which Max Weber had once believed "unshatterable," were consolidated and extended in 1937 by a comprehensive civil service "reform." By this reform, the traditional standards of the governmental bureaucracy were perverted; the standards of the party bureaucracy, such as loyalty to the Führer and to Nazi ideology, were made the ultimate tests of official conduct. This process is the cue to that de-bureaucratization of which we spoke at the outset. (134b)

In terms of the concept of bureaucracy, defined above, we find developing under Hitler a dualism of governmental and party bureaucracies, which found symbolic expression in the fact that Hitler was both Chancellor and leader of the party. This is not an unfamiliar situation in constitutional systems, such as Britain and the United States. But since, in these systems, the party and its leader are only "in power" as long as the electorate supports them in free elections, the government functionaries are largely independent of them in their day-to-day operations; the party's control finds expression through the adoption of laws which the official is, of course, bound to obey, that is, to execute and to apply. But under Hitler, the party had come to stay (see Chapter 3). With its various branches and extensions, such as the Security Police, the Hitler Youth, the National Socialist Civil Servants League, and others, it permeated and infiltrated the government service. This meant, as we have already said, that the governmental bureaucracy was de-bureaucratized in the following ways: the centralization of control (the hierarchy) was continually subject to challenge by party functionaries; the functions of various government officials were impinged upon by party offices (for example, the Foreign Office by the Rosenberg-led Office for Foreign Policy Questions of the Party and by another such office in Himmler's SS); recruitment into and promotion in the government bureaucracy depended more and more upon positions in the party and its formations rather than upon "qualification for office"; objectivity was denounced in favor of "ideological conformity"; neither precision nor continuity were permitted when they conflicted with the exigencies of the moment, including the Führer's whims; official secrets were continually leaked with impunity to party functionaries who made such use of them as they saw fit, including the publishing of articles in ideologically oriented publications, such as the SS' *Das Schwarze Korps* (The Black Corps).

Behind these corrupting influences we find, of course, the terror. Any attempts on the part of an official to maintain former standards of legality and objectivity were seen as attempts at endangering the security of the people, its party, and its government, and correspondingly were punished by removal from office, concentration camp, and death. At first these cases were rare, but as the Hitler regime became more totalitarian, such actions became more numerous, until after 1942 they were the order of the day. (For all this see Part IV.) The result was, of course, that the more ordinary officers soon adopted an attitude of ready compliance with party directives of the most arbitrary kind. (54c) It is easy to picture a government councillor—timid though devoted to his task, conventional though well-educated and professionally competent, secure in his routine and trembling for his job, the security of which was once in his youth one of the main reasons for becoming a government official— yielding to a party official strutting back and forth in his full battle regalia of, say, an SS *Sturmbannführer* (major), and demanding in the name of the party's ideology and interest the alteration of a decision, which the hapless official had made in accordance with existing law. One needs to recall in this connection that Hitler had, at the time of the Blood Purge of 1934, proclaimed himself the "supreme law lord" (oberster hoechster Rechtsherr) of Germany.

The position of the courts, traditionally considered separate from the executive and hence the bureaucracy, deserves some further comment. Under Hitler, the judges were at first slow to yield to Nazi pressure. Having played a rather conservative, not to say reactionary, role under the Weimar Republic, they prided themselves on their independence from "democratic" influences. Like the army, they believed in their "neutrality," that is to say, their remoteness from politics. But the National Socialists could not, of course, permit such an independent judiciary. They rapidly transformed the judiciary, and more especially the criminal bench, into organs of the terror. (16) By the beginning of the forties, when the regime had become thoroughly totalitarian, a prominent Nazi jurist could write: "In the field of crime prevention the judge no longer merely administers justice. His . . . activity approaches that of an administrative official. He no longer looks for justice alone, but also acts in accordance with expediency. Judge and administrator, judiciary and police, often meet . . . in the pursuit of identical objectives. This change in the character of some judicial activity has led to a decline [in the importance] of judiciary." (127) The United States military tribunal at Nuremberg brought suit against one such set of judges in the case of *U.S. v. Josef Altstötter et al.,* in which the whole range of the corruption of the judiciary was laid bare. It is clear from this record, as well as many records in German Denazification Courts, that the judiciary had essentially become a branch of the administrative service, subject to continuous interference by the party. But this was not enough. In order to handle certain kinds of criminal prosecutions, which even this kind of judiciary would not attend to, the Nazi regime organized the *Volksgerichte,* or People's Courts, special tribunals resembling the revolutionary tribunals under the French terror as well as institutions in the USSR, in which only expediency in terms of Nazi standards served as a basis for judgment. (81.2)

If we turn from these developments under the Hitler dictatorship to the Soviet Zone of Germany (59.2), we find that basically the SED (Socialist Unity Party) has continued, or revived, after it turned totalitarian, the techniques and practices of the Nazis. The officialdom in the government offices is subservient to the party bureaucracy to an even greater degree, in accordance with Soviet practice. Administrative law provides for a strict subordination of the governmental to the party bureaucracy. One of the main agents of this ascendancy is the attorney of state, who has become the whiphand of the secret police. Divorced from all court control, he operates on the basis of a vastly expanded concept of security, hunting down deviationists in the complex bureaucracy, not only in the government proper, but in the network of enterprise of which the socialized economy is composed (see Chapter 19). The courts themselves have become appendages of the administration. In the statute establishing the new court system, the SED completed the process initiated by the Hitler regime of depriving the courts of their independence and of superimposing upon them the notion of administrative and political expediency, as contrasted with the constitutional principle of *nulla poena sine lege*. Indeed, the jurists of the Soviet Zone have gone one step further, in keeping with Soviet conceptions of "law"; they have introduced the notion that decisions of courts which have already been pronounced with legally binding effect may be annulled by judicial decree within the year. It is by perversion of the French concept of *cassation,* or review, that the attorney-general-of-state (as well as the president and vice-presidents of the Supreme Court) can request cassation if the decision "violates a law," or if it is "decidedly in error" in the penalty it inflicts, or if it "decidedly contradicts justice." Clearly political considerations can be, and have in fact been, the basis of this cassation. (172; 214)

In Italy, the problem of bureaucratization presented itself in a somewhat different form. As we have seen, the Fascists proclaimed the doctrine of the strong state. Such ideologues of Fascism as G. Gentile insisted that the party was subordinate to the state, and should serve as its conscience. Mussolini stressed the point when, in his article on Fascism (150b), he asserted that "everything is in the State, and nothing human or spiritual exists, much less has value, outside the State. In this sense, Fascism is totalitarian, and the Fascist State, the synthesis and unity of all values, interprets, develops and gives strength to the whole life of the people. Outside the State there can be neither individuals nor groups (political parties, associations, syndicates, classes)." In terms of such a concept, the governmental bureaucracy, and more especially the high civil servant, assumes an independent role vis-à-vis the party and the corporate bureaucracy of business. In rejecting the view that Fascism was the arm of big business, G. Salvemini wrote that there were no less than three bureaucracies: the officers of the regular army, the civil service, and the officials of the Fascist Party. He estimated that the members of these three bureaucracies constituted about one-twelfth of Italy's adult males. (180a) He then proceeded to describe vividly the attitude of the civil servant bureaucrat toward the big businessman who seeks government aid, and observed, "When a disagreement arises between a big business man and a high civil servant, Mussolini's immediate inclination is to favor the high civil servant. The person who repeats to him that the state must 'discipline' private initiative is sure of awakening a sympathetic echo in his soul. For what is the state if not Mussolini?" (180b)

When it came to clashes between the party and the governmental bureaucracy, Mussolini's inclination was likewise to favor "the state," but this might mean now the high civil servant, and now the Fascist "spiritual conscience of the state." In any case, it is evident that the Fascist emphasis on the state tended to foster genuine bureaucratization. The symbolic expression of this was the "train on time" of which the Italian Fascists made so much in the early years. Yet, in spite of Mussolini's greater emphasis on the state, it would be a mistake to underestimate the continuous impact of the party bureaucracy on the governmental bureaucracy. Through its control of the associations of civil servants, and through the requirement of party membership for advancement in the governmental bureaucracy, the party wielded a powerful influence, reinforced by a system of spies. In 1932 it succeeded in effectuating a purge of the entire top layer of officialdom in the Ministry of the Interior. It also managed to secure substantial representation on the *Consiglio di Stato* (Council of State), which was not abolished by the Fascists, but continued to adjudicate problems of administrative law involving the conduct of officials. (88.2) The Corporate State which extended the rule of officialdom or bureaucracy to all phases of economic life (see next chapter) meant, therefore, total bureaucratization in the light of Mussolini's conception of the state as the all-engulfing guardian of the national life.

In conclusion, it might be said that whether in the name of the state, of the party, of the nation, or of the proletariat, the totalitarian dictatorship steadily expands the role of bureaucracy. At the same time, however, it must be borne in mind that this feature of totalitarian dictatorship is paralleled by a steady expansion of bureaucracy and bureaucratization in all industrial nations. The trend appears to be connected with the growing size of organizations. What is distinctive in totalitarian dictatorship, apart from the lack of any institutional pattern of responsibility, is the sharp dualism of governmental and party bureaucracy. Hence, this expansion creates serious problems of conflicting bureaucratic cadres fighting among themselves for supremacy and thereby de-bureaucratizing the governmental service in those countries where this service had already achieved a high degree of bureaucratization. The extension in size is bought at the price of a deterioration in quality, at least temporarily. What all this implies for the economic life of the country is the problem to which we must next turn.

Chapter Eighteen

Plans and Planning

A totalitarian economy is centrally directed and controlled. In order to execute such central direction and control, there must be a plan. Since the economy has become one gigantic business enterprise, and yet an enterprise that does not get its incentives from the desire to make a profit nor from the consumers' needs and demands as expressed in the price system, its managers must be *told* what measuring rods to apply in determining what should be produced, and consequently how the scarce resources available for production should be distributed between the various branches of productive capacity. The slogan, "Guns rather than butter," is only a crude indication of the vast range of decisions which have to be made. The decisions involved in arriving at such a plan are the most basic decisions which a totalitarian regime has to make. Hence the Five Year Plans of the Soviet Union, the Four Year Plan of Hitler Germany, the Two and Five Year Plans of the Soviet Zone, and so on, are focal points of political interest.

Characteristically, in a totalitarian dictatorship, the leader or leaders at the top, men like Stalin, Hitler, or the Party Presidium, make the basic decision in terms of which the plan is organized. This basic decision was, in the case of the Soviet Union, that of industrializing the country; in the case of Nazi Germany, that of preparing immediately for a war of aggression; in the case of China, again industrialization, but combined with "land reform" (see Chapter 21); and in the case of the Soviet Zone of Germany that of providing the large-scale reparations the Soviet Union demanded.

Such a basic decision provides the starting point for a system of priorities which can be utilized in making allocations of raw materials to the different sectors of the producing economy.

It is the absence of such a basic decision and indeed the impossibility of securing it that has led many to conclude that constitutional democracy is incompatible with planning, or, to put it in another way, that any attempt to enter upon planning constitutes in effect a "road to serfdom." (55f; 74) This is true, if planning is understood in a total sense, and it is often so defined, especially by economists. Actually, the planning process in a democracy is very different, and contingent upon the democratic process as a whole, whose outstanding characteristic is the continuous review of all decisions, including basic ones, by the people and its representatives. (55g) In autocratic systems, and more especially in totalitarian dictatorships, the end or purpose of the plan is determined by the autocratic leader or ruler(s) and implements their basic decision. It is carried forward by a bureaucracy which has the full backing of the terrorist and propagandist apparatus of the totalitarian dictatorship. Consequently, little if anything can be learned from the planning procedures of totalitarian societies in molding the planning process in democratic societies. But an understanding of the process is essential for an understanding of totalitarian dictatorship. The great advantage which a fixed goal or purpose possesses from a technical standpoint is counterbalanced by the disadvantage of not having the planning respond to the reactions of those affected by it. Which is the greater disadvantage only experience can tell.

A comparison of the planning experience in totalitarian dictatorship brings to light some very striking contrasts, as well as similarities. In the Soviet Union, a number of years passed before the central importance of planning was fully realized. Before the revolution, Russia was far behind Western Europe in its industrial development. Marx and Engels had not been greatly concerned with this problem. They had stressed control of the economy, rather than industrialization and the increase in production, because they had assumed that the communist revolution would occur in societies which had reached a high stage of industrialization; indeed it was to be the culminating point of capitalist development when the means of production would, through trusts and vast monopolies, have become concentrated in "fewer and fewer hands," so that this shrinking group of exploiters would be confronted by an ever larger proletariat. All that the proletariat would have to do, consequently, would be to take over and run this gigantic productive apparatus. But in Russia, over 80 per cent of the population lived on farms at the time of the revolution, and a similar situation prevails in China today. This fact was so completely at variance with Marxist anticipation that novel approaches had to be developed.

This question preoccupied the Bolsheviks throughout the twenties and gave the post-Lenin struggles for power a marked theoretical flavor. A number of solutions was advocated, ranging from left-wing emphasis on immediate efforts to increase industrial output, even at high cost and considerable coercion (expounded most clearly by Preobrazhensky), to right-wing advocacy of adjustment to a temporary, transitional capitalist stage (as, for instance, voiced by Bukharin). The ensuing policy, based more on the requirements of the situation than ideological dogma, was one of compromise and postponement of the radical solution.

Planning, accordingly, developed slowly and modestly. On February 22, 1921, a State Planning Commission (*Gosplan*) was set up. It was charged with the task of working out an over-all state economic plan and preparing the technical and managerial staffs and know-how necessary to its success. (269a) In fact, however, Gosplan's immediate tasks were more restricted and concentrated on developing the state plan for the electrification of Russia (*Goepro*), which had been prepared some time earlier and was to serve as the basis for further centralized planning. In addition, Gosplan assumed control over some sectors of the economy which were subject to crises and vital to economic survival, like the railroads. Thus despite the very broad grant of planning and controlling power, Gosplan, during the NEP period, did not vitally influence the Russian economy. It concerned itself rather with collecting statistics, studying existing economic trends, and laying the groundwork for an over-all plan.*

The big impetus to centralized state planning came with the political decision to launch a large-scale industrialization and agricultural collectivization program. The era of the Five Year Plans began in 1928. Since then Soviet economic life has been revolving

---

* The first comprehensive plan, but not implemented by the government, appeared in 1925 as *Control Figures of National Economy for 1925–1926.*

around these broad, comprehensive schemes, developed in keeping with the policy-decisions of the leadership by planners of the Gosplan. Indeed, the inauguration of the First Five Year Plan can be described as the beginning of the real totalitarian revolution in Russia. Stalin's program, borrowed in many respects from the left-wing opposition, inevitably encountered resistance from the established peasantry and other groups. As resistance mounted, so did coercion. Society being a complex and overlapping cluster of interests, the totalitarian revolution inevitably embraced almost the entire society. The launching of the Plan, however, despite certain initial failures (camouflaged by scapegoat trials of engineers), fired to a great extent the imagination of the more youthful members of the party and raised the sagging morale of the whole party. Its initial results, therefore, were not unimportant politically.

The Gosplanners were now in their element. The coercive pow-- ers of the government and party were put at their disposal and the process of rapid industrial development, concomitant with the collectivization of agriculture, was pushed ahead at full speed. (For further treatment see Chapter 21.) The planning apparatus expanded accordingly. By 1938 it grew to a central staff of 1,000 planners organized in 54 departments of the Gosplan. (9) In addition, planning officials are to be found on subordinate levels, from the republics down to the regions, and even districts and towns. The plans that they prepare thus include not only the over-all Five Year Plan, but also economic plans for all levels of Soviet society, from that of the RSFSR to even a small plant in Yakutsk. The Gosplan, known since 1948 as the State Planning Committee, is organized into departments dealing with regional planning, and finally into departments charged with integrating the work of the two preceding types of planning departments. Gosplan committees are also attached to regional Executive Committees, which in turn supervise the work of the district and town-city planning committees. Gosplan, in addition to planning that is worked out through lengthy processes of estimating and struggling with subordinate organs, determined to avoid excessive quotas.

Gosplan is concerned also with the problem of allocating resources. This is an important matter, since Soviet managers operate constantly in a situation of scarcity, and adequate allocation is the prerequisite to plan achievement, and resulting bonuses. Indeed, one of the primary reasons for evasion is to be found in the unending competition between managers for scarce materials. In 1948 an effort was made to divest the Gosplan of the allocating function and to assign it to a separate body (*Gossnab*). Apparently, the experiment was not successful and in 1953 the Gosplan again took over the allocation function.

Supervision of the execution of the plan is becoming an increasingly important aspect of Gosplan work. This supervision essentially involves the twin tasks of detection of failures and evasions, and the check-up on the general development of the plan and analysis of the portents. A great deal has recently been said in the USSR on the urgent need to uncover the growing number of managers and officials who, having learned the game, have become skillful in keeping their quotas down by underestimating the capacity of their plants and, on the other hand, lowering quality for the sake of achieving quantity. (471) However, equally important, if not more so, is the necessary task of keeping in touch with the development of the plan in order to be able to make necessary adjustments. Soviet leaders were at first unwilling or unable to perceive the necessity of elasticity, and many of the failures of the earlier periods can be ascribed to a rigid insistence on plan fulfillment. The 1955 measures to give lower echelons a greater say in planning and the efforts to make a meaningful distinction between long-range and short-range planning are probably a further step in the direction of increasing the economic value of centralized state planning.* But it still remains essentially totalitarian in character and coercive in method, particularly in view of the current agricultural-industrial campaigns. (252c)

Principles of Soviet economic planning have also been imposed on the captive nations of central Europe. With Soviet experience serving as the beacon, the satellite communist parties did not go through the preliminary stage of controversy which the fight between Preobrazhensky and Bukharin highlighted, but as soon as the consolidation of power was completed they proceeded to launch economic planning on the Soviet model. In Poland, for instance,

* In June 1955, on the basis of the former USSR State Planning Committee the Council of Ministers' State Commission for Long-Range Planning (the Five Year Plans) and the Council of Ministers' State Economic Commission for Current Planning (annual) of the National Economy were formed.

the State Commission for Economic Planning (PKPG) operates as a superministry which supervises and co-ordinates the economic life of the country, with the right to issue directives to individual ministries. It has also been charged with nationalization of private enterprises, an important task in a country only recently taken over by the communists. The PKPG is also in charge of the Main Statistical Administration, the Central Administration of Professional Training, the Patent Office, and the Main Administration of Measures. (248; 261) Polish planning, on Soviet insistence, has been co-ordinated in recent years with that of Czechoslovakia and Hungary, and industrial development in these countries is to result in complementary and mutually dependent economies. In particular, the development of the Silesian basin in terms of electric energy and coal output has been made subject to close Polish-Czech cooperation. Also, as a reaction to the Marshall Plan, a so-called Molotov Plan resulted in the setting-up of a co-ordinating committee of the heads of the planning boards of all the satellite regimes and of the USSR for the purpose of working out joint plans. That such plans are not devoid of political significance is seen, for instance, in the development of a new industrial town in Poland, Nowa Huta, constructed next to the old and highly conservative city of Cracow, to a great extent according to Soviet plans.

The Communist Party of China faced, upon seizure of power, an economic situation less favorable than that of the USSR in 1928 or of any of the satellites in 1946–1949. However, after the totalitarian control of the regime was firmly established, a decision rapidly to industrialize soon followed and a somewhat vague Five Year Plan was announced in 1953. Apparently a series of regional plans are gradually being evolved into an over-all national plan, which, according to present indications, will aim at rapid industrialization at all cost. That there might have been some opposition within the party to such a drastic collectivist solution is indicated by the virulence of Liu Shao-chao's attack, in February 1954, on party factionalism. (173a) Unlike the situation in the USSR in the twenties, however, no open voice has been heard in China urging a go-slow policy, while in the words of Hsiueh Mu-Chiao, a member of the Chinese State Planning Committee, the party must "suppress all intrigues of imperialists and class enemies within the country. Only in this way can we successfully accomplish the task of socialist industrialization in China." (271i)   All indications point, therefore, at least at present, to a "Stalinist" line of development.

The situation was very different in Nazi Germany. In keeping with what we have already said, Franz Neumann wrote: "National Socialism has coordinated the diversified and contradictory state interferences into one system having but one aim: the preparation of imperialist war." (148c)   The documentary evidence which has come to light since 1945 amply supports this statement. For after his protestations during the early days of his regime, Hitler soon made it clear that he proposed a policy of preparation for large-scale war. Alan Bullock has shown how very definitely Hitler planned the war which by 1937 he considered "inevitable." (22c) The entire Four Year Plan, so-called, initiated in 1936, was geared to this objective. In a council of ministers, Hermann Goering, whom Hitler had put in charge of the plan, declared in 1938 that the plans and planning "start from the basic thought that the showdown with Russia is inevitable . . . all measures have to be taken just as if we were actually in a state of imminent danger of war." (22d)

It was essentially a matter of shifting production to war needs, and doing this not by throttling the consumption and standard of living of the masses, but by increasing production. At the same time, the memory of the blockade of 1916–1918 was still vivid enough to make it seem desirable to have Germany become as independent as possible from outside supply sources. This objective was highlighted in the slogan of "autarchy," which in turn was reinforced by the notion of "living space." This living space, related as it was to aggressive designs against Germany's eastern neighbors, was to round out the Greater German Reich into a self-supporting and independent polity. The course of the war showed, of course, that this objective was not only not obtained, but was indeed unattainable. The preparation for war under the Four Year Plan was quite inadequate (22e; 90), and after a transitional period, Hitler, in 1942, made Albert Speer the key planner, but it was too late for "planning." All in all, one is obliged to conclude that, due to the incompetence of Goering and to Hitler's lack of understanding of economic problems, the planning of the Nazi dictatorship never became effective. But to argue that for this reason the Hitler regime was not a totalitarian dictatorship (146; 59f) is going too far;

the measures it took in subordinating business and labor to the Führer's war policy were decidedly totalitarian and the failure of the central plan was a result of lack of time. It is well-known that the Five Year Plans of the Soviet Union also involved great failures at the outset.

It is interesting to see how planning has developed in the Soviet Zone of Germany since the war. We find here, in contrast to the Hitler regime, a plan originally directed toward a predominantly economic objective—securing reparations for the Soviet Union. Of course, in a way the entire enterprise of the military occupation of Germany was one gigantic "plan," a plan for the demilitarization, de-industrialization, and democratization of Germany. (72) But this "plan" remained in a very primitive state, as far as the effective planning procedures were concerned, and it soon broke apart as the policies of the Allies began to diverge and eventually it was made obsolete by the re-emergence of the Federal Republic of Germany as a self-directing polity. Here the liberal, free-enterprise policy of the Adenauer-Erhard line developed a sharp hostility toward all forms of planning, except for the purpose of freeing the economy from wartime and postwar restraints.

In the Soviet Zone of Occupation, the development has taken the opposite course. Here the entire economy is subject to planning. As mentioned, the centrally controlling Planning Commission is directly co-ordinated by the Gosplan and its successors in Moscow, or at least that was true until 1955. But whether or not one accepts this interpretation of Soviet Zone realities, it is clear that the State's Planning Commission is directly under the Presidium of the Council of Ministers and in a position to give orders to all ministries and other administrative organs of the government. (223) Actually not only the Planning Commission itself, but the Presidium of the Council of Ministers and the so-called Coordination and Control Offices directly attached to it are involved in the planning process. On the whole, this process follows Soviet precedents and practice. The orders, ordinances, and regulations of the Commission have, after approval by the respective Coordination and Control office, the "force of law." Failure to obey these orders constitutes an "economic crime" punished by such very high penalties as long prison sentences. The Control Office has a right to demand arrests and therefore works closely with the Security Office (Secret Police).

In connection with this control, statistics become an instrument, as they are based upon an elaborate system of reporting all up and down the line. But the work proper of the Planning Commission, like that of the Gosplan, is surrounded by secrecy; only top-level personnel have access to its findings; the statistical information furnished, usually in terms of percentages, is misleading, to say the least, since the basis of comparison is continually shifted. The middle and upper personnel is entirely composed of members of the SED and systematically trained along party and ideological lines. It runs into many hundreds, a large part of them very young men and women who have been specially indoctrinated and who are better paid than personnel in industry.

In summary, then, we may observe that totalitarian planning is formulated on the basis of ideologically determined goals; that their scope, in the final analysis, is total; and that effective time limits are absent, the usual four- or five-year periods being mere accounting devices. Totalitarian planning is a necessary concomitant of the total revolution that these regimes set in motion—without it they would easily degenerate into anarchy—and it is this *political* quality that sets it apart from democratic economic planning.

Chapter Nineteen

Battle for Production and Industrial Expansion

Within the context of a total bureaucracy and of total plans, the battle for production must be seen as the decisive test of the totalitarian economy. If the plans call for conquest and war, the pre-existing system of production for peacetime consumption must be revamped to provide the essential transformation. If the plans call for industrialization, controls must be set up and maintained for forcing a substantial part of the social product into capital goods, even when the standard of living and level of consumption of the people is quite low. In either case, we have what has been aptly called, by Germans, a "command economy." In the case of the Soviet Union and its satellites, this command economy consists of a vast combine of state enterprises, competing with each other to some extent, but devoid of the profit motive as known in other economies. In fascist countries, and more especially in Nazi Germany, the economy was on the industrial side largely cartellized and subject to much monopolistic or oligopolistic control.* The achievements of the command economy under either of these arrangements have been impressive, as far as the realization of the announced goal is concerned. The failure to satisfy consumer needs and demands cannot, strictly speaking, be held against these systems, since they did not operate with the purpose of satisfying the consumer.

SOVIET INDUSTRIAL DEVELOPMENT SINCE 1927–28

	1927–28	1932	1937	1941
1. Coal (1,000 m.t.)	35,510	64,664	127,000	171,160
2. Electric power output (mil. kwh.)	5,007	13,540	36,400	53,957
3. Steel (ingots & castings) (1,000 m.t.)	4,250	5,927	17,729	22,400
4. Aluminum (m.t.)	0	855	46,800	———
5. Crude oil extracted (excl. natural gas) (1,000 m.t.)	11,472	21,413	28,501	34,602
6. Passenger cars & ½-ton trucks	580	7,511	137,016	131,000

Industrial progress in the Soviet Union since 1927–28, the date of the First Five Year Plan, may be indicated by the accompanying table. (87) The war resulted in a considerable retardation of Soviet industrial development. Destruction was particularly heavy in the industrial areas occupied by the Germans and hence sub-

* Oligopoly is the technical term modern economics has developed to indicate a situation where a *few* control the market, as contrasted with strict monopoly, where one does, but in popular parlance any such excessive control is called monopolistic.

jected, first, to Soviet scorched-earth policies and then to German looting and destruction prior to evacuation. The Stalinist regime made rapid industrial recovery its priority goal and, despite its many sacrifices and sufferings, the Soviet population was called upon to devote all its energy to new industrial drives. The second table of figures, covering the same items as the first table, testify eloquently to the scale of these efforts and to their undeniable impressiveness.

Item	1945	1951	1953	1955
1.	148,000	282,000	320,000	390,000
2.	44,900	102,900	133,000	166,000
3.	12,200	31,400	38,300	45,000
4.	——	——	——	——
5.	19,500	42,300	52,000	70,000
6.	83,000	364,000 (in 1950)	——	445,000

(241b; 271j; 245b) Thus, in six years of admittedly intensive efforts, Soviet production, in terms of the items cited, not only made up for the war losses, but in some cases even doubled the top output of 1941.

Since then Soviet industrial expansion has continued unabated, despite the temporary consideration given in 1953 to the increase in output of consumer goods. (271k) In the January 1955 session of the Central Committee of the CPSU such views were characterized as "anti-Party slander," and the Central Committee journal, *Partiinaia zhizn'*, attacked the economists sponsoring them for "anti-Leninist right-wing opportunism." (265e) Both charges rank high in the Soviet lexicon of deviations. Industrial expansion, therefore, remains the dominant goal of the Soviet system. Indeed, it has been the unique quality of the communist dictatorships, sprouted as they have done in backward areas, to stress rapid industrialization as the vital economic and political objective of their regimes.

Soviet industrial achievements, as seen above, are in fact imposing. From an industrially backward country the Soviet Union has, through unprecedented sacrifice and terror, pushed itself to the forefront of the world's industrial powers. It did so by sacrificing the human element and the freedom to which it allegedly aspired. It did so also without foreign capital and, after the mid-thirties, with relatively little outside technical assistance. Soviet capital investment has been largely supported by the national budget (the average ranging from about two-thirds to three-fourths of the funds for capital construction), and the standard of living has suffered accordingly.

The turnover tax (*nalog s oboroty*) has been the most important source of revenue, accounting on the average for somewhat more than half of the budget receipts in the USSR. The turnover tax is borne by the consumer, as each commodity price has an unspecified turnover tax included in it. This tax is particularly high on consumer goods, in some items accounting for 75 per cent or more of the actual sale price. The second, but much less important, source is the profits tax (*podokhodny nalog*) levied on those enterprises which actually make a profit in excess of their quotas.

Soviet industrial output is still lagging behind that of the United States, but the swift increases in the volume of production and the general emphasis of the regime on technocratic achievement are accompanied by a vast and intensive training program for young engineering talent. From a meager 26 higher educational establishments offering engineering training in 1928, Soviet training facilities have expanded by 1955 to 175 with some 300,000 students, as compared to the former 52,000. (The United States has about 194,000 students taking engineering in 210 colleges.) Between the years of 1928 and 1955 the Soviet Union produced 630,000 engineers of all types, or the equivalent of 25 per cent of graduates of its higher institutions. (While the number of United States graduates was twice as high, the number of engineers was only 480,000 or 9 per cent of the total.) (242) Such figures indicate a tremendous capacity for further industrial expansion.

Soviet industrial expansion, as suggested before, has important political and social consequences also. It gives a semblance of truth to the Marxist prophecy that a communist society arises out of the proletariat. It destroys existing traditional bonds, creates a situation of great social fluctuation, and results in population shifts and weakening of national lines. Thus an important aspect of Soviet industrial development has been the conscious attempt, motivated partially by geopolitical factors, to shift the industrial concentration from the regions of the Donbas and Moscow to other areas, relatively untouched by industrialization. A close observer of Soviet economic developments has summed up the situation thus:

the Russians in their current plans are still pursuing a policy of differential economic development, strongly favoring the central regions (Central Russia, Ukraine, Volga and Urals). Within this industrial heartland, hydroelectric power and water transportation would reduce the need for close conjunction between industry and mining. The decision to emphasize the central regions is clearly based on political and strategic considerations, rather than purely economic; for both the western regions of European Russia and Soviet Asia afford major opportunities for industrial growth. (251)

The thousands of novice workers who come to the newly constructed factories, torn from their traditional environment and thrown into the mass barracks of the new construction sites, find themselves in an environment of strict discipline and centralization of command. It need not be pointed out that all the factories are state-owned, and that the managers who run them are state officials, subordinate to the ministry controlling this particular branch of industry. With the expansion of the Soviet industrial machine there has come a great proliferation of such ministries; as early as 1940 there were the following People's Commissariats dealing with industry: Heavy Industry, Oil Industry, Coal Industry, Power Stations, Electrical Engineering, Ship-building, Heavy Metallurgy, Nonferrous Metallurgy, Chemical Industry, Building Materials, Heavy Engineering, Medium Engineering, General Engineering, Defense Industry, Aviation, Armaments, Munitions, Food Industry, Meat and Dairy Industries, Fisheries, Light Industry, Textiles, Timber Industry, Cellulose and Paper Industries. In 1953 a drastic reorganization cut down the number of economic ministries, but by 1955 the number had again grown to about thirty. Under the Ministry there is the so-called *Glavk,* or Main Administration, either of a territorial type (administrating enterprises in a given region) or of an industrial type (administering specific types of industrial enterprises). Furthermore, in some cases the Glavk administers trusts or combines which are an intermediary stage between the factories and the Glavks. This is particularly true of fields where smaller, more numerous enterprises prevail. In some cases involving particularly important and large factories, on the other hand, both the trust and the Glavk levels are skipped, and such factories are directly subordinate to the responsible ministry.

The factory itself is run by the state-appointed director. The director is responsible to the head of the level directly above him, i.e., a trust director to a Glavk director to the minister. The various shop heads and foremen are subordinated in turn to the factory director. The principle of *edinachalstvo* is thus firmly followed, and the factory director is fully responsible for his factory. This, in cases of accident, failure to achieve quotas, or technical inefficiency, can have rather unpleasant consequences for a director who is then held responsible. Indeed, the practice has been to consider serious accidents as evidence of failure and/or sabotage and cases of directors being tried have been frequent, particularly during the purge periods. In recent years, there has been a tendency toward less stringent punishments (financial penalties, restitution of damage, demotion), but the director still remains liable whenever anything unforeseen happens.

The director, however, is not only driven forward by fear. Productive success has very tangible attractions for him, as he is given a sizable share in the profits that follow from an overfulfillment of quotas. Large bonuses are given to those directors who have been "successful," and interviews with former Soviet managers indicate that they attach the greatest importance to such premiums, as "the difference between 99 per cent of plan fulfillment and 100 per cent means a difference of up to 30 per cent in income." (273b) The workers too share in these premiums, but the percentage is considerably scaled down on their level. Such incentives, however, result in a phenomenon known as the *shturmovshchina*—a last-minute attempt at breakneck speed to meet the quota and share in the dividend. In the words of the annual report of the Soviet industry,

One of the chief shortcomings in industry was that, as a result of unsatisfactory management, many industrial enterprises were not working rhythmically. They were turning out much of their production at the end of the month and permitting a fall-off in activity at the beginning of the following month. The absence of a rhythmic work schedule led to workers and machinery being idle at certain times, to an increase in personnel beyond the planned number of employees, non-productive expense on overtime work, overexpenditure of the wage fund, a higher percentage of scrapped production and an increase in cost of goods. (271l)

The temptation to share in the premiums has led some directors, whose plants failed to meet their quotas, to falsify results, or even to bribe state control officials. A number of incidents of this type have appeared in the Soviet press and have been confirmed by interviews with former Soviet officials. (252d)

In his efforts to maximize production the factory director is assisted by the factory party organization, by the secret police Special Section, and by the local trade union (see Chapter 20). The party organization, encompassing all the party workers in the factory, holds regular meetings at which production levels are discussed, encourages self-critique on the part of the workers and the administration, attacks laggards, watches the political morale of the personnel, and finally supervises the director himself. The Special Section makes certain that sabotage is prevented, that disloyal elements are ferreted out and that enemies of the people are exposed. It organizes regular networks of informers both among the workers and the managerial staffs. Occasionally it may serve as a stimulant to increased efforts by arresting known slackers or those expressing antiparty opinions. The factory, in a sense, is thus a small-scale replica of the pattern of controls and of the hierarchy of decision-making characteristic of the Soviet Union in general.

The imposition of communist power in central Europe and in China has resulted in similarly drastic efforts to push industrial expansion. This was as true of the relatively advanced economies of Czechoslovakia and Poland as of Bulgaria or Jugoslavia (in 1946). It was only as a result of the marked failures of such programs in the more backward states of central Europe that the Soviets decided in 1947–48 to encourage a slower industrial development in such places as Bulgaria and Jugoslavia (which was one of the reasons for the Tito-Cominform tension, since Tito was quite anxious to industrialize rapidly), and a closer cooperation of these states with the more advanced areas in the Soviet bloc. Industrialization, however, has been pushed very forcefully in Poland, where the natural wealth of the Silesian basin makes it an ideal site for the creation of a second Ruhr. Steel production and coal output have tripled over the prewar figures and a steady expansion is evident from day to day. Similarly, the Chinese decision to industrialize this extremely backward country has as its goal, in a broad sense, to reach by 1957 the level of production attained by the Soviet Union in 1928, that is, at the beginning of the First Soviet Five Year Plan. (290)

As far as the Fascist and Nazi systems are concerned, the record is somewhat less easy to analyze. For one thing, in Germany the foreign trade, essential to the well-being of this overpopulated country, rapidly declined. In 1933 exports still exceeded imports by almost 700 million marks, but by 1935 the surplus had shrunk to 100 million marks, and this trend continued. The situation was to some extent the natural consequence of the National Socialist government's policy of self-sufficiency or "autarchy," for it meant that the country's economic resources, limited as they were, had to be organized in such a way as to render the country as independent of foreign supplies as possible. Since the ulterior goal was readiness for war, this policy was carried out irrespective of the intrinsic viability of the activities when measured by standards derived from the world market. Mining operations for low grade ore were extended, and oil borings carried through. The synthetic production of such materials as rubber and fibres was vigorously pursued. As a result, a good deal of additional work was provided for Germans who were now producing these goods, instead of importing them from abroad. Of course, self-sufficiency, or autarchy, was never fully achieved while the Nazis were in power, but it increased considerably. Hitler once admitted Germany's limitations: "We know that the geographical situation of Germany, a country poor in raw materials, does not permit of autarchy. It must be emphasized again and again that the government is anything but hostile towards exports." (41) Nonetheless, the policy was pushed as hard as circumstances would permit in order to make Germany ready for war, when imports might be cut off. *Wehrwirtschaft,* or an economy for defense, was the euphemistic expression employed to describe this military economy which was based on the subordination of commercial motives to national military needs. (See Chapter 18.)

In the light of the objective, it is extraordinary how little Germany was prepared for the world war in which Hitler's policies were eventually to plunge the country. The only explanation is that the Nazis, in view of Hitler's conception of a lightning war (*Blitzkrieg*), did not expect the war to last very long nor, even less, to turn into a *world* war.

As an illustration of what this search for war materials, combined with the policy of self-sufficiency, meant, one might cite the

Hermann Goering Werke—plants intended to exploit low-grade iron ores found in central Germany and not economical in the usual sense. These works were part of a rapidly increasing business activity of the party and its agencies. Publishing, printing, and real estate had, of course, been important party activities even in the days of the Weimar Republic, but to these were added in the thirties a considerable number of other fields. Among these, the Goering Works, or more fully the *Reichswerke, A.G. für Erzbergbau und Eisenhütten, Hermann Göring,* with a capital of 75 million marks, was the most important. From the original mining and steel-making, it soon branched out in many other directions. It has been called a gangster organization "to steal and rob" as many other businesses as possible, especially in conquered and occupied territories, such as Austria and Czechoslovakia. (148e) Originally the capital for this enterprise was gathered by Goering using every means at the disposal of a totalitarian dictator, especially intimidation. Since the venture had no capitalist appeal and hence could not command credit, Goering intimidated bankers and industrialists into contributing their share (155 million out of 400 million in 1939). This brings us to one of the key aspects of the Nazi economy.

The substitution of fear for convenience fundamentally alters the nature of the economy. It ceases to be "capitalist." *Credit* derives from the Latin word *credo* or "I believe you"; since here we find substituted "I fear you," such a system might well be called a *timet* system. (165a) Such a *timet* system did, in fact, constitute the basis of government finance under the Nazis. Not only industrial enterprise, but the whole field of public borrowing, came to depend upon the intimidation of the public. The consequent vast increase in Germany's public debt, eventually reaching nearly 500 billion marks (100 billion dollars), was the consequence. It raised, of course, a serious question of how to go on. One ingenious professor, presumably with tongue-in-cheek, suggested just before the war that this was Hitler's great invention in the field of public finance, and offered an opportunity to every German to help the Führer achieve the goals which his genius sought to realize. (208) The question of ultimate limits to such a system of forced borrowing he answered by saying that at some point there must be made a "creative sacrifice." This sacrifice would consist of every loyal German accepting the cancellation of the Reich's indebtedness, so as to free the Führer's hands for further ventures. This was a neat, sycophantic way of describing state bankruptcy, but it turned out that the sacrifice was quite uncreative and resulted from the collapse and liquidation of the Hitler regime. But while the system lasted, it gave the government a good deal of capital which it might not otherwise have been able to secure. In a sense, the fiscal operation of a totalitarian economy may thus be compared to that of a constitutional system at war, when large-scale financing of the government is carried out on the basis of patriotic appeals, backed by a good deal of pressure from various sources.

Under this *timet* system there was, obviously, no natural limit to an increase in the government's indebtedness, and the result was a steadily mounting debt. It rose on an ascending scale as shown by the following figures (in rounded billion marks): 1932, 11; 1933, 12; 1936, 15; 1938, 20; 1939, 30. (202) It was the application of this *timet* system to foreign trade negotiations that really constituted the essence of Hjalmar Schacht's dealing with the smaller countries, especially in the Balkans. Here, too, threats were employed to extract goods and loans in connection with their delivery which could not have been secured on the basis of free bargaining. (148d) The threats were primarily in the field of foreign trade itself, such as stopping all imports from a particular country, but at times they went a good deal further. "The aim of Germany's trade policy thus became exceedingly simple: to buy from a country as much as you can . . . but without paying," Franz Neumann very aptly wrote. Thus Germany became more and more of a debtor nation under a clearing system which concentrated all control over foreign trade balances in the hands of the government. (138)

Franz Neumann makes this point as part of his detailed analysis of the Nazi economy. His central concern is to show that this economy was neither socialist nor state capitalist. To be sure, the law gave the government "unlimited power"; it could do almost anything and could expropriate anybody, but this law, he thought, in fact hid the reality, and the economy remained "capitalist." Not only does he minimize the role of planning, but he sees the economy as compounded of two parts which he calls the "monopolistic economy" and the "command economy." The first part is characterized by a vast increase in cartels and monopolies which, aided and abetted by the government and the party, maximized profits. "The motivating power of expansion is profit. The structure of the German economy is one of a fully monopolized and cartellized economy" in which the small businessman and the worker are at the mercy of the big tycoons. (118) The second part, the command economy, is that section where the interfering and regimenting "state" is at work. Neumann, after examining the several aspects of this part of the economy which might "decisively change the picture" comes to the conclusion that it is not changed. Neither the direct economic activities of the state, in the nationalized sector, and of the party, nor the control of prices, of investments and profits, of foreign trade, and of labor constitute "state capitalism," and he argues that this is so "in spite of the fundamental changes that are the inevitable consequence of regimentation." Words like "state capitalism," constituting a type of economy that Neumann did not actually define clearly, may be useful for political propaganda, but obscure the scientific insight. If a more clearly defined criterion is used, a better understanding may result. We said in Chapter I, page 10, that, characteristically, a totalitarian dictatorship possesses "the central control and direction of the entire economy through the bureaucratic co-ordination of its formerly independent corporate entities, including typically most other associations and group activities." Such central control and direction was indeed characteristic of the Nazi regime. It is not only not disproved by the fact that key figures in the Nazi control setup were at the same time businessmen, but it is this fact that clinches the argument. Neumann describes in detail how the key posts in many directorates of banks and industrial combines were occupied by men who at the same time were powerful figures in the Nazi hierarchy; he means to argue that such participation of businessmen proves that the "state" was not in full control. His thought is evidently the result of a traditional German notion that the "state" is, or at any rate ought to be, something apart from, if not over and above, mere business. In the Hegelian-Marxist tradition he presumes that an intermeshing of the two precludes both "state capitalism" and "socialism"; this, as we said, is a matter of definitions. It does not preclude the central direction and control of the entire economy, but in fact aids it considerably. Neumann's own analysis suggests it and the vast amount of additional evidence brought to light since by the United States Bombing Surveys and the Nuremberg trials proves it. (60)

European countries have traditionally let certain sectors of the economy be operated by the government. Democratic Switzerland no less than autocratic Prussia runs its railroads, telephone, and telegraph services as government monopolies. This policy of letting the government participate in the economy, especially where natural monopolies present the problem of effective control in the public interest, has been greatly expanded since the war. In Britain, France, and other countries, banking, mining, and other basic economic activities have been placed under government control. These economies are, therefore, neither capitalist nor socialist in any strict sense, though they are obviously less socialist than the Soviet Union. The term "mixed economies" has been suggested for them. The fascist regimes, in a sense, also operated such mixed economies. But under such regimes no part of the economy is free from government interference. The central direction and control is concentrated in the hands of the party and its ruler-dictator, and no popularly elected parliament or other representative body is there to interpose its views between the government and the economy. The government is consequently not subject to extended criticism and the rival proposals of alternating party majorities. This does not by any means preclude the influence of businessmen who are members of the party and its ruling groups; quite the contrary. In the case of the Hitler regime, such businessmen were able to manipulate the corporate system, with its cartels and monopolistic trusts, as well as the control of prices, of investments, profits, and foreign trade, to their personal advantage on a large scale. The careers of men like Frick, who was brought to trial at Nuremberg, show how extensive were the possibilities for personal enrichment along these lines. (90b) But such personal careers are incidental to the over-all pattern; they correspond to the careers of skilled managers in the Soviet Union —men like Saburov or Malyshev, or the fallen-from-grace Voznesensky. The over-all pattern is one of central control and direction; it came to full fruition in Hitler Germany only during the war, when Albert Speer was invested with dictatorial powers of direction (see Chapter 18).

The focus of this central direction and control went through three different stages. They were the stage of work-creation programs; the stage of preparation for war under the Four Year Plan; and the attempt at total mobilization during the war. In each of these stages, various decisions were taken which constituted interventions in the operations of a free market economy, and deflected economic development into the channels desired by the totalitarian rulers. It is true that some nontotalitarian countries have, within the context of constitutional democracy, attempted similar central direction—subject to extended public criticism and, therefore, party competition and rivalry leading to substantial alterations and even abandonment—but this does not alter the fact that interference by central control, combined with the other typical features which have been discussed, is characteristic of totalitarian dictatorship, and would not be possible in a free market economy. Such central direction and control operates differently (but not necessarily better!), when accompanied by ideological and one-party leadership, by secret police terror, and by government monopoly of mass communications and weapons. For the inherent potentialities of corruption which such a system entails by its large-scale bureaucratization are greatly enhanced by these totalitarian features. The detailed record now available shows that this potential corruption was in fact at work in both the Nazi and Italian fascist systems. Therefore such data as the increase in undistributed profits, in consequent share values and in dividends (on the basis of statistical averages), which Neumann marshals in support of his contention that the nazi economy was a "capitalist" economy, do not in fact support the contention, but show rather that it was a "vampire" economy, rapidly getting bogged down in a morass of special favors, such as are the very opposite of the workings of the price mechanism of the open and competitive market economy. (165b)

The situation in Fascist Italy under the corporative system is particularly revealing. The essential effect of this system was to put all of Italian industry into one big pool, make the pool, that is, the government, assume responsibility for a minimum profit, and concede it in return the power to direct all investment and hence the future development of industry. (180c) That such an arrangement, based as it is upon guaranteed profits, does not constitute a competitive market economy is evident. The stress on profits, as can be seen, is altogether misleading.

In conclusion, it is readily conceded that the differences between the fascist-nazi type of industrial arrangement and the communist one are many and obvious. In one case the totalitarian system is superimposed on an established industrial structure, in the other the industrial structure is built almost from scratch. In the fascist and nazi economies the ownership of the means of production is formally left intact and the same "tycoons" continue to preside at board meetings (with the exception of government-sponsored enterprises such as the Goering works), while in the communist economies industry is state-owned and the managers are state-appointed officials. (Or, as in some earlier cases, former owners are temporarily kept as state managers.) But these, and some others, do not appear to be really fundamental differences. One needs to go beyond the surface and ask: who controls the industrial development, who sets its quotas and allocates resources, who determines the ultimate objectives of industrial production, who regulates rewards, who controls the personnel, who establishes political standards of loyalty for all those involved?

The answers to these questions suggest that the modern totalitarian regimes are basically alike in recognizing the vitality of the industrial process, and in considering it as the key to political success, domestic or external. As a result they have made the "battle for production" a central theme of their action programs, and to achieve it they have penetrated and subordinated the industrial machine to the requirements of the regime. Such questions as who holds formal title to property, how "profits," that is to say, rewards, are determined, and whether former owners and decision-makers continue to hold positions, provided they conform to the regime's commands are of relatively minor significance. What is decisive is the overpowering reality of totalitarian central control by the dictator and his party.

Chapter Twenty

Labor: Bond or Free

The centrally directed economy, and the bureaucratic co-ordination of all associations and corporate entities that possess a degree of autonomy and self-government under a constitutional democracy, engulf, of course, the organizations of labor. This fact is, in a sense, the most disillusioning aspect of socialism from the viewpoint of the laboring man. Labor has been told and is still being told that socialism as envisaged in Marxism, that is to say, socialism based upon the dictatorship of the proletariat, means the liberation of labor from capitalist oppression and exploitation. What labor finds, however, is that in reality the all-powerful government, which acts on behalf of the proletariat and presumably embodies its "dictatorship," deprives the organizations of labor, the unions, of their former independent status, and transforms them into adjuncts of the governmental bureaucracy. The same thing happens under facism and Nazism; here too the "socialist" dictatorship is prepared to co-ordinate the unions and to synchronize their actions with the policies of the government.

In the last hundred years, trade unions became important organizations in those countries in which industrialism and capitalism developed. Being in effect the successors to the guilds of medieval craftsmanship, they were built upon the common workmanship and the common interest of workers in a particular "trade." The many highly specialized unions of the American Federation of Labor are typical of this early unionism. Later, as industries grew and plants became larger and larger, there also developed more inclusive unions, less concerned with workmanship and more preoccupied with the common interests of all the workers in a particular industry, of which the Congress of Industrial Organizations is typical. The recent merger of the A.F. of L. and the C.I.O. is based upon the recognition that all workers, no matter how organized, have certain common interests and tasks. (55h)

In the earlier period and down to the very end of the nineteenth century employers resented and opposed the free labor unions, and in some countries do to this day. It has become increasingly clear to management in all advanced countries that labor was not only theoretically entitled to form its own free associations, if it chose to do so—that in a constitutional democracy labor had the right to be organized—but that it was actually of great advantage to management in industry to have free unions to deal with. Modern labor relations are based upon the freely negotiated contractual relationship between "capital" and "labor," which collective bargaining has brought into being. The idea of a "company union" organized and dominated by the employer and management has been superseded by the free union, because its paternalistic conception proved inadequate to the task of representing the workers, who were free citizens in a constitutional and democratic society.

Among the most important, and for a long time the most hotly contested weapon of the organized worker, was his right to strike, that is to say, collectively to refuse to continue working, until a bargain had been arrived at between his representatives, typically the officers of his union or unions, and the employer. This right to strike, while not found in the constitutions of eighteenth- and early nineteenth-century vintage, has made its way into more recent constitutional documents, for instance, a number of the American states, France, Italy, and the Federal Republic of Germany. It is also contained in the Universal Declaration of Human Rights issued by the United Nations. No doubt the assent of the Soviet Union and the satellites was secured, because this declaration lacks all enforcement machinery; for no such right is recognized in the USSR.

Strange as it may seem from an ideological viewpoint, the USSR, the country in which the worker is supposed to be in effective control of the government, rejects the right to strike, along with the idea of a free and independent union. The argument advanced for this policy is basically very simple. Why, it is said, should there be a right recognized for one group of workers to force its demand upon the rest of the workers, when all of them together control the means of production? The argument would be unanswerable if the workers' control were effective, from a democratic standpoint, instead of being embodied in the monolithic power of the Communist Party, which monopolizes the representation of all the proletariat, including even the farm workers. As a matter of fact, this problem of workers' participation in the control of industry at first presented itself in the Soviet Union in simple syndicalist form. Soviets were formed in each plant, and the management of the plant entrusted to these councils. But the efforts at building a comprehensive structure from the ground upward soon ran into snags. The position of the unions and the form of their effective participation proved, in the twenties, to be the real touchstone of Soviet organization.

As early as 1920, at the Tenth Party Congress, strong opposition developed among some trade unionists against the markedly centralizing, statist tendencies of the newly established dictatorship of the proletariat. Led by Shliapnikov and Mme. Kollontai, the so-called "Workers' Opposition" came out strongly for an egalitarian utopia run by workers organized into trade unions. At the other extreme, they were opposed by the "statists," led by Trotsky and Bukharin, who urged immediate absorption of the trade unions by the state, on the ground that no conflict was possible between a state of the workers and the workers themselves (a prophetic viewpoint later accepted by the Stalinist regime). Lenin, after briskly attacking the "Workers' Opposition" for engaging in "anarchistic, syndicalist" and non-Marxist agitation, responded with the "transmission-belt" theory, according to which the trade unions are to act as intermediaries between the dictatorship of the proletariat and the working masses:

Trade Unions are the reservoirs of state power, a school of Communism, a school of management. In this sphere the specific and main thing is not administration, but "contacts" between the central state administration, national economy and the broad masses of the toilers. (113g)

Such a defintion obviously changed entirely the nature of the trade union from an institution of workers into an agency of the government. The history of the Soviet trade unions from this moment on is one of steady decline in independence and of their transformation into a bureaucratic institution for dealing with labor problems.

For a while, during the NEP period, the unions remained active on behalf of the working masses, but on the eve of the Sixteenth Party Congress the trade-union leadership was accused of Menshevism and purged. The Congress proclaimed the no-conflict theory previously postulated by Trotsky, and rapid development of industry was declared to be the workers' primary interest. The trade unions were told to help the party increase labor productivity, and the process of trade-union submission to the political requirements of the regime was, broadly speaking, put in final form. At the same time, the newly launched policy of industrialization resulted in a rapid expansion in the number of industrial workers, giving rise to numerous problems of administration, organization, welfare, and so on. From 14.5 million industrial workers in 1930, the total grew by 1940 to 30.4 million and by 1948 to 33.4 million. (220)   It became the function of the trade unions to give these masses an organizational framework and leadership.

In the words of a Soviet student of constitutional law, "The Soviet trade unions are not a formal party organization but, in fact, they are carrying out the directives of the party. All leading organs of the trade unions consist primarily of communists who execute the party line in the entire work of the trade unions." (34) This frank comment thus makes no secret of the fact that the Soviet trade unions are mere agencies of the CPSU. Their organization, like that of the party, is hierarchial and centralized. Real power lies not with the nominally all-powerful Congress, but with a much smaller body, the Presidium of the All-Union Central Council of Trade Unions. All unions are in the end subordinate to this body and subject to its instructions. The tasks of the Soviet trade unions, apart from that of raising productivity and struggling relentlessly "for complete elimination of the rotten practice of equal wages" (103b) include the administration of the state program of social insurance, of sanatoria and workers' rest homes, supervision of food served at work and of factory housing conditions, control of the level of political consciousness, participating in planning, and finally limited grievance intervention on behalf of the workers. Thus, with the exception of the last item, the broad pattern of trade-union functions indicates clearly the extent to which it has become absorbed into the workings of the totalitarian system.

Worker-management grievances are adjudicated by Norms and Conflicts Commissions (RKK). The majority of such cases arise either because of alleged management injustices or as a result of varying interpretations of existing labor regulations. According to Fainsod—

The retention of limited grievance procedure in the Soviet factory is an indication of its usefulness to the party leadership. The well-publicized cases in which workers' complaints lead to corrective action have important propaganda significance. They help to instill faith in the sense of equity of the regime, and they provide a symbolic justification for the sacrifices that the industrialization program imposes. Even though the grievance machinery is greatly restricted in scope, it provides a partial outlet for the frustrations of Soviet factory life. The relief it affords is a positive contribution to the strength and productive efficiency of the regime. (47m)

Since 1947 the trade unions have been empowered to negotiate collective agreements with management, but here again the right is more illusory than real. Such agreements must follow the standard form prescribed by the given industrial ministry, while the broad pattern of wages and salaries is centrally determined and decreed by the Council of Ministers. The so-called collective agreements, therefore, tend to become little more than a repetition of the existing prescriptions for the given industrial branch, to which is added a specific statement, incorporated in the agreement, as to the quotas and production goals to be achieved by the workers and management. The agreement hence becomes a reminder to the workers of what is expected of them rather than a protection of their interests. The Soviet workers are not allowed to forget the fact that the Code of Labor Legislation states explicitly that "when a worker fails to fulfill by his own fault the established norm, his wages are paid according to the quantity and quality of his actual output without a guarantee to him of any minimum wages whatsoever" (art. 57). Unlike his capitalist counterpart, according to Soviet legislation "an employer is not obliged to support the worker." (103c)

The Soviet worker, furthermore, toils under severe restrictions imposed upon him by the state. His eight-hour work day explicitly makes no allowance for time off for meals, hence the actual time spent at work is longer. He works six days a week.* According to Soviet legislation, he is subject to severe penalties for late arrival at work. During the war and until recently, tardiness of even twenty minutes could result in imprisonment.† A Ministry of Labor Reserves, set up in 1947, was given the right to assign workers to priority industries. Workers could be frozen in the jobs and denied the right to quit. Noncompliance in either of the two alternatives could result in prosecution by the state. Since December 1938, Soviet workers have been obliged to carry with them special labor books which include, apart from their personal data, a brief statement of their background, employment record, transfers, and reasons for them. No one can be hired without such a book. Managers, furthermore, retain the labor books during the workers'

---

* In Feb. 1956, plans were announced to reduce the working week.

† There were indications that this policy had been modified since Stalin's death. This was officially confirmed in May 1956; see *Vedomosti Verhovnogo Soveta SSSR*, no. 10, May 1956.

employment, and a worker who quits without authorization is thus deprived of this vital document. In more vital industries the worker is also obliged to hand over his passport—a document which every Soviet citizen must have for *internal* travel and identification.

While at work, the workers are constantly exhorted by their party organizations and by the trade unions to engage in "socialist competition" among themselves, and collectively with the workers of other factories, trusts, or institutions. Special rewards are given to those who excel in overfulfilling their norms, the so-called "shock-workers"; since the thirties the successful shock-workers have been known as Stakhanovites, after Stakhanov, a shock-coalminer. The Stakhanovites receive special medals, and badges, as well as financial rewards. They are entitled to certain privileges, such as free railroad travel, while in some cases their children are entitled to free education. It was estimated that in 1948 some 87 per cent of the labor force in the USSR was engaged in "socialist competition." (283) Labor class solidarity under such circumstances is difficult to maintain.

No account of Soviet labor would be complete without at least a brief reference to the State Labor Reserves mentioned above. The State Labor Reserves give training, under a draft system, to youths over fourteen who are not continuing their studies. After completion of such training they are assigned by the government to specific occupations where they are needed most. Evaders are prosecuted. The system, apart from its important distinction between those who continue higher education, either through scholarship or, until 1956, by paying the fees, and those who do not, gives the government a cheap and steady supply of manpower to be used for urgently needed projects. Furthermore, the system serves to break the youth away from their rustic environment and to transform them into urban proletariat.

In all this the Soviet trade unions tend to play a role similar to that of the government under radical *laissez faire*—the role, that is, of a policeman stepping in only in the case of extreme abuse but not actually and positively striving to help the cause of the working man. The trade unions admittedly render some important services to the labor masses, particularly in terms of health and leisure facilities and in helping out on the lowest levels of labor disputes, although the total regimentation of leisure time is a significant and, in some ways for the average man, perhaps the most obnoxious aspect of totalitarianism. In any case, their over-all function is entirely oriented in terms of the economic objectives of the system and the political requirements of the regimes. To repeat, they are not agencies of Soviet labor, but bureaucratic institutions of the Soviet government for labor matters.

Beyond this general subjugation of labor in the Soviet totalitarian system there exists the outright slavery of the labor camps. It is perhaps the most paradoxical feature of a political system erected in the name of Karl Marx that these labor camps should exist. For had it not been the most bitter reproach of Karl Marx to the "capitalist system" that under its so-called "iron law of wages" there was kept in existence a large pool of unemployed, the "reserve army of industry" who, because they were eager for jobs, kept the wage level down near the minimium of existence. The labor camps that today contain millions of people are the communist totalitarian equivalent of the "reserve army of industry." They are composed of all kinds of people whom the regime for one reason or another does not like, including so-called slackers—men and women who do not slave hard enough for the minimum wages which the regime actually pays to many of its workers, though some favored classes of workers are quite well paid—these labor camps provide workers for projects which are run so uneconomically that even the minimum wages of the Soviet Union are not available for the workers who operate them or who build them.

Conditions in these labor camps are so appalling that their existence has become a concern of the United Nations. An *Ad Hoc* Committee, constituted by UNESCO and the International Labor Organization, was set up in 1952, and, after hearings and presentations by such interested organizations as the Mid-European Study Center, published a report. (5a) While the system originated in the Soviet Union, where, in conjunction with a crime wave in the mid-twenties and the later collectivization, an ever larger group of people was incarcerated by the regime, it gradually has spread over the entire orbit of the Soviet empire. Today all the satellites, Poland, Czechoslovakia, Hungry, Bulgaria, Rumania, Albania, and the Soviet Zone of Germany employ the system, and it is found in Jugoslavia and China, too. It was in full swing by 1928 when the peasant resistance to forced collectivization in connection with the first

Five Year plan produced millions of "criminals." A secret "State Plan for the Development of the National Economy of the USSR in 1941" captured by the Germans during the war shows that a substantial portion of Soviet output was produced by slave labor.

What is the size and importance of this slave labor in the Soviet economy, and what can be credited to it? In 1941 slave labor produced 5,325,000 metric tons of coal; 34,730,000 cubic meters of commercial timber and firewood, or 11.9 per cent of Soviet production; 14.49 per cent of all furniture; 22.58 per cent of railroad ties; 40.5 per cent of chrome ore, and so on. (5b) Road building and rail construction and mining in remote regions, like Siberia, have been carried through by this slave labor. The estimates as to the number of persons involved in this gigantic "industrial reserve army" varies between 8 and 14 million. To these must be added the satellite labor camps, but no reliable estimates have been made. (5c; 32) If we accept a figure of 10 million for the USSR alone as a broad estimate for the Stalinist period, we must conclude that about 5 per cent of the Soviet population was thus "employed," a figure which just about corresponds to Karl Marx's industrial reserve army. It is in the light of these facts that the Soviet claim for "labor peace" and their proud boast that "no unemployment" exists in the Soviet Union must be seen and evaluated. The contrast between a western unemployed eking out a meager existence on the basis of his unemployment insurance payments and an inmate of a Soviet slave labor camp, systematically starved and brutalized beyond the imagination of civilized man, shows the full measure of difference between democracy and totalitarianism.

The Fascist and Nazi dictatorships did not go the whole length of this development before the war, but the Nazi system of slave labor evolved during the war was essentially the same kind of totalitarian reserve army. In any case, both dictatorships arrived at the subjugation of all free trade unions to the party and government. The only difference was in the ideological motivation. The Fascists did not claim that the elimination of the class struggle was the result of its consummation, as is the case in the Soviet Union; they rather insisted that it must be suppressed. The class-struggle doctrine of orthodox Marxism was, in fact, one of the key points of the Fascist attack. The bitterly denounced division of the nation into classes was alleged to be the result of the Marxist–socialist–communist agi-

tation, and hence after the liquidation of these disturbers of the social peace, a new organization of industrial and labor relations
would reunite the nation. The Fascist solution was essentially part
of the corporative organization, the Nazi one that of the Labor
Front. In both, to be described presently, the conflict of interest
between labor and management-capital was "resolved" by making
the assumption that the plant, factory, or industry was a "community" and to apply the pattern of community organization typical for its own kind of totalitarianism to this set of communities.
In Italy this was a matter of subjecting both management and labor
to the controlling direction of the "state," while in Germany the
employer was made the Führer (leader) of his workers. It was
what an old folk saying calls "making the goat the gardener."

The National Socialist policy of establishing a "labor front" which
would transform the contractual relations of labor and management
into communal relations cannot be said to have been a success. Yet
it completely destroyed the freedom of the unions. (148g; 270) It
must be seen in conjunction with related policies of declaring the
plant a community in the so-called "Charter of Labor" of January
20, 1934 (148h), of organizing leisure time in "strength through joy"
activities, and of compulsory work assignments. The Labor Front
was a party "formation" which included virtually every gainfully
employed person, management as well as employees, 25 million in
all. It was led by Dr. Ley, one of the early leaders of the Nazi
party. At the outset, it took over the entire trade-union structure,
including all its property. The utter failure of the unions to fight
back has been attributed to their bureaucratization under the Weimar
Republic, which transformed their leadership into an unenterprising
officialdom. Whether they actually could have accomplished much
may be doubted. In the Soviet Union, as we have seen, the attempt
to maintain some measure of independence, even under Communist
leadership, proved unsuccessful. (148i) The same may be said of
the small units or cells which the National Socialists had organized
originally to infiltrate the unions. They too would not maintain the
independence of the unions. Instead, the Labor Front assumed
the task of indoctrinating labor in National Socialist ideology, according to which the employer was made the "leader" of his workers, who became his "followers." These plant communities were
grouped according to industries into national communities (*Reichs-*

betriebsgemeinschaften), each of which was subject to an office of the National Labor Front. Since the *Führerprinzip* was applied throughout, it is clear that in a sense every worker in every plant in Hitler's Reich was a cog in the vast bureaucratic hierarchy. The union dues which the Labor Front continued to collect were in fact taxes, considering that the Front did not represent the workers, but the party bureaucracy. (148j)

It might be well to say a word more, therefore, about the "plant community" of the Charter of Labor. It states the concept as follows: "In the plant, the enterpriser as leader and the employees and workers as followers work together for the accomplishment of the objectives of the plant and for the common good of the nation and the state." In the light of this general concept, it further provided that "the leader of the plant decides all matters concerning the plant, as regulated by statute," and that "he [the leader] shall look after the welfare of the followers, while the latter shall place full confidence in him." The latter notion, namely, that the employer is responsible for the welfare of his workers, was a traditional notion in Germany (26), based, however, on the fact that as owner of the plant he must look after those who work in it, much as a houseowner is responsible for those who enter his house. It had been somewhat shaken by the development of the Works Councils (in the Weimar Republic), which the courts considered ground for asserting that the responsibility was now a joint one—a rather extraordinary view considering their very limited functions. They were a feeble beginning of democracy in industry—the councils now set up under the Codetermination Law in the Federal Republic constitute a further extension of it—and hence the Nazis immediately transformed them in accordance with their totalitarian leadership notions. Renamed Advisory Councils (*Vertrauensräte*), they were nominated by the manager and the leader of the party cell in the factory, and approved by acclamation of the followers. One cannot but agree with Neumann's conclusion that the Nazi innovations in the labor field, as we have sketched them here, were "devices for the manipulation of the working class." (148k) The system was rounded out by two other features, already mentioned, namely, the leisure-time activities ("strength through joy") and the compulsory assignment. The latter began under the Four Year Plan in 1938, and became more onerous, as the country faced war and defeat. The contractual relationship as the basis of work became a mockery under these assignments: when a worker is assigned to a plant, he is assumed to have entered into a contract, subject, of course, to general labor law. At the same time, workers became tied to their place of work, as they were forbidden to leave without permission from the government's Labor Exchange. Firing was likewise made subject to government veto. In short, the freedom of both employer and employee to choose was almost completely destroyed; as in the USSR, the workers constituted a vast reserve army to be assigned at pleasure to the managers of plants operating within the context of the government's plans and directions. Since the government also assumed the right to fix both minimum and maximum wages at the outset of the war, and to regulate all other conditions of work, it is evident that to speak of this economy as "capitalist" in the sense of a free, competitive market economy is untenable: the labor market was neither free, nor competitive. It is therefore not surprising that the efforts of the Nazis to increase productivity and, thereby, self-sufficiency failed. While labor productivity rose steadily in the United States between 1933 and 1939, no such development took place in Germany. Instead of increasing productivity, the businessmen exploited labor ruthlessly with the aid and encouragement of the Hitler regime.

To draw a veil over this sordid drama, the Nazi Party developed the "strength through joy" program of organized leisure time. It was actually patterned on the Italian *dopolavoro* program, carrying it merely to greater length and surrounding it with a great halo of innovation. It is perhaps too much to say that leisure time was "regimented," because workers were free to participate or not, to some extent, but it certainly was a palliative to sugarcoat the loss of the genuine rights that German labor had possessed to a marked degree as a result of the efforts of its free unions over many decades. Claiming that it too was a community, an official Nazi put it thus: "to win strength for daily work was therefore the final goal which the new creation sought to achieve." Thus the leisure organization "After Work" became the National Socialist community, "Strength through Joy." (1481)

In Italy, the workers were organized as one of the "pillars" of the corporative organization. Indeed, the corporate organization evolved out of the peculiar Fascist unions, or "syndicates," unions which were actually developed in competition with the free unions and gained ascendancy, under the skillful leadership of Edmondo Rossoni, after the Fascists had seized power. The original radical notion, derived from older syndicalist thought, that the union would take over the plants by absorbing management, was in typical Fascist fashion superseded by the idea that "corporations" composed of both employers and employees would accept direction and control of the state. The thought underlying the Fascist corporative setup was in fact to some extent akin to older conservative and Catholic thought; but whereas the papal encyclical *Rerum Novarum* (1891) had put forward the idea of a corporative structure along medieval lines, that is to say, decentralized and localized in authority, the Fascist conception was "hierarchical" and all authority was derived from the head of the corporative state, the minister of corporations, Benito Mussolini. It was the Italian version of "co-ordination" under which all associations became Fascist. As Herman Finer put it many years ago: "The dictatorship is the necessary rack and screw of the Corporate system." (50h; 120d) The corporative system was initiated by the Charter of Labor, of April 21, 1927, which the Grand Council of Fascism adopted as a party measure (it was then a party organ). It was, of course, soon transformed into a governmental policy by statutory enactment and judicial decision. Under it, Italian workers lost all the rights and privileges which their unions had fought for and won, in exchange for a paternalistic governmental control. For throughout the Charter and its subsequent implementation the government was supreme. The key passages assert that "since the private organization of production is a function of national concern, the organizer of the enterprise is responsible to the State for the direction of production . . . The employed . . . is an active collaborator in the economic enterprise, the direction of which belongs to the employer, who bears the responsibility for it." (50i) Measures of social welfare, such as health protection, scholarships for children, and insurance against disability, illness, and old age, as well as governmental control of minimum wages, holidays, and vocational education, among others, ought not to deceive anyone about the basic change: both workers and management lost their autonomy, but, in view of labor's weaker position, this was the most serious aspect of the solemn mockery of this "Charter." Proclaiming the "freedom of the syndicates" the Charter asserted that "only the legally recognized syndicate, subjected to the control of the State, has the right to represent legally all the employers and employed." (50j)   It comes almost as an anticlimax when one learns that "strikes are criminal offenses."   Only a percentage of the workers participated in this sham organization; but under Fascist pressure, it ran as high as 87 per cent in industry. (50k)   Leaving aside the employers, one can readily see that the unions had ceased to be representative and militant organs of the workers and had become instruments for the disciplining of labor, run by thousands of Fascist officials completely subservient to the government.

It is within this context that *Dopolavoro* must be seen.   It amounted in fact to transforming the rich free associational life of the Italian people in all the different spheres of cultural and social life into bureaucratically controlled appendages of the government. Music and art, literary and social leisure time activities, including mandolin societies and the like, became Fascist by being absorbed into the huge network of Dopolavoro.   In his wonderfully sardonic portrayal of all this humbug, G. Salvemini, after reporting that exactly 1,155,365 excursions, musical performances, sports exercises, and so on had been taking place under Dopolavoro in 1934, concludes: "The Fascists have not yet come to the point of publishing statistics on the number of kisses exchanged under the auspices of Dopolavoro, but these will soon be counted, and the staggering total will be attributed to the genius of Mussolini."

In conclusion, it seems very clear that labor has lost its freedom and independence, that its organizations have become bureaucratic agencies of the government, and that not only in his working hours, but in his leisure time as well the worker has become a cog in the totalitarian centrally directed economy.   To complete the paradox of his "workers' paradise," any worker who fails to live up to the standards set by the regime is in danger of being made a slave in one of the many labor camps of the regime.   Thus the industrial reserve army of capitalism which aroused Marx's indignation has been transformed into an army of "men in bond."

Chapter Twenty-One

The Battle for Bread and Butter

Agricultural production has been as central a concern of the totalitarians as industrial production. But the problems to be faced and the policies adopted have been quite different between the regimes and within them. The Bolsheviks started with an appeal based on treating the peasants as the brothers of the workers; the Fascists and National Socialists did the same. Yet for the communists this was a concession based upon a sharp differentiation between the poor peasants who were part of the toiling masses, and the more well-to-do ones who were soon denounced as kulaks and lumped together with capitalists. The Fascists, and even more the Nazis, on the other hand "idealized" the peasantry under such slogans as "blood and soil." The concrete situation with which different totalitarian regimes were confronted also played a role: in the Soviet Union more than 80 per cent of the population were peasants in 1917, while in Italy only around 60 per cent, and in Germany perhaps 30 per cent. The situation in the satellite countries—Poland, Hungary, Rumania—resembles that in Italy, while in Czechoslovakia the peasantry constituted about 55 per cent. In China, finally, the population is so very largely of the peasant type that the Communist leadership there actually found it necessary to alter the ideology of communism somewhat to take account of the situation, at least, in the revolutionary stage. (185b)

The actual policies pursued by the totalitarian regimes in the field of agriculture cannot be understood unless one appreciates fully the role of the peasantry in the countries concerned. The related issue of the need for "land reform" must also be considered at the start. Only after these two topics have been dealt with can agricultural operations of the totalitarian regimes be adequately analyzed by comparative evaluation. Before we turn to the peasantry, the problem of "land reform" needs to be briefly sketched. Throughout the world, the problem of large-scale landed estates, in many instances the result of preceding "feudal" conditions of land ownership (44), has become a focal point of attack for widely demanded reforms.

Throughout Asia, "land-lordism" has become a battle cry of the embittered peasant masses who have been kept in conditions of abject poverty. The same may be said of considerable areas of Europe, especially in the east and south. Land reform, meaning essentially the distribution of these estates among independent farmers each receiving a parcel sufficient for effective operation (varying from 20 to 100 acres, depending on conditions of climate, soil, and marketing) and thus providing him with the necessary "means of production," should have been the policy of regimes aspiring to democratic rule. Unfortunately, time and again, the landed proprietors have employed their vested wealth and entrenched social position to thwart the efforts of progressive democratic elements at such land reform. Thereby they prepared the ground for totalitarian movements, both communist and fascist. The communists adopted the "land reform" slogan—distribution of land to the peasants—as their most potent weapon in building effective mass support, while the fascists, both in Italy and Germany, not to speak of Rumania, Hungary, and the rest, though in fact allied with the big landholders, talked much of their interest in the peasantry and its rights. Everywhere it is the same story: a land-hungry peasantry, deeply disappointed in the failure of presumably democratic regimes to provide them with the means for making a living, turning to the totalitarians in the hope of a solution, and eventually finding themselves trapped and turned into slaves of the totalitarian party and government, who control the means of production and more especially the land, either through outright proprietorship or indirectly by means of an elaborate pattern of bureaucratic techniques.

The peasants, then, demand land reform. What actually is this peasantry? The peasantry, in fact, presents a most perplexing issue. As a human type, the peasant is preindustrialist and precapitalist. Americans are apt to see him in comic opera perspective, as clad in quaint costumes, singing old folk songs and dancing folk dances. This image is not wholly in error; for throughout Europe and Asia the peasantry has been the guardian of older, more earthy traditions, habits and beliefs. But politically speaking, the most significant feature of the peasant is his attitude toward the land and toward the methods of production he employs in tilling it. Typically, the peasant is not market-oriented, but tradition-oriented. The focal point of his outlook is not what brings the best results, in terms of market requirements, but what does so in terms of ancestral practices. Frequently, the peasant is decidedly fixed, indeed immobile, in his attitude toward the land. Unlike the American or Australian farmer, or even the Danish or Swiss farmer, the peasant thinks of his land not as "capital" of a certain value, but rather as a heritage handed down by his forebears and to be handed on to future generations.

This rootedness, this attachment to the land as a timeless possession, makes the peasant a misfit in modern industrial society, rejected and despised by its protagonists, idolized by romantic adversaries of industrial society. (88.1) Political parties have had difficulties in assimilating him—the rightist ones, because of their tie-up with big landowners, the leftist ones because of their hostility to property, the liberal and middle-of-the-road ones because of their friendliness to industrial capitalism. As a result of all this, the peasant has been the stepchild of democratic parliamentary politics. From time to time, he has formed his own party; peasant parties had come to play a significant role, particularly in the Slavic countries now overrun by the USSR, such as Poland.* But these were, of course, minority parties, and since they were led by responsible agrarian leaders they were no challenge to the demagoguery of the totalitarian movements, for both the Bolsheviks and the fascists made the peasant a major focus of their mass propaganda and continue to do so. Indeed, Mao has made the role of the peasant the main point of his adaptation of Marxist-Leninist orthodoxy to the Chinese situation. (185c) But the Bolsheviks, confronted with the peasant masses of Russia, appealed to the peasants as well as the workers, and in the early years of the regime, the "soviets" or councils, were workers' *and* peasants' councils. All this, of course, soon proved a hollow sham. The peasants who had been happy to distribute the land of the big estate owners among themselves were decidely hostile to the Soviet government's coercive policy of regimenting the farmers' food deliveries. After the failure of an initial effort at conciliation—the New Economic Policy of Lenin 1922–1928 (NEP)—Stalin turned against the peasantry and under the

* Strange as it may seem, these parties actually carry on even after emigrating, and have formed an International Union which publishes a Monthly Bulletin very representative of the democratic peasants' viewpoint. They speak of themselves, in contrast to the red International of the workers, as the "green" international.

First Five Year Plan undertook the wholesale liquidation of this class. This process was ideologically rationalized by dividing the peasantry into rich and poor peasants and by claiming that the fight was only directed against the former. Actually, they were only the first line of attack and in developing the collectivist forms of agriculture, the independent peasant was largely eliminated from the Soviet scene (128); the same process is at present being repeated in the Slavic satellites and in the Soviet Zone of Occupation.

The collectivization in the Soviet Union was largely a forcible one. The peasants were pressed into collective farms by open coercion, and flying squads of party activists, Komsomolite and GPU detachments, and even army units roamed through the countryside to subdue the recalcitrant peasants. The so-called kulaks, or the richer peasants, were rounded up and deported in great numbers to outlying districts of the USSR, where they were forcibly settled on barren land and forced to farm collectively. Some were sent directly into forced labor camps, and the history of the forced labor camps really begins on a large scale in this period. Resistance and oppression were particularly severe in the Ukraine, where the soil is rich and the peasants had the greatest vested interest in their landholdings. The regime utilized the technique of deportation on a vast scale here, and as a partial result the notorious Ukrainian famine of the early thirties took place. Literally hundreds of thousands died from starvation, and the general decline in food-production affected the entire Soviet Union. Starving peasants, long queues, beggars—these were common on the Soviet scene at that time. This process went so far that Stalin was forced to apply remedial measures, and his "Dizzy with Success" speech was designed to put a halt to this rapidly deteriorating situation. The broad pattern of collective agriculture had been established, however, and the next few years saw the gradual elimination of the remaining farmers. By 1934, 84.5 per cent of agriculture had been collectivized; by 1939, the figure was 93.5 per cent. (189; 190c)

World War II and the collapse of Soviet power in the Ukraine and Byelorussia resulted in the destruction of the collective farm system in the most important agricultural areas. At the same time, the exigencies of the war effort forced the party to ignore some serious abuses of the collective system which were developing in other areas of the USSR. Private plots (which collective farmers are allowed to retain on a very small scale) tended to be enlarged by stealth, the livestock of the collective farms was frequently and illegally divided by the peasants, and so forth. In addition, rumors were circulating that the party was planning to abandon the collective system altogether and restore land to the peasants (Chapter 16). The party, however, had no such intentions. As early as 1943 a decree was issued outlining the measures to be followed in the reconstruction of the collective farm system in the newly re-occupied areas. (99a) As the Germans retreated, the returning Soviet administration immediately set itself the task of recapturing any land taken over by the peasants. After the conclusion of the hostilities, an all-out campaign was launched to reinvigorate collectivized agriculture, and in a very much publicized decree, entitled, "On Measures to Liquidate the Violations of the Regulations of Agricultural Artels in Collective Farms," (99b) the party charted the struggle for discipline, intensified production, and full collectivization.

The prewar pattern of agricultural organization was thus re-established. It consisted of some 250,000 collective farms, where the workers allegedly owned the land in common, were paid by labor-days (by amount of work they actually performed), and shared the profits and losses of the collective farm, depending on the harvest; a smaller number of state-owned farms, where the farmers worked as if industrial workers, that is, were paid normal wages irrespective of the harvest; some 8,000 Motor-Tractor Stations (MTS) which served the various farms with their machinery, tractors, and technical assistance on a contractual basis. The party leadership, however, was still plagued by the fact that the large number of collective farms made central political direction difficult, whilst it also resulted in tremendous administrative inefficiency and overlapping. Accordingly, in the early fifties a policy of farm amalgamation was launched, and in four years the number of collective farms was reduced to some 95,000 superfarms, serviced by about 9,000 MTS. More recently, in 1955, in order to increase the operational efficiency of these farms, measures were adopted to grant them greater autonomy in crop selection and in planning.* The collective farms are, however, in a broad sense subject to the over-all state plan and their quotas are set by the state planning agencies.

* "Changes in the Practice of Agricultural Planning," decree (in translation) of the Central Committee of the CPSU and of the Council of Ministers, March 2, 1955.

Soviet agriculture, however, has lagged far behind industrial development. This fact has become a source of major worry to Soviet leaders who cannot fail to note that, while industrial production had doubled since 1940, agricultural output is at most 10 per cent higher. The situation appears even more catastrophic when Soviet agricultural statistics for 1954 are compared to 1928, the last precollectivization year.· Cattle is 15 per cent down, cows 27 per cent, while the population has grown from some 150 million to 215 million. Agricultural production standards are also extremely low when compared to western norms: for example, average milk yield per cow in 1954 in the USSR was 1,100 litres as compared to 2,865 in West Germany and 2,531 as early as 1937 in Sweden. (135) Similarly, corn yield per bushel per acre, is 17.8 in the USSR, while in the United States it is 37.1. (262b) Many other statistics could be cited, but these are sufficient to illustrate the gravity of the situation, particularly if one also considers the rapid growth of the urban population in the USSR.

The Central Committee of the Party, therefore, ordered "a considerable improvement in the productivity of stock raising, an acceleration in the rate of cattle increase, an improvement in breeding and, in the next two or three years, a sharp increase in the output of meat and dairy produce." (271m) Soon afterwards, under the aegis of Khrushchev, a vast project for cultivating underdeveloped or entirely virgin lands was launched. It was made necessary not only by the considerations sketched above, but also by the fact that agriculture in the USSR is concentrated in regions subject to great weather hazards. The need to spread the risks had become apparent to the Central Committee. Kazakhstan, in particular, and central Asia in general became the foci for this new push for which the energies of the youth were to be mobilized. Thousands of young Komsomolites left the cities, some willingly, others pressured into "volunteering," to work on the virgin soil. They were to live on newly set-up state farms, a development suggesting a further extension of the factory-production system into agriculture. (271n)

The scope of this new program is really vast. It envisages a tremendous "young man, go *west*" movement which, within a few years, will result in a republic like Kazakhstan becoming a predominantly Slavic-populated region. This, of course, will also have important political repercussions in breaking down the resistance of these regions to centrally directed innovations. This resistance is rooted in their national traditions. In the years 1954–1956, the Soviet regime hopes to bring under cultivation some 28–30 million hectares of virgin land, some 19 million of which are in Kazakhstan alone. The area under cultivation in Kazakhstan will accordingly increase from about 10 million hectares to 28.5. (2710) This project naturally has created a great need for outside settlers, who can come only from the overpopulated regions and urban centers in Russia and the Ukraine. Whether this undertaking will succeed in relieving Soviet agricultural problems remains to be seen, but it does suggest that the regime has not yet found an adequate solution, despite its many boasts.

Nonetheless, there is absolutely no intention on the part of the Soviet regime to abandon its commitment to a policy of collectivization, and the Soviet pattern has become the model for satellite development, albeit a somewhat more moderate one. The excesses and brutality of the early thirties have not been repeated by the satellite regimes, where more subtle methods of coercion, such as excessive taxation, discrimination, and occasional show trials, have been adopted. As a result, progress in collectivizing has been slow. According to a recent study of Polish economy, "the share of socialized agriculture in the total areas in agricultural use . . . increased from about 8 per cent in 1947, nearly all in state farms, to about 20 per cent in 1953, of which about 12.8 per cent was in state farms and the remainder in producer cooperative farms." (1) By 1955 the percentage grew to only 27.* Still the Soviet pattern and regulations are followed closely, and have been made the basis for satellite agricultural policies. (263b) In China, similarly, once the revolution was achieved, the peasants became the less favored partners in the worker-peasant coalition, the great pressure has been put on them to enter into the agricultural producers' cooperatives. This is to be accompanied at the same time by the process of industrial expansion. One may expect, therefore, in China also a duplication of the Soviet experience, with its coercion, economic dislocation, and suffering. (222)

* The figures for the other captive nations are higher, although still below the comparable Soviet rate of collectivization: by the end of 1955, 45% of the arable land was collectivized in Czechoslovakia, 35% in Rumania, 33% Hungary and East Germany. The most "advanced" was Bulgaria: by May 1956 some 75% of the arable land was collectivized.

The Fascists and National Socialists repeated the demagoguery of the Bolsheviks on a grander scale, as far as the peasants are concerned. They, too, of course, proclaimed themselves workers' parties, but among the workers the peasants held, for them, a special place. There is a sound psychological and sociological reason for this: the peasants have, through their attachment to the land, a peculiar affinity to nationalism. To be sure, theirs is a defensive nationalism, and when the dictatorship launches forth into foreign wars, the peasantry becomes restive and abandons the regime (291), though there may be occasional exceptions like the Ethiopian war which the Italian peasants are said to have supported. This was also the case at the time of the French Revolution. It was the peasantry that turned from the radicalism of the revolutionaries to Napoleon, but deserted him when he set out to conquer Europe. But after all is said and done, it still remains a crucial factor in the fascist movements of our time that the peasantry, hostile to both the internationalism and the industrialism of the socialists, inclines toward supporting fascist movements because they claim to be hostile to industrialism (anticapitalist) and hostile to internationalism (nationalist). The peasantry feels strongly about its possession of the land; it likewise feels strongly about the defense of the homeland, the fatherland. It was recently claimed by peasant leaders in Italy that the peasantry did not really support fascism. In a deeper sense this is true; for the aggressive imperialism and big-business monopolism with which Italian Fascism developed was deeply antagonistic to peasant interests and peasant views. But in the early stages, the peasants provided substantial support to Fascism. Mussolini always claimed that the peasants were his staunchest supporters. In the case of Hitler, we can even prove the proposition statistically. The largest part of Hitler's electoral support came from the peasantry in the early days. Curiously enough, the very regions in which the democratic movement had been strongest among the peasants, Holstein and Baden, were the ones that turned toward Hitler, whereas in the staunchly conservative and Catholic regions of Upper Bavaria the peasantry remained hostile. A similar phenomenon can be observed in Italy in the contrast between Tuscany and southern Italy that is now being repeated in the struggle between communism and Christian Democracy. (272) This peasant support is frequently overlooked in analyses that stress the "middle class" support of fascism, which, while undoubtedly a fact, would not have provided the necessary votes for the building of an electoral following of nearly 40 per cent by Hitler.

But if the peasants were wholly deceived by the Bolsheviks and by their support decreed their own death warrant, they were nearly as much disillusioned by the National Socialist regime. To be sure, the regime protested its love for the peasants throughout. It developed a special facet in its official ideology, the "blood and soil" (BLUBO) line. Under this banner of Blubo the racial purity of the peasants was linked to their attachment to the land (*Boden*) as proof of their high value for the folk community. National festivals were held, with a sumptuous display of costumes and folk dances, and at the great party rallies or *Parteitage,* the peasants were conspicuous participants. But behind this façade of make-believe, the reality of Nazi agrarian policy turned out to be decidedly contrary to the peasants' interest, and not only in terms of international adventures. It has been rightly observed that agriculture was more strictly regimented than any other field of economic activity. The party organization invaded the villages and bestowed leadership upon the most loyal party members rather than upon the most respected tillers of the soil. Since farming is a very exacting business, the best farmers are rarely much occupied with politics, and the peasants deeply resented the extent to which the Nazis placed a premium upon political activity. The Nazi frontal attack upon the churches (see Chapter 23) added fuel to the fire. In the end peasant support for the regime almost completely disappeared.

But it may be well to sketch briefly the agrarian policy of the Hitler regime. At the center we find the organization of the Reich Food Estate (*Reichsnährstand*). This term, derived from older romantic and feudal views about the revival of a medieval corporate order (see Chapter 13), did in fact designate a complete bureaucratization of the agrarian sector of the economy. The formerly autonomous "chambers of Agriculture" were transformed into dependent arms of the government and its ministry of agriculture and of the party and its corresponding organs. Walter Darré, the architect of this Reich Food Estate, and its effective leader under Hitler, professed the official peasant ideology of Blubo. But in fact, he attempted to convert all agricultural producers into National Socialists who would help to win the "battle of food." His policy toward the peasantry had three major features: the control of prices; the control of inheritance; and the control of planting. In all of them, the technique employed was that of bureaucratic coercion and terrorist police and party work rather than economic incentives. As far as prices were concerned, both direct and indirect fixing were practiced, making the farm operations dependent on government *fiat* rather than on the free market. Since the peasant had never really accepted the free market, this change seemed at first a gain for the peasantry, but as the price-fixing soon proved to be motivated by the military and industrial needs of the regime, rather than the interests of the farmer, it resulted in noncooperation and eventually even sabotage. Its potentialities for large-scale corruption discredited the regime.

More extraordinary than the price-fixing, though perhaps economically less significant, was the forcible entailing of farm property. Cast in terms of protecting the peasant against losing his farm, since bankruptcies had, as in the United States during the great depression, caused widespread agrarian unrest, this legislation had an initial appeal. (178) But it soon turned out to be another link in the chain by which the peasantry was enslaved to the party and the government. The laws provided that a farmer could not sell or pass on his farm without securing the assent of the local government and party officials. He could also lose his farm if the local party boss was not satisfied with the way he was operating it. In short, the proprietary rights were made dependent upon bureaucratic discretion. An incidental result was that farmers could no longer get credit; the government stepped into the breach and provided credit facilities, thereby welding another link in the chain. Finally, the government could take over the farm, if in the judgment of the local Nazi farm leader the property was not being administered "in conformity with demands which must be made on farming in the interest of the feeding of the people." The Nazis developed legislation concerning the planting of certain crops, often in disregard of local climatic and soil conditions, thereby also arrogating to themselves this crucial function of farm management. Now, some of these policies will be recognized as fairly common in democratic countries, including the United States, but the decisive difference is, as always, one of method. In democratic countries, such policies result from extended debates in representative assemblies in which all relevant interests are fully represented; they are subject to continuous revision and they typically rely upon such economic incentives as subsidies to accomplish results. The agricultural policies of the Nazi regime were, on the other hand, decreed by government and party bureaucrats in accordance with the leader's over-all policy decisions. While, therefore, the outward forms of peasant proprietorship remained, at least within the narrow limits left by the legislation we have just described, the actual substance of an independent peasantry completely disappeared. But the peasants were not liquidated, as in the Soviet Union, with the very significant result that after the defeat of the Nazis, the peasantry could re-emerge as a significant factor in the German social structure. As a result the Communist rulers of the Soviet Zone of Occupation have had to undertake the task of liquidation, as they have in the Slavic satellites. The process is not yet very far advanced; while *kolkhozes* have come into existence, they are not yet the predominant form of agricultural enterprise as in the Soviet Union.* But the very fact that they had to be instituted shows that the Nazi policy had not destroyed the peasantry.

In Italy the process was not carried so far. This is because the Italian Facists, like the Nazis, failed to tackle the task of land reform. Since Italy was a country of large agricultural estates (*latifundia*), its true need was land reform on a considerable scale, such as is now being tackled, at last. The Fascists, though well aware of the problem, substituted a vast program of reclamation, such as that in the Pontine marshes which the previous regimes had instituted. The total effect upon the position of the Italian peasantry was, of course, minimal, but it lent itself to dramatic proclamations on the part of Mussolini. (180e)

In conclusion, it is fairly clear that the agricultural sector of the totalitarian economy presents peculiar difficulties to the rulers of these regimes. The nature of agricultural production is such that it is unsuited to large-scale organization and control, but, at the same time its product, food, is vital, for even totalitarians have to eat. The drive for additional land presents itself as a way out of the dif-

---

* There is a persistent rumor that the policy of the Soviets in making the farms too small for effective operation, when dividing the big estates (8 hectares or less), was aimed at forcing these "independent" farmers into *Kolkhozes* as an escape from their troubles.

ficulties involved in making the available land more productive. This drive, epitomized in the German "space" (*Raum*) ideology, reinforces the totalitarians' propensity to foreign conquest. Considering the disastrous consequences of such expansion, as far as the support of the peasantry is concerned, the peasantry may well, in fact, have been the "Achilles' heel" of the fascist regimes. Whether the lag in agricultural production by which the Soviet Union is afflicted will serve to play a similar role there—leading either to the collapse or to the radical modification of totalitarianism—remains to be seen. In any case, the natural requirements of agricultural production, namely, many small-scale independent proprietors working the soil on their own responsibility, seem to present a major obstacle to totalitarian rule. Is it an accident that, as Jefferson among others insisted, precisely such a population of farmers is the best foundation for a free and democratic society?

VI

Islands of Separateness

Chapter Twenty-Two

The Family

Nora Waln, in *Reaching for the Stars,* tells of a visit to a clergyman's family in Nazi Germany. The father and breadwinner had been thrown into concentration camp for his convictions. Mother and children were out in the field, working to raise vegetables, trying to subsist. After Miss Waln had sympathized with their lot, the talk turned to the Nazis and what they might be doing to the father. Then the youngest spoke up and declared, simply and quite firmly, "We are praying for them that God may help them." This moving story, told as part of a series of sketches about life under a totalitarian dictatorship, shows what we mean by "islands of separateness." For even within the grip of a total demand for total identification with such a regime, some people manage to maintain themselves aloof, to live in accordance with their personal convictions, and perhaps to organize some minor opposition to the regime. All expectations that they could overthrow the totalitarian regime are utopian delusions. But these islands are not only eloquent testimonials to the strength of human character, but are also capable of preserving human beings for a better day, when the scourge of totalitarian terror is dead and gone. Among these islands of separateness, we propose four which have proved to be of particular tenacity: the family, the churches, the universities, and the military establishment. Among these, the family is the most important, the most universal, and the most elementary. Hence we start with it.

There was originally a striking contrast in the approach of the communist and fascist ideologies to the family, but this difference has been replaced by a common approach, or at any rate by approaches which closely parallel each other, characterized by an emphasis upon the family as the procreator of children who will strengthen the regime. In other words, the family is seen as essentially an instrument for enhancing the power of the totalitarian dictatorship; family policy becomes an element of population policy. It is fitted into the over-all planning of the regime's social and economic efforts. At the outset, however, this was not the view of the Bolsheviks. On the contrary, they tended toward the depreciation of the family. The family was seen as an institution linked to private property and typically bourgeois in nature. This dogmatic view was, perhaps, reinforced by the bohemian style of living of many of the ideologues of the Marxist movement, but it had its roots in the preoccupation with the strictly economic phases of social structure and dynamics. As Marxism had a blind spot when it came to assessing the bureaucratic prospects resulting from the socialization of the means of production, so it also did not perceive the importance of stable personal relations within such a bureaucratic structure. Hence, at the outset, the communists made not only divorce and abortion easy, but they encouraged sexual promiscuity on a large scale. (224c) The disruptive potential of such policies, clearly perceived by Lenin who denounced it, became increasingly apparent during the twenties, with the result that after extended "discussion" in the early thirties, the trend was sharply reversed. In 1933 homosexuality was made a criminal offense and decrees against abortion followed in 1936. Severe restrictions on grounds for divorce were imposed in 1944, and since then Soviet publications have been at great pains to emphasize the importance to the regime of the family unit.

The role of the family is especially great in the development in the child of Soviet patriotism . . . Parents who are patriots develop in their children love for their native language, for the profound beauty of the national folklore and songs, and for the native country and scenery . . . Love of country begins to blend in his [the child's] consciousness with love for the socialist people and State regime and for the Bolshevik Party and its leaders. (243)

The Soviet people, the Communist Party and government tirelessly concern themselves with strengthening the family, with the proper rearing of the younger generation. (252e)

In 1955 the Soviet press launched an extended discussion of the nature of "socialist morality" which again made manifest both the current "victorianism" of Soviet morals as well as the importance that the regime attaches to the institution of the family. Citing numerous cases of broken families, the press reiterated the duty of the party members to act as watchdogs for family unity and maintenance of "socialist morality." Such a policy is decidedly more in keeping with totalitarian needs, especially once the regime has become fairly confident that the family is no longer the center of antiregime hostility. The 1955 provisions once again legalizing abortion can also be viewed in that light: the regime is assured that natural increase in population is high enough, it is encouraging family life, and at the same time it wishes to eliminate secret, and often fatal, illegal abortions. (252f)

The fascists sought from the very beginning to strengthen the family. The argument was usually cast in terms of the role of women. More especially Hitler, in keeping with his *Blut und Boden* ideology, announced with his customary coarseness that women belonged in the kitchen and should devote themselves to the raising of children. Actually, here again he merely echoed Italian views. Mussolini had voiced similar opinions long before him, and both movements had faithfully repeated the slogans. In *Mein Kampf* Hitler wrote: "The object of woman's education must be immovably directed to making the future mothers." At the same time, the Fascists and Nazis wanted women to take a keen interest in their politics, to be totally committed to their ideology. Hence they would also proclaim: "Intellectual women? No! But those whose interests in life do not reach beyond the limits of the household are not fit to become the forebearers of the kind of new generations which the Reich needs." (207)

In keeping with these ideological proclamations, Fascists and Nazis offered various kinds of assistance: loans to young couples seeking to get married, prizes for mothers with many children, aid during pregnancy especially for women who were working. In the late thirties, civil servants in Fascist Italy were required to be married and all bachelors in government employ were discriminated against and heavily taxed. A hot debate raged over whether to expel bachelors from the party altogether. Mussolini was very fond of arguing that Italians had to reproduce more rapidly in order to become "great" and "found an empire." The very same type of assistance is now being offered in the Soviet Union and in the Soviet Zone of Germany.

The Soviet government gives special allowances to mothers of illegitimate children or, if the mother so desires, provides special state institutions to care for them. Mothers of large families receive, apart from Medals of Motherhood for six or seven children and

Medals of Maternal Glory for more than seven, substantial income awards. They are indicated in rubles in the accompanying table. (103d)

Number of Children	Birth Allowance	Monthly Allowance
3	250	0
4	650	40
5	850	60
6	1,000	70
7	1,250	100
8	1,250	100
9	1,750	125
10	1,750	125
each additional	2,500	150

The government also gives special consideration to working mothers, giving them leaves of absence with pay usually for about 112 days. (252h) Generous allowances are also provided by the satellite regimes. In Hungary, the government has even decreed a special tax on bachelors, as did the Italian Fascists before them.

All these forms of assistance are concentrated upon hastening and reinforcing the procreative function of family life. Beyond this, the totalitarian dictatorship by its very nature is obliged to pursue policies hostile to family life and family cohesion. Its desire for total absorption of the man, or woman, in the totalitarian mass movement propels it into efforts to counteract, indeed to break down, the closed circle of the family.

Since the dawn of political thought, the family has been recognized as the most elementary of social groups, and by many political thinkers the family has been considered the essential underpinning of organized political systems. Aristotle in particular stressed this view, in combating Plato's radical proposals for organizing a political elite on the basis of a community of wives and property, and a communal education of the young. (2; 158) Indeed, in the course of the centuries it became one of the most frequent commonplaces of political thought, and writers of the most divergent schools, Thomas Aquinas and Marsilius, Bodin and Althusius, Harrington and Montesquieu, Kant and Hegel, all agreed on this basic function of the family. In spite of this almost universal agreement among political philosophers, there was relatively little discussion of just what were the characteristics of this basic institution, and the term "family" has stood for a great variety of social groupings, from the many-numbered patriarchal family to the small contemporary union of man and wife, rearing one or two children and united in romantic love for each other. Only fairly recently have anthropology and sociology devoted detailed scientific attention to the complex variety of structural models and the problems resulting from them.* At the same time, family policy has become the concern of legislative bodies, and important enactments have been the result in, for example, Sweden and Switzerland. (145; 94) These developments are due to the fact that it is increasingly recognized that the intimate group must be strengthened and protected as a counterbalance to the alienation and isolation of man resulting from the increasing size of organization, both political and economic, in the contemporary world. Totalitarianism is, as we have tried to show, the extreme projection of these trends. Consequently, totalitarian dictatorship has in various ways sought to break up the cohesion of the intimate family grouping. We have described the way in which more particularly the mass organization of youth and the propagandist development of the school have been employed for this purpose. Besides, the encouragement of women working in industry, the continuous appeal for men to attend meetings, and to participate in collective enterprises, the whole governmental effort at organizing leisure time activities—all these various undertakings have tended to weaken the family by depriving it of its functions. Also, as we have seen, in the early stages of the totalitarian regimes measures are taken to facilitate divorce, to weaken the unity of the family. The following Supreme Court decision in Poland is but one of many characteristic of this particular stage in the development of totalitarian society.

[The Supreme Court has considered] the District Court wrong in holding that the petitioner's claim that serious political differences had sepa-

---

* Without detailed reference, the work of the following may be mentioned: Briffault, Burgess, Calhoun, Frazier, Groves, Malinowski, Mead, Morgan, Ogburn, Thurnwald, Westermarck, Zimmermann. A recent survey of American writings is given by Ernest R. and Gladys H. Groves, *The Contemporary American Family* (Philadelphia, 1947), especially ch. 2; more especially the kinship problem is treated within a systematic context by Talcott Parsons, *The Social System* (Glencoe, 1951), ch. 5.

rated him from his wife could not be a ground for divorce . . . A marriage must be based on ideological unity which cannot prosper if there are conflicting views on basic political and social problems, especially if one partner represents a progressive, the other however a reactionary creed . . . (160)

In breaking up the family group totalitarian dictatorship has merely completed a cycle that started under industrial capitalism, when the factory began to take men out of their homes for the greater part of the day and, by paying them wholly inadequate wages, further encouraged the work of women and children. These consequences of industrial capitalism have been extended, by the methods described above, to the middle classes, who had maintained a rigid family system during the earlier phases of industrial capitalism.

But in spite of these policies hostile to family cohesion, the family has proved a haven for the persecuted, and has served to counteract the tendency of our time to isolate and eventually to collectivize the individual. Consequently, the totalitarian movements, and more particularly their secret police systems, have tried to break into the charmed circle of the family. Indeed, members of families have been encouraged to testify against other members and such betrayal of the most intimate relationships has been praised as "patriotism" and loyalty to the totalitarian leadership. It is not an accident that one of the official heroes of the Soviet youth movement is one Pavlik Morozov, who earned his place in the galaxy of Soviet heroes by denouncing his parents to the NKVD. It appears that his father, a farmer, was opposed to the collectivization, and young Pavlik reported this fact to the local secret police officials. The father was duly "unmasked" and liquidated as an enemy of the people. Unfortunately, however, young Pavlik was subsequently murdered by his fellow villagers, who were enraged at this display of Soviet loyalty. His "marytrdom" earned him a lasting place in the manuals of the Pioneers and the Komsomolites. (268) Former Soviet citizens testify that at the height of the terror in the thirties it was dangerous to discuss political matters even in the family circle, as the young were constantly exhorted by the party not to hesitate to denounce even their closest relatives. And while such views may easily be exaggerations induced by the all-pervading atmosphere of fear, they do serve to reveal the type of atmosphere that a totalitarian regime tries to generate even within the family circle itself.

It would, however, be a great mistake to see the family in the perspective of these cases. They are, in a sense, as untypical as the Stakhanovs and the Hennekes, and are the exceptions to the rule. The annals of the resistance movements are replete with stories of the aid offered by the family to the man or woman who seeks to fight the regime. (169b; 12; 107a) But these are merely the very dramatic expression of a much more general phenomenon, namely, that the anxiety-ridden subject of a totalitarian dictatorship, in his isolation and alienation from all ordinary community living, seeks refuge in the intimate relations of family life. It is, of course, difficult to document this generalization adequately, for the anonymous life of every man is not recorded for the social scientist to inspect. However, where we do catch glimpses of this situation, it confirms the general impression. Thus, investigators of the development of the postwar German family have been able to show, on the basis of extended interview material, that the family cohesion was strengthened by the Nazi effort to weaken it, and that among quite a few families a conscious effort at broadening family ties was made. (182; 235) Both tendencies were further intensified during the postwar debacle, when the total collapse and break-up of country and social structure left the family as almost the only dependable "community group."

The same was true of the earlier Soviet days. The family, according to the testimony of many former Soviet citizens, became the sole refuge where anticommunist sentiments were freely voiced and where religious rites were maintained. Many Soviet emigrés recall that their parents attempted to counter the official propaganda to which the children were exposed in the schools and in the communist youth organizations. Some recall sharing their parents' indignation at the purge policies of Stalin. One, for instance, tells us that:

in 1937 in connection with the execution of Tukhachevsky and the military conspiracy, I stopped believing in the Soviet regime . . . These people had great merit . . . My father told me often about Yakir. He served in his division during the civil war. And what he told me about him was always good. He became indignant when all this happened, and I was indignant with him. (18i)

The transmission of parental feelings against the Soviet regime was particularly marked in the agricultural areas, where the influence of

the regime had been the slowest in making itself felt, and where collectivization had left the deepest wounds. In time, however, the
family attitudes themselves underwent a change. It became more
and more apparent that the Soviet regime would not collapse and
more and more parents, out of consideration for their childrens' future, became inclined not to impede their children's adjustment to
the new system. This theme is repeated quite frequently by Soviet
emigrées. Furthermore, the process of urbanization and industrialization tended to weaken family bonds and to deepen the abyss between the prerevolutionary and the postrevolutionary generations.
Of course, such things as arrests or executions always tended to bind
the family together, but it appears that generally the process has
been in the direction of weakening the role of the family as an antiregime influence. Indeed, some emigrés openly admit that they became alienated from their parents because it seemed that the parents
had "counterrevolutionary" views. Anti-Soviet sentiments thus
served sometimes as a further method of weakening parental influence, giving the party full control of young minds. By now, most
Soviet parents are themselves of the postrevolutionary generation,
and the problem of the family tends to recede into the historical past,
except, of course, for the satellite areas. There, as in the early days
of the USSR, the family still remains a bastion to be stormed and
subdued. (62; 61; 254)

It is perhaps not without interest that, even in the Soviet Zone of
Occupation in Germany, the same general trends can be observed.
But the situation is complicated by the extent to which family
bonds extend westward into the Federal Republic. Again, the regime seeks to reorganize and at the same time strengthen the family. (46) Again, the family finds itself battered by the demands of
the regime upon all its subjects, but more particularly upon the
youth whom it has organized extensively and seeks to influence
through the propaganda carried on in the schools. But again, we
also find the family providing the essential "castle," the haven of
refuge not only for those who are persecuted and those who resist,
but also for large numbers of isolated and alienated men and
women who have retreated into this group's intimacy as an escape
from the totalitarian demands.

In conclusion, it might be said that the family, because of its basic
and universal nature, because of the intimacy and human warmth of

its bonds, has been a true oasis in the sea of totalitarian atomization. It has not only resisted this atomization, but the totalitarians have found themselves obliged to make substantial concessions to family stability, primarily in order to buttress their search for ever larger reservoirs of human manpower needed for their totalitarian enterprise.

Chapter Twenty-Three

The Churches

"Religion is the opium of the people!" This famous slogan of the Communist-Marxist movement conveys a good part of the essence of the totalitarian approach—its hostility to all organized religion. The communists especially were inclined to see the churches as willing helpmates of the established capitalist order, and the faith they encourage as merely "superstition" nurtured for the purpose of misleading the common man and of preventing him by a belief in a nonexistent God and by fear of a nonexistent afterlife from taking a rational view of government, history, and the economy. The Fascists and National Socialists, committed in this as in so many other matters to an ideological opposition to the Communists, denounced this doctrine of Marxism, and as a result were mistaken by quite a few observers to be defenders of the church and of the Christian religion. In candid programmatic declarations, however, both Mussolini and Hitler made it very clear that they were equally hostile—clear, that is, to him who still knew and understood the meaning of the Christian faith and of the church which exists for the purpose of its practice on this earth. This must be said in spite of the fact that high-ranking dignitaries in both the Catholic and the Protestant churches, in both Italy and Germany, failed to perceive this basic conflict and sought to strike compromises built upon an acceptance of Fascist and Nazi ideology.

It is true, however, that the Fascist and Nazi movements at the outset pursued policies which seemed to be radically at variance with the well-known Godless movement of the Bolsheviks, who openly attacked and eventually undertook a large-scale liquidation of the ecclesiastical organization of the Russian Orthodox Church. In their

policies, the Bolsheviks were guided by the known Marxist position
on the subject of religion, and by the violent policy declarations of
Lenin. To quote but two such statements:

Religion is a kind of spiritual vodka in which the slaves of capital
drown their human shape and their claims to any decent human life.
(113h)
All oppressing classes of every description need two social functions to
safeguard their domination: the function of the hangman, and the function of a priest. The hangman is to quell the protest and the rebellion
of the oppressed, the priest is to paint before them a perspective of miti-
gated sufferings and sacrifices under the same class rule . . . Thereby
he reconciles them to class domination, weans them away from revolutionary actions, undermines their revolutionary spirit, destroys their
revolutionary determination. (111b)

So instructed, the Bolshevik regime launched, in the twenties, an intensive antireligious campaign, which lasted, with some relaxations
and oscillations, until the end of the great purges in 1936–1938. The
most violent periods involved the years 1922–23, 1929–30, and 1937–
38. The first attack was designed to decapitate the Russian Orthodox clergy and involved the temporary arrest of the Patriarch and
the deportation of the acting patriarchs. At the same time, "spontaneous" local actions on the part of zealous communists were encouraged, resulting in the pillaging and closing of the churches.
Local religious communities were "encouraged" to vote for decisions
to close their churches and to transform them into museums or halls
of culture. In 1925 a League of Militant Atheists was set up to give
this campaign more effective expression. This was followed by
an intensification in the antireligious campaigns carried on in the
schools. Violence became quite open during the "Yezhovshchina"
and large numbers of the clergy were indicted for "antirevolutionary
wrecking." The Russian Orthodox clergy was intimidated and subdued, and the church no longer represented an effective impediment
to totalitarian rule.

The Fascists and Nazis claimed to fight this policy, which had
aroused the indignation of the Western world, by erecting a totalitarian dictatorship strong enough to withstand the Bolshevik on-
slaught. But in conjunction with this claim they propounded views
which made religion purely a function of political needs. They in-

sisted upon a "political faith" which must be the cardinal point of reference.* Adolf Hitler put this quite clearly and unequivocally in *Mein Kampf:*

For myself and for all true National Socialists there exists only one doctrine: nation and fatherland. What we have to fight for is to make secure the existence and the expansion of our race and of our nation, to rear its children and to keep pure the blood, the freedom and the independence of the fatherland, so that our nation may get ripe for the mission which the creator of this universe has assigned it. *Every thought and every idea, every doctrine and all knowledge have to serve this purpose.* (82b)

Mussolini was no less explicit in expounding such a "secular religion." In his doctrine of fascism, we read:

Fascism is a religious conception in which man is seen in his immediate relationship with a superior law and with an objective will that transcends the particular individual and raises him to conscious membership of a spiritual society. . . The man of Fascism is an individual who is nation and fatherland, which is a moral law binding together individuals and the generations into a tradition and a mission . . . the nation is created by the state which gives the people, conscious of its own moral unity, a will and therefore an effective existence . . . knows no limit to its development and realizes itself in testing its own limitlessness . . . Fascism, in short, is not only the giver of laws and the founder of institutions, but the educator and promoter of spiritual life. (150c)

But these views do not preclude accepting religion, or even the churches, as useful helpmates in the struggle for power that is politics. Both Hitler and Mussolini admitted, and the latter indeed stressed the value of religion within this context: "In the Fascist State religion is looked upon as one of the deepest manifestations of the spirit; it is therefore not only respected, but defended and protected," Mussolini wrote, and he added that fascism did not vainly seek to expel religion from the minds of men, as Bolshevism had tried to do. But what if the church, what if the religion which the church "embodies," demands something different than the fascist state? The fight of fascism with the church over the education of youth is typical here, and it is because of this potential clash be-

* For this "political faith" see Chapter 2, which shows this faith to be ideology, that is to say a weapon in the fight for power.

tween the two that the totalitarian dictatorship considers the problem a serious one. The church is another island of separateness that cannot be allowed to remain separate and apart, which must be subjugated and co-ordinated.

From the other side of the dilemma, the Soviet Union found itself in the position of acknowledging the role of religion and the value of ecclesiastical organization, provided it could be made the hand-maiden of the totalitarian dictatorship, so that eventually the two ideologies, seemingly worlds apart at the outset, met upon a common ground that is in keeping with the inner rationale, the dynamism, of the totalitarian society. But this rationale is confronted in the sphere of religion, as in that of the family, with "limits," resulting from the very nature of the total claim which religion makes upon the man who confesses it. Hence the story of religious opposition, suffering, and resistance to the inroads made by totalitarian political demands. As one writer put it very well: "Had Hitler really known the Christian church, there would have had to exist a deathly enmity from the first day on." (20a) As it was, Hitler, like Mussolini, pretended to be defending the church against Marxism, and to be protecting it against its being corrupted through participation in politics. He even claimed to be creating the "conditions for a truly deep, inner religiosity." (131; 20b) What is to be thought of this concern of Hitler's for truly inner religiosity can be seen from one of the conversations Rauschning has reported to us:

What do you think, will the masses ever become Christian again? Never! . . . but the priests . . . will betray their God to us . . . and replace the cross by the swastika. They will celebrate the pure blood of our nation instead of the blood of their previous redeemer . . . (163)

We find the very same views expounded in his *Secret Talks* where we find such views as "the party does well to keep its distance from the church"; "I do not care for articles of faith," and "I do not permit priests to concern themselves with secular matters." (86c; 84f) He criticized S. H. Chamberlain for believing in Christianity as a spiritual world, and Mussolini for having made compromises with the Catholic Church. "By himself he is a free spirit," he said of Mussolini, meaning that he agreed with himself that Christianity was a "dying branch." He remarked that he would "march into the Vatican and carry out the whole bunch." (86d) It is necessary to face these brutally frank sentiments of the true Hitler in order to grasp the purely tactical meaning of expressions like that cited, which are meant to suggest that fascism considers religion an important factor in national life. In *Mein Kampf* he had written that "the movement sees in both churches (the Protestant and the Catholic) equally valuable supports for the continued existence of our people." Hitler planned to tackle the problem of the churches after the war as "the last great problem" and to transform them into organizations for celebrating the racial "faith" in which he believed. (86e; 84h)

In the light of all the evidence, one might well ask whether the frank and frontal attack of the Bolsheviks was not the lesser evil. Neither in the Soviet Union in the twenties, nor more recently in the satellites has there been the same amount of danger that the churches are caught in the meshes of totalitarian religious corruption, although the recent tendencies in the Russian Orthodox Church are disturbing. But they are probably the consequences of the Soviets adopting a line of approach more nearly akin to that of the fascists: allowing the churches to operate on a very restricted basis and forcing them to abstain from all concern with secular issues in exchange for supporting the regime. The Soviet regime has thus been able to capitalize on the traditional submissiveness of the Russian Orthodox Church to state authority, dating back to the tsarist period. The Russian Orthodox clergy had spinelessly supported tsarism, and after the period of persecutions had little stamina left for opposing the Soviet regime.

This turn in the church-state, or rather church-party, relations in the USSR came during the war, when the regime liberalized its religious policy and the church gave its blessing to the "Great Fatherland War" against the German invader. It was at that time that Stalin characterized himself, in an interview with a fellow-traveler American priest, as "an advocate of freedom of conscience and freedom of worship" and even suggested the possibility of cooperation with the Pope "in the struggle against coercion and persecution of the Catholic Church." (200) Although this cooperation never materialized, the treatment of the Russian Orthodox Church never returned to its prewar severity, and the church became more and more an appendage of the party. Before the 1953 elections to the Supreme

Soviet, the Moscow Patriarchate stated that nowhere in the world was the church as free as in the USSR, and gave its blessing to those who cast their votes for the Communist bloc of candidates. The clergy has also been extensively utilized for propaganda purposes in connection with the various "peace" campaigns sponsored by the Soviet regime, and the patriarchs have been active in sponsoring these petitions abroad.

The Russian Orthodox Church has justified its cooperation with the Soviet regime, which some of the church members may possibly dislike, in terms of God's will and "giving unto Caesar what is Caesar's." The type of theological gymnastics which its submission to communism involves is well illustrated by an article of Rev. V. Radzyanko in the Journal of the Moscow Patriarchate, *Zhurnal Moskovskoi Patriarkhii,* in which he states: "Glory be to God for the separation of church and state, for the confiscation of church lands and property, and even for the persecutions and the closing of churches; for all this has been in accordance with the will of God. Struggle against all this would have been opposition to the designs of God." (286b) Under these circumstances it came as no surprise that in 1955 the Soviet government decorated high Russian Orthodox clergymen for their "patriotic work and . . . role in the peace movement." (252g)

Opposition to the Soviet antireligious policies, however, existed and still persists. In the twenties there were many cases of underground religious movements, of brave priests of all creeds preaching the word of God at the risk of their lives, religious congregations meeting secretly, youth groups set up to maintain the faith among the young. Even secret theological study groups operated in order to fill the gaps created by the arrests and deportations of the clergy. (286c) The war, resulting in the opening of the churches under the German occupation and in the liberalization of the Soviet policy towards the churches, also served to re-awaken religious activity. Even several theological seminaries were opened, and old, prerevolutionary theological scholars permitted to teach in them. Despite the fact that the life of a priest in the USSR is one of the greatest uncertainty, including always the possibility of arrest, the number of applicants exceeded the capacity of these schools, suggesting that even after several decades of Soviet rule there are young people willing to risk serving God. At first, however, the regime was inclined to feel that religion would soon disappear once the church had been taken over and the young denied religious instruction in the state schools. That this did not happen, however, is evidenced by efforts of the regime's propagandists to rationalize the persistence of religious feeling among some circles of the population. According to a recent Soviet explanation, the presence of "religious survivals" is due to the fact that:

the consciousness of the people . . . usually lags behind the changes in the life of society . . . This applies particularly to religion, a form of social consciousness which lags behind the base more than all other elements of the superstructure and possesses a greater degree of independence. Another cause of the tenacity of religious survivals is the influence of capitalist encirclement. (188)

Old religious ways have been particularly strong in resisting Soviet atheism in the Moslem areas of the USSR, which include some thirty million Moslems. The Soviet regime has been engaged repeatedly in violent campaigns to break up the influence of the mullahs by closing the places of worship and subjecting the clergy to persecution. In Crimea, for instance, long a center of Moslem tradition, not a single temple was open by 1941. Yet, immediately after the German occupation, some fifty mosques were spontaneously set up by the former congregations. (286d) More recently, Soviet propagandists have been linking Islam with "colonialism" and "imperialism," and stating that "Islam reflects the social yoke and the views of the exploiters." (292)

Accordingly, in 1954 the antireligious campaign was again stepped up. The Central Committee of the Party issued a decree, exhorting its members and the Komsomols to engage in more active antireligious propaganda and to combat the "last remains" of religious survivals. The committee's decree, "On Errors in Conducting Scientific-Atheistic Propaganda Among the Public," however, was not designed to stimulate a new period of open repression. Rather, it was to guide the party members in their atheistic indoctrination while not disturbing the relationship of state or party with the church, since the church had become useful to them. Commentaries on this decree, therefore, stressed the fact that such propaganda must be careful not to degenerate into violence which, in effect, might be more harmful to the party. *Partiinaia zhizn'*, the or-

gan of the Central Committee, emphasized that the method was
now one of education and not of coercion. (265f)

And the regime could well afford its moderation. The previous
coercion destroyed any will to resist among the higher clergy, who
now usefully serve the state. The process of urbanization has
broken up the established village routine that involved religious
ritual also. The new urban centers, with their new modes of life,
leave little room for religion, and Soviet efforts aim to make certain
that this remains so. Thus, while some religious feeling may continue, religion no longer finds in the USSR an institutional expression which could challenge the supremacy and the monopoly of the
party, even in the nonmaterial aspects of life.

In the communist satellites, antireligious activity seems to have
learned a great deal from Soviet experience. Thus in communities
where religious feeling was either weak or the church was not
strong, suppression was rapidly applied. In countries like Poland,
where the church has a long history of national struggle, more cautious measures have been adopted. Thus in Poland, despite the arrests of some hundreds of priests, religious activity by the Roman
Catholic Church continues on a large scale, new churches have
been built, and old ones rebuilt. Even a Catholic university still operates in Lublin. But at the same time, the regime is steadily working to subvert the independence of the church. A collaborationist
group, known as "patriot priests," has been organized, ostensibly
to defend Poland against German aggression. The Primate of Poland, Cardinal Wyszynski, known as an outspoken opponent of
communism, was forcibly removed to a monastery. In 1952 and
1953 the first arrests occurred among the bishops, and some were
charged in public trials with being American spies.* The government, on its own authority, appointed "patriot priests" to fill their
sees. The process of subjugation, although still not as far advanced
as in Jugoslavia or Hungary (where the cardinals were sentenced to
prison), is thus following the Soviet model, although it encounters
much more resistance from both the clergy and the population.
(191)

* See, for instance, the stenographic transcripts of court proceedings against
Bishop Kaczmarek "and other members of the antistate and antipeople's center" in
Warsaw, and against Father Lelita "and other agents of American espionage" in
Krakow in 1953: *Proces Ksiedza Biskupa Kaczmarka i innych* . . . (Warsaw,
1953); *Proces Ksiedza Lelity i innych* (Cracow, 1953).

These remarkable efforts of the churches in the captive nations resemble what the churches, or rather groups within the Protestant and Catholic churches, attempted under the Nazis (and to a very limited degree under Mussolini). The story is an involved one. During the early days of the movement and immediately after its seizure of power, there was very substantial support for it from the Protestant clergy. Its links with pre-Weimar Germany, and its anti-socialist and anti-Catholic outlook had made many of them look with favor upon a movement that claimed to fight these forces and to seek the re-establishment of a conservative, Christian order of things. Their traditional authoritarianism and nationalist patriotism inclined them to overlook the un-Christian views and actions of the movement, and as a matter of fact a substantial number among this Protestant clergy remained National Socialists to the bitter end.

But there soon arose a most vigorous opposition within its ranks. The fight was kindled in part by an issue which struck at the very heart of Hitler's ideology: the racial issue. No Christian who understood the teachings of the church, and more especially no clergyman, could possibly accept the Nazi view that a member in good standing must be excluded from the church because he, or his father or grandmother had been a Jew. Men like Pastor Niemöller, himself originally a National Socialist, rebelled at this flagrant violation of Christian teachings.

Perhaps even more important, though, was the issue of ecclesiastical self-government. The party's interference in the churches' affairs aroused their immediate opposition. Among Protestants this opposition was further intensified by the movement of the "German Christians," which culminated in a scandalous speech by one Krause in the *Sportpalast* on September 26, 1933. (20c) The German Christians were essentially National Socialists who favored a creed which was only nominally Christian, but in fact a replica of the Nazi ideology: fight against Marxism, Jews, cosmopolitanism, and freemasons, and for the purification of the race, and such. The Protestant clergy had to wage their fight against these perverters of the Christian faith. Since the German Christians had the advantage of the political support of the Nazi state and party, this resistance was most difficult and dangerous, but it was carried on relentlessly and at great personal sacrifice. When the German Christians gained control of the Church and elected the Reich Bishop, the opposing clergy, high and low, formed in March 1934 the "Confessional Church" (Bekennende Kirche),* which held its first synod in Barmen-Wuppertal, May 29–31. This synod arrived at a pointedly oppositional agreement:

In opposition to the attempts to unify the German Evangelical Church by means of false doctrine, by the use of force, and of insincere practices, the Confessional Synod declares: the Unity of the Evangelical Churches in Germany can only come into being from the Word of God in faith through the Holy Ghost.

They further maintained that the introduction of alien principles threatened the unity of Protestant Christians and that only those who remained true to the gospel and the creed of the church (in contrast to the German Christians) represented the legitimate church. Denouncing the German Christians, they continued:

We reject the false doctrine that the Church might and must acknowledge as sources . . . besides the one word of God . . . other truths as God's revelation . . . We reject the false doctrine that there are realms of life in which we belong not to Jesus Christ, but to other masters . . . We reject the false doctrine that the state should or could go beyond its special task and become the sole and total order of human life . . .

This was clearly a declaration of war against the very essence of the totalitarian dictatorship, and the Council of Brethren (Bruderrat), which was formed to carry forward the fight, constituted a true resistance to the regime. Besides Niemöller, Bishop Meiser of Bavaria and Bishop Wurm of Württemberg, as well as Karl Koch, who had headed a "Gospel and Church" group of opponents of the Nazi trends, were leaders of this movement. We cannot trace in detail here the complex story of this opposition. It lasted from the beginning to the end of the regime, with various advances and retreats on both sides, but maintaining intact, on a large scale, the essential Christian teachings. It was responsible for the fact that a large majority of the Protestant clergy became unsympathetic if not hostile to the regime, that, of the 18,000 Protestant pastors, approximately 10,000 spoke out in 1935 against the regime's "Church Law,"

---

* The literal translation would be "Confessing Church" and it may be the more correct one since the views of the church's members have nothing to do with the confessional.

and that 11,000 again rejected the regime's attempt to settle the conflict in January 1939. Approximately 6,000 Confessional Brethren confronted the 2,000 German Christians among the clergy, and these men were subjected to vigorous persecution by the regime, and considerable numbers perished in concentration camps. It would seem that only a minority of the Protestant pastors supported the regime actively, with nearly a third being in opposition. If proof were needed beyond the figures made available since the war, it is contained in a Gestapo report of February 15, 1938. "The Confessional Front embraces by far the largest majority of Protestant theologians and likewise the majority of believing church members." (20d) No other organization, unless it were the Catholic Church, was able to mount a comparable opposition, to resist as it were a totalitarian system for twelve full years. It was a true "island of separateness," resting upon the strength of Christian convictions among Protestants, stirring them into new life and genuine dedication. (80; 70; 40; 137a; 91; 236)

But what about the Catholic Church? We find here a somewhat different picture. Considering the leading role of the Center Party in the Weimar Republic, and the great vigor of Catholic lay activity under it, the Catholic clergy at first maintained not only a standoffish but an openly hostile attitude toward the Nazi movement, going so far as to declare in 1932 that a good Catholic could not be a member of the party. United through its episcopate in a way unconceivable for Protestants, the Catholic Church stood firm against the movement until it actually achieved power. Thereafter, unfortunately, they sought to accommodate themselves, in the manner of the Church in Italy, hoping for a while to be able to secure an effective modification of the movement's totalitarian goals. At the initiative of Hitler, and through the agency of Franz von Papen, a Concordat was indeed concluded between the Reich and the Church (July 20, 1933). However, the experience was similar to that of the Church in Italy; the provisions of the Concordat, guaranteeing the Church its essential autonomy, were honored mostly in the breach; for example, in education, both school, university, and adult, the Church could only with the greatest difficulty retain some of the controls the Concordat had envisaged. Similarly, the Catholic press and associations were put under severe pressure, and the bishops protested in a pastoral (1934). As the regime became more fully totalitarian, the clashes increased until eventually in January 1935, the Nazis launched a full-scale attack against the Catholic Church, seeking to destroy the Catholic press, Catholic education, Catholic associations, and even the influence of the priests over the faithful. They succeeded with press, education, and associations, but the congregations stood firm behind their pastors, as in Protestantism. The press was abolished or "censored," education was driven from the schools, while confessional schools were virtually eliminated, and the associations were "co-ordinated," like all others. The pretenses used by the Nazis in explaining these attacks were first, currency violations by ecclesiastical bodies, and second, sexual and other crimes by priests, monks, and lay brethren. The small amount of genuine evil which these accusations involved was, in typical totalitarian propaganda style, blown up to assume the significance of an essential characteristic. (107b) They served to discredit the church to some extent, until a substantial group of ecclesiastical dignitaries, under the leadership of Clemens August Count von Galen, Bishop of Münster, and Konrad Count von Preysing, Bishop of Berlin, insisted on taking a stand. Galen liked to spice his sermons of defiance with such remarks as "they can take my head, but not my convictions." There were also Bishop Sproll of Rottenburg and Bishop Bornewasser of Trier, as well as the redoubtable Cardinal Archbishop of Munich, Michael von Faulhaber.

But when speaking of these high dignitaries, we must not forget the vast number of more humble ecclesiastics, priests, monks, and nuns, who actually suffered more violent persecution, since the Nazi government never quite dared to take vigorous action against the high dignitaries of the church; that they would have done so after a victory in the war is highly probable. Both *Hitler's Secret Conversations* and *The Goebbels Diaries* refer several times to this prospect. (84h; 67c) In any case, they did not show much forbearance with regard to the rest of the clergy; by the end of 1939 approximately 5,700 priests had been arrested, and nearly half were still in concentration camps then. (124; 147a) This is about a fifth of the entire Catholic clergy. In short, the struggle was quite an open one, and the Catholic Church, like the Protestant, mounted a vigorous campaign of resistance. Churchmen, high and low, spoke out against the outrages of Nazi doctrine and action. They had their own "Catholic Niemöller," Jesuit Father Mayer, who though protected by Cardinal Faulhaber was arrested in 1937. When this happened, the Cardinal ordered protests to be read from every pulpit in the diocese.

However, the nature of the Catholic struggle was different from the Protestant, for it rested upon the Church's hierarchical authority. Therefore it took clear and decisive form only after Pope Pius XI issued his encyclical *Mit Brennender Sorge,* which was read from every Catholic pulpit on March 21, 1937. In it the Pope said:

> With deep anxiety and increasing dismay, we have for some time past beheld the sufferings of the Church and the steadily growing oppression of those men and women who have remained true to her . . . He who takes the race, or the people, or the state, or the form of government, or the bearers of the power of the state, or other fundamental elements of human society, which in the temporal order of things have an essential and honorary place, out of the system of their earthly valuation and makes of them the ultimate norm of all, even of religious values, and deifies them with idolatrous worship, perverts and falsifies the order of things created and commanded by God.

The Pope said also that the church's efforts at accommodation had been made in the hope of preserving the essential basis of work for the Christian church, but that it had become clear that the true intention of the Nazis was to destroy Christianity, as indeed it was. It has been suggested that the Catholic shift was in part motivated by the vigorous opposition which the Confessional Church was making to the Nazis; perhaps so. But there was enough provocation given by the Nazis themselves in their mounting attacks on the church to produce a reversal of the policy of accommodation. The Catholic clergy had been divided from the beginning, as had the Protestant, and it was in fact a matter of the opposing minority gaining papal support that turned the tide in favor of outright opposition. (63; 203a; 25; 39) In this respect, the Catholic Church had a distinct advantage, counterbalancing its slower start: once the authorities of the Church had taken a clear and definite stand, the unity of action of most Catholic clergy was pretty well assured.

Catholic authorities were faced with a most curious contrast when Austria and Poland were taken over by Hitler. In the former case, an abject subjection on the part of Cardinal Innitzer and the Catholic clergy had to be counteracted by the Holy See in order to bring the Austrian episcopate into line with the German episcopate, many of whom were outraged by the action of their Austrian colleagues. In Poland, on the other hand, the persecution of the church, as of the people, was so violent that after a report by Cardinal Hlond in December 1939, the new Pope Pius XII became even more firmly committed to a radical anti-Nazi position than his predecessor; in the sequel it also became an anti-Fascist position. In Poland particularly the Nazis gave full vent to their anti-Christian feelings, and subjected the Catholic Church to a policy of unmitigated terror. At first, the most intense violence was restricted to those parts of the clergy which were in the western part of Poland, arbitrarily incorporated into Germany itself. As these territories were to be considered as German in character, the presence of Polish Catholic clergy was highly inconvenient. Accordingly, mass arrests occurred in 1939, and the clergy was exposed to a policy of persecution until the end of the war. This policy soon spread to the other occupied parts of Poland, too, and mass deportations of the clergy to concentration camps took place. All in all, the Nazis arrested and placed in concentration camps 3,643 priests, 341 monks, 389 novices, and 1,117 nuns. Of these, 2,517, including 4 bishops, succumbed to Nazi tortures or were executed. (170)

As a matter of fact, after the Nazis plunged Germany into war, the Catholic hierarchy, like the Confessional Church, was confronted with a difficult problem. They did not wish to be unpatriotic by seeming hostile to the fatherland, yet the intensification of totalitarian trends under the impact of war necessitated a sharper rejection of Hitler and his movement. Among the most moving documents portraying this conflict are the sermons of Bishop Galen after the bombardment and destruction of Münster. Virtually from among the rubble, the staunch anti-Nazi denounced the "tyranny of the Secret State Police [Gestapo]." In one of his sermons he said:

The right to life, to inviolability and to liberty are an indispensable part of every moral social order . . . Any state which oversteps these limits imposed by God and which permits or causes the punishment of innocent men undermines its own authority and the respect for its dignity . . .

And he compared the church to the anvil that must resist and will survive the hammer that is striking it. The same line was taken by the Bavarian bishops who in 1941 issued a pastoral which said: "We

German bishops protest against each and every violation of personal freedom . . . we are concerned not only with religious and Church rights . . . but also of all men, the God-given rights of men"—ancient Catholic doctrine, but often forgotten in more recent times! (203b; 194; 137b; 206; 23a) It all culminated in a protest by the entire episcopate, foregathered at Fulda on March 22, 1942, which was immediately suppressed by the Nazis, but distributed widely:

For years a war has raged in our Fatherland against Christianity and Church . . . We emphasize that we stand up not only for religious and clerical rights . . . but likewise for the human rights bestowed by God on mankind . . . We demand legal evidence for all sentences and the release of all fellow citizens who have been deprived of their liberty without such evidence . . . The Nazis wish to destroy Christianity, if possible . . . Before the soldiers whose Christian faith gives them the strength for heroic battles and sacrifices return home . . . we call upon you . . . to support our efforts . . . Decisively and firmly we refuse the suggestion that we should prove our patriotic faith through faithlessness toward Christ and His Church. We remain eternally true to our Fatherland just because and at any price we remain faithful to our Saviour and our Church. God bless our country and our holy Church. God grant an honest, happy, lasting peace to the Church and to the Fatherland. (262c; 23b)

This in turn was followed by a pastoral of August 29, 1943, which recited at length the violations of Christian doctrine by the actions of the totalitarian dictatorship and more especially the killing of "unproductive" persons, which Himmler had initiated on orders from Hitler, and which had aroused not only the ire, but the most vigorous action of protest by bishops, especially Galen. The same was done two weeks later in a pastoral entitled: "The Ten Commandments as Living Law of all Nations." (147b)

While the Catholic Church did not assist Fascism's rise to power, she later entered into rather close and unfortunate relations with the regime. Many lay Catholics, of course, became Fascists, and a number of the higher clergy, notably Cardinal Schuster of Milan, became outspoken in their advocacy of fascism. The high point of these relations was reached with the conclusion of the Lateran treaty in 1929. This treaty seemed favorable to the church on paper, but it carried with it the church's endorsement of the regime. Soon afterwards difficulties arose in connection with the education of youth (see Chapter 12), but at the outbreak of the Ethiopian war, priests enthusiastically welcomed the war as "carrying Christian civilization" to a barbaric people (Schuster). Soon afterwards, new difficulties arose in connection with racialism, and Pope Pius XI spoke sharply against such radicalism. He even considered repudiating the treaty, but died before he took this step. Nonetheless, throughout the war, the clergy supported the regime, although a significant minority developed a resistance movement which played a key role in the liberation and provided many of the Catholic lay leaders of postwar Italy. The church's relation may therefore properly be described as an ambivalent one, with the hierarchy retaining the right to criticize and even to condemn the regime, which sharply differentiates their position from that of the Russian church with its abject dependence on and subjection to the Bolshevik government. (64g)

In conclusion, we can say that the Christian churches have shown themselves to be a real bulwark against the claim to absolute power of the totalitarian dictatorship, perhaps more real than any others. Whether Protestant or Catholic, the genuine Christian cannot accept totalitarianism. For Christianity claims the whole man and the last word with regard to man's values and man's destiny. This claim the totalitarians cannot accept. They may temporarily seek to compromise, but if they accepted this claim, they would cease to be totalitarians. There is an interesting recent confirmation of this clash. When Peron showed signs of turning into a totalitarian dictator, he quite typically and logically began to attack the Catholic Church. Significantly, the "boiling popular soul"—in the shape of mobs—was at hand to attack and burn churches; vigorous action by a part of the military, inspired by these threats to the church and to other vested interests turned into a complete *coup d'état*. At least that is the appearance of these recent disturbances, especially when seen in the light of the past history of totalitarianism.

It would be pure speculation to try to delineate the parallel problem in countries like China. To date there is no indication that the Confucians or Buddhists have been able to mount a defense comparable to that of the Christians. But this may not mean that these peoples are prepared to accept a "secular religion" of the totalitarian kind forever. Perhaps the family will show itself the comparable bulwark of human dignity, especially since it is itself the most living embodiment of the Confucian faith. (173b) By contrast the islands of separateness, represented by the Christian churches as guardians of the individual conscience and its religious freedom, are likely to outlast even a longterm totalitarian dictatorship. Just how they still exist in the genuine form in the Soviet Union is rather uncertain. But it may well be asked at this point whether their challenge does not spell the doom of totalitarianism as a lasting form of government.

Chapter Twenty-Four

The Universities and the Sciences

The attitude of the totalitarians toward science and hence toward the universities is an ambivalent one, because, on the one hand, their ideology is supposed to rest upon scientific foundations, while, on the other, the antidogmatic attitude of all true science fits ill into the totalitarian scheme of things. Their escape takes the form of a crude utilitarian view of science as merely a means to an end. It cannot be denied that this ambivalence permits the existence of another "island of separateness," especially in those fields of learning which are somewhat remote from the totalitarian ideology. Yet even these tended to be invaded by the totalitarian dogmatism, as shown by Stalin's efforts in the field of language and literature (see Chapter 12) and the Nazis' denunciation of Einstein's theory of relativity.

Science and the universities occupy a very special role in Western culture and society. If we take science in the broad (and proper) sense of any field of learning which is distinguished by a method or methods upon which a group of scholars are agreed as the most suitable for treating a particular subject, whether it be life, government, or the human anatomy (55i), then the very autonomy of such groups of scholars clashes with the totalitarian conception, as it does indeed with all authoritarian conceptions of government. The degree of authority exercised affects the seriousness of the clash, however, and it is bound to be the most serious in a totalitarian society. Yet Western culture has developed many of its distinctive traits, and more especially its technology, as a consequence of its dedication to learning in the distinctive sense of modern science. Indeed, human culture all over the globe is being not only profoundly affected, but revolutionized as a result of the impact of modern technology. And as we have tried to show, totalitarian dictatorship is itself the "logical" outcome of some of these technological trends. This is not true in the sense of modern technology's having "caused" totalitarianism, but in the sense of having made it possible. Without it, several of its distinctive traits, more especially propaganda, the terror, and central planning, would be quite impossible; the dictatorships set up by Lenin, Mussolini, and Hitler would merely have been autocracies of the older despotic or tyrannical variety (for which they were and are mistaken by many, both friend and foe). This undeniable fact that totalitarian dictatorship rests upon modern science and technology produces an inner contradiction of truly Hegelian proportions. It means that totalitarian dictatorship, in throttling science, saws off the branch it is sitting on, especially as long as it competes in the world at large with free societies, in which the progress of science is unimpeded.

It is fairly clear from the record that the totalitarian societies were and are parasitic, as far as science is concerned. They avail themselves, that is, of its fruits without contributing fully toward the maintenance of the plant that feeds them. This parasitism takes two forms. On the one hand, there is the exploitation of past scientific and technological work. Both Mussolini and Hitler lived by the attainments of the societies, which they at the same time sought to liquidate. The universities and the teaching staffs, their libraries and laboratories, were "taken over" and put to work within the context of the regime, like so many other existing things (especially the economy, embodying past technological advance). They continued to function, with certain slow-downs and breakdowns, in their accustomed manner, continued to provide education, to produce new knowledge and so on, even though the regime did not feed them, but starved them, from a spiritual viewpoint. On the other hand, there is also the parasitism that exploits the progress and the inventions of free societies. There is no intrinsic parasitism involved in the free exchange of scientific knowledge; quite on the contrary. But when this exchange becomes largely a one-way traffic, the parasitic nature of the recipient is made evident. The contributions of Soviet science to the general progress of science are very limited indeed. (59g; 142c) All the violent proclamations of the Bolsheviks and their claque celebrating the "triumphs" of Soviet science cannot hide the fact that the USSR has continually fed upon scientific progress in the free countries. The most dramatic expression of this fact are the efforts of the Soviets to secure the essential data on atomic and hydrogen physics by the most elaborate kind of espionage. The way in which science in all its reaches declines under totalitarian impact can be seen in particularly striking fashion in the successive depletions under the Nazis and the Communists in the Soviet Zone of Occupation, as described in a recent detailed study. (144a)

In order to be able to engage in this kind of parasitic activity, the totalitarian dictatorship must, nonetheless, have the cooperation of "bourgeois" scholars who are willing to continue their work. Indeed, this continuation of scholarly work aroused the dismay and indignation of outsiders and victims of these regimes, who felt that the guardians of truth and scholarship ought to rise in wrathful resistance against the totalitarian dictatorship (227; 73), or should at least depart and refuse to lend a helping hand in keeping the totalitarian regime going. There is much to be said for this viewpoint, at least in general moral terms. The fact is, however, that scientists and scholars, by the very nature of their task and training, are the least likely men to mount an effective resistance to a totalitarian regime. There are, to be sure, quite a few cases of noble, if somewhat ineffectual, efforts on the part of scholars, but these are exceptions and they occurred rather late in the evolution toward a totalitarian system, at a time when resistance was no longer effective. One of the main reasons is that the very antidogmatism of science causes scholars to be puzzled and perplexed in the face of so startling a development as a modern dictatorship. There are, of course, those numerous ones who are driven away by the totalitarian masters, but their position is that of victims of the regimes, not fighters in the cause of freedom.

Hitler's views on science and the universities are a curious reflection of the totalitarian ambivalence. He mingled the harsh contempt of the man of action for the man of thought with a ready dependence on science to support him in his pseudoscientific biologically inspired views. In this connection, he repeatedly spoke of the "humility" which science instills in man, as it shows him the limits of his knowledge, and he even betrayed an awareness for the nondogmatic, tentative character of science. He showed himself all ready to voice some of the popular slogans of scientific progress in the manner of Haeckel, and even at one point exclaimed that "the truth will win out in the end." (86f; 84k) But this "truth" that is going to win out in the end, is, in Hitler's more usual view, no such transcendent reality (82c; 92), but rather a tool which is to be employed by the practical man of action for the purpose of realizing "the iron laws of nature," which he contrasted with the "ideas of some crazy ideologues." Rarely has a man written his own epitaph in more persuasive form. And Hitler's confusion on the point is due to his basic failure to fathom, or even to grasp superficially, the conditions for the growth of modern science.

Such truly scientific and scholarly activity is, of course, of great long-range benefit to the totalitarian dictatorship. In a sense, therefore, the preservation of this island of separateness could even be justified by the key leadership. We find occasional observations of that sort, not only in the Soviet Union, but also in Nazi Germany. In such grudging recognition of the role of the independent scholar the totalitarian ambivalence regarding science and scholarship finds its subtler expression. (142d)

The inner contradictions of Soviet thinking on this subject of science are similar, though more elaborate. We have already had occasion to deal with *Diamat* (Chapter 7) and with Stalin's notions on linguistics (Chapter 12), as well as the Lysenko case involving the inheritance of acquired characteristics. But since Marx's and Engels' pretensions to scientific insight are much more insistent (and also better founded) than those of Mussolini and Hitler, the Soviet approach to science and the universities has been one of slow evolution. A considerable number of leading Russian scholars fled, of course, being evidently part of the bourgeoisie, while others lent their hand in providing the essential underpinning of communist ideology; the most striking instance is Pavlov, whose experiments on the influence of environment tended to support the radical environmentalism of the reigning ideology, and who remained to transform the universities into cooperative instruments of the regime. Barrington Moore builds his analysis of the scientist in the Soviet Union on the identification of five primary premises or assumptions in the fields of scientific endeavor. (142e) These are materialism, antiformalism and antisymbolism, verification through practical results, the partisanship of science, and the need of modifying scientific dogma only through action of the political leadership. His able discussion of these several premises and their kinship with certain Western trends culminates in two propositions which display the inherent ambivalence of Soviet doctrine: first, there does not appear to be any significant difference between a decision in regard to scientific orthodoxy and a decision on foreign policy or domestic politics; and second, during the last years of his lifetime Stalin himself was often quoted as reasserting the theme that science cannot advance except through open, free, and creative discussions. (142f) The apparent contradiction of these two views as stated remains unresolved. "The Bolsheviks do not, and perhaps cannot, fully realize the instrumental nature of scientific knowledge, since they try to make science the anchor of their total belief system." It is equally true, however, that the Bolsheviks do not, and perhaps cannot, fully realize the nature of scientific truth, since they make a truth a function of the political order. And yet they need to know the truth as much as their competitors.

For this reason one of the recurrent themes in Soviet writing on scientific research is the emphasis both on ideological orthodoxy and on the importance of the quest for knowledge, including also open and even controversial discussion. But the obvious contradiction between the two postulates, given the totalitarian setting, usually results in the stifling of free thought to the detriment of scientific advance.* That the Soviets are not unaware of the dangers of this situation is suggested by the following pleas in *Literaturnaia gazeta*:

Why is it sometimes so difficult to organize one or another discussion? Why are certain of our scientific disputes more like personal quarrels and altercations than like serious and principled discussions of the essence of great scientific problems? Why is it that with us valuable works, if they are opposed to the views of the leading "school," are not always noticed? What can explain the mistakes made in a number of cases in awarding prizes in science? . . . It seems to us that one of the reasons for all this is the canonization of certain scientific trends . . . (259a)

---

* As much has been recently admitted in Soviet discussions on the Lysenko theories. See the *Current Digest of Soviet Press*, vol. 7, no. 1 (February 16, 1955), pp. 4–11, 22. This matter is much more fully treated in *Academic Freedom Under the Soviet Regime, A Symposium* (Munich, 1954).

The party theoretical journal, *Kommunist,* re-echoes this by claiming that "a struggle of opinions, professional controversies, and discussions are more and more becoming the norm in our scientific and scholarly groups," and adds "this is undoubtedly to the good." Yet, in the very same article, *Kommunist* states explicitly that "discussion of any scientific problem should be based above all on the Leninist principle of the party nature of science and scholarship, and participants in a discussion must approach the solution of all disputes from a position of Marxist-Leninist methodology, the only scientific basis for cognition of the objective world. Fruitful discussion can be based only on the Marxist outlook." (255c; 253b)

The result of this inner contradiction has been that universities and other institutions of higher learning have been greatly expanded under totalitarian dictatorship, while they have at the same time been "politicized," that is to say, on the one hand subjected to a variety of political controls, on the other hand, fitted into the over-all planning of the regime. It is easy to misinterpret these developments, if their true nature is obscured by a "progressive" Western terminology. The most striking instance of this sort of danger is perhaps the work of Sidney and Beatrice Webb (224d; 29), but many others have committed similar errors. Basically, the policies of the communist and fascist dictatorships in the field of higher education are remarkably alike. They consist of the following measures. The universities are deprived of their autonomy and are subjected to rigid bureaucratic controls. More particularly, the rectors (presidents) and deans are made appointees of a special government agency and the teaching staff is made removable at pleasure. At the same time, programs of ideological indoctrination are instituted in which the "true science" of certain laws is expounded to faculty and students alike. In all institutions of higher learning, party and youth group cells are instituted (Komsomols, FDJ, HJ, GUF), which control, and terrorize, not only their fellow students, but also the faculty. Ideological and party qualifications are given increasing weight in the selection of students, as well as faculty. In addition to these "politicizing" aspects of totalitarian university life, there is the stress on technological specialization in response to the needs of the regime's over-all planning. It has been called "polytechnization" in the Soviet Union, and it means that there is, especially among the communists, but also, though less so, among the fascists, an insistence upon narrow specialization of the student, and the steady increase in specialized schools of one sort or another. In addition, and this is peculiar to the USSR and its satellites, there is an enormous expansion of higher technical training (see Chapter 19). Admittedly, the Soviet Union started from a small base, and its rapid industrialization has greatly increased its need for technical "cadres." Still the figures are imposing and are shown in the accompanying table. (37b)

SOVIET HIGHER EDUCATIONAL ESTABLISHMENTS

	Total number (universities in parentheses)	Enrollment Regular	Extension
1913	95 (9)	125,000	none
1928	152 (20)	177,000	40,000
1935	514 (20)	525,000	negligible
1939	750 (22)	620,000	250,000
1946	792 (31)	653,000	212,000
1950	853 (32)	841,000	406,000
1954	814 (33)	1,087,000	645,000

It will be noted, however, that while universities quadrupled in number, other institutions of higher learning and the student body increased about tenfold. It is in keeping with this general outlook that we find that the Five Year Plan for the Soviet Zone of Occupation in Germany specifies an increase from 19 to 26 universities and institutions of higher learning and an increase of students from 27,700 (in 1951) to 55,000. (144b) But all of this increase is accompanied by the insistence on *training,* with fixed curricula, a tenmonth academic year, and narrow specialization, as we have said, combined with a great deal of political indoctrination.

In what sense can institutions of higher learning and more especially its faculty and students remain "islands of separateness"? It would seem on the face of it as if they were completely coordinated and integrated into the regime and hence incapable of any "separateness." The answer must be found in the nature of scientific and scholarly work. The preservation of some of the spirit of free inquiry is something both more precious and more elusive than any kind of political resistance, though the latter may spring from it. Thus, recently fifty-eight professors of the University of Rostock pro-

tested against the Sovietization of the universities of the Soviet
Zone by the SED. Many similar acts of individuals and groups occurred during the Fascist and Nazi dictatorships, and presumably
more could be found in the Soviet Union and the satellites, if the
records were thrown open. There is no point in reciting the individual acts, such as harboring a Jewish colleague, fighting the Nazi
student group over a boycott, attending religious services of a man
belonging to the Confessional Church, and so on. In themselves they
are unimportant, but in the aggregate they add up to a manifestation
on behalf of freedom. Perhaps more important are such acts as the
participation of a number of professors at the University of Frei-
burg, including Gerhard Ritter, Constantin von Dietze, Walter
Eucken, and Erik Wolf in the uprising on the twentieth of July, or
the student-led underground at the University of Munich, which resulted in the execution of Hans and Sophie Scholl, as well as Professor Huber, or the leadership provided by Professor Chabod to the
partisans in the Val D'Aosta, and the courageous fight carried on by
Professor Carlo Antoni and his friends at Rome. (179d; 174c; 39c;
144c)

But the real issue is of a different kind. As we have already said,
it results from the very nature of scientific work. It primarily affects the teacher, but it also involves the student, and the artist and
writer into the bargain. One can dramatize the issue in terms of
the apocryphal remark of Galileo: "And yet she moves!" (59h; 181)
For the man who knows, according to this anecdote, cannot be
made by the decision of a political authority to forget and un-learn
what he knew. Yet this is precisely what is implied by the fifth
principle of the Soviet approach to science, namely, that all basic
principles are to be decided upon by the key totalitarian leadership,
or the dictator. We know today that there remained in the German
and Italian universities considerable numbers of scholars, teachers
and students, who quietly continued their work along genuine scientific lines, who accepted Einstein and not his Nazi detractors, who
taught Christian principles, even if they had to do so in esoteric
terms, who realized that Hitler was a psychopath, even if they were
prevented from saying so (the professor of psychiatry at Heidelberg
who did say so in 1933 was forced out of his position), and so forth.
An anecdote might illustrate this. When in the summer term of
1933 a National Socialist speaker appeared at the University of Hei-

delberg to expound the view that Luther's views were essentially National Socialist and more particularly racialist—a demonstrable falsehood—no one in the audience dared to protest but one visitor from America. In a gathering afterward at the home of one of the professors, those present all congratulated the American most emphatically for having spoken out "against this nonsense." This kind of experience, often repeated afterward, does not perhaps add to the moral stature of German professors (whether professors of other nationalities do much better, the record to date would lead one to doubt), but it shows that the scholar can retreat into the inner sanctum of the intimate group and the esoteric communication that permits him to preserve an "island of separateness" in the totalitarian sea. In other words, the totalitarian, like other authoritarians before him, finds it impossible to penetrate the invisible walls which surround the sacred haven of scholastic enterprise, even though he can reduce the number of men and women truly belonging to it. Such objectivity, has, therefore, occasioned great anger on the part of the communists.

A regular "struggle against objectivism" characterizes all the totalitarian dictatorships, but especially the USSR. Besides the well-known phrases on this score uttered by fascists in the past, we have this kind of statement by contemporary Communism:

The struggle against the reactionary bourgeois ideology prevalent in the universities . . . is essentially identical with the struggle against objectivism . . . Objectivism serves directly the ideological war-preparation of American imperialism . . . With the help of objectivism the American imperialists and their German minions seek to break down the moral resistance of the German people and more especially its intelligentsia . . . Bourgeois objectivism is not compatible with true science and objectivity. It denies the fact of continuous progress in nature and society; for this development takes place through the ineluctable struggle of the New which is coming against the Old which is dying . . . because such objectivism places the old and the new as equally deserving of attention upon the same footing. Thus objectivism wishes to produce the appearance of nonpartisanship . . . In fact, objectivism is thus the most devious, the most insincere form of partisanship for the Old, the Outlived, that is to say it is the ideology of the Reaction. We must unmask it . . . and fight it and take the side of the New, the Progressive . . . We must take the part of the laboring class which is the most progressive class of mankind and the part of that science which expresses labor's interests, and which is therefore the most progressive science—Marxism-Leninism. (250)

Passages such as these make it quite clear why the totalitarian cannot be accepted by the scholar and scientist.

But it also makes it clear why the scholar and the scientist cannot stay away completely from the totalitarian system without cutting himself off from his work. Many scholars, therefore, pay lip service to the ideological trappings that such quotations as the one cited above demand. The introduction and the conclusion of their books become, then, symbolical rituals by which the scholars make their act of obeisance to the regime, while continuing their search for the truth in the substance of their work. The success of such attempts depends on the degree of personal courage, diplomatic tact, and the esoteric nature of the research involved. It is no accident that recent years have seen a remarkable revival in the academic circles of the satellite states of interest in ancient and medieval history, in literature, and in the mathematical sciences. That some Soviet scientists escape into obscure subjects is illustrated by the following dissertations allegedly submitted to the Moscow Institute of Economics of the Academy of Sciences: "Investigation of the Size of Spots on the Lady Bug," "'Inquiry into the Length of Fish Gills." (262d) Every relaxation in government control reveals the extent to which the academicians attempt to maintain the separateness between their own values and those that the regime requires. For instance, after Khrushchev's attack on Soviet architecture, a violent architectural debate arose in Warsaw, and many noncommunist architects came out with sharp criticisms of the Soviet-type ornamental architecture which the regime imposed upon Warsaw reconstruction between 1949–1954. Referring to that period as "the hermetically-sealed one," the architects insisted that more attention be paid to recent Italian and South American styles, and repudiated the arbitrary standards of taste imposed upon them. That such pressures develop in free societies as well can be denied by no one who has lived through recent events in the United States. But they are passing phenomena that cannot penetrate the "castle" that is the modern university. It is these "castles" which the totalitarians seek to conquer. Stalin once said: "We are confronted by a fortress. The name of this fortress is science with its innumerable branches. We must conquer this fortress. Youth must take this fortress, if it wishes to build the new life, if it wishes to replace the old guard."

But it seems that the fortress is unconquerable. Why? Because it is no fortress at all. Science is a method of human beings who are engaged in the search for truth, and that truth is a hard mistress who expects to be wooed in accordance with her nature. As the totalitarians marshal youth to try and conquer her, they are likely to find those youth who are capable of pursuing the truth, who have the imagination and the sensitiveness and sharpness of mind to discover new truths, become new recruits for a value which transcends their totalitarian enterprise. As they enter the island where the quiet of study and inquiry reigns, they become separated from the loud battle cries of the totalitarian regime.

Chapter Twenty-Five

The Military Establishment

The degree to which a totalitarian movement succeeds in politicizing the army is indicative also of the extent to which the society itself has become totalitarian. Indeed, not the least striking distinction between modern totalitarian regimes and traditional dictatorships is the different ways in which they treat the armed forces. In the case of the latter, the army usually provides the actual power basis for such regimes, and to a great extent retains its autonomy of action. Most of the traditional dictators of our age, like Pilsudski, Kemal Pasha, or even Franco, not only based their power on the army, but had actually come to power from the army and through the use of the army. Naturally, under such circumstances, the army tended to remain in a sacrosanct position, jealously watching its many prerogatives and privileges, and retaining a distinct political identity of its own.

In a totalitarian system, this relationship is startlingly reversed. The totalitarian movement is the source of the dictator's power, despite occasional expedient compromises with other elements, particularly in the early stages of its development. As soon as power is seized, efforts are made to neutralize, and then to integrate the armed forces into the totalitarian fabric. Indeed, in terms of the mature type of totalitarian system, the ultimate goal is to make the armed forces into a mere branch of the totalitarian party. The army would be then a sort of totalitarian militia, supporting the external policies of the regime in much the way the totalitarian secret police buttresses the regime's domestic policies.

Political necessity, however, creates its own imperatives. When Hitler seized power in 1933, the political situation was such that any immediate effort to limit the influence of the Reichswehr would have been disastrous for the NSDAP. The totalitarian dictator realized that he held power thanks, to some extent, to the tolerance and benevolent neutrality of the armed forces, and he was not yet in a position to do away with his benefactors. Another factor of paramount importance in temporarily maintaining the integrity of the Reichswehr was the internal struggle for power between Hitler and Goering on the one side and the more radical, revolutionary elements led by Roehm and his storm troopers (SA) on the other. Roehm's program of integrating the army into the SA so as to create eventually a party praetorian guard played into Hitler's hands, but also aided the continued maintenance of Reichswehr independence. It played into Hitler's hands, for it induced the army to back him in the final showdown. Precisely because Hitler needed this backing, he was unable to act vigorously against the army in the fashion in which he acted against the other Weimar institutions. The attack on the army had to wait.

The army was thus able to resist, passively at least, the process of totalitarian subjugation. Nazi foreign policy goals, furthermore, postulated the need for strong armed forces, to be built up as rapidly as possible. This again made it inexpedient for the Hitler regime, even after solidly entrenching itself in power, to attack the army. Such an effort would have produced obvious dislocation and confusion, and would have most likely impaired the fighting capacity of the new Wehrmacht. The officer corps, on the other hand, while often not masking its suspicions of the domestic political objectives of the regime, could not fail to note that at long last it was getting all the sinews of war it needed. The marriage of convenience was thus bearing fruit.

In fact, as the Nazi controls were gradually being strengthened, it became fashionable to remark that so-and-so has "emigrated into the Army," clearly implying that there, at least, one was relatively free from totalitarian control and could pursue, to a degree, one's career on a purely professional basis. Such a situation, however, was anomalous and could not last within the framework of a totalitarian revolution. Even before the outbreak of the war in 1939, a number of leading German generals, such as Blomberg, Beck, and Fritsch, were removed from command and replaced by more spineless officers. At the same time, young Nazi stalwarts were being increasingly introduced into the lower command echelons. This process, naturally, became more marked as the war casualties took their toll, while the later reversals and defeats resulted in the appointment of Nazi partisans to the top command posts.

This process of penetration of the army with politically devoted elements was not the only method used by the Nazis first to neutralize and then to integrate the armed forces. The fact is that, despite all these efforts, the Nazi leadership was never fully certain of the loyalty of its officer corps, and the events of July 1944 bore out the correctness of their suspicions. For this reason, even while strengthening the Wehrmacht, the German political leadership set busily about developing a parallel military structure which was to be the praetorian guard of the National Socialist movement and a countervailing force to the professional army. The SS (Schutzstaffeln-Security guards), accordingly, became a second army, independent of the *OKW* (High Command), and at its peak could boast of over 800,000 elite troops, organized in some forty divisions.

The unsuccessful uprising of July 20, 1944, further enhanced the position of the SS, and Himmler was given the task of commanding all the Reserve Armies on the home front. At the same time, a thorough and bloody purge took a heavy toll of the Army High Command, a large number of whom were implicated. (230a) A particular effort was made to humiliate the condemned officers, and some of them were hanged in the nude on meat hooks. In an effort to institutionalize direct party controls in the armed forces, Martin Bormann, the Party Secretary, was given command of a network of political officers of the commissar type, known as NSFO (National-Sozialistische Fuehrungs-Offiziere—leadership officers). Their task was to make certain of the political loyalty of the military. The Party Secretary, and not the military, was also charged with the task of creating the Volkssturm, a sort of Home Guard of old men and youngsters, for the purpose of a last ditch stand. This process of complete politization of the army, however, came too late, for within ten months the German military machine itself fell apart under Allied blows.

In Italy, as in Germany, the totalitarians, after seizing power, had to cope with an established army and a professional officer corps. Here, throughout the Fascist era, the army remained a haven for royalist sentiments and a source of latent, and finally active, opposition to Mussolini. Indeed, the very fall of the dictator in the summer of 1943 was engineered by the combined resources of the royal court and the military high command. Mussolini, after being dismissed as Capo del Governo by King Victor Emmanuel, was arrested on the steps of the Quirinale palace and transported away in a military ambulance. These technical arrangements of the coup were symbolic of the military forces that Fascism had shrunk from destroying.

At the time of the march on Rome, the Italian army was the only force capable of defending the liberal and democratic order against the rising power of the Fascists. Mussolini, therefore, was extremely careful not to offend the armed forces, and at every occasion emphasized both his hostility to pacifism (exemplified by his military service and wounds) and Fascist admiration for the "Army of Victory." Even after the seizure of power and the reorganization of the original *squadristi* (armed guards of the Fascist Party, like the SA in Germany) into the Milizia Volontaria per la Sicurezza Nazionale (MVSN), the army leaders were assured that the MVSN was merely an auxiliary arm of the Fascist Party and would not threaten the army's monopoly of the uniform and the sword. "The officers of the militia are the chiefs of the revolution; the officers of the army are the architects of the military machine which won the war. Mussolini does not intend to use the army as a political arms," said an early Fascist statement. (49)

As in the case of Germany, foreign ambitions of the regime made necessary a strong army with a high professional morale. For this reason the Fascist regime felt it inexpedient to engage in a headlong clash with the military circles that were needed for the expansion of the armed forces and that appeared to be content with the fascist program of rapid armament. An unstated *modus vivendi* therefore seems to have developed and, although since the military reorganization of 1926 the Duce had been in command of the armed forces with the Chief of Staff directly responsible to him, no direct process of politicizing the military was launched. In fact, during the rapid expansion of the army during the thirties, although MVSN was not integrated into the regular units as shock troops, its units were, during the Ethiopian war, placed under the command of army officers. During World War II efforts were made to promote young Fascists to leading posts, but to the very end senior officers of a royalist orientation generally remained part of the professional cadres. The fact that the top staffs were not members of the Fascist Party made possible the secret negotiations between the Allied and Italian High Commands in 1943, prior to the official surrender of Italy. For a brief spell afterwards, Mussolini, upon his spectacular release from captivity by Skorzeny's Nazi paratroopers, attempted to build up, on the basis of the former MSVN, his own Republican Fascist Army under the command of one of the few higher officers who remained true to Fascism, Marshal Graziani. These efforts, however, were merely the last gasps of Fascism.

Italian Fascist experience with the armed forces, as well as the ambivalent attitude of the Fascist movement toward the monarchy, raises once more the important question whether Italy may legitimately be included as an example of a totalitarian system. On the one hand it is important to point out that the Fascist movement in Italy never fully succeeded in mastering and politicizing the military. On the other, party and military agents influenced military policy, promotions, and the like, as brought out in the Bastrocchi trial. There prevailed a genuine dualism between army and MVSN until the outbreak of World War II, the army being much smaller than the MVSN with its 700,000 men. After the outbreak of the war, the position of the party rapidly deteriorated. No such organization as the Waffen-SS was developed in Italy, but then Italy only "joined" the war, and became increasingly dependent upon Germany in the course of it. Yet, until 1939, the party and its militia effectively held the army in check, and no such coup as the one in Argentina which overthrew Peron's dictatorship would have been possible. (64h) When the impact of outside blows and military defeats made it clear that Fascism was leading Italy to ruin, the military, with the collusion of the monarchy, were able to shake off the controls superimposed upon them by the Fascist leadership, and take effective action of the type that their colleagues in Germany were not able to initiate successfully.

The situation in Russia was quite different from that of Germany or Italy, after the totalitarian seizure of power. The tsarist army disintegrated completely under the stresses of the war and domestic sedition. The Bolshevik revolution was achieved with scattered, unequipped and illtrained Red Guards and the Kronstadt sailors. The great masses of the soldiers merely drifted home, casting away their weapons. The army of the *ancien régime* was no more. But this, initially at least, did not trouble the Bolsheviks. For many years the army had been in their eyes the symbol of imperial oppression, and Marxist theory emphasized frequently that this coercive tool must be destroyed, together with the state which it buttressed. Lenin, for instance, declared: "A standing army is an army that is divorced from the people and trained to shoot down the people . . . A standing army is not in the least necessary to protect the country from an attack of the enemy; a people's militia is sufficient." (113i)

As in the German case, however, political imperatives intervened. The Civil War, efforts to invade the Baltic states, and the Russo-Polish war could not be fought with rabble. A revolutionary army had therefore to be created to defend the revolution against counter-revolutionary coups and to spread the red banner to adjoining areas. This revolutionary army had to have leaders, and the only available officers were former tsarist commanders. The Bolsheviks had no choice but to accept them and give them the command of the newly created Red Army of Workers and Peasants. Trotsky, the organizer of the Red Army, rationalized it thus: "As industry needs engineers, as farming needs qualified agronomists, so military specialists are indispensable to defense." (211) Some 48,000 former tsarist officers were accordingly given command posts in the revolutionary army.

The regime, however, was fearful of a Bonapartist coup and was determined to prevent it. One of the first steps taken in connection with the admission of former officers into the ranks of the new army was to decree that political commissars would supervise the operations of the military commanders. The commissars were given power to countermand orders and even to arrest the commanders whenever it was deemed necessary. Their function was defined as follows:

The military commissars are the guardians of the close and inviolable inner bond between the Red Army and the workers' and peasants' regime as a whole. Only irreproachable revolutionaries, staunch champions of the proletariat and the village poor, should be appointed to the posts of military commissars, to whom is handed over the fate of the Army. (221)

Following the conclusion of hostilities, the new Soviet regime at first decided not to set up a centralized military organization, but rather to rely on a decentralized territorial militia-type army. This plan, however, soon proved to be inefficient and by the mid-thirties energetic efforts were being made to develop a centralized, hierarchically commanded army. By then most of the tsarist officers had been weeded out, and a Soviet-trained officers' corps had replaced them. (231b) Still, Stalin continued to suspect the army command and between 1936–1938 most of the higher ranking Soviet officers were eliminated in a series of lightning and fierce purges. The situation was thus radically different from both the German and Italian cases.

During the same time the regime was making certain that the officer corps was composed of loyal elements, an institutional framework of controls was being constructed to insure that loyalty. In its present form it combines a tripartite network of political officers, party cells, and secret police agents. (19a) The political officers, who are no longer known as commissars, but *Zampolits* (abbreviation for Deputy Commanders for Political Affairs), operate in every unit starting with the company, and are responsible to their own superiors for the political loyalty of their men as well as the officers. At the apex of the political officers' network stands the Main Political Administration of the Soviet Armed Forces (GPUVS), which is also a section of the Central Committee of the Communist Party. The Zampolits wield considerable power, and are particularly important through their periodic assessments of the state of political consciousness of the officers and men. In order to stimulate that consciousness they organize constant political activities and conduct regular indoctrination study courses.

The party cells organize the activities of the party members serving in the armed forces and are the nerve centers for propaganda and agitation among the troops. "The party organizations of the armed forces are an organic part of the Bolshevik Party . . . They enlightened the Red Army men, cemented their ranks, implanted strictest discipline among them, rallied them around the Bolshevik Party and educated them in the spirit of selfless devotion to the motherland and the cause of Communism." (257) The party members are also urged to report all shortcomings and negative reactions to their cells or the zampolit. Party members are likewise charged with organizing small study circles to read party literature. They sponsor special movies for the troops, and devote their leisure time to the indoctrination of the noncommunist military personnel. The party organizations thus provide the necessary support to the official functions of the political apparatus in the army, and it was with a degree of satisfaction that the Nineteenth Party Congress reported that 86.4 per cent of Soviet officers are party or Komsomol members. (271p)

In the event that these controls fail to ensure a positive and enthusiastic approval for the Soviet regime, the matter is taken over by the secret police. Secret police officers operate in all units, starting with the regiment, and are charged with the general task of security. They are to make certain that no "disloyal" elements penetrate the Soviet armed forces, and in this they cooperate closely with the zampolit and party secretary. According to former Soviet officers, the secret police tries to have its own informants in every platoon, and during the war the secret police sections in the army were notorious among the troops for their brutal and arbitrary handling of suspects. Lt. Col. I. Dmitriev, a former Soviet officer, stated that during his entire military career he never heard "of a single enemy spy being apprehended in any regiment or brigade. But there are many examples of the special sections arresting soldiers and officers for expressing critical views, not infrequently qualifying such expressions as hostile activity." (19b) The secret police special sections operate independently of the authority of the zampolits and the party officials, and report directly to their own command in Moscow.

The purpose of all these controls is to prevent the armed forces from developing a distinct identity of their own. They are to be, rather, an integral part of the totalitarian system, living in an atmosphere of an armed camp, surrounded by enemies. Of the totalitarian systems subjected to analysis in this chapter, it is the Soviet handling of the army which comes closest to the model image of the complete integration of the military into the totalitarian movement. Such a process is not without obstacles, and former Soviet military personnel testify to constant strains and tensions which these controls themselves generate. It is very doubtful, however, that the existing impediments to political indoctrination and integration are in themselves sufficient to produce anything like a major crisis in the totalitarian control of the armed forces, as long as the totalitarian system is not itself subjected to a major challenge from the outside. Only then could latent dissatisfaction and hostility develop into a positive reaction against totalitarian control. But even under such circumstances, if both Nazi and Soviet experience during World War II has any meaning, the likelihood of a successful military coup is doubtful. (51a; 230b) This, in itself, constitutes a significant difference between totalitarianism and the older type of traditional dictatorship.

Chapter Twenty-Six

The General Problem of Resistance

In the preceding chapters we have had occasion to speak of groups that manage to offer some resistance to totalitarian rule. The family, the churches, the universities and other centers of technical knowledge, the military establishments—each in response to the rationale of their being, must, if they are to survive, resist the total demands of the totalitarians. As we have seen, the totalitarian dictatorship seeks to divide and rule in the most radical and extreme way: each human being should, for best effects, have to face the monolith that is the totalitarian rule as an isolated "atom." By being thus atomized, the people with its many natural subdivisions becomes the "mass" and the citizen is transformed into the mass man. This mass man, this isolated and anxiety-ridden shadow, is the complete antithesis to the "common man" of the working free society. (58c)

But men resist this totalitarian effort—not only those within the particular structures of university, church, and military establishment, but all kinds of individuals. If one studies, for example, the social composition of the July 20, 1944, uprising, one finds that persons of all walks of life were involved. It was by no means a "generals' putsch"; in fact the generals were rather late and reluctant participants in an undertaking that had extended antecedents which went back as far as 1938. (174d; 169c) The same is true, of course, of the French resistance and of the Polish resistance from 1939 to 1945, the latter taking the dramatic form of a veritable political organization of the underground. (135.2)

In exploring the human motivations which lead to resistance, one finds that they are as varied as human personalities. Moral indignation and thwarted ambition, religious scruples and personal revenge, patriotic fervor and class antagonism, these and many other contrasting impulses, ideas, and convictions have entered into the complex skein of resistance movements and acts. We say "acts" because it is important to realize that a great deal of resistance consists of isolated individual acts of protest. The old German lady demonstratively shopping at Jewish stores on boycott day, the Polish peasant helping to derail a train, the French shopkeeper going out into the street in the dark of night and writing on an empty wall, "À bas Vichy!"—these and many other similar token acts constitute what one might call the symbolic resistance. As one studies the Gestapo records, it becomes evident that there was a great deal more of this kind of thing going on, and presumably is now going on, than becomes known to the outside world.

Throughout Soviet history, the record clearly shows, there have been such symbolic acts of resistance. In addition, actual plots and conspiracies to overthrow the Bolshevik regime—quite a few, doubtless, fabricated by the secret police for the sake of eliminating inconvenient elements (18j), but others probably genuine—have accompanied the rise of totalitarian dictatorship. The course of recent Soviet history actually could be traced in terms of constant plots, conspiracies, and efforts to overthrow the Soviet regime. There is incontrovertible evidence that for many years after the revolution, sporadic outbreaks against the Communist regime continued to occur. Individual acts of resistance took the form of industrial sabotage, efforts to foil state delivery quotas, defection to the outside world, and others. Former Soviet citizens have often testified that their parents made great efforts to impregnate their children against

Soviet propaganda. Similarly, the press in the satellite regimes often refers to acts of individual resistance among students or clergymen.

It is evident that none of this activity seriously threatens the power of a totalitarian regime. But there have also been cases of larger groups of persons engaging in concerted acts of sabotage. We find especially among the farming and working population extended use of the slow-down as a weapon employed to combat the collectivization program which the peasants in Russia, and lately in Central Europe, violently opposed. There have been numerous cases of communist officials being assassinated, local party buildings burned, collective farmers assaulted by noncollectivized peasants. Stalin himself testified to the violence of the collectivization period in the USSR in his conversations with the Western leaders during World War II. Even more serious in nature were the efforts by the various non-Russian nationalities of the USSR to assert their national distinctiveness through separatism and eventual statehood. To this day, one can read in the Soviet press virulent denunciations of "bourgeois-nationalists" in the national republics, and periodic purges of such resistors are a common feature of the Soviet scene. (18k) But after all is said and done, this sort of activity does not seriously threaten the stability of the totalitarian regime. It serves rather to maintain the self-respect of those participating because they share a common danger.

It must be remembered, however, that this national type of resistance is not entirely resistance to totalitarian dictatorship. Rather it is rooted in the sense of national freedom and patriotism which was also the central "motif" in the resistance movements against the German conquerors during World War II in France and elsewhere, as it is a mainspring in the Soviet Zone of Germany today. Such resistance, especially when supported vigorously from the outside, as was the French movement after 1942, has a psychological basis quite different from the hopeless resistance to totalitarianism with which we are here primarily concerned. (135.2) But the distinction is not a sharp one, as shown by the story of the uprising of the German workers of June 17, 1953. Starting from a labor demonstration against excessive work demands, the uprising spread like wildfire throughout the Soviet Zone of Germany, since it was misinterpreted as being in keeping with the New Course of the Soviet Union. It

was not directed against the foreign occupying power, although the
deep resentment aroused by the USSR policies no doubt played its
role. Rather it was mounted to overthrow the East German Communist regime and to reorganize the Soviet Zone along more democratic lines. (15.2) The history of all such genuine antitotalitarian
resistance remains to be written.

There are those more elaborate undertakings, known as resistance
movements, in which extended preparations are made by large
numbers of persons with the purpose of overthrowing and destroying the totalitarian dictatorship and replacing it by some freer system. Such movements are more likely at the beginning and at the
end of a totalitarian dictatorship. The extended civil war in Russia, after the Bolsheviks seized power, is perhaps the most sizable
effort of this kind. It must be noted, however, that the democratic
forces in Russia found themselves, in the course of the civil war, between the hammer and the anvil. On the one side there was the
Bolshevik dictatorship, with the flaming and bloodthirsty rhetoric
of Trotsky; on the other, the reactionaries Denikin, Wrangel, and
Kolchak. These representatives of the old order succeeded in retaining control over large portions of the former tsarist army, and
were able to launch a large-scale fight against the Bolshevik government, established in Petrograd. Not until 1920, after two
years of continued battles, did the Bolsheviks succeed in establishing effective control over the former tsarist empire, and they
were still faced with the problem of national separatism in the Caucasus. (156) However, one of the most unfortunate results of tsarism was the weakness of organized resistance to Bolshevism once
it did establish itself in power. The instances mentioned earlier
were the last gasps of the old system, but its final heritage was a new
tyranny.

Large-scale resistance to totalitarian power has thus been much
more in evidence when the totalitarian system is challenged from
without by a force powerful enough to encourage organized resistance from within. The uprising of July 20 occurred at a time when
the doom of the Nazi regime was a foregone conclusion for all but
the most fanatical followers of Hitler. Nonetheless, it was a remarkable undertaking in which there really culminated a protracted
series of efforts to remove the Hitler regime by force. In spite of the
failure of several earlier attempts, the main leaders of the movement

carried on. They came from all classes of the population except the peasantry. Workers and clergymen, businessmen and army officers, government officials, professors and students formed part of the far-flung conspiracy which almost succeeded. By a mere chance, Hitler was not seriously hurt, and the Nazis drowned the effort in blood. More than 2,000 men and women were executed, often after brutal tortures and public humiliation. (53; 240.2; 169; 39d) But although this most extended effort at violent resistance against a native totalitarian ruler failed, it nevertheless served an important moral purpose after the collapse of the regime. This spiritual end, however, must be weighed against the frightful loss of valuable democratic leadership.

The comparable effort of General Vlasov never achieved the scope of the July 20 uprising. The Vlasov defection from Stalin in the early stages of the Nazi-Soviet war, as well as local efforts to aid the Germans in their military activities, could count on the greatest mass support in the period of the German successes on the battlefield. If it had not been for the stupidity of the Nazi leadership, a most effective movement against the communist regime might have been stimulated. (51b) Greater in scope and more spontaneous in its development was the Polish resistance, considered the most effective in Europe, and which culminated in the Warsaw uprising of 1944. This resistance movement, although it was launched immediately after the Nazi-Soviet partition of Poland in 1939, at first was designed to provide the skeleton institutions of a Polish state in readiness for the allied victory. However, as German atrocities mounted, it took more and more the form of an underground state, waging organized warfare against the occupant. A Civil Directorate of Resistance organized a vast network of underground publications, schools, and universities, even police and courts. This High Command of the Home Army directed, by 1944, the operations of a field army of some 300,000 men engaged in guerilla activities, as well as urban squads designed to carry out sabotage, diversionary activities, and executions of particularly oppressive Nazi officials. In August 1944, when the Soviet troops were approaching Warsaw, the Polish Home Army units in Warsaw—numbering some 30,000 men—seized the city after several days of bloody streetfighting against the retreating Wehrmacht and the SS. However, for political reasons, the Red Army halted its advance, leaving the rebellious city to its own resources. After 63 days of lonely house-to-house resistance, the city finally fell, and was razed to the ground on Hitler's orders. (93b; 101b; 15) No really significant movement of this kind crystallized in Italy until the Allied armies had conquered a substantial part of Italian soil. The partisans who were organized to assist the Allied armies did put up a heroic struggle at the end, but it was a fight waged in close cooperation with these armies. (178.2)

It can be seen that generally the Nazi dictatorship stimulated much more violent resistance than the Soviets, not only at home but also in areas made captive by these regimes. This fact is only partially due to the greater sophistication of the police methods of the MVD and the ability of the communists, because of their ideological position, to recruit local cadres of support. The Nazi program, particularly in the occupied countries, was a thoroughly negative one. The entire population soon became aware that they were doomed to a position of perpetual subjugation, inferiority, and, in some cases, total extinction. This the Nazis proclaimed openly and their subsequent measures bore out the sincerity of their proclamations. The populations, with their schools closed, career opportunities liquidated, and their national economy ruined and exploited, had no choice but to resist. And resist they did *en masse,* stimulated by open atrocities. The Soviets on the other hand, mask most carefully their atrocities (the secret executions of Katyn being only one example), loudly proclaim their friendship for "the people," and give the population certain positive goals to strive for, such as industrialization with all its subsequent career opportunities and hopes. The political opposition is thus caught on the horns of a bitter dilemma: to resist might mean to harm the national economy, by driving the Soviets into more violent measures. The youth, even if opposed to the regime, still cannot fail to notice the positive advantages of cooperation, especially on a nonpolitical plane. Nonresistance soon finds a most convenient rationalization.

Resistance to Soviet tyranny has thus been most effective when a common basis for such resistance was evident. Most violent expressions of it accordingly occurred on a national basis where the local communities became convinced that they were being destroyed by Soviet settlers, by Russians flocking into new cities. Similarly in the captive nations, open resistance, sabotage, and guerilla activity decreased once the period of open Soviet plundering stopped, around

1946–47, and more refined methods of economic and political "integration" were developed. At the same time, the populations could not fail to note the large-scale efforts to build factories, the rebuilding of Warsaw, which the Poles considered a national shrine, the often fantastic projects for a glorious future, to be achieved even by the most stupendous labors. All that, however, is a potent weapon in the communist arsenal for the weakening of political resistance.*

It can be seen from all these experiences that the chances of success in overthrowing a totalitarian regime are slim indeed. The only strong case of a would-be totalitarian regime being overthrown is that of Argentina. But this was due to the regime's failure, for many complex reasons, to develop effective totalitarian control of the armed forces.

Many outsiders have been unjust in demanding, and unwise in expecting, the growth of such resistance movements in more developed totalitarian systems. People used to ask one of the authors of this book in the thirties: "Why doesn't some German shoot Hitler?"—to which he usually replied: "Why don't you?" the point being that it is extremely difficult to mount an effective opposition to a totalitarian dictatorship precisely because it is totalitarian. Its total control of all the means of mass communication, and others, (post, telephone, telegraph, and so on); its complete monopoly of all weapons (except in so far as the military can manage to establish some measure of independent control); finally, its all-engulfing secret police surveillance, which utilizes every available contraption of modern technology, such as hidden recording devices, as well as the older methods of *agents provocateurs* and the like—these and related features of totalitarianism make any attempt at organizing large numbers of people for effective opposition and resistance well-nigh hopeless. People have criticized a man like Goerdeler for his foolishness in preparing lists of people and formulating

---

* That anticommunist resistance was, nonetheless, very strong in Poland was finally admitted in 1956 by the regime itself, which stated that "enemies of the people" killed some 30,000 of its supporters in the years 1945–1956. This book was already in press when the Poznan uprising of June 1956 occurred. Starting as a labor demonstration (much like the Berlin uprising of 1953) it became a genuine attack on the communist dictatorship, though probably not planned in advance. The party headquarters, the prison, and the radio stations were attacked, the secret police administration building was subjected to machine-gun fire. Hundreds were killed and wounded. This again illustrates both the hopelessness and the tenacity of anti-communist resistance among the masses.

written programs for action both before and after the overthrow of
the regime. This sort of criticism is not without good foundation,
but what the critics fail to do is to show how they would organize
any large number of people without even these rudimentary devices
for effective communication. What the critics, in other words, are
really saying is that no resistance movement has any reasonable
prospect of success, and that therefore anyone undertaking it is lacking in judgment. The only answer is that which Berthold Schenk
Graf von Staufenberg gave his wife six days before the attempt to
kill Hitler: "The most terrible thing is to know that it cannot succeed and that, in spite of that, it must be done for our country and
for our children." (107c) If this is true, and we believe it is, that
no effort at resistance is likely to succeed, then no outsider has a
right to adopt an attitude of righteous indignation at the failure of
the people living under a totalitarian dictatorship to offer such resistance. It is one of the most central rules of all sound ethics, a
rule stressed by such a rigorous moralist as Immanuel Kant, that no
one is obliged to undertake actions which are beyond what he can
do (*ultra posse nemo obligatur*). At this point, the will to become
a martyr for a cause begins, and to do so is always "beyond the call
of duty." (12.2)

There is little disposition in free America to dispute the *right* of
resistance to totalitarian tyranny, even though resistance to established government is hardly regarded with tolerance when directed
against the American government. With Lincoln, Americans are
inclined to say that there is no appeal from ballots to bullets . . .
But against totalitarian violence, resistance seems to them not only
allowed, but morally required. It is often forgotten that the problem of a right of resistance has been a serious concern of political
thinkers for hundreds of years, and that the weight of religious doctrine has been against it, though some exceptions have been allowed.
On the whole, though, passive resistance is about all that both Protestant and Catholic moral teachings will permit. For the rest, the
sufferings which the abuse of governmental powers inflict are to be
endured as a scourge by which God chastises a sinful mankind.
However, the insistence of the churches that the people, even though
obeying totalitarian regimes, must not accept totalitarian values
places the churches in fact in opposition to these regimes. In the
light of this situation, it is not surprising that so much of the im-

petus toward building an effective resistance has originated in religious circles. It has usually been the result of a profound internal struggle, a veritable "revolution in the conscience." This struggle has been the most intense where the actual killing of a totalitarian leader was being envisaged. (12b, 17e) When this side of the problem is given due attention, any demand on the part of people living in freedom and security that the subjects of totalitarian rule rise and overthrow their tormentors appears quite preposterous.

VII

Conclusion

Chapter Twenty-Seven

The Stages of Development and the Future of Totalitarian Dictatorship

In much of the foregoing discussion, there have been some implicit notions about the stages or phases of totalitarian development. From time to time, explicit statements have been made regarding them. At the very outset, we suggested that totalitarian dictatorship does not come into existence by a "seizure of power," as is assumed in so much of the literature regarding the subject. What is seized is the control of the existing government, customarily referred to as the state, and a dictatorship is set up in order to realize the totalitarian ideology of the party movement which has "seized the power." But the total transformation of the existing society that this ideology calls for quickly runs into numerous and formidable obstacles. The series of critical situations thus created give rise to the swift enlargement of power, and the totalitarian radicalization of the means of control; in the course of this process the totalitarian dictatorship comes into being.

In view of this gradual emergence of the totalitarian features of these dictatorships, it is evident that these totalitarian systems were not the result of intentional action. (81) True, the total character of the ideology led to a dim appreciation of the difficulties, and a corresponding ideological acceptance of force and violence. The acceptance of violence also carried with it the acceptance of fraud, and more especially propagandistic fraud on a large scale, as a more special form of violence, namely, that done to mind and sentiment. But force, fraud, and violence have always been features of organized government, and they do not constitute by themselves the distinctive totalitarian operation. This operation we have defined in terms of a syndrome of interrelated traits or model features, the emergence of which signalizes the consummation of the totalitarian evolution. It is easy to identify these features, once they have come into full play: Italy, Germany, Russia—they all had emerged by about

1936 as totalitarian dictatorships; China and a considerable number of satellites have followed suit in the years since the Second World War. All these exhibit the six traits we have identified as characteristic: a total ideology, a single mass party, a terroristic secret police, a monopoly of mass communication, a monopoly of weapons, and a centrally directed planned economy.

The collapse of two of these totalitarian dictatorships occurred as a result of war and foreign invasion. If we study these wars, we find that they were the natural consequence of the ideologies of these particular dictatorships. Demonstrably, the ideologies themselves, with their glorification of violence, were at least in part responsible for the grave errors in judgment which launched the leadership into their belligerency. Other difficulties contributed to the defeat; some of these are once again definitely traceable to ideological and other defects of these regimes. More particularly the concentration of all power in a single man's hands, when combined with the absence of any sort of continuing critical evaluation of governmental operations, greatly enhanced the probability of erroneous judgments with fateful consequences.

But the end of these particular regimes, linked as they were to some specific features of their ideology, must not mislead one into readily assuming the early demise of totalitarianism. One need not go so far as to envision with George Orwell a world which in 1984 will be divided between three warring sets of totalitarians in order to appreciate the possibly lasting qualities of totalitarian dictatorship. More particularly the inroads of totalitarianism into the Orient, where despotic forms of government have been the rule for thousands of years, ought to give one pause, and prevent any too optimistic estimate of the totalitarians' lack of capacity for survival. We noted at the outset that autocratic regimes have often lasted for centuries, even when their oppressive practices became ever more pronounced. Therefore the mere maturing of the totalitarian autocracy into regularized patterns of organized violence need not spell their destruction; quite the contrary. Hence, since the end of totalitarian dictatorship is purely a matter of speculation to which we may return at the end of this discussion, let us start with its beginning.

As we just noted and indicated at various points in our study, the totalitarian dictatorship in our meaning of the term emerges some time after the seizure of power by the leaders of the movement that had developed in support of the ideology. The typical sequence is therefore that of ideology, movement, party, government. The point of time when the totalitarian government emerges may be reasonably fixed and delimited. It is that point at which the leadership sees itself obliged to employ open and legally unadorned violence for maintaining itself, most particularly against internal opposition due to ideological dissensions arising from within the movement's own ranks. In the Soviet Union, this point is marked by Stalin's liquidation of his erstwhile colleagues in the USSR's leadership and more particularly by his epochal struggle with Trotsky. In Nazi Germany, Hitler's bloody suppression of Roehm and his followers represents this totalitarian "break-through." In Mussolini's Italy, the Matteotti murder and its sequel are one turning point, the attack on Abyssinia another. In China, the totalitarian government seems to have emerged full-fledged, which is due to the fact that a kind of dictatorial government had been in existence for a considerable time prior to the Communists' establishment of control over all of China, namely, in those provinces that they had controlled and developed in their war against the Japanese. But even here, the true totalitarian maturation may be fixed at the point where the purge of any competitors to Mao Tse-Tung's absolute dictatorial control occurred.

The development in the Eastern European satellites of the USSR follows a definite pattern, too, culminating in the totalitarian break-through some time after the seizure of control by the Communists. However, in these regimes it may be claimed that the establishment of a totalitarian dictatorship was definitely willed at the outset. We do not know for sure, and there are indications that at least the local leadership had some illusions expressed in notions about the more democratic form which the Communist regimes would take in Poland, Czechoslovakia, and Hungary. But it is likely that the Soviet leaders had definite plans for the structuring of the society concerned in their own image, to become "people's democracies" in their own parlance, totalitarian dictatorships in ours. This inference is supported at least in part by the remarkable parallelism in the development of all these regimes. On the other hand, highly authoritative voices from within the Soviet Union took a line which makes it conceivable that the Soviet leadership itself was uncertain, and only "crossed the Rubicon" toward the totalitarian break-through in the light of the actual situational need. Thus we read, in an article by E. S. Varga, "The social order of these states differs from all states known to us so far. It is something completely new in the history of mankind." (266)   A. Leontiev even went so far as to claim that neither Marx nor Lenin foresaw or could foresee such a form of state, the reason being that these regimes were organized in response to a specific and novel historical situation. (269b)   But whether intentional or not, here too the totalitarian features came into existence not immediately upon the seizure of power, but some time afterward, and regularly in connection with the purging of dissident elements in their own ranks, presumably men who had questioned the need for setting up a regime in the image of the Soviet Union.

In a recent study (129; 187), it has been possible to show that the totalitarian dictatorship in the satellites developed in accordance with a definite pattern. The spark which set off the totalitarian break-through was the defection of Tito from the Cominform. It highlighted, as in the corresponding situations in older totalitarian systems, the dangers inherent in the survival of potential centers of dissent from the Soviet-controlled Communist movement. It brought on the total dominance of the several societies by the Russian-directed Communist Parties, except of course in Jugoslavia, where it enabled the anti-USSR group of the Communist Party to establish totalitarian predominance (59i).

If one inquires how this break-through was conditioned, one finds two antecedent stages in these regimes. During the first, the totalitarian movement achieved a key position within an as-yet nontotalitarian political environment. It therefore entered into coalitions with other parties to form a government. It was maintained that this represented a novel and unique form of democracy, unlike the USSR, and that its political task was to liquidate the old ruling class, and to seize control of the major instruments of power: the resistance movements, trade unions and other associations, the armed forces, land reform and socialization, and the key ministries such as Interior, Justice, Communications, and Education which would yield control of the police and courts, as well as mass communication and propaganda. It is evident that this pattern corresponds to the features characteristic of a totalitarian dictatorship as we have analyzed it. Hence it is hardly surprising that in the second stage, the government is definitely molded in the image of the totalitarian dictatorship. Hence the pretense that these regimes were novel and unique was dropped and their kinship with the USSR as a model for building the communist society frankly proclaimed, as well as their dependence upon Soviet political and military support readily acknowledged. During this phase, opposition was destroyed and dissenters purged from the party coalitions. Opposition leaders fled or were liquidated, while their parties were either reduced to impotence or dissolved. During this process, the Soviet Union itself shifted gradually from moderation and tolerance toward tight control and intransigence, preparing the ground for actual total control at the point of the break-through.

The reason for sketching these recent developments in the satellites is that they throw some light on the evolution of totalitarian dictatorship in the major countries. For without drawing sharp lines we find the coalition with nontotalitarian parties in Italy and Germany, the compromise with remaining bourgeois and "rich" peasants' groups in Russia, as well as Hitler's and Mussolini's "deals" with "big Business," with the churches, and so on, and an insistent emphasis on the democratic features of the new regime. If it was stressed later in the discussions on the satellites that their "road to socialism" was easier than had been that of the Soviet Union, there was an element of truth in such an assertion; for the lack of a "model" had indeed been a striking feature of the development of totaliarian dictatorship in the Soviet Union, as we have stressed at the outset. The lack of such a model cannot be claimed with quite the same justification in the case of the Fascists and Nazis; for while they doctrinally rejected the Soviet Union altogether, there is a good deal of evidence that they followed its example in a number of respects concerning vital features of the totalitarian system. When they instituted the secret police and the monopoly of propaganda, the corresponding transformation of education, and the organizing of the youth, and finally the central planning, and when they developed the technique of a rigidly hierarchical party apparatus, the Fascists followed essentially Soviet models. To what extent this was a matter of conscious imitation does not seem very important, since these features are inherent in the dynamics of the totalitarian movement. It may, however, be well to trace this "phasing"

through some of its distinctive component fields, more especially
ideology, party, and secret police. This sketch provides a summary
of what has been discussed in greater detail before.

We saw when discussing ideology that the radical change which
a totalitarian ideology demands necessarily occasions adjustments
and adaptations to reality and its situational needs when an attempt
is made to "realize" such an ideology. The totalitarian revolutionaries are, in this respect, in no different situation than have been
other revolutionaries before them. In the French revolution, especially, the violent controversies over the ideological "meaning" of the
revolution led to the *Terreur*. But since the ideology lacked that
pseudoscientific ingredient which has enabled the Communist and
Fascist totalitarians to insist on the "mercilessness of the dialectics"
(Stalin) and the "ice-cold reasoning" (Hitler), a totalitarian ideology did not develop. Whether its exponents are convinced or
merely pretending, the totalitarian ideology requires that it be maintained even while it is being "corrupted." It is at this point, when
the inner contradictions of the totalitarian ideology become evident,
that the totalitarian break-through occurs. For since there is no
longer any possibility of maintaining the logicality of the ideology
on logical grounds, total violence must be deployed in order to do so.

In the development of the party, which is closely related to this
ideological evolution, an analogous process takes place. In the original movement, when the party fights for success against an hostile
environment, all the leader's authority, or a very large part of it,
springs from the genuine comradeship which unites the effective
participants. After the seizure of power, this relationship continues
to operate, but—due to the new situation confronting the leadership
with the vast tasks of a government that aspires to accomplish a total change and reconstruction of society—it becomes rapidly bureaucratized. Not only the government but the party is transformed
into an increasingly formalized hierarchy. As is always the case,
the *apparat* acquires its own weight and operates according to its
inherent laws of large-scale bureaucracy. At the point of the totalitarian break-through, purges of former "comrades" reveal that it is
no longer a matter of "belonging" to a movement, but one of submission to autocratic decisions which determine a person's right to
belong to the party.

Hand in hand with this development goes that of the secret police. In order to become the instrument of total terror which the police system is in a matured totalitaran system, it must acquire the requisite knowledge of its human material, the potential victims of its terroristic activity. Centers of possible opposition have to be identified, techniques of espionage and counterespionage have to be developed, courts and similar judicial procedures of a nontotalitarian past have to be subjected to effective control. Experience and observation show that the time required for these tasks varies. In the Soviet Union, the tsarist secret police provided a ready starting point, and hence the Soviets got under way in this field with their Cheka very quickly. The entrenched liberal tradition in Italy allowed the Fascists to organize the secret police effectively only in 1926, and it took another two years before it really "got hold" of the situation. The Nazis, although anxious to clamp down at once, did not perfect their secret police system until well after the Blood Purge of 1934, when Himmler first emerged as the key figure in the manipulation of this essential totalitarian ingredient.

It is at the point at which the totalitarian break-through occurs that the total planning of the economy imposes itself. For it is at this point that the social life of the society has become so largely disorganized that nothing short of central direction will do. In a sense, this total planning is the sign of the culmination of the process. In Soviet Russia, it is the year 1928, in Nazi Germany that of 1936, while in Italy it comes with the instituting of the corporative set-up in 1934 (it had been grandiloquently announced in 1930), though perhaps the Ethiopian war was even more decisive. It is not important in this connection to what the planning effort amounts; it will vary in significance in inverse proportion to the economic autonomy of the country concerned. The crucial point is that this total planning imposes itself as the inescapable consequence of the totalitarian evolution in the economic field. It is therefore not surprising that plans should have sprouted all over the satellite region, and that even Red China should have produced a "plan," announced in 1952 and starting in 1953, even though many of the essentials of planning are absent in that vast and unorganized country, where not even the statistical basis for planning exists, actually.

If we view these several factors or determinants in combination, we find that roughly speaking the totalitarian break-through occurs sometime after the seizure of power, depending upon the various conditions, both favorable and unfavorable. What can be said about the projection of totalitarian dictatorships into the future? We exclude here the problems raised by the possibility of a world-wide conflict between totalitarian and nontotalitarian regimes; such a war, while possible, is too speculative in its military and political implications to allow reasonable reflections. But the internal evolution of the totalitarian dictatorships, given some species of peaceful coexistence, allows for some projection on the basis of past experience.

One possibility should be excluded, except in the satellites: that is the likelihood of an overthrow of these regimes by revolutionary action from within. Our entire analysis of totalitarianism suggests that it is improbable that such a "revolution" will be undertaken, let alone succeed. (59j) The records of the resistance in the several totalitarian regimes which have collapsed reinforce this conclusion. When the characteristic techniques of a terroristic police and of mass propaganda are added to the monopoly of weapons which all modern governments enjoy, the prospect of such a revolutionary overthrow becomes practically nil. This may be true, though one doubts that, "even if opposition were less savagely repressed, the people of the totalitarian countries, no matter how badly off or how dissatisfied they are, would not want to engage in any large-scale struggle—they seem to feel that disorder, chaos, and destruction would make them even worse off." (59k) The doubt is suggested by the events of June 17, 1953, in the Soviet Zone of Occupation (German Democratic Republic), and those of June 1956 in the Polish province of Poznan. But the dismal failure of these upheavals unfortunately confirms the conclusion that revolution is not likely to succeed even if it is begun.

What then is going to be the course of totalitarian development? If one extrapolates from the past course of evolution, it seems most likely that the totalitarian dictatorships will continue to become more total, even though the rate of intensification may slow down. This view is questioned by those who expect the requirements of the bureaucratic organization to assert themselves and to lead to a less violent form of autocratic regime. (142g) In this connection, it is argued that the technological needs of an advancing industrial civilization will also play a decisive role. There is the possibility here of an inherent conflict between industrialization and totalitarian dictatorship, through the rise of a class of managers and technicians, who, when they allied themselves with the military, might wish to abandon the ideology and the party and thus bring the totalitarian dictatorship to an end. This development is conceivable, but not very likely. It may be doubted that such managers and technicians have any imaginable conception of the ground upon which the legitimacy and hence the authority of their continuing power might be built. (240.3)

One feature of the probable future course that can be predicted with some confidence is related to totalitarian foreign policy. In the past, when tensions and partial breakdowns in autocratic systems increased, the employment of violence likewise increased in order to solve these tensions. As part of this general pattern, autocratic organizations have tended to turn to violent aggression as a way of solving their difficulties. In totalitarian regimes, it appears that ideology plays a greater role in this respect. In the case of the Nazi regime, one of the initial decisions after the seizure of power was to gear the national economy to a large-scale war preparation. Internal developments, as well as actual strength, were largely ignored by the dictator. In the case of the Soviet Union, there is no doubt that the Soviet leaders have tended to emphasize international relaxation at times of internal difficulties. This was as true in the days of the "Popular Front" as it is in the era of "the spirit of Geneva." At the same time, however, the ideological doctrine of class war can be utilized to develop aggressive belligerency in subject populations throughout the world. The Soviet regime, by maintaining a sham sense of identity with these populations, can abet their revolutionary efforts and exploit them politically.

The degree of direct Soviet involvement in such "revolutions" varies; in some areas, as in Europe, such upheavals were in fact created by Soviet armies; in others, as in Asia, the communists have merely exploited and channeled a stormy situation. When the United States military strength blocked further Soviet advance in Europe, Stalin, in response to this, intensified the totalitarianization of the captive nations, and encouraged the Chinese Communists in their revolutionary activity. It seems likely that in the future the Chinese Communists will continue, on the Soviet pattern, to encourage revolutionary movements in Asia and to give them ideological and institutional backing. The Soviet Union, especially since the "spirit of

Geneva" formally limits the opportunity for direct action, will continue to attempt to exploit the current relaxation to undermine the military barriers built up against it in Europe and to mobilize some of the sympathy existing for the USSR in European intellectual circles.* There is also no doubt that areas of conflict and unrest in the Middle East will provide the Soviet Union with ample opportunities for political maneuvers to set in motion a revolutionary chain of events. And all of this will be carried on without direct clash with the still preponderant military might of the United States, while at home energetic efforts will be pursued to solve the agricultural and related problems.

It therefore appears as we have observed, that the Nazi and Fascist regimes, drawn into a policy of war, on the traditional pattern, by the ideological blindness of their leaders, committed themselves in advance to an open conflict the outcome of which was more than doubtful. Except for a very few areas, such as Austria, their opportunities for creating revolutionary upheavals which they could exploit were limited. The Communists, launching a broad economic and social revolution at home, can combine these domestic measures with a foreign expansion, short of war. It is therefore rather unlikely that they would launch a major and open campaign of aggression because of internal difficulties. They accept such difficulties as part of the revolutionary process. Their refined, yet often brutal, system of controls dooms any effective resistance in advance (see Chapter 25). The possibility of open war will increase, however, as the Communists gain in military preponderance.

Whether it is possible, in terms of a developmental construct, to forecast the probable course of totalitarian evolution seems more doubtful. We prefer the simple extrapolation of recent trends, and the estimate of broader potentials in terms of long-range observation of autocratic regimes throughout history. (59l) Considered in such terms, the prospect of totalitarian dictatorship seems unclear. Leaving aside the possibility of liquidation by war, there might conceivably be internal transformation. "It is possible," as one highly qualified observer said, "that the 'wave' of totalitarianism has reached its high water mark. And it may well be that in the not too distant future it will start rolling back." (59m) It may be. But if one such totalitarianism disappeared, others may appear to take its place, due

---

* See R. Aron, *Opium des Intellectuels.*

to the endemic conditions which have given rise to them. [Totalitarian dictatorship, a novel form of autocracy, more inimical to human dignity than autocracies in the past, appears to be a highly dynamic form of government which is still in the process of evolving. Whether it will, in the long run, prove to be a viable form of social and political organization remains to be seen. Nonetheless, large portions of mankind may have to pass through its crucible, before becoming ready, if they survive the ordeal, for more complex forms of political organization.

Some Bibliographical Notes
Bibliographical References
Index of Names
Index of Subjects

Some Bibliographical Notes

Any study of totalitarianism should involve, in great measure, original research. Fortunately, recent years have seen intensive efforts to tap the available research data, and the books in English cited below represent some, but not all, of the more serious efforts to shed light on the problems with which our book has been concerned. However, a great deal of original research still remains to be done, and a student of totalitarianism would find it extremely rewarding to explore some of the available original sources. To mention but a few: the proceedings and documentary evidence of the Nürnberg War Crimes Trials represent a rich fount of information on the Nazi system. Easily available and thoroughly indexed, they are "a must" for anyone undertaking to examine the Nazi system. Similarly, such materials as *Hitler's Secret Conversations* or even *The Goebbels Diaries* shed a great deal of light on the thinking of the most important Nazi figures. *Voelkischer Beobachter, der Stuermer,* or *das Schwarze Korps,* and other Nazi publications (each major institution had its own) are almost indispensable to this type of research. Similarly in the case of the USSR, the Soviet press, both national and local, is extremely helpful to research on current and past problems. Thus *Partiinaia zhizn,* the party journal, reflects many of the current problems faced by the leadership, *Kommunist* gives the ideological flavor, *Voprosy ekonomiki* discusses economic matters, *Vedomosti Verkhovnogo Soveta SSSR* gives texts of official decrees, etc., not to mention *Pravda* and *Izvestia* for day to day coverage. The list of available publications runs into many tens. Party congresses and conferences, compiled in lengthy stenographic reports, are absolutely invaluable to research not only on the party but on the state and economy. One could stretch such lists *ad infinitum,* but the above should suffice as a preliminary guide for a student undertaking serious study of the totalitarian problem.

Such research and analysis will, of course, benefit from available studies of totalitarianism, and the number of such studies in English is rapidly multiplying (for the foreign studies, see page 313). Remarkably few of them, however, have attempted to undertake a broad synthesis of the problem in terms of the admittedly distinct experience of the Fascist-Nazi and of the Communist experiments. An able effort to do so was made some fifteen years ago by S. Neumann in his *Permanent Revolution* (1942), a book deserving of close scrutiny by a student of totalitarianism. In it Neumann undertakes to detect the unifying element of such varying systems as the Nazi and the Soviet and finds it in the permanent revolution. A more recent undertaking is that of the collective volume on *Totalitarianism* (1954), edited by C. J. Friedrich, consisting of a series of papers presented at a conference of the American Academy of Arts and Sciences in March 1953. The authors include H. Arendt, R. Bauer, C. J. Friedrich, A. Inkeles, G. Kennan, H. D. Lasswell, and other outstanding authorities, and a specific effort is made by them to consider the totalitarian problem in its entirety. In so far as more general theoretical works on the rise of totalitarianism are concerned, one must mention H. Arendt's challenging and stimulating volume on *The Origins of Totalitarianism* (1951), as well as J. Talmon's very scholarly, although controversial, *Totalitarian Democracy* (1952). Both try to find the meaning of totalitarianism in terms of certain intellectual traditions of the western experience.

There are more books available on specific totalitarian systems, both from the institutional-operational and the theoretical standpoint. M. Fainsod's treatment, in his *How Russia is Ruled* (1953), of party controls in Soviet institutions is the outstanding study of Soviet totalitarianism in action. B. Moore's *Soviet Politics—The Dilemma of Power* (1950) is a well-documented and very thoughtful analysis of the relationships between theory and practice in the development of the Soviet system. His later *Terror and Progress—USSR* (1954) is a model of reflective consideration of projected trends of political development. W. Kulski's *The Soviet Regime* (1954), an encyclopedic collection of basic data, casts light on almost every facet of life under that system. J. Towster's *Political Power in the USSR* (1948) has useful material on the institutional development of the USSR, while Z. K. Brzezinski's *Permanent Purge—Politics in Soviet Totalitarianism* (1956) analyzes the political process in totalitarianism as manifested in the party purges. In so far as the historical aspects of the USSR are concerned, one might suggest E. H. Carr's monumental, even though somewhat doctrinaire, volumes on *The Bolshevik Revolution;* R. Pipes's *The Formation of the Soviet Union* (1954), dealing particularly with Soviet absorption of central Asiatic and Caucasion regions, as well as N. S. Timasheff's *The Great Retreat* (1946), written under the impact of wartime compromises in Soviet policies. In terms of biographical studies which cover the working of totalitarian dictatorship, one may well refer to I. Deutscher's and also to B. Souvarine's volumes, both entitled *Stalin* (1949 and 1939 respectively), as well as B. Wolfe (see below). Students of Soviet affairs can also take advantage of a number of scholarly journals, devoted almost exclusively to the study of communism. Leading among them are *Problems of Communism, The American Slavic and East European Review, Russian Review,* as well as *The Current Digest of the Soviet Press,* an excellent source for Soviet material.

Comparatively thorough treatment of the Nazi system is to be found in F. Neumann's *Behemoth* (1942), although its analysis is marred by the author's Marxist bias. *The Dual State—A Contribution to the Theory of Dictatorship* (1941), by E. Fraenkel, focuses on the persistence of a complex legal order in spite of the arbitrary action emanating from the totalitarian leadership. A UNESCO study, edited by M. Baumont, *The Third Reich* (1955), is the most recent attempt to discuss the nature and institutions of the Nazi system, but on the whole it suffers from inadequate documentary research and fails to utilize, among other things, sociological tools of analysis. Important for the international aspects is *Hitler's Europe,* edited by Arnold & Veronica Toynbee (1954). In general, coverage of Nazi Germany lags behind that currently available for the USSR. Biographical studies, which are in fact historical surveys of the regime focused on the person of the dictator, also are useful for a better understanding of the Nazi system: outstanding among them are A. Bullock's *Hitler—A Study of Tyranny* (1952) and the earlier work by K. Heiden, *Der Fuehrer—Hitler's Rise to Power* (1944). O. Dietrich, the Nazi press chief's recent reminiscences, *Hitler* (1955), is subjective and impressionistic. In so far as Italy is concerned, there is a great need for further work to supplement the earlier studies by Max Ascoli (with A. Feiler) *Fascism for Whom?* (1938), G. Salvemini, *Under the Axe of Fascism* (1936), H. Finer, *Mussolini's Italy* (1935), and G. A. Borgese, *Goliath—The March of Fascism* (1937). D. Germino's Ph.D. thesis (Harvard, 1956), "The Party as an Instrument of Totalitarian Rule: The Partito Nazionale Fascista, 1925–1939," provides an excellent beginning.

One should also mention in this connection works dealing with some other dictatorial and totalitarian regimes, such as the Chinese, the satellite, or the Argentinian before 1955. Literature on them is still rather sparse. However, B. Schwartz's *Chinese Communism and the Rise of Mao* (1951) and R. Walker's *China under Communism* (1955), as well as A. Ulam's *Titoism and the Cominform* (1951), constitute significant contributions to scholarship. H. Blanksten, in his *Peron's Argentina* (1953) gives an early assessment of the then-budding Argentinian totalitarianism. F. Borkenau's *European Communism* (1953) deals more broadly with communist totalitarian movements in Europe, as does M. Einaudi in his *Communism in Western Europe* (1951). E. Nettl's *The Eastern Zone and Soviet Policy in Germany* (1951) provides a specific treatment of one of the Soviet satellite regimes. Similar studies are available, or are being prepared, on the other regimes of the captive nations in Europe.

Problems of theory, in terms of specific totalitarian regimes, come in also for their due share of consideration. Naturally, there is no substitute for the original works: the so-called Marxist classics of Marx, Engels, and Lenin. Certainly, Stalin and Trotsky are relevant also. Similarly, Hitler's *Mein Kampf,* Rosenberg's *Der Mythos des Zwanzigsten Jahrhunderts* (1930), as well as Mussolini's more limited contributions, call for careful study. There is a great abundance of interpretative works, based on the above, which deal with a number of facets of the respective ideologies. Among the more recent studies, one may point to A. Meyer's *Marxism—The Unity of Theory and Practice* (1954), L. Haimson's *The Russian Marxists and the Origins of Bolshevism* (1955), and J. Plamenatz's *German Marxism and Russian Communism* (1954). B. D. Wolfe's *Three Who Made a Revolution* (1948) is a biographical classic on the earlier days of Lenin, Trotsky, and Stalin, and recounts the ideological clashes of the prerevolutionary era. *The Appeals of Communism* (1954), by G. Almond, is an important attempt to relate the role of ideology to the personal viewpoint and experience of party members in several selected countries. Somewhat of that type, but dealing more specifically with central Europe, written in a literary style of high order, is C. Milosz's *Captive Mind* (1953), perhaps the best treatment available on the intellectual under communism. The problem of continuity and discontinuity finds exhaustive treatment in the collective volume on *Continuity and Change in Russian and Soviet Thought* (1955), edited by E. Simmons. Needless to add, the above list is highly selective, and mentions merely some of the more recent works.

Nazi ideology, probably because of the inherently primitive nature of its system of thought, has attracted fewer thinkers to a critical exposition of its meaning. An early attempt to understand the essence of Nazism was made by H. Rauschning in his *The Revolution of Nihilism* (1939). R. A. Brady developed a general exposition of Nazism in *The Spiritual Structure of German Fascism* (1937) from a Marxist standpoint. The collective volume on the Third Reich (Baumont) also deals in part with problems of ideology, but a systematic treatment of this subject still offers a fruitful field for further work. The same is largely the case with Fascism. Fascist ideology is treated in the general works cited previously, and there is an early piece by A. Rocco, *The Political Doctrine of Fascism,* which is rather expository and formal. No overall, thorough examination and critique of the theoretical tenets of Fascism is available in English.

As we have noted in our book, terror and propaganda occupy a central place in the totalitarian scheme of social reconstruction. Most of the general works cited above do discuss them, although frequently failing to show the inherent connection between them. In addition to them one might cite a few selected books dealing with this particular aspect of totalitarianism; again, our list is highly selective. Among personal recollections of Soviet prisons and camps, the following may be suggested: G. Herling, *A World Apart* (1952); J. Gliksman, *Tell the West* (1948); A. Weissberg, *The Accused* (1951); F. Beck & W. Godin, *Russian Purge and Extraction of Confession* (1951). The first two deal with Soviet camps, the latter two essentially with prisons. More recent accounts of released German prisoners confirm the pattern of life as presented in these accounts, although some institutional changes have been noted in our Chapter 15. Some more specific aspects of Soviet terror are treated in the gripping accounts of the Katyn forest massacre of 4,000 Polish officers by J. Mackiewicz in *The Katyn Wood Murders* (1951); Z. Stypulkowski in his *Invitation to Moscow* (1951) tells the story of Soviet "brainwashing" in preparation for a Moscow show-trial; N. Leites and E. Berhaut, in *The Ritual of Liquidation* (1954), analyze fully the confessions of the great trials in the thirties; while D. Dallin's *Soviet Espionage* (1955) gives a thorough treatment of that aspect of Soviet operations. An up-to-date study of Soviet forced labor is to be found in the report edited by R. N. Baldwin in 1953, entitled *A New Slavery—Forced Labor: The Communist Betrayal of Human Rights* (1953), while A. Inkeles gives a complete description of Soviet propaganda in his *Public Opinion in Soviet Russia* (1950), covering radio, press, and oral indoctrination. For an example of its consequences, see F. Barghoorn's *The Soviet Image of the United States* (1950). The process of remaking the Soviet man, including his training, finds coverage in R. Bauer's *The New Man in Soviet Psychology* (1951) and in N. De Witt's *Soviet Professional Manpower* (1955).

The German equivalent for the above, apart from the general works cited previously, is more than adequate and constitutes mute testimony to German proficiency in these areas. First of all, most of the governments of the wartime occupied countries published detailed accounts of the atrocities committed in them. In addition to these, we may recommend E. Kogon's excellent study of the concentration camp system, somewhat "overtitled" as *The Theory and Practice of Hell* (1950). For sociological aspects of the same problem, consult *Human Behavior in the Concentration Camp* (1953), written by a Dutch psychiatrist, E. Cohen, on the basis of personal experience in the camps. A general treatment of Nazi terror and atrocities is to be found in the *Scourge of the Swastika* (1954) by Lord Russell of Liverpool. As one of the many accounts of personal experiences we can recommend the recollections of a Jewish girl who wrote, under the name of Ka-tzetnik 135633 (the number tattooed on her), a stirring indictment entitled *House of Dolls* (1955). Nazi propaganda operations are described in D. Sington & A. Weidenfeld, *The Goebbels Experiment—A Study of the Nazi Propaganda Machine* (1943), while an "inside" look can be had from the Goebbels and Dietrich diaries. For the process of creating a new "Nazi-man" one might also consult E. Mann's *School for Barbarians* (1938) and the official British document on *Education under Nazi Rule* (1940). A worthwhile study on the Fifth Column, *The German Fifth Column* (1956) by De Jong has been published recently.

The problem of the armed forces under a totalitarian regime is given a historical survey in F. D. White's *The Growth of the Red Army* (1944), while the specific matter of political and police controls is summarized in a series of accounts by Soviet officers in Z. K. Brzezinski's *Political Controls in the Soviet Army* (1954). Ideology and strategy are discussed fully in D. Garthoff's *Soviet Military Doctrine* (1954). The relationship of the German army to Nazi totalitarianism is given detailed treatment in Wheeler Bennet's *The Nemesis of Power* (1953) and in T. Taylor's *The Sword and the Swastika* (1952), both of which add much, though neither are without bias, to the wartime treatment by H. E. Fried, *The Guilt of the German Army* (1942); a broader historical perspective of this entire problem can be found in G. Craig's *The Politics of the Prussian Army* (1955).

For economic aspects of the totalitarian problem, one may turn to the studies by H. Schwartz, *Russia's Soviet Economy* (2nd ed., 1954), N. Jasny, *The Socialized Agriculture of the USSR* (1949), and H. Dinerstein, *Communism and the Russian Peasant* (1955). Other aspects, particularly the industrial and the fiscal, are considered in D. Hodgman's *Soviet Industrial Expansion 1928–1951* (1954) and F. Holzman's *Soviet Taxation: The Fiscal and Monetary Problems of a Planned Economy* (1955). Again in so far as the Nazi experience is concerned, worthwhile materials and analysis can be found in L. Lochner's *Tycoons and Tyrant* (1954), who refutes the "big bosses made Hitler" myth, G. Reimann's *The Vampire Economy* (1939), M. Sweezey, *The Structure of the Nazi Economy* (1941), as well as in the more general works cited previously.

Certainly the works cited in the notes to the text of the book constitute reference sources for a number of problems raised by us but not covered in these bibliographical comments. In addition, we might suggest that a student of totalitarianism would benefit by consulting the growing literature on this subject appearing lately in foreign languages, particularly in French and German, and to a lesser extent in Italian. For instance, among the French studies, we may point to J. Monnerot's

Sociologie du Communisme (1949), subsequently translated into English, which is an extremely interesting analysis of the ideological aspects of the problem, although drawing a somewhat forced analogy between communism as a secular religion and Mohammedanism (cf. our chapters on ideology); H. Chambre's *Le Marxisme en Union Sovietique— Ideologie et Institutions, leur évolution de 1917 à nos jours* (1955) is, as the lengthy title suggests, an attempt to consider theory with reference to practice, and points to the instrumental character of Soviet ideology: C. Bettelheim's detailed *Les Problèmes Théoretiques et pratiques de la planification sovietique* (1951) gives an uncritical party-line assessment of Soviet planning. R. Aron's *L'Opium des Intellectuels* (1955) is a provocative indictment of the intellectuals' response to communism, while Jean Lacroix in his *Marxisme, existentialisme, personnalisme* (1950) discusses critically the new Soviet man. Broad discussions of Marxism are to be found in H. Collinet's *La tragédie du marxisme* (1948) and J. Romeuf's *Permanence de la doctrine marxiste dans l'evolution economique et sociale d'USSR* (1946). Maurice Merleau-Ponty addresses himself specifically to the problem of the purge trials in his *Humanisme et terreur* (1947), while A. Rossi's *Physiologie du Parti communiste français* (1948) is the best available study of that totalitarian movement. There is also considerable literature in French on Fascist totalitarianism. A remarkable study of Nazi leader psychology is François Bayle, *Psychologie et Ethique du National-Socialisme— Etude Anthropologique des Dirigeants SS* (1953). G. Castellan's *La DDR* (1955) is the latest and most detailed study of the Soviet satellite regime in East Germany. On the whole, available French works tend to emphasize the theoretical and ideological aspects of modern communist totalitarianism, but much of it is rather on the doctrinal side, and not in line with more recent thought on totalitarianism. We might mention Jacques Bainville, *Les Dictatures* (1935), Daniel Guérin, *Fascisme et Grand Capital* (6th ed., 1945), A. Rossi, *La Naissance du Fascisme* (1938), Marcel Prélot, *L'Empire Fasciste* (1936), and F. L. Ferrari, *Le Regime Fasciste Italien* (1928). Besides these, two recent works of a rather unusual cast deserve the attention of the student of totalitarian dictatorship: Alfred Fabre-Luce, *Histoire de la Révolution Européenne* (1954) and Louis Rougier, *Les Mystiques Economiques— Comment on passe des Démocraties Libérales aux Etats Totalitaires* (1949). We note also the volume entitled *L'Etat* (Vol. X) of the *Encyclopédie Française* by de Manzie, Bertrand de Jouvenel's *Du Pouvoir* (1947, also in English), and the *Cours* of George Vedel at the Institut d'Etudes Politiques, dealing with totalitarian dictatorship.

Students wishing to consult German studies will do well to acquaint themselves with the *Zeitschrift für Zeitgeschichte,* published by the Institut für Zeitgeschichte in Munich since 1953 and containing many significant monographs. The same institute has also been publishing special studies. Other pertinent studies in German, as well as in Italian and Russian, can be found in the bibliographical references that follow, and there is no need to recite them here once more.

Bibliographical References

These references are arranged alphabetically by authors with the particular reference to the pages grouped by letters in parentheses. The asterisk (∗) introduces subsequent references to the entry.

BOOKS

1. Alton, T. P., *Polish Postwar Economy,* New York, 1955, p. 198.
2. Aristotle, *Politics,* Book I.
3. Arendt, Hannah, *Origins of Totalitarianism,* New York 1951. ∗(a) *passim.* ∗(b) *passim.* ∗(c) esp. pp. 387ff, concerning the role of the secret police; and also p. 76 in Friedrich (ref. 59). ∗(d) p. 130. ∗(e) p. 400.
4. Aron, Raymond, *L'Opium des Intellectuels,* Paris, 1955. ∗(a) pp. 315ff. The author argues this case with persuasive insistence for the French Left, whose ideology, or myths, he compares with that of the Right, asking finally whether the age of ideologies is coming to an end. ∗(b) Part I, pp. 15–114, where the *mythes* of the French Left are subjected to a searching critique.
5. Baldwin, Roger N., ed., *A New Slavery—Forced Labor: The Communist Betrayal of Human Rights,* New York, 1953. ∗(a) *op. cit.* ∗(b) p. 53. ∗(c) p. 60.
6. Bauer, Raymond A., *The New Man in Soviet Psychology,* Cambridge, Mass., 1952. See ref. 69.
7. Beloff, Max, *The Foreign Policy of Soviet Russia, 1929–1941,* London, 1947; see ref. 57.
8. Bertalanffy, Livon, *General System Theory: A New Approach to the Unity of Science,* 1951. A system is characterized by three features: it consists of several parts that are quite distinct and different from each other; these parts bear a defined functional relation to each other; and typically the destruction of some of these parts (the essential ones) entails the destruction of the system as a whole. Such systems may be composed of physical entities, of animated beings, or of thoughts. A social or cultural or political system is typically a combination of all three.
9. Bienstock, Gregory, S. M. Schwartz, and A. Yugow, *Management in Russian Industry and Agriculture,* London, 1947.
10. Bischoff, Ralph F., *Nazi Conquest through German Culture,* Cambridge, Mass., 1942.

11. Bottai, G., *Vent' anni e un giorno,* Rome, 1949, esp. p. 96. See also ref. 64f.
12. Bonhoeffer, Dietrich, *Letters and Papers from Prison,* ed. by E. Bethge, trans. by R. H. Fuller, London, 1954. See also Ritter (169b).
12.2 Borch, Herbert von, *Obrigkeit und Widerstand,* 1954.
13. Borgese, G. A., *Goliath, The March of Fascism,* New York, 1937, pp. 271–344. For a bitter criticism of this tendency, see Emil Ludwig's *Mussolini* (119), p. 231.
14. Borkenau, F., *European Communism,* London, 1953, for a detailed treatment of this period.
15. Bor-Komorowski, General T., *The Secret Army,* London, 1951. See also Karski (93) and Korbonski (101).
15.2. Brant, Stephen, *Der Aufstand, Vorgeschichte, Geschichte und Deutung des 17. Juni 1953,* Stuttgart, 1954.
16. Brecht, Bertold, *Furcht und Elend des III. Reiches,* New York, 1945, for a pointed indictment. Unfortunately, the author, as a communist, fails to draw the obvious parallel with the USSR and the activities of men like Vishinsky.
17. Brown, Macalister, "Expulsion of German Minorities from Eastern Europe: The Decision at Potsdam and its Background," Ph.D. thesis, Harvard University, 1952.
18. Brzezinski, Z. K., *The Permanent Purge: Politics in Soviet Totalitarianism,* Cambridge, Mass., 1955. *(a) chapter 9 for a thorough discussion of this conflict. *(b) chapter 9. *(c) chapter 9. *(d) chapter 9. *(e) chapters 4, 5, 6, and 7. *(f) for a general theoretical treatment, as well as specific Soviet data; see also ref. 64f. *(g) p. 133. (h) chapter 4 for more detail; see ref. 252b. *(i) p. 216 for quotation cited. *(j) chapters 1, 2, and 7. *(k) chapters 5 and 8 and Appendix II.
19. Brzezinski, Z. K., ed., *Political Controls in the Soviet Army,* New York, 1954. *(a) for a detailed treatment. *(b) p. 54, I. Dmitriev.
20. Buchheim, H., *Glaubenskrise im Dritten Reich,* Stuttgart, 1953. *(a) p. 83. *(b) pp. 81–83, for discriminating commentary; see also ref. 131. *(c) pp. 124ff, for this event and its antecedents. *(d) p. 78, for Richtlinien, as summed up. *(e) pp. 13–17, for penetrating comments; see also ref. 82c.
21. Buhler, N. and S. Zukowski, *Discrimination in Education in the People's Democracies,* New York, 1944, quotation from *Lidove Noviny,* April 27, 1951. Their study is a useful handbook on the iniquitous practices followed by the satellite regimes.
22. Bullock, Alan, *Hitler—A Study in Tyranny,* London, 1952. *(a) *passim.* *(b) p. 367, and also p. 349. *(c) chapter 9, esp. pp. 469ff. *(d) chapter 18, p. 328, for citation of Minutes of the Council of Ministers, September 4, 1938. *(e) p. 328.
23. Burns, Findley, Jr., "The Roman Catholic Church in Germany and National Socialism," unpublished seminar report, Harvard University, 1951. *(a) see ref. 203b. *(b) quotation from Burns.

24. Carr, E. H., *The Bolshevik Revolution, 1917–1923*, New York, 1951–1954. *(a) Vol. IV, "The Interregnum." *(b) Vol. IV.

25. *The Catholic Church, Persecution in the Third Reich: Facts and Documents*, London, 1940; see also ref. 63.

26. *Civil Code (BGB)* (German), para. 616–618.

27. Clay, Lucius D., *Decision in Germany*, New York, 1950, pp. 358–392. See also ref. 241a.

28. Counts, G. S. and N. Lodge, *I Want to Be Like Stalin*, New York, 1947, translation of a Soviet propaganda textbook on civic training. See also *Il Libro della IV classe elementare*, Rome, 1941, which shows how the Fascists used even the grammar section for propaganda purposes.

29. Crowther, J. C., *Industry and Education in Soviet Russia*, London, 1932.

30. Curran, Joseph, *President's Report on the State of the Union*, Sixth National Convention of the National Maritime Union (C.I.O.), September 22, 1947, p. 108, for a case study; see also ref. 188.

31. Czech-Jochberg, E., *Hitler—Eine deutsche Bewegung*, Oldenburg, 1930.

32. Dallin, David and Boris Nikolaevsky, *Forced Labor in Soviet Russia*, New Haven, 1947, esp. chapter 6; see also ref. 5c.

33. Danev, A. M., *Narodnoe Obrazovanie: Osnovie Postanovlenia, Prikazy i Instruktsii*, Moscow, 1948, p. 123, quoted in Kulski (103a), pp. 491–492.

34. Denisov, A. I., *Sovetskoe Gosudarstvennoe Pravo*, Moscow, 1940, p. 60.

35. De Jong, Louis, *The German Fifth Column*, Chicago, 1956.

36. Deutscher, I., *The Prophet Armed*, New York, 1954, p. 158.

37. De Witt, Nicholas, *Soviet Professional Manpower: Its Education, Training and Supply*, Washington, D.C., 1955. (a) pp. 58–61. (b) chapters 4, 5.

38. Dietrich, Otto, *Zwölf Jahre mit Hitler*, Munich, 1955 (English ed., *Hitler*, Chicago, 1955). (a) *op. cit.* (b) p. 154. (c) translation our own.

39. Dulles, Allen Welsh, *Germany's Underground*, New York, 1947. (a) p. 136 and elsewhere; see also ref. 174a. (b) see ref. 174b. (c) pp. 119ff; see ref. 179d.

40. Duncan-Jones, A. S., *The Struggle for Religious Freedom in Germany*, London, 1938; see also 80.

41. *Economic Conditions in Germany: A Report to the Department of Overseas Trade*, Washington, D.C., 1936, p. 2.

42. Elliott, William Y., *The Pragmatic Revolt in Politics*, New York, 1928, chapter 4; see also ref. 195.

43. *Encyclopedia Italiana*, Mussolini's essay, quoted by Herman Finer (50), p. 175, presumably in Finer's translation. (a) *op. cit.* (b) see Oakeshott (150).

44. *Encyclopedia of the Social Sciences*, article on Feudalism. Vol. VI, pp. 203ff.

45. *Entsiklopedicheskii Slovar*, Vol. I, Moscow, 1953, p. 355, for figures for 1936–1951.

46. *Entwurf des Familiengesetzbuches der Deutschen Demokratischen Republik*, Bonn, 1955.

47. Fainsod, Merle, *How Russia is Ruled,* Cambridge, Mass., 1953. ✳(a) p. 166. ✳(b) chapter 6 for detailed treatment. ✳(c) p. 179. ✳(d) p. 529; also *Kommunisticheskoe vospitanie v Sovetskoi shkole,* Moscow, 1950, pp. 313ff. ✳(e) chapter 9 for a more detailed treatment, both in terms of historical outline and organizational pattern. ✳(f) *passim.* ✳(g) chapter 13 for a thorough discussion of the Soviet secret police. ✳(h) pp. 384–387. ✳(i) p. 152. ✳(j) pp. 152–180 for a detailed treatment of the growth of party bureaucracy. ✳(k) p. 329. ✳(l) p. 341. ✳(m) p. 436.

48. Fanelli, G. A., *Idee e polemiche per la scuola fascista,* Rome, 1941; see also ref. 50e.

49. Fasoni, I., *Esercito e Milizia, con pensieri di S. E. Mussolini e di S.A.R. il Duce d'Aosta,* Mantua, 1923, p. 14.

50. Finer, Herman, *Mussolini's Italy,* New York, 1935. ✳(a) p. 185. ✳(b) pp. 175–176. ✳(c) pp. 180–181. ✳(d) pp. 471–472. ✳(e) pp. 475ff. A good recent Italian study on this subject has not been published, but there are interesting sidelights on it in Luigi Salvatorelli (179); among Fascist writings, we note Fanelli (48) and Malfi (122), as well as the study of Gentile, edited by Vittorio Vettori (218). ✳(f) esp. Part III, for adequate stress on the passion for unanimity. ✳(g) pp. 321ff. ✳(h) p. 499; he says there, "That the observer of this system cannot escape the impression that the term 'Corporative' has been used, if not invented, to rouse a sense of wonder in the people, to keep them guessing, to provoke inquiry and to contrive, out of the sheer mystification of an unusual word, at once to hide the compulsion on which the dictatorship finally depends and to suggest that a miraculous work of universal benevolence is in the course of performance." This impression or conclusion of the direct observer was strikingly documented by G. Salvemini (180). ✳(i) pp. 503–504; Articles 7 and 9 of the Charter. ✳(j) Article 3. ✳(k) p. 506, footnote 1.

51. Fisher, George, *Soviet Opposition to Stalin,* Cambridge, Mass., 1952. ✳(a) see also Wheeler-Bennett (229). ✳(b) for a detailed study.

52. Fischer, Louis, *The Soviets in World Affairs,* second ed., Princeton, 1951. See also ref. 57.

53. FitzGibbon, Constantine, *20 July,* New York, 1956; see also ref. 174b.

54. Fraenkel, Ernst, *The Dual State—A Contribution to the Theory of Dictatorship,* New York, 1941. ✳(a) *passim.* ✳(b) *passim.* ✳(c) these problems have been made the focal point of his penetrating study of the Hitler regime, though his distinction of a "legal" and a "prerogative" state is not identical with that of government and party. The title is unfortunate, however, since neither the old bureaucracy nor the Nazi Party was, properly speaking, a "state." But the dualism was unquestionably there.

55. Friedrich, C. J., *Constitutional Government and Democracy,* Boston, 1950. ✳(a) chapter 9—"The Constitution as a Political Force." ✳(b) p. 419; Lasswell's definition (106), p. 169, is inapplicable to the totalitarian party altogether, since it stresses the formulating of issues and

elections. Max Weber's definition is found in *Wirtschaft und Gesellschaft* (225), p. 167. ✳(c) pp. 548ff, for greater detail and the literature cited there. ✳(d) pp. 564ff. ✳(e) chapter 2, a development of Weber's conception; see also ref. 225b. ✳(f) pp. 652ff; see also ref. 74. ✳(g) chapter 23, for a further discussion of the problems and experiences of democratic planning. ✳(h) chapter 22, and more especially the literature cited there. ✳(i) chapters 2 and 19. ✳(j) esp. chapters 7–9.

56. Friedrich, C. J., *Die Philosophie des Rechts in historischer Perspektive,* Heidelberg, 1955, chapter 8.

57. Friedrich, C. J., *Foreign Policy in the Making,* New York, 1938. For an early assessment, see also Beloff (7), and Fischer (52).

58. Friedrich, C. J., *The New Image of the Common Man,* Boston, 1951. ✳(a) chapter 3. All attempts at defining propaganda in terms of the content of the communications or the psychological effect tend to obscure these crucial political features. For further detail, see chapter 3, where the implications of these insights for democratic theory are explored. ✳(b) chapter 3 on this problem in its broadest aspects. ✳(c) esp. the prologue.

59. Friedrich, C. J., ed., *Totalitarianism,* Cambridge, Mass., 1954. ✳(a) H. Arendt, p. 76. ✳(b) P. Kecskemeti, pp. 345–360, for interesting, if somewhat contrasting, discussion. ✳(c) J. Gliksman. ✳(d) pp. 274–275; see also ref. 247d. ✳(e) H. D. Lasswell, p. 367. ✳(f) P. Nettl, pp. 296–307; see also ref. 146. ✳(g) H. J. Muller, pp. 232–244, primarily concerned with the Lysenko case. ✳(h) George de Santillana, pp. 224–262. ✳(i) A. Gyorgy, pp. 381ff, does not share this view and argued that neither ideologically, nor in relation to the secret police, has the totalitarian nature of these regimes been established, but the evidence he adduces is unconvincing. ✳(j) P. Kecskemeti, pp. 345–360, where the decline of the revolution as a form of political action has been argued persuasively on purely observational grounds. The reason for revolution becoming "an extinct political form" appears to be the weapons monopoly. ✳(k) p. 359. ✳(l) H. D. Lasswell, pp. 153ff, deems the emergence of a world of one or more "garrison states" as probable. In the course of his analysis he qualified his former concept of the garrison state and introduced that of a garrison police state that is, in effect, a totalitarian dictatorship. The only alternative he allowed was that of a world federation of constitutional democracies; the continuation of something like the present situation he did not include among his alternatives. ✳(m) P. Kecskemeti, p. 360.

59.2. Friedrich, C. J. and Associates, *The Soviet Zone of Germany,* printed as a manuscript by the Human Relations Area Files, Yale University, 1956.

60. Galbraith, J. K., *U.S. Bombing Survey,* Washington, D.C., 1946.

61. Geiger, H. K., "The Changing Political Attitudes in Totalitarian Society: A Case Study of the Role of the Family," *World Politics,* January 1956.

62. Geiger, H. K., "The Urban Slavic Family and the Soviet System," Ph.D. thesis, Harvard University, 1954.

63. *German Foreign Policy, Documents on,* Series D, Vol. I, 1949, esp. pp. 940ff.

64. Germino, Dante, "The Party as an Instrument of Totalitarian Rule: The Partito Nazionale Fascista," Ph.D. thesis, Harvard University, 1956. *(a) p. 71. *(b) p. 57. *(c) chapters 1 and 2 for detailed analysis based entirely on Italian materials. It was called Opera Nazionale Fascista (O.N.B.), and was subdivided according to the several age groups into the sons and daughters of the wolf (Figli and Figlie della Lupa), the Balilla and Piccole Italiane (9–14), the Avanguardisti and Giovane Italiane (14–18), the Giovani Fascisti and Fasciste (18–21); besides there were the Gruppi Universitari Fascisti (18–28). *(d) translation from Regime Fascista. *(e) pp. 280ff. *(f) esp. pp. 116ff, regarding the "Changes of the Guard," and p. 102. *(g) see also D. A. Binchy, *Church and State in Fascist Italy,* London, 1941, and A. C. Jemolo, *Chiesa e Stato in Italia negli ultimi cento anni,* Turin, 1954. *(h) we are indebted to Mr. Germino for this evaluation of the Italian situation. See also E. Canevari, *La Guerra Italiana,* Rome, 1949, and Q. Armellini, *La Crisi Dell' Esercito,* Rome, 1946.

65. Gilbert, Felix, *Adolf Hitler,* New York, 1950.

66. Gliksman, J., *Tell the West,* New York, 1948; see also ref. 79.

67. *The Goebbels Diaries,* trans. and ed. by L. Lochner, London, 1948. *(a) p. 519. *(b) *passim.* *(c) see ref. 84i.

68. Greene, William C., "Platonism and its Critics," Harvard Studies in Classical Philology, Vol. LXI, Cambridge, Mass., 1953; see also ref. 161.

69. Grundel, E. G., *Die Sendung der jungen Generation,* München, 1932, esp. pp. 327ff. The literature on these several kinds of "new man" is considerable. In critical perspective, these views are seen in Bauer (6); cf. also Leites (109), esp. chapters 4–9.

70. Gurian, Waldemar, *Hitler and the Christians,* New York, 1936; see also ref. 80.

71. Harper, Samuel N., *Civic Training in Soviet Russia,* Chicago, 1929.

72. Harris, Seymour E., *Economic Planning,* New York, 1949, chapter 2; Harris does not give attention to the authoritarian quality of this "plan," since he generally fails to differentiate between democratic and autocratic planning.

73. Hartshorne, Edward Y., *The German Universities and National Socialism,* Cambridge, Mass., 1937.

74. Hayek, Friedrich A., *The Road to Serfdom,* Chicago, 1944.

75. Heberle, Rudolf, *From Democracy to Nazism,* Baton Rouge, La., 1945.

76. Heimann, Eduard, *Vernunftglauben und Religion in der modernen Gesellschaft,* Tübingen, 1955, p. 160; apart from this point, Heimann's brilliant analysis of Marxist "theocracy" largely fits our presentation here. See also Schwartz (185).

77. Henderson, Sir Nevile, *The Failure of a Mission,* New York, 1940. *(a) p. 282. *(b) pp. 258–301.

78. Hensley, Francis H., *Hitler's Strategy,* Cambridge, 1951, pp. 238–239.

BIBLIOGRAPHY

79. Herling, G., *A World Apart*, trans. by Joseph Marek, New York, 1951.
80. Hermelink, Heinrich, *Kirche im Kampf: Dokumente des Widerstands und des Aufbaus . . . 1933–1945*, Tübingen, 1950, p. 499. The literature has become fairly extensive, for example, Gurian (70), Duncan-Jones (40), Micklem (137); for documents, W. Jannasch (91). Our interpretation was materially aided by a study made under our seminar direction by Parker D. Wyman in 1952, "The Protestant Churches of Germany and National Socialism" (unpublished).
81. Heuss, Theodor, *Hitler's Weg—Eine historische-politische Studie über den Nationalsozialismus*, Stuttgart, 1932.
81.2. Hippel, Fritz von, *Die Perversion von Rechtsordnungen*, 1955.
82. Hitler, Adolf, *Mein Kampf*, München, 1925–1927. *(a) *passim*. *(b) p. 234; in Hitler's text, the whole first passage is italicized, but in our view it is the second that deserves special emphasis. The translation is ours. *(c) pp. 293, 316, and 418 and the penetrating comments by Buchheim (20), pp. 13–17, who shows that Hitler drew a sharp contrast between "Programmatiker" and "Politiker," between the "theorist" and the "politician," and that in the end the politician wins out, because only he can "from the realm of the eternally-true and the ideal take that which is humanly possible and let it take form." Here the pragmatic utilitarian conception of truth is particularly striking; cf. Jaspers (92).
83. Hitler, Adolf, *My Battle*, trans. by E. T. S. Dugdale, Boston, 1933. *(a) p. 24. *(b) p. 25. *(c) pp. 75–81.
84. *Hitler's Secret Conversations, 1941–1944*, ed. by H. R. Trevor-Roper, New York, 1953. *(a) *passim*. *(b) *passim*. *(c) pp. 341–342. *(d) pp. 389–390; see also ref. 86b. *(e) pp. 117–118; see also ref. 86c. *(f) pp. 74–75, 448–451; see also ref. 86e. *(g) pp. 447–448. Hitler's comments in *Tischgespräche* (86), pp. 370–375, show that he considered the Concordat "eigentlich hinfällig" (actually invalid) and intended to proceed against the church after the war; cf. also pp. 355–357. *(h) pp. 69–71; see also ref. 86f. There also appeared a German edition, not as complete as the English, to which reference is made as follows.
86. Hitler, Adolf, *Tischgespräche*, ed. by H. Picker, Bonn, 1951. *(a) chapters 4–7. *(b) p. 128; see also ref. 84d. *(c) pp. 339ff; see also ref. 86c. *(d) p. 349. *(e) pp. 370–375. He mentioned his intention to cancel the Concordat, as he had refused to consider it applicable to conquered territories; see also ref. 84f. *(f) "Science is nothing but a ladder which one climbs. With each rung one sees a bit further," p. 340; "In the subconscious everyone has a sense of limits of human power," p. 341; "One understands that man has the ability to understand these laws (the laws of nature). Then one must become humble," p. 352; cf. also pp. 344–345; see also ref. 84f.
86.2. Hitler, Adolf, *Speeches, April 1922–August 1939*, trans. and ed. by Norman H. Baynes, Oxford, 1942.
87. Hodgman, D. R., *Soviet Industrial Production, 1928–1951*, Cambridge, Mass., 1953, pp. 194–208.

88. Homans, George C., *English Villagers of the Thirteen Century,* Cambridge, Mass., 1941, for a recent and detailed analysis of the peasantry in the middle ages. How unrelated these idealized images are to the actual reality has often been pointed out.

88.2 *Il Consiglio di Stato nel quinquennio 1936–1940. Relazione al Duce del Fascismo Capo del Governo,* 2 vols., Rome, 1942—for the major decisions of the Consiglio di Stato during Fascism's most totalitarian period. The Consiglio di Stato has not only continued under the Italian Republic but its personnel remained virtually identical with that of the Fascist regime.

89. Inkeles, Alex, *Public Opinion in Soviet Russia,* Cambridge, Mass., 1950. *(a) for a thorough analysis of the institutions and operations of Soviet propaganda and agitation. *(b) p. 275. *(c) p. 248. *(d) p. 333.

90. International Military Tribunal. *(a) see testimony of Speer. *(b) Hans Frick trial data: I, 24, 27, 72, 298–301; XXII, 544–547, etc.

91. Jannasch, W., *Deutsche Kirchendokumente: Die Haltung der Bekennenden Kirche im Dritten Reich,* Zurich, 1946; see also ref. 80.

92. Jaspers, Karl, *Die Wahrheit,* Bonn, 1953; see also ref. 82.

93. Karski, J., *The Story of a Secret State,* Boston, 1943. *(a) *op. cit.* *(b) *op. cit.*

94. König, Rene, *Materialien zur Soziologie der Familie,* Bern, 1946, esp. pp. 165–179; see also ref. 145.

95. Kogon, Eugen, *Der SS-Stat—Das System der Deutschen Konzentrationslager,* Berlin, 1946. (Abbr. Eng. ed., *The Theory and Practice of Hell: The German Concentration Camps and the System Behind Them,* London 1950.) Cf. also David Rousset (176). Important also are the various novelistic accounts contained in the works of writers such as Koestler, Silone, Sengers. Their portrayal was confirmed by what was found in the Kz's after the war, and what was brought forward in the trials of criminals, both war and other. (See the volumes on the SS trials and Rohde-Liebenau, W., "Heinrich Himmler" (169.2).

96. Kohn, Hans, *Panslavism—Its History and Ideology,* Indiana, 1953.

97. Kohn, Hans, *Revolutions and Dictatorships,* Cambridge, Mass., 1939, pp. 200–210.

98. Koestler, Arthur, *Darkness at Noon,* New York, 1951; see also ref. 95.

99. *KPSS v Rezoliutsiiakh i Resheniiakh S'ezdov, Konferentssii i Plenumov TsK,* Vol. III, Moscow, 1954. *(a) pp. 437–474. *(b) pp. 495–501.

100. *Kommunisticheskoe vospitanie v Sovetskoi shkole,* Moscow, 1950, pp. 313ff; see also ref. 47d.

101. Korbonski, S., *W Imieniu Rzeczypospolitej,* Paris, 1954. *(a) for a complete account by one of its political chiefs, the head of the Directorate of Civil Resistance. *(b) *op. cit.*

102. Kramer, G. G., in *The Third Reich* (UNESCO), New York, 1955; see chapter 18.

103. Kulski, W. W., *The Soviet Regime,* Syracuse, 1954. *(a) Danev quote,

pp. 491–492, *(b) p. 513. *(c) quote from *Voprosy Trudovovo Prava*, p. 414. *(d) p. 319. The official rate of exchange is four rubles to a dollar. The purchasing power, however, ranges somewhere between ten to forty rubles to a dollar.

104. Laffan, Robert G. D., *The Crisis over Czechoslovakia*, London, 1938, for the progress of negotiations; see also ref. 85.

105. Lange, M. G., *Totalitäre Erziehung*, Frankfurt, 1954. *(a) p. 30. *(b) pp. 39ff, where this law is discussed.

106. Lasswell, Harold D. and Abraham Kaplan, *Power and Society*, New Haven, 1950. *(a) para. 3.1, 6.1, and 6.3. For the meaning of myth and symbol, see below Chapter 5, where the views of Parsons and Lasswell are further analyzed. *(b) p. 103. *(c) p. 169; see also ref. 55b.

107. Leber, Annedore, *Das Gewissen steht auf—Lebensbilder aus dem deutschen Widerstand 1933–1945*, Berlin, 1954. *(a) see ref. 169b. *(b) It is worth observing how many of the leaders of the political resistance were basically motivated by religious convictions; this striking fact is convincingly documented here. *(c) p. 126.

108. Leites, Nathan C. and E. Bernaut, *Ritual of Liquidation: The Case of the Moscow Trials*, Glencoe, 1954, for a thorough study.

109. Leites, Nathan C., *A Study of Bolshevism*, Glencoe, 1953. *(a) p. 24. "The party aims at a radical transformation of the world." The study is based upon such a concept of ideology, or rather that aspect of it which Leites calls its "operational code." *(b) chapters 4–9; see also ref. 69.

110. Lemkin, Raphaël, *Axis Rule in Occupied Europe*, New York, 1944, pp. 15ff.

111. Lenin, V. I., *Sochinenya*, Moscow, third ed., 1935. *(a) Vol. XXIV, p. 293. *(b) Vol. XVIII, p. 296. *(c) pp. 443–444. *(d) Vol. IV, p. 468. *(e) 4th ed., Vol. XII, p. 143.

112. Lenin, V. I., *Revolutionary Army and Revolutionary Government—1905*, New York, 1943, Vol. III, p. 313.

113. Lenin, V. I., *Selected Works*, New York, 1943. *(a) "State and Revolution," Vol. VII, p. 24. *(b) "Revolutionary Army and Revolutionary Government," Vol. III, p. 313. *(c) "War and Peace," Vol. VII, p. 297. *(d) "Proletarian Revolution and Renegade Kautsky," Vol. VII, p. 123. *(e) "What is to be Done," Vol. II, p. 152. *(f) Speech to the VII CPSU(B) Congress, 1918, Vol. VIII, p. 318. *(g) Vol. IX, p. 70. *(h) "Socialism and Religion," Vol. XI, p. 658. *(i) "To the Rural Poor," Vol. II, p. 281.

114. *Leninsko-Stalinskii Komsomol-Vernyi Pomoshchnik i boevoi rezerv Kommunisticheskoi Partii*, Moscow, 1952, for a Soviet account.

115. Lerner, D., *The Nazi Elite*, Stanford, 1951.

116. Leto, Guido, *Memoirs*.

117. Leto, Guido, *OVRA. Fascismo-Antifascismo*, second ed., Bologna, 1952, for an apologetic descriptive account of the operations of OVRA, published since the war by one of its officials.

118. Lochner, Louis P., *Tycoons and Tyrant*, Aurora, 1954, for a contrasting view.

119. Ludwig, Emil, *Mussolini*, Berlin, 1932, for a bitter criticism of this tendency. See ref. 13.

120. McKinder, Halford J., *Democratic Ideals and Reality*, New York, 1919. This geopolitical kind of approach to Russia is highlighted by its famous hypothesis about the heartland of the Eurasian plain and its world-historical destiny.

121. Machiavelli, Niccolò, *Il Principe*.

121.2. Mackiewicz, J., *The Katyn Wood Murders*, London, 1951.

122. Malfi, Erasmo, *Scuola e G.I.L.*, Rome, 1939. *(a) see ref. 184. *(b) According to him the school is a political institution, and school and youth organizations together form the unitary instrument of Fascist education.

123. Mannheim, Karl, *Ideology and Utopia: An Introduction to the Sociology of Knowledge*, Oxford, 1936, 1950. *(a) *passim*. *(b) p. 50. *(c) p. 111. *(d) p. 238. *(e) p. 239.

124. Martin, Hugh, *Christian Counter-attack: Europe's Churches against Nazism*, London, 1944, p. 25. This figure may be compared with the figure 1,493, given for a single concentration camp, Dachau, for March 15, 1945, and covering 25 nations, among which the Germans supplied 261, the Poles 791, French 122, Czechs 73, Austrians 64, and so on. See J. Neuhäusler (147), p. 349. Neuhäusler also gives (pp. 336-348) a long list of clergy in the Dachau concentration camp in 1943, based on a report of an inmate, which was smuggled out. Altogether, Neuhäusler's account is the most detailed story of individual and group efforts of Catholics to resist the Nazification of the Church.

125. Marx, Karl, *Das Kapital*, Hamburg, 1867, Vol. I., pp. 23-24.

126. Marx, Karl and Friedrich Engels, *Die Deutsche Ideologie*, Berlin, 1953, pp. 35-36 and elsewhere.

127. Maunz, T., *Gestalt und Recht der Polizei*, Hamburg, 1943, pp. 51-52.

128. Maynard, John, *The Russian Peasant*, London, 1943. The brutal violence of this process is not given adequate attention in this book.

129. Medalie, Richard J., "The Stages of Totalitarian Development in Eastern Europe," *Public Policy* Volume VII, Cambridge, Mass., 1956. Earlier Hugh Seton-Watson attempted to generalize upon the more conventional subject of the "seizure of power." See his *The East European Revolution* (187). We benefited greatly from Medalie's discussion of these phenomena.

130. Mehnert, Klaus, *Weltrevolution durch Weltgeschichte; die Geschichtslehre des Stalinismus*, 1953 (*Stalin Versus Marx; The Stalinist Historical Doctrine*, London, 1952), gives a more balanced analysis of this "nationalist" trend and the way in which Stalin developed it out of the ideological transformations required by the exigencies of the Soviet Union. Mehnert links the trend to such phenomena as Stalin's *post mortem* purge of M. N. Pokrowsky, the historian, and of N. Ia. Marr, the linguist. In these changes Mehnert surmises to have been embodied a new

"messianic" conception of Russia's role as the "savior" of mankind; and he cites Stalin's toast of May 24, 1945, as one of the striking bits of evidence in support of his general contention. At the same time, he stresses, as we do, that this kind of Marx-derived messianism must not be confused with the older mystic and panslavist versions, in spite of the kinship between them.

131. Meier-Beneckenstein, Paul, ed., *Dokumente der Deutschen Politik,* 1935, Vol. I, p. 39.

132. Merriam, Charles E., *The Making of Citizens,* Chicago, 1931, the leading volume of a series that dealt in separate monographs with Switzerland, Great Britain, France, Italy, and others. These studies are of somewhat uneven value, but they are all built upon the assumption underlying Merriam's entire enterprise, that the "making of Fascists" and the "making of citizens" is essentially the same kind of undertaking. Actually the difference is as great as is that between "liberating" and "enslaving" a man.

133. Merriam, Charles E., *Political Power, its Composition and Maintenance,* New York, 1934, pp. 104–105, for a similar list; Merriam here discusses the importance of ceremonialism in politics.

134. Merton, Robert K., *et al., Reader in Bureaucracy,* Glencoe, 1952. *(a) see C. J. Friedrich, "Some Observations on Weber's Analysis of Bureaucracy," pp. 27–33. See also ref. 225. *(b) see Frederic S. Burin, "Bureaucracy and National Socialism: a Reconsideration of Weberian Theory," who stresses this point; but he builds his analysis partly on the semantically misleading terminology of Karl Mannheim—"functional" *versus* "substantive" rationality—and partly on the notion that the party and SS bureaucracy may be called an "ideological" bureaucracy, and yet, he said, not to be concerned with "substantive" rationality. But if the party apparatus is an ideological "bureaucracy," then its distinctive feature is precisely its concern with "values" or "ends"— the distinctive feature of "substantive reality"—rather than with being rational in terms of legally fixed ends. All these terminological difficulties, occasioned by Max Weber's cumbersome conceptual scheme, do not prevent Burin from making a very useful analysis showing the decomposition of the bureaucracy of the government. *(c) see ref. 127.

135. Mertsalov, V. S., *Politika krutogo pod'ema i selskoe khoziaistvo SSSR,* Munich, 1955, p. 37.

135.2. *Michel, Henri, Histoire de la Résistance,* Paris, 1952.

136. Michels, Robert, *Political Parties: A Sociological Study of the Oligarchical Tendencies of Modern Germany,* New York, 1915, 1949; he argued that there is no such thing as a democratic, cooperative party, that all parties are "oligarchic." He overstated a good point.

137. Micklem, Nathaniel, *National Socialism and the Catholic Church, 1933–1938,* London, 1939; see also ref. 80. *(a) see ref. 80. *(b) see ref. 203b.

138. Miller, Douglas, *You Can't Do Business with Hitler,* Boston, 1941, p. 73,

gives a description of the clearing system: "Exporters in Germany would
ship, for example, to Jugoslavia and be credited in dinars by the central bank in Belgrade, with the two banks balancing accounts. Pay-
ment was credited to the exporters in each country in their local
currency, and at the turn of the year the balance would be carried forward in favor of one or the other country to apply against next year's
transactions."

139. Milosz, Czeslaw, *The Captive Mind,* New York, 1953, p. 231.
141. Moore, Barrington, *Soviet Politics—The Dilemma of Power: The Role
of Ideas in Social Change,* Cambridge, Mass., 1950, p. 406. *(a) p.
406. *(b) chapters 8 and 12 for a more detailed discussion of this.
*(c) pp. 280–281. The above total includes all Soviet workers em-
ployed in bureaucratic activities. *(d) p. 163.
142. Moore, Barrington, *Terror and Progress USSR,* Cambridge, Mass., 1954.
*(a) chapter 7, p. 194. *(b) *passim.* *(c) chapter 5, for a thoughtful, balanced treatment. *(d) chapter 5, p. 129. Moore recognizes
this point, and shares the belief that "the Soviet scientist still retains a
substantial degree of autonomy in spite of all the planning." *(e)
chapter 4, esp. pp. 100ff. *(f) pp. 110–111; quotation from p. 112.
*(g) *passim.* This view has been for some time espoused by George F.
Kennan and others.
143. Mora, S., and P. Zwierniak, *Sprawiedliwosc Scwiecka,* Rome, 1945; see
ref. 204.
144. Müller, Marianne, and Erwin Egon, *Stürmt die Festung Wissen-
schaft,* Berlin-Dahlem, 1953. *(a) *op. cit.* *(b) p. 213, quoting an
article by Walter Ulbricht in *Neues Deutschland,* July 23, 1950.
145. Myrdal, Alva, *Nation and Family: The Swedish Experiment in Democratic Family and Population Policy,* New York, 1941.
146. Nettl, Peter, *The Eastern Zone and Soviet Policy in Germany, 1945–50,*
London, 1951 (German ed., *Die Deutsche Sowjetzone bis heute,*
Frankfort, 1953), pp. 1–35.
147. Neuhäusler, J., *Kreuz und Hakenkreuz: Der Kampf des Nationalsozialismus gegen die Katholische Kirche und der Kirchliche Widerstand,*
Munich, 1946. *(a) p. 349, and pp. 335–348; see also ref. 124. *(b)
Vol. II, pp. 68ff.
148. Neumann, Franz, *Behemoth,* New York, 1942. *(a) also Maxine B.
Sweezey, *The Structure of the Nazi Economy,* Cambridge, Mass., 1941,
and R. A. Brady, *The Spirit and Structure of German Fascism,* New
York, 1937. Neumann's analysis is much the ablest of the three. The
"imperialist" interpretation ties in with Thorstein Veblen's earlier analysis of German and Japanese militarism and imperialism. *(b) Neumann is perhaps the leading writer stressing the charismatic character of
Hitler. *(c) p. 360. *(d) pp. 327ff. *(e) pp. 298ff. *(f) pp. 349–
361. *(g) pp. 337–349 and 413–428. What is otherwise a well-
informed discussion of this problem is marred by his preoccupation with
proving that, in spite of the destruction of the free unions, capitalism

continues to exist. He admits that capitalism requires "free labor," but undertakes to escape from the clear consequences of this fact by introducing a distinction between three different concepts of "freedom" which are said to correspond to "stages" in capitalist development. The distinctions have a degree of validity, but they do not succeed in supporting his main argument. For a detailed analysis of the labor front, see also Taylor Cole (270), utilized by Neumann. The German literature, given by both, should also be consulted. *(h) p. 613, footnote 14, for German literature regarding this. *(i) pp. 403–413. Neumann writes with bitterness of this failure, but, communism apart, it is not clear just what the Social Democratic Party and the unions should according to him have done. *(j) p. 418. Neumann rightly concludes that "the Labor Front has driven the process of bureaucratization to its maximum." *(k) p. 425. *(l) p. 429, for quotation, with inadequate references.

149. Neumann, Sigmund, *Permanent Revolution*, New York, 1942. *(a) p. 77. *(b) p. 79. *(c) p. 83.
150. Oakeshott, Michael, *The Social and Political Doctrines of Contemporary Europe*, Cambridge, 1939. *(a) pp. 164ff for reprint of this. *(b) pp. 164ff, esp. p. 166; translation of *La Dottrina del Fascismo* (1934). *(c) reprint of article on Fascism (1932).
151. Orlov, A., *The Secret History of Stalin's Crimes*, New York, 1953. See also ref. 204.
152. Pareto, Vilfredo, *The Mind and Society*, trans. by A. Bongiorno and A. Livingston, New York, 1935 (trans. of *Trattato di Sociologia Generale*, Florence, 1923, last ed.), esp. pp. 389–480.
153. Parsons, Talcott, *The Social System*, Glencoe, 1951. *(a) p. 349. *(b) p. 10. *(c) p. 11.
154. Parsons, Talcott and A. M. Henderson, *Max Weber, The Theory of Social and Economic Organization* (ed. and intro. by Parsons), New York, 1947; esp. pp. 329–341; see also ref. 225b.
155. Peralta, Jeronimo M., *Peron y la Revolución Justicialista*, Buenos Aires, 1951, for an "authorized" analysis. Chapter 10 contains the Twenty Basic Tenets of the movement.
156. Pipes, Richard, *The Formation of the Soviet Union: Communism and Nationalism, 1917–1923*, Cambridge, Mass., 1954.
157. Plamenatz, John P., *German Marxism and Russian Communism*, London, 1954, pp. 8–36, who points out that the communist emphasis on *Diamat* is often merely lip-service. What communists refer to as dialectical materialism is not that at all, but historical materialism. Genuine dialectics has little to do with it.
158. Plato, *The Republic*, Book V.
159. *P.N.F., Atti del*, 16 vols., Bologna, 1931–1939, Vol. III, 1934, p. 312. (Includes *Fogli di ordini* and *Fogli di disposizioni* of the national party secretary.)
160. Polish Supreme Court, Judgment of a civil division of the PSC of 11–29

December 1951—Reference No. C 1083/51, Law Publishing Company, Warsaw, 1953, Vol. II.

161. Popper, Karl R., *The Open Society and its Enemies*, London, 1945, Vol. I, perhaps the most outspoken of the Platonic critics. This aspect of Plato's philosophy is the genuine link with the views of the totalitarians of our time. It has given rise to a heated controversy over whether he was or was not a totalitarian. In terms of our criteria, he clearly was not.

162. Raschofer, Hermann, *Die Sudetenfrage, ihre völkerrechtliche Entwicklung vom ersten Weltkrieg bis zur Gegenwart*, Munich, 1953, pp. 144–164.

163. Rauschning, Hermann, *Gespräche mit Hitler*, New York, 1940 (Eng. ed., *Hitler Speaks* 1939), p. 51. We used our own translation from the original. We agree with Alan Bullock and Trevor-Roper that Rauschning's account is confirmed by later evidence, and hence an important source.

164. Rauschning, Hermann, *Hitler's Speeches*, New York, 1942.

165. Reimann, Gunther, *The Vampire Economy*, New York, 1939. *(a) for greater detail; the term is our own coinage. *(b) Reimann stressed this aspect.

166. *Report of the Case of the Anti-Soviet and Right-Trotskyite Bloc* (Sudebnyi Otchet po Delu Anti-Sovetskogo i Pravo-Trotskistkogo Bloka), Moscow, 1938, p. 697, Andrei Vyshinsky's address.

167. *Report of the Proceedings of the Anti-Soviet Trotskyite Centre*, Moscow, 1937, pp. 162–163, Shestov's last plea.

168. *Report of the Proceedings of the Case of the Anti-Soviet Trotskyite Centre*, Moscow, 1937, p. 127.

169. Ritter, Gerhard, *Carl Goerdeler und die deutsche Widerstandsbewegung*, Stuttgart, 1954. *(a) see ref. 174b. *(b) pp. 388–434. Merely as illustrations we mention Carl Goerdeler's brother as his most intimate associate, and the brothers Bonhoeffer (cf. Dietrich Bonhoeffer's *Letters and Papers from Prison*, ref. 12; the most important letters are to his parents). But perhaps most impressive of all is the record that has been presented from Gestapo records by Annedore Leber (107), where again and again the crucial support is shown to have come from the family. *(c) for a more detailed background of the key leader, Carl Goerdeler.

169.2. Rohde-Liebenau, Wolfram, "Heinrich Himmler," unpublished seminar paper, Harvard University, 1951. See also ref. 95.

170. *The Roman Catholic Church in People's Poland*, Warsaw, 1953, p. 105.

171. Rosenberg, Alfred, *Der Mythos des zwanzigsten Jahrhunderts*, Munich, 1930, p. 2.

172. Rosenthal, Walter, Richard Lange, and Arwed Bomeyer, *Die Justiz in der Sowjetischen Besatzungzone*, third ed., Bonn, 1955; for the concrete evidence of the perversion of judicial administration see ref. 214, covering, in two parts so far, the period down to and including 1943.

173. Rostow, W. W., *et al., The Prospects for Communist China,* Cambridge, Mass., 1954. *(a) *passim.* *(b) pp. 116–123; unfortunately, Rostow speaks of the "complex value system" of traditional Chinese society as an "ideology."

174. Rothfels, Hans, *The German Opposition to Hitler,* second ed., Chicago, 1948. *(a) esp. pp. 85ff. *(b) this was by no means the only motivation. See also Dulles (39). There is a growing literature on the Twentieth of July; among these, the recent study on the key leader, Carl Goerdeler, by Ritter (169) is outstanding. *(c) p. 101 and elsewhere. *(d) *passim.*

175. Rounds, Frank, *A Window on Red Square,* Boston, 1953, pp. 46–48.

176. Rousset, David, *The Other Kingdom,* New York, 1947. See also ref. 95.

177. *Royal Commission's Reports on Espionage in Canada, 1946, and Australia, 1955,* for excellent source material.

178. von Salomon, Ernst, *Der Fragebogen,* Hamburg, 1951, for a dramatic description of this little-known phase of Germany's revolutionary situation.

178.2 Salvadori, Massimo, *Storia della Resistenza Italiana,* 1955; this avoids the communist bias of some other recently published interesting studies on the Italian resistance.

179. Salvatorelli, L. and G. Mira, *Storia del Fascismo,* Rome, 1952. *(a) *op. cit.* *(b) p. 745. *(c) see ref. 184. *(d) for the Italian record and for the Germans, Hans Rothfels, *The German Opposition to Hitler,* Chicago, 1948, p. 101 and elsewhere. Dulles' account (39), pp. 119ff, is too preoccupied with political resistance and "guilt," and contains some grave errors, notably about Albrecht Haushofer. On the Soviet Zone resistance, cf. Müller and Egon (144), pp. 282–284, who also give a number of individual cases.

180. Salvemini, Gaetano, *Under the Axe of Fascism,* New York, 1936. *(a) p. 383. *(b) pp. 385–386. *(c) Salvemini rightly stressed the corrupt features of corporativism, but failed to bring out this inherent "rationale" of the corporate state. See L. R. Franck, *Les Étapes de l'économie fasciste italienne,* Paris, 1939, and Carl T. Schmidt, *The Corporate State in Action,* New York, 1939. *(d) *passim,* see also ref. 50h. *(e) pp. 294–295.

181. de Santillana, George, *Galileo Galilei—Dialogue on the Great World Systems,* Chicago, 1953 (learned introduction, pp. xi–lviii). See also the essay on "Phases of the Conflict between Totalitarianism and Science," ref. 59h.

182. Schelsky, Helmut, *Wandlungen der deutschen Familie der Gegenwart,* second ed., Stuttgart, 1954. See also Wurzbacher (235). The two works were done in conjunction and complement each other, Schelsky, broadly speaking, dealing with the external, Wurzbacher with the internal, relations of the family since 1945. In all, 180 families were studied intensively.

183. Schneider, Herbert W., *Making the Fascist State,* New York, 1928, p. 228.

184. Schneider, Herbert W. and Shepard Clough, *Making Fascists,* Chicago,

1934, chapter 5; see also Finer (50) pp. 475ff. A good recent study on this subject has not been published yet, but there are interesting sidelights on it in Salvatorelli (179). Among Fascist writings, we note Fanelli (48) and Malfi (122), as well as the study of Gentile (218).

185. Schwartz, Benjamin, *Chinese Communism and the Rise of Mao,* Cambridge, Mass., 1951. ✻(a) see also ref. 76. ✻(b) *passim.* ✻(c) pp. 191–199.

186. Seabury, Paul, *The Wilhelmstrasse,* California, 1954.

187. Seton-Watson, Hugh, *The East European Revolution,* second ed., New York, 1952; see also ref. 129.

188. Selznick, Philip, *The Organizational Weapon: A Study of Bolshevik Strategy and Tactics,* New York, 1952, pp. 171–214, for a broader analysis. See also ref. 30.

189. *XVII S'ezd VKP (b),* Stenographic Report, Moscow, 1934, p. 15.

190. *XVIII S'ezd Vzesoiuznoi Kommunisticheskoi Partii (b),* Stenographic Report, Moscow, 1939. ✻(a) p. 28. ✻(b) for details, particularly the reports of Molotov and Kaganovich. ✻(c) p. 19.

191. Shuster, G. N., *Religion Behind the Iron Curtain,* New York, 1955.

192. Silone, I., *Bread and Wine,* London, 1936; see also ref. 95.

193. Sington, Derrick and Arthur Weidenfeld, *The Goebbels Experiment—A Study of the Nazi Propaganda Machine,* London, 1942. ✻(a) esp. chapters 2 and 3. ✻(b) p. 17. It may, however, be argued that the real dualism was that between Goebbels and Dietrich. In the party, Dietrich's position was equivalent to that of Goebbels; he was Reichsleiter as press chief of the Reich, and although he was Goebbels' subordinate as secretary of state in the Ministry of Propaganda, he wore another hat as press chief of the government, which gave him direct access to Hitler.

194. Smith, Patrick, ed., *Clemens August von Galen—The Bishop of Münster and the Nazis,* London, 1943, sermons. See also ref. 209b.

195. Sorel, Georges, *Réflexions sur la violence,* second ed., Paris, 1910. (Eng. ed., trans. by T. E. Hulme and J. Roth, *Reflections on Violence,* Glencoe, 1950.) See the interesting introduction by Edward S. Shils in the English edition. Very significant also for his early recognition of the important doctrine of the myth—Elliott (42), chapter 4.

196. Spirito, Ugo, *Capitalismo e Corporativismo,* Florence, 1936. Reviews: Critica Fascista and Lavoro Fascisto.

198. Stalin, J. V., *Anarchism or Socialism* (1907), in Collected Works, Moscow, 1952, Vol. I, pp. 294–295.

199. Stalin, J. V., *Problems of Leninism,* Moscow, 1940. ✻(a) pp. 659–699. ✻(b) pp. 115–116, "The October Revolution and the Tactics of the Russian Communists," 1924. ✻(c) pp. 591–597, "Dialectical and Historical Materialism." ✻(d) p. 451.

200. Stalin, J. V., *"Soviet Policy during the Great Patriotic War* (Materials and Documents),*"* New York, Vol. II, pp. 79–80. Interview between Stalin and Rev. S. Orlemanski, May 12, 1944.

201. Starlinger, W., *Grenzen der Sovietmacht,* Kitzinger-Main, 1954. ✻(a)

op. cit. ✳(b) for interesting and supporting evidence where the disintegration of the MVD "state" is described. Starlinger is inclined to interpret the system of camps as a "state within the state" in line with Kogon (95). ✳(c) *passim.*

202. Sternberg, Fritz, *From Nazi Sources: Why Hitler Can't Win,* New York, 1939, p. 73.

203. Strobel, Ferdinand, ed., *Christliche Bewährung: Dokumente des Widerstands der Katholischen Kirche in Deutschland, 1933–1945,* Altero, 1946. ✳(a) this, together with Neuhäusler, supersedes the earlier, meritorious document collection published in 1940 in London and entitled *The Persecution of the Catholic Church in the Third Reich: Facts and Documents.* ✳(b) p. 299 for quote; cf. also Smith (194), which gives his sermons. See also a few works especially concerned with Catholicism. Micklem (137) is best for the prewar period, but Teeling (206) is important because of its critical view of Catholic failings, by a Catholic. A recent comprehensive assessment from which we have profited greatly was prepared for our seminar by Findley Burns, Jr. (23).

204. Stypulkowski, Z., *Invitation to Moscow,* London, 1951. See also Orlov (151) and Mora and Zwierniak (143).

205. Tasca, A., *Nascita e avvento del Fascismo,* Rome, 1950. Mussolini's attitude toward democracy was ambivalent. Fascist theory was much more frankly elitist than Nazi ideology.

206. Teeling, William, *Crisis for Christianity,* London, 1939; see also ref. 203.

207. Tell, Rolf, *Nazi Guide to Nazism,* Washington, D.C., 1942, for quotation from *Volk im Werden,* 1934. This "guide," compiled during the war, was evidently edited with a view to arousing indignation, yet the contradiction in the Nazi approach to the family becomes apparent in the quotations offered.

208. Thoma, R., *Die Staatsfinanzen in der Volksgemeinwirtschaft,* Tübingen, 1937.

209. Timasheff, N. S., *The Great Retreat: The Growth and Decline of Communism in Russia,* New York, 1946.

210. Trotsky, L., *Itogi i Perspektivy,* p. 42; see also ref. 36.

211. Trotsky, L., *Kak vooruzhalas revolutsia,* Moscow, 1923–1925, Vol. I, p. 29.

212. Trotsky, L., *Nashi Politicheskie zadachii,* Geneva, 1904, p. 23. In the same publication, Trotsky decried Lenin's "malicious and morally repulsive suspiciousness."

213. Trotsky, L., *Sochinenya,* Moscow, 1927, Vol. XIII, pp. 6–14, quoted in Deutscher (36), p. 450.

214. *Unrecht als System—Dokumente über planmässige Rechtsverletzung in der Sowjetzone Deutschlands,* published by the Untersuchungsausschuss Freiheitlicher Juristen, so far in two parts, covering the period down to and including 1954 (Part I also in English).

215. Ulam, Adam, *Titoism and the Cominform,* Cambridge, Mass., 1951, for a penetrating analysis.

216. Vagts, Alfred, *Hitler's Second Army*, Infantry Journal, Washington, D.C., 1943, chapter 12.

217. Veblen, Thorstein, *Imperial Germany and the Industrial Revolution*, New York, 1915, 1939, 1954; see also ref. 148a.

218. Vettori, Vittorio, *Giovanni Gentile*, Florence, 1954; see also ref. 184.

219. Vögelin, Eric, *The New Science of Politics*, Chicago, 1952.

220. Voznesensky, N. A., *Voiennaia Ekonomika SSSR*, Moscow, 1948, p. 66.

221. *V Vserossiiskii s'ezd sovetov rabochikh, krest'ianskikh, soldatskikh i kazach' ikh deputatov*, Stenographic report, Moscow, July 4–10, 1918, p. 213.

222. Walker, R., *China under Communism: The First Five Years*, New Haven, 1955, chapter 6.

223. Walther, Otto, *Verwaltung, Lenkung und Planung der Wirtschaft in der Sowjetischen Besatzungszone*, Bonn, 1953.

224. Webb, Sidney and Beatrice, *Soviet Communism: A New Civilization*, New York, 1935. *(a) *passim.* *(b) chapter 10 (1), pp. 887ff; note esp. p. 921, where these facts are made the basis of a "justification" of the Soviet regime by Harold Laski in *Revolution.* *(c) pp. 1054ff. *(d) esp. chapter 10 (c), pp. 887ff. Progress is here defined in terms of "literacy" (p. 894), number of schools (p. 892), or "learning by doing" (p. 898). For the last, Crowther (29) is cited as authority, and the concept is related to a principle presumably enunciated by Samuel Butler (Thoreau stated it considerably earlier); but what a difference between the reality to which the term refers in the West, and the regimented assignment to work-places in the USSR and the satellites.

225. Weber, Max, *Wirtschaft und Gesellschaft*, Tübingen, 1925. *(a) p. 167; see also ref. 55b. *(b) esp. pp. 128–133, 650–678, and the corresponding sections in Parsons (154), pp. 329–341. Cf. also ref. 226, esp. pp. 196–244, 416–444. See also C. J. Friedrich's development of Weber's conception (ref. 55, chapter 2), which is further explicated in a chapter in Merton (134), upon which the analysis is based.

226. Weber, Max, *From Max Weber: Essays in Sociology*, trans., ed., and intro. by H. H. Gerth and C. Wright Mills, Oxford, 1946. See also ref. 225b.

227. Weinreich, Max, *Hitler's Professors—The Part of Scholarship in Germany's Crimes against the Jewish People*, New York, 1946. For a less emphatic treatment, see Hartshorne (73).

228. Wertheimer, Mildred S., *The Pan-German League, 1890–1914*, New York, 1924, for an older but still largely adequate study.

229. Wheeler-Bennett, John, *The Forgotten Peace*, Brest-Litovsk, 1918 (and New York, 1939).

230. Wheeler-Bennett, John, *The Nemesis of Power: The German Army in Politics, 1918–1945*, London, 1953. *(a) Part III. *(b) *passim.*

231. White, Fedotoff, *The Growth of the Red Army*, Princeton, 1944. *(a) *op. cit.* *(b) *op. cit.*

232. Widmeyer, E., "The Communist Party and the Soviet Schools, 1917–1937," Ph.D. thesis, Harvard University, 1952; see also ref. 71.

233. Weizsäcker, Ernst von, *Memoirs,* Eng. trans., 1951, *passim;* see also ref. 186.

233.2. Wittke, Karl, *Democracy is Different.*

234. Wolfe, Bertram D., *Three Who Made a Revolution,* New York, 1948, *passim.*

235. Wurzbacher, Gerhard, *Leitbilder des gegenwärtigen deutschen Familienlebens,* Dortmund, 1951; see also ref. 182.

236. Wyman, Parker D., "The Protestant Churches of Germany and National Socialism," unpublished seminar paper, Harvard University, 1952, see also ref. 80.

237. Yakovlev, B., *Konsentratsionne Lageri SSSR,* Munich, 1955, for a recent attempt to identify, locate, and describe the Soviet camps.

238. Yaroslavsky, R., *Bolshevik Verification and Purging of the Party Ranks,* Moscow, 1933, p. 13, quoting Lenin, addressing the combined session of the All-Russian Central Executive and the Moscow Soviet, April 4, 1919.

239. Yaroslavsky, E., *Kak provodit chistku partii,* Moscow, 1929, for an early discussion.

240. Yoffe, A. A., *Mirnye peregovory v Brest-Litovske* (official Soviet record), Moscow, 1920, p. 104.

240.2. Zeller, Eberhard, *Geist der Freiheit,* second ed., München, 1954.

PERIODICALS AND ARTICLES

240.3. *American Political Science Review,* Z. Brzezinski, "Totalitarianism and Rationality," 3 (50), September 1956.

241. *Annals of the Academy of Political Science.* ✳(a) J. Bennett, "The German Currency Reform," 267:43–54 (January 1950); see also ref. 27. ✳(b) A. Bergson, J. H. Blackman and A. Erlich, "Postwar Economic Reconstruction and Development in the USSR," 263:52–72 (May 1949); see also ref. 271j, ref. 245b.

242. *Aviation Age.* N. De Witt, "Russia Threatens US Engineering Leadership," February 1955, for all the data in this paragraph.

243. *Bol'shevik.* ✳(a) no. 17 (1948), p. 51. ✳(b) V. Kolbanovsky, "Ukrepleniie semii v sotsialisticheskom obshchestve," no. 17 (September 1949), pp. 53–63.

244. *Buletinul Oficial,* no. 51 (June 9, 1950), decree no. 583.

245. *Bulletin of the Institute for the Study of History and Culture of the USSR.* ✳(a) vol. 2, no. 1 (1955), p. 10. ✳(b) vol. 2, no. 3 (1955), p. 5. ✳(c) vol. 3, no. 2 (1956), p. 11.

246. *Common Ground,* C. J. Friedrich, "Foreign-Language Radio and the War," 3:65–72 (1942).

247. *Confluence.* ✳(a) C. J. Friedrich, "Religion and History," vol. 4, no. 1 (1955), pp. 105–116. ✳(b) C. J. Friedrich, "Authority and Loyalty," vol. 3, no. 3 (1954), pp. 307, 316. ✳(c) Friedrich, *ibid.,* and the literature cited there.

248. *Dziennik Ustaw, R.P.* no. 22 (1950), p. 188; see also ref. 261.

249. *Fogli Di Ordini,* p. 244.

250. *Forum,* Wolfgand Schubardt, "Der Kampf gegen den Objektivismus an den Universitäten und Hochschulen unserer Republik," March 21, 1951, p. 3. (Communist publication of students.) See also the comment in Müller (144), pp. 219ff.

251. *The Geographical Review,* D. B. Shimkin, "Economic Regionalization in Soviet Union," vol. 42, no. 4 (October 1952), p. 611.

252. *Izvestia.* ＊(a) July 11, 1955. ＊(b) August 10, 1930; see also ref. 18h. ＊(c) May 26, 1955, p. 2, on the setting up of the USSR State Planning Committee to guide long-range planning and the USSR Economic Committee to guide short-range planning. ＊(d) April 6, 1955. ＊(e) January 23, 1955. ＊(f) November 30, 1955, for decree. ＊(g) August 7, 1955, on the award of the order of the Red Banner of Labor to the Metropolitan of Kolomna. ＊(h) March 27, 1956.

253. *Journal of the History of Ideas,* Lacey Baldwin Smith, "English Treason Trials and Confessions in the Sixteenth Century," vol. 15 (October 1954) (Humanities, no. 10, Department of Humanities, M.I.T., 1954).

254. *The Journal of Social Issues,* A. Inkeles, "Social Change and Social Character: The Role of Parietal Mediation," vol. 11, no. 1 (1955), pp. 12–23.

255. *Kommunist.* ＊(a) M. Strepukhov, "Powerful Instruments for Mobilizing the Masses to Carry Out Party and Governmental Decisions" (translated title), no. 6 (April 1955), pp. 91–102. ＊(b) no. 10 (July 1955), p. 4. ＊(c) no. 7 (May 1955), pp. 117–128. Compare this with the following statement (translated) in *Literaturnaia gazeta* (259b): "'Cautious' people, who consider the appearance and establishment of different trends in one and the same field of knowledge 'dangerous,' generally declare that this, as they say, may lead to the appearance or reanimation of reactionary trends which contradict the Marxist-Leninist outlook."

256. *Komsomolskaia pravda.* ＊(a) March 24, 1954, p. 2. ＊(b) March 30, 1954. ＊(c) 1954 figures, March 20, 1954, p. 1.

257. *Krasnaia Zvezda* (official army paper), October 22, 1946.

258. *Lidove Noviny,* April 21, 1951, quoted by Buhler and Zukowski (21).

259. *Literaturnaia gazeta.* ＊(a) January 11, 1955, p. 1. ＊(b) see also ref. 255c. January 11, 1955, p. 1.

260. *Look,* "Interview with Elliott Roosevelt," February 4, 1947.

261. *Monitor Polski,* A-45, p. 519; see also ref. 248.

262. *New York Times.* ＊(a) L. Dubrovina, RSFSR Deputy Minister of Education, August 30, 1955. ＊(b) July 24, 1955, p. 6E. ＊(c) June 7, 1942; for quotations of striking passages of pastoral letter. These are curiously not contained in Neuhäusler's account, though he quotes others from a "gemeinsame Hirtenbrief." ＊(d) August 25, 1955, p. 4.

263. *Nowe Drogi.* ＊(a) January 1947; the Secretary-General of the Party, Wladyslaw Gomulka (subsequently purged), went as far as to claim that there was no need of a dictatorship of the proletariat in Poland as communism in Poland would arrive through an evolutionary process. ＊(b) July–August 1948, p. 17, the resolution of the Cominform on the situation in the Communist Party of Jugoslavia.

264. *Nowa Kultura,* no. 34 (282), August 21, 1955, pp. 4–5; S. Sobocki, "Egzamin."
265. *Partinaia zhizn.* ✳(a) no. 5 (March 1955), pp. 8–13. ✳(b) no. 6 (1955), pp. 30–34. ✳(c) no. 5 (March 1955). ✳(d) no. 3 (1955), pp. 60–61. ✳(e) no. 6 (March 1955), pp. 1–2. ✳(f) no. 15 (November 1954), pp. 9–15.
266. *Mirovoe Khoziaistvo i Mirovaya Politika,* E. S. Varga, "Demokratiya Novogo Tipa," 1947, p. 3.
267. *Pergale,* no. 4 (April 1950), p. 52.
268. *Pionerskaia pravda,* September 12, 1952.
269. *Planovoie Khozjaistvo.* ✳(a) no. 2 (1941), pp. 5–6. ✳(b) A. Leontiev, "Ekonomischeskie Osnovy Novoy Demokratii," no. 4 (1947), p. 69.
270. *Political Science Quarterly,* Taylor Cole, "The Evolution of the German Labor Front," 52:532–558 (1937), and literature cited there; see also ref. 148g.
271. *Pravda.* ✳(a) December 29, 1936, p. 2. ✳(b) October 9, 1952, p. 2. ✳(c) July 4, 1947. ✳(d) October 9, 1952, Malenkov, report of the CC of CPSU(B). ✳(e) April 16, 1953. ✳(f) November 7, 1947, speech on the thirtieth anniversary of the Revolution. ✳(g) December 18, 1917. ✳(h) October 9, 1952, p. 6, Nineteenth Party Congress, credentials report; see also ref. 47j. ✳(i) June 22, 1954, article on China on the path of socialist industrialization. ✳(j) July 17, 1955. ✳(k) January 21, 1955; for 1954 achievements, the annual report of the Central Statistical Administration ('TsSU), "Results of the State Plan for the Development of the National Economy of the USSR in 1954" (translated title). ✳(l) January 21, 1955. ✳(m) September 19, 1953. ✳(n) February 23 and 24, March 6, 1954, for Khrushchev's report, and stories on Komsomolites leaving for the East. ✳(o) October 27, 1954. ✳(p) October 10, 1952, p. 5. ✳(q) April 11, 1956. ✳(r) *op. cit.*
272. *Public Opinion Quarterly,* C. J. Friedrich, "The Agricultural Basis of Emotional Mass Nationalism," 1937, pp. 50–61, for the Nazi situation.
273. *Quarterly Journal of Economics.* ✳(a) J. S. Berliner, "The Informal Organization of the Soviet Firm," 46:342–365 (August 1952). ✳(b) *ibid.*
274. *Radio (Moscow),* September 1954.
275. *Regime Fascista.* ✳(a) March 1, 1930. ✳(b) November 23, 1938, p. 1, as translated by Germino (64d).
276. *Review of Politics.* ✳(a) Hannah Arendt, "Ideology and Terror: A Novel Form of Government," 15:309ff (1953). The antecedents in earlier discussions of the law of nature are inadequately recognized, since Miss Arendt takes only the normative (scholastic) law of nature into account. ✳(b) *ibid.,* pp. 303ff. In this interesting paper, Miss Arendt advances the thesis that it is not merely the utopian nature of the ideology, but its alleged logicality, that leads to the terror. Based on a "scientific" law of movement, these ideologies are "literally the logic of an idea" which is carried through with "ice-cold reasoning"

(Hitler) or with the "mercilessness of dialectics" or the "irresistible force of logic" (Stalin). We believe the point Miss Arendt makes to be a significant aspect of totalitarian ideology, but not to have the broad importance she attributes to it. *(c) Karl Wittfogel, "The Historical Position of Communist China: Doctrine and Reality," 16:463ff (1954), for further detail.

277. *Socialisticka zakonnost,* no. 4 (1953), special supplement.
278. *Sovetskoie gosudarstvo i pravo,* *(a) no. 6 (1954), pp. 16–23. *(b) *ibid.*
279. *Sovetskaia Kultura,* January 18, 1955, p. 2, for a recent attack on "huligany," *i.e.,* "huliganism."
280. *Sovetskaia pedagogika,* no. 1 (1955), holiday work plan for students in an agricultural area.
281. *Trybuna Ludu,* June 7, 1953.
282. *U. S. News and World Report,* reports of N. and H. Dodges, September 16, 1955. This is also the conclusion of two American educators who have recently spent some time in the USSR studying the Soviet educational system.
283. *USSR Information Bulletin,* October 20, 1948.
284. *Vechernaia Moskva,* August 12, 1955.
285. *Vedomosti Verkhovnogo Soveta SSSR,* no. 9 (827), June 20, 1954, pp. 259–267.
286. *Vestnik instituta po izucheniiu istorii i kultury SSSR.* *(a) P. Sencha-Zalesky, on the Soviet school, no. 2 (1955), p. 69. *(b) "Po stranit-sam Zhurnala Moskovskoi Patriarkhii," no. 1(14), 1955, p. 76. *(c) D. Konstantinov, "Sovetskaia molodezh v borbe za Tserkov," no. 1(14), 1955, pp. 61–72. *(d) E. Kyrymal, "Polozhenie musulmanskoi religii v Krymu," no. 2(15), 1955, pp. 55–68.
287. *Vierteljahrshefte für Zeitgeschichte.* *(a) Karl O. Paetel, "Geschichte und Soziologie der SS," 2:15–17; however, he neglects the Italian Fascist antecedents of this kind of conception. *(b) *ibid.,* p. 3. *(c) *ibid.,* pp. 1–33.
288. *Voprosy filosofii,* F. N. Ileshchuk, "Religious Survivals and Ways of Overcoming Them," no. 6 (1954), p. 79 (translated title).
289. *Voprosy Trudovovo Prava,* N. G. Aleksandrov and V. M. Dogadov, p. 241; quoted in Kulski (103), p. 414; see also ref. 103c.
290. *World Politics,* A. Eckstein, "Conditions and Prospects for Economic Growth in Communist China," vol. 7, no. 1 (October 1954).
291. *Yale Review,* C. J. Friedrich, "The Peasantry—the Evil Genius of Dictatorship," vol. 26, no. 7 (1937), pp. 724–740.
292. *Zaria vostoka,* L. Klimovich, "Origin and Reactionary Essence of Islam," October 10, 1954 (translated title).
293. *Zentralinstitut für Erziehung und Unterricht,* Deutsche Schulerziehung (ed. Rudolf Benzed), 1940, containing a report about the development of German schools between 1933 and 1939.

Index of Names

Index of Subjects

In an analytical index for a systematic study such as this, it is not possible to list every instance where a general term, like "revolution," occurs. An effort has been made to include those instances which seem of more general significance. The bibliography is not covered by this index.